This book is dedicated to all the friends, family, and coworkers who have been so helpful, supportive, understanding, and generous with their time over the past year and a half. It's a long list, in no particular order: Roxanne, Nicole, Sarah, Meredith, Paula, Barb, Christina, Shirley, Cyndi, Sommar, Brian, Gary, Heather, Rich, Gina, Mike, Kay, Janice, David, and everyone at Peachpit Press.

A BUSHEL—THAT'S FOUR WHOLE PECKS—OF THANKS TO…

Rebecca, Nancy, and Nancy, for making this project happen. And for continuing to work with me time and again.

Robyn, for managing the project, and for being so pleasant and well organized.

Jay, for providing a top-notch technical review, and a couple of good jokes, to boot.

David and Myrna, for magically converting a handful of random materials into something that walks and talks like a book.

Patricia, for the sharp proofreading eye.

The indexer, Valerie, who makes it easy for readers to find what they need to know without wading through all of my blather.

Terri and Aren, for the snazzy interior and cover design work.

All the readers who requested that I write this book and provided detailed thoughts as to what they would and would not want this book to be. I hope it's what you were looking for!

Gary at Kona Earth coffee (**www.konaearth.com**) for the ton of feedback. And for the truly excellent coffee!

Templates.com (**www.templates.com**) and spyka Webmaster (**www.spyka.net**) for permission to use their templates in the book's examples.

Jon, for permission to use his "Architecture by Hand" stencil for some of the book's figures (**www.jonathanbrown.me**).

Karnesha, for entertaining the kids so that I can get some work done, even if I'd rather not.

Zoe and Sam, for being the kid epitome of awesomeness.

Jessica, for doing everything you do and everything you can.

EFFORTLESS
E-COMMERCE
with PHP and MySQL

LARRY ULLMAN

New Riders

Effortless E-Commerce with PHP and MySQL
Larry Ullman

New Riders
1249 Eighth Street
Berkeley, CA 94710
510/524-2178
510/524-2221 (fax)
Find us on the Web at: www.newriders.com
To report errors, please send a note to: errata@peachpit.com

New Riders is an imprint of Peachpit, a division of Pearson Education.

Project Editor: Rebecca Gulick
Editor: Robyn G. Thomas
Technical Reviewer: Jay Blanchard
Production Coordinator: Myrna Vladic
Compositor: David Van Ness
Proofreader: Patricia Pane
Cover Designer: Aren Howell Straiger
Interior Designer: Terri Bogaards
Indexer: Valerie Haynes Perry

ISBN 13: 978-0-321-65622-3
ISBN 10:   0-321-65622-9

9 8 7 6 5 4 3 2 1

Printed and bound in the United States of America

CONTENTS

INTRODUCTION

Electronic commerce has been an important and viable part of the Internet for well over a decade now. From the behemoths like Amazon.com to the mom-and-pop online stores, e-commerce is performed in a number of ways. Despite the dozen, or hundred, of failures for every single commercial success, e-commerce can still be an excellent business tool when done properly. And yet, surprisingly, there are very few books dedicated to the subject.

Using two concrete examples, plus plenty of theory, this book covers the fundamentals of developing e-commerce Web sites using PHP and MySQL. Emphasizing security, a positive customer experience, and modular, extendable programming, this book presents tons of detailed solutions to today's real-world e-commerce demands. Whether you've been creating dynamic Web sites for years or just weeks, you're bound to learn something new over the course of the next 11 chapters.

WHAT IS E-COMMERCE?

In the broadest sense, the term *e-commerce* covers the gamut of possible online commercial transactions. Any Web site with the intention of making money for a business could fall under the "e-commerce" label. Of course, such a liberal definition encompasses the vast majority of existing Web sites. On the opposite end of the scale, e-commerce can be defined as strictly the online act of taking money directly from customers. And that's the kind of e-commerce this book addresses.

There are two key differences between a site hoping simply to *make* money and one intending to *take* money:

■ How comfortable the customer needs to be

■ How secure the site needs to be

A site can make money from selling ads, in which case all that's required of the customer is that they visit. Or a site could make money from referrals, where the hope is that the customer will use a link on the site to purchase something from another site. In both cases, what's being asked of the user is insignificant. But when a site wants a customer to provide their full name, address, and credit card information, that becomes serious business. The customer must be respected, their questions answered, their concerns addressed, and their fears mitigated in order for the site to succeed in the endeavor.

When it comes to e-commerce, I can't overstress the importance of security. To protect both the business and the customers, a site must be designed and programmed so as to establish and maintain an appropriate level of security. As you'll see, especially in Chapter 2, "Security Fundamentals," the overall security of a Web site is impacted not just by the code you write but also by some of the initial decisions that you make, such as the chosen hosting environment. With this in mind, security concerns are presented in the book from the big picture and the general theories down to the nuances of specific code. You can rest assured that the book's examples have no known security holes. Moreover, there's plenty of discussion as to how you can make specific processes even more secure, as well as warnings as to what you shouldn't do, from a security perspective.

ABOUT THIS BOOK

The goal of this book is to portray the widest possible range of what e-commerce can be, in terms of PHP code, SQL and MySQL, and a Web site's user interface. Toward that end, the book is broken into three parts, cleverly named Part One, Part Two, and Part Three (and in that order, no less!).

Part One, "Fundamentals," has just two chapters. They:

- Discuss the fundamental theories and issues surrounding an e-commerce business

- Examine what decisions will need to be made up front

- Lay out critical aspects of online security

In Part Two, "Selling Virtual Products," an entire e-commerce site is developed. This site sells virtual products, namely access to content. With virtual products, there's no inventory management or anything to sell. The business just needs to accept payment from customers and ensure that access is denied to nonpaying customers. For this example, PayPal will be used to handle customer payments. PayPal is a wise choice for beginning e-commerce sites, because it's easy to integrate, has a name that almost all customers will be familiar with (and therefore, trust), and minimizes the security risks taken by the site itself.

Part Three, "Selling Physical Products," creates an entire e-commerce site for the sake of selling physical products. This means: inventory management, an online catalog, shopping carts, order history, and more. For that example, the Authorize.net payment gateway will be integrated directly into the Web site, creating a more seamless and professional experience.

By using two examples with different goals and features, the book presents a smorgasbord of ideas, database designs, HTML tricks, and PHP code. The intention is that, after completing the book, you'll feel comfortable implementing any number or combination of features and approaches on your own e-commerce sites.

Technologies Used

This book, as its title implies, uses the PHP scripting language (**www.php.net**) and the MySQL database application (**www.mysql.com**) as the foundation of the Web site. The book uses version 5.3.2 of PHP and version 5.1.44 of MySQL, although you should have no problems with any of the code so long as you're using PHP 5.2 or greater and MySQL 5.0 or greater. In places where newer versions of these technologies are required, you'll see alternative ways to accomplish the same tasks.

As with any modern Web site, HTML is involved (of course), as is CSS. The book does not explain either in great detail, but does show some best practices in terms of their use.

In Part Three of the book, you'll encounter some JavaScript, involving the jQuery framework (**www.jquery.com**). In those few instances, jQuery is used to enhance the site and add some functionality, but the JavaScript itself is not complicated.

Part Three of the book also taps into some of what the Apache Web server (**http://httpd.apache.org**) can do. As with the JavaScript, the Apache particulars are not too complex, but are still very useful and worth knowing.

Getting Help

If you have any problems with, or questions about, what is said or done in this book, there are several resources to which you can turn, starting with, naturally, the book's corresponding Web site, **www.DMCInsights.com/ecom/**. There you can find all the files, code, and SQL commands used in this book.

At **www.DMCInsights.com/phorum/** is a support forum dedicated to this book. If you post a question or comment there, you'll get a relatively prompt reply, from others or me.

Finally, as this book was designed to be both modular and extendable, I came up with literally dozens of additional ideas or alternative approaches as I created the two examples. As time permits, these extras will be discussed, and sample code provided, through the book's corresponding Web site.

WHAT YOU'LL NEED

Just as e-commerce is a transaction between a customer and a Web site, a book can be viewed as a transaction between the writer and the reader (just not one that takes place in real time). I've already presented a short sense of what this book is, but who do I imagine you to be and what will you need?

Some Fundamental Skills

The goal of this book is to demonstrate the application of PHP and MySQL to the task of creating an e-commerce site. Although I expect that even a seasoned Web developer will learn a lot, the book does not, nor cannot, teach the absolute fundamentals of either PHP or MySQL. If you're not already somewhat comfortable with these two technologies, this is not the book for you. If you have no problems executing a MySQL query using PHP and then handling those query results, you'll be fine.

The same must be said for the secondary technologies involved, namely HTML and CSS. If the definition of an HTML form is foreign to you, you should learn those basics before getting immersed in this book's material.

As for the JavaScript, jQuery, and Apache work that you'll come across, no previous experience with them is expected.

A Web Server

In order to develop a Web site using PHP and MySQL, you'll need a Web server, which is to say a computer running PHP through a Web server application (such as Apache or IIS, Internet Information Server) and the MySQL database application server. Fortunately, you can install all these on your own computer, at absolutely no cost. The easiest way to do so is to use an all-in-one package, such as XAMPP (**www.apachefriends.org**) or MAMP (**www.mamp.info**). If you already have a Web site being hosted on a live server, that will work as well.

And a Bit More

A Web server will let you *run* a dynamic Web site, but you need additional tools to *develop* one: at the very least, a decent text editor or Integrated Development Environment (IDE). A commercial IDE like Adobe Dreamweaver (**www. adobe.com/go/dreamweaver**) is fine, as is an open-source IDE like Aptana Studio (**www.aptana.com**) or a plain-text editor such as TextMate (**www.macromates.com**). Just use something with more features than Notepad!

It really doesn't matter what Web browser you're using, although Firefox (**www.mozilla.com**) has better debugging tools available (such as Firebug, **www.getfirebug.com**) than the others.

And that's really it! If you've already done some PHP and MySQL development (which is a requirement for following along with this book), you probably already have everything you need. So let's get started!

PART ONE
FUNDAMENTALS

GETTING STARTED

Just as the process of building a house does not begin with a hammer, creating an e-commerce site does not start with your computer. Well, you'll probably use your computer for research, but actual coding is a step that comes much later. In this chapter, you'll learn how to get started developing your e-commerce site. The goal is to explain two things:

- The actual steps you'll need to take

- The perspective I have on e-commerce, which is also to say the perspective of this book

While the point of this book is to provide concrete answers and usable code, there will be some subjects, especially over the next few pages, for which I cannot tell you what to do. In such cases, I try to identify what questions you'll need to answer and how you might go about doing so.

At a root level, the success of any type of Web site, whether or not it's intended to make money, depends upon its reliability and performance: If people are attempting to use the site, can they? In this chapter, you'll encounter many of the decisions you'll need to make that impact your site's availability. The choices you make aren't permanent, but as with most things, not having to make big changes further down the road is preferable.

The success of an e-commerce site further depends upon security. This chapter touches upon a few security issues, but security is addressed in more detail in the next chapter, and then throughout the rest of the book.

The last thing to note is that you may be creating an e-commerce site under one of two scenarios: for yourself or for someone else. When creating a site for yourself, you'll need to make most of the decisions. When creating a site for someone else, they'll be the ones making most of these decisions and your part in the process is, at best, advisory. Take, for example, the business's goals...

IDENTIFYING YOUR BUSINESS GOALS

Before you do anything, anything at all—mock up a Web design, identify your Web host, or even buy the domain name—you need to identify your business goals. For an e-commerce site, the goal is to make money, which you can do in different ways:

- Selling goods or services directly

- Advertising on the site

- Promoting goods or services that can be purchased elsewhere

In this book, I'm using the term *e-commerce* to refer to sites that directly accept money from end users. I've limited myself to that scope, because it demands a level of security well beyond other types of sites. Say you wanted to create a site that reviews music: You might give all the content away for free but hope to make money by displaying ads on your site and/or by using affiliate links to other sites that actually sell music. In either case, the security issues you would have are no bigger than those for most other non-e-commerce sites. As another example, my company's Web site, **www.dmcinsights.com**, supports and augments the books I write, which ideally increases the sales of the books; however, the site itself does not take money directly. The goal in this book is to create sites that sell goods or services directly to customers.

There are many facets to achieving a business's goals. The focus of this book is strictly on manufacturing the online experience; you'll need to follow through on your own with the other key issues, such as:

- Creating a legal business entity

- Properly handling business taxes

- Accounting

- Coordinating with vendors

 tip

A good way to get people to your site is to offer something, almost anything, for free!

- Marketing your business

- Managing employees and payroll

- Controlling physical inventory

- Managing shipping and returns

In short, just creating the Web site is not all you'll need to do. Most importantly, know going into this that **even if you make a *fantastic* e-commerce Web site, that alone is no guarantee of business success.**

So stop reading right now and write down your business goals. What do you hope to achieve? What are your short-term goals? What are your long-term goals? Try to be realistic about them.

 tip

Give people a reason to visit your site even when they're not shopping, so they might buy something on impulse or think of your site first when they do want to make a purchase.

Next, write down (on a large piece of paper!) everything you think you'll need to do and have in order to achieve those goals. How much money can you invest up front? How much time? Who will help you? How will they be compensated? From where will you get more money when that need arises? Who is going to handle the bookkeeping? How will you get people to visit your site? If you're selling physical products, where will they be stored? How will you perform the actual shipping of the merchandise?

Clearly, there are a lot of questions involved, even for the most basic of goals. There is one key question I can answer for you: How do you create a good, secure e-commerce site? Answer: Read this book!

RESEARCHING LEGAL ISSUES

Rightfully so, whenever you're dealing with other people's money, and whenever you're creating your own business, there are plenty of legal issues to consider. This is a big area in which I can be of little assistance: I'm not a lawyer, and I don't know in which country, state, province, territory, or city you live. But this doesn't mean I can't point you in the right direction.

National and International Laws

The legal issues involved differ when the Web site is for your business and when you're creating it for a client. When working for a client, you need to sign a sound, legal contract. In particular, the contract should limit the liability you personally have should something go wrong. As a general rule, good contracts limit your liability to the amount of money you made on the project itself, should you be at fault. Also, you should define a process for how to handle change requests. Normally, my clients get one round of requests after the initial version of the site is complete. Secondary requests, or any additions unreasonably beyond the original scope of the contract, must be renegotiated.

If you have your own business and there is no client, then there are tons of other legal issues to investigate, having nothing to do with the e-commerce site itself. For these, start by contacting every applicable governmental depart-ment to see what you must know and do. Many cities and states have small business branches dedicated to helping people like you navigate the maze of legal necessities.

In either case, you must be knowledgeable about legal issues specifically addressing online commerce. Again, your local and national governments should be able to provide you with this information. The particulars will dif-fer greatly from one country to the next. They may even depend upon where you're located, where the client is located, where the customers are, where the site is physically hosted, where the associated bank can be found, and so forth. In the United States, the Federal Trade Commission (FTC) oversees many aspects of e-commerce. On their Web site, **www.ftc.gov**, they provide guide-lines for e-commerce, international sales, security, and more.

As another example, in the United Kingdom, there are exact requirements as to what information should be available on the Web site, as well as on order forms and in emails. This includes:

- The company's physical address

- The company's registration number

- Any trade associations

- The Value Added Tax (VAT) number

Because you'll be storing information about the customers, there are other laws involved. The European Union has specific regulations as to how personal data is stored and used. The United States also has precise rules about using customer email addresses for advertising, promotional emails, and how to handle disclosures. All these laws just apply to basic personal information; if you're storing credit card data (and you really shouldn't), more laws apply.

You'll also need to know whether or not Internet sales should be taxed and, if so, at what rate. In the United States, this is currently a hotly debated topic and varies from state to state. And if you're shipping physical products, there

tip

All laws aside, treat the customer and their personal information as you would hope sites treat you and your information.

tip

Many payment gateways allow for recurring payments, meaning you can charge a customer multiple times, still without storing their payment information yourself.

are rules about when you can actually charge the customer based upon when the order ships. If part of the order ships, you can only charge the customer part of the order total at that time.

Should the worst happen—your system be hacked and the data be breached—laws may apply as well. The state of California, for example, has very specific and strict laws as to what you must do once you find a security violation. Part of planning—a big part, really—is preparing yourself should the worst happen, so that you're not scrambling to find answers in the middle of a crisis.

PCI Compliance

Another legal issue on which you should be extremely well versed is PCI DSS, short for Payment Card Industry Data Security Standard (**www.pcisecuritystandards.org**). This is a specific set of rules for ensuring secure, proper handling of credit cards by all commercial vendors. Any company that processes, stores, or transmits credit card information must follow these guidelines, thereby being *PCI compliant*.

By following the code in this book, you'll neither store nor process any credit cards yourself, which is really for the best. **You absolutely do not want to store the user's credit card information!** There are companies that do that, yes, but that's their full-time job and they have the knowledge, resources, and money to do that properly. Still, even taking credit card information on your site and passing it off to another company means you should be PCI compliant. The specific requirements differ based upon what you actually do with credit cards and how many transactions per year you process. I'll get into those requirements in the next chapter.

If your site is not PCI compliant and there is a security breach, several bad things could happen (beyond the effects of the security breach itself). First, the credit cards companies will likely escalate your security requirements to a higher level, such as requiring external security scans of your system. This means more work and likely more money. Second, the credit card companies that created the PCI DSS—Visa, MasterCard, American Express, Discover, and JCB—could make you pay any damages they incur because of your security breach. They may even fine you as well. Third, those same companies could deny you the option of accepting their cards, which will pretty much shut down your business.

Now technically, the PCI DSS is not a law, but some parts of the specification may also be an applicable law in your country, state, province, or territory. And, the potential penalties that the credit card companies can impose can be just as scary as any legal repercussion.

CHOOSING WEB TECHNOLOGIES

Over the past 20 years, the Web has changed in many ways. It has changed significantly in just the past five! But some things still remain the same. For starters, there's HTML (HyperText Markup Language). Whatever else has changed, whatever image types you use, video options, and server-side technologies, the end user first interacts with HTML. This book does not, and cannot, teach HTML. Pick up a book on that subject, such as the de facto standard, Elizabeth Castro's *HTML, XHTML, and CSS: Visual QuickStart Guide, Sixth Edition* (Peachpit Press, 978-0-321-43084-7), if you need more information along those lines.

With modern Web browsers, much of a site's layout and design comes from CSS (Cascading Style Sheets). I'll be using CSS in this book, too, and just like with HTML, I don't explain it in much detail. Still, I won't be using CSS in any super-fancy way, so it shouldn't be a problem following along.

When I first began doing Web development in the late 1990's, there was this annoying little thing called JavaScript. At that time, JavaScript was largely used for petty and cutesy tricks. JavaScript was almost entirely unnecessary. Today, things are quite different, thanks to Ajax, Web 2.0, and other marketing terms that people throw around. Now, JavaScript, when properly used, greatly improves the user's experience. Many Web-site features that people appreciate, such as being able to present lots of content in a limited space, being able to add something to a cart without leaving the page, and so forth, use JavaScript. While JavaScript is valuable, it's really an "extra."

Another way to create a rich user interface in the browser is to use Flash, a platform of tools and software managed by Adobe. Flash has a mixed reputation, largely because it can be used for really distracting advertisements, but people's misuse of a technology does not mean the technology itself isn't worthwhile. You might be surprised to know that Flash-based e-commerce applications have a higher success rate (in terms of sales) than non-Flash sites. In part, this is because the different client-server model used in Flash can result in a more seamless process, giving the user fewer reasons not to complete the sale. All that being said, e-commerce with Flash would be an entirely different book.

 note

This book doesn't teach HTML, CSS, JavaScript, PHP, SQL, or MySQL; instead it demonstrates real-world application of these technologies.

 tip

If you are curious about programming Flash content, consider my *Effortless Flex 4 Development* (New Riders, 978-0-321-70594-5).

note

After this chapter, I'll stop recommending other books to buy, I promise!

On the server-side of the equation, unlike in the client, you have a vast range of Web technology to consider. This book uses PHP as the programming language of choice and MySQL as the database application. These are my personal favorite server-side technologies, and if you're reading this book, I assume you think so as well. I'm going to forgo the sales pitch on PHP and MySQL, and move on. If you aren't already well-versed in PHP and MySQL, you might have difficulty with some of this book's code. Consider my *PHP 6 and MySQL 5 for Dynamic Web Sites: Visual QuickPro Guide, Third Edition* (Peachpit Press, 978-0-321-52599-4) to learn more about these technologies.

EASY E-COMMERCE ALTERNATIVES

In this book, you'll learn how to write an e-commerce application from scratch, using a combination of HTML, CSS, JavaScript, PHP, SQL, and MySQL. There are, however, faster, less custom approaches you can use.

If you just want to get an e-commerce site online quickly, or if you don't actually know any of the listed technologies, you can use "turnkey" e-commerce sites that Yahoo!, Google, and others provide. By answering some questions and using their interface, you can create a basic e-commerce site in a day. It'll even be tied automatically into a payment system. But make no mistake: Although you'll get up and running in no time, the end result will be rather amateurish and very limited.

A middle-ground solution between using an entire third-party system and creating your own custom one is to use an off-the-shelf e-commerce package, such as ZenCart (**www.zen-cart.com**) or osCommerce (**www.oscommerce.com**). They provide all the functionality, from creating a catalog or a shopping cart to administration, which can then be tied to one of several payment systems. These tools have been around for years, are quite solid, and well supported, but will still have some limitations compared to writing your own e-commerce site, especially when it's time to add features that will be uniquely yours. At the same time, these packages will also be bogged down with lots of features that you might not ever use.

SELECTING A WEB HOST

In order to make your Web site available for the public to access, it needs to be hosted on a server. A server is just another computer whose hardware and software are oriented for network use.

tip

You will need to put your site on a hosted server in order to test it with PayPal.

In theory, you may be able to use your personal computer as a server, but you absolutely do not want to do this. First, doing so may violate the terms of your Internet provider's service; ISPs are in the business of providing you access to the Internet, not hosting Web sites. Second, most ISPs change your IP address on a regular basis. Getting any domain name to work with a dynamic IP address requires extra know-how and effort. Third, even if you can overcome those first two hurdles, the resulting performance for the end user will be terrible. The Internet access you have at home, no matter how fast, will likely have an upload speed that's a fraction of the download speed. It's this upload speed that'll impact the end user, as they'll be uploading the site's content—HTML, CSS, JavaScript, and media—through that narrow connection.

To be clear, you can *develop* the entire site using just your personal computer. You can install all the necessary tools—a Web server, PHP, and MySQL—on your own computer, then develop the database, write the code, test, and so on. Developing on your personal computer is faster (because you don't have to upload files), cheaper (because you're not paying for hosting during this time), and more secure (because incomplete, potentially unsecure code won't be online).

Hosting Options

With regard to hosting, you can generally say that you get what you pay for, and I say that as a person who's generally inclined to go the cheapest route whenever possible. I've used probably five or six hosts for my own Web sites and dealt with many others for clients. The old adage says that you have to spend money to make money and finding a cheap host is a bad way to go about making money.

Hosting plans vary based upon:

- Price
- Features
- Performance
- Amount of control

The *price* is directly related to the quality of the other three attributes. If you spend more, you'll get more.

To be honest, the *features* don't really matter. Well, some do and many don't. Most hosting plans will offer around 56 features, of which you'll need 10. This even goes for disk space and bandwidth limitations: Hosting plans will offer you more of these than you'll ever need, thereby tempting you with trivialities. The minimally required features are PHP, MySQL, a mail server (to send and receive email), and security software, such as a firewall, a virus detector, and so forth. Additionally, beneficial features include regular backups and excellent—truly excellent—customer support. When it comes time to compare one hosting option to another, decide what really counts—like uptime, backups, security, and customer service—and ignore the rest.

 note

Do not attempt to host your Web site from your home!

tip

Buy cheap beer if you must, but never purchase cheap Web hosting!

The *performance* of a server will depend upon the type of hosting involved, the server's specific hardware—amount of RAM, disk types, processor types, the number of processors, and the server's network connection. As I say in the beginning of this chapter, the site's performance is hugely important, but it's unfortunately something that's not easily determined in advance.

The *amount of control* you have over the server will depend upon the hosting type. Different Web-hosting companies offer different plans, but the basic hosting options are:

- Free

- Shared

- Virtual Private Server (VPS)

- Dedicated or colocation (colo)

 tip

You'll eventually come to regret using free or very cheap hosting plans for your Web site, so save yourself that headache!

Free hosting plans are harder to come by now than they used to be, but you shouldn't even consider them for an e-commerce site. You may have a free site possibility with your .Mac account or from your ISP, but you probably can't even use your domain name on them.

Shared hosting plans are the most common and the cheapest (of the paid choices). Shared hosting involves putting tens of clients and possibly hundreds of Web sites on a single server. Shared hosting is inexpensive—decent plans range from $10 to $20 (all prices in the book will be in U.S. dollars) per month and may be a reasonable way to start. However, because there are multiple users on each server, your Web site will only be as secure as the weakest security link in any site on the server. The performance of the site will also suffer, as the demands are so high. Finally, you'll have little to no control over how the server runs. You won't be able to use a particular version of PHP, enable certain PHP settings or features, or tweak how MySQL runs. Shared hosts are not likely to make any changes that might adversely impact the other clients on the same server. Still, shared hosting may be appropriate for smaller, less demanding sites without higher security concerns.

A happy medium between shared hosting and dedicated is the *Virtual Private Server* (it's what I've personally used for a couple of years). Instead of having tens of clients on a single server, there may be only a couple or a handful, each running their own virtual operating system. Although all the server's hardware is still being shared, limitations can be placed so that you'll always get a minimum amount of RAM, thereby guaranteeing some performance no matter what happens to the other sites on the server. From a security perspective, each virtual server is a separate entity, so what some other client does with their VPS cannot impact yours. And since the VPS is yours alone, you can do whatever you want with it in terms of installing and configuring software. VPS hosting plans run from as cheap as $30 per month to around $100 per month.

A *dedicated* or *colocated* server is on the other end of the hosting spectrum. This kind of hosting puts an entire computer—its software and hardware— under your command, but the server is physically housed at the hosting company's location. That location, unlike your home, should have multiple, fast connections to the Internet, redundant power supplies with battery backups, secure physical access to the server rooms, climate control, and so on. (The technical difference between dedicated and colocated hosting is that the host typically owns a dedicated server whereas you typically own a colocated one.)

The other hosting types cannot match the amount of control, the number of features, or possibly the performance of running your own entire server. But the cost of a dedicated or colocated server will be much, much higher—from a couple of hundred dollars per month to several hundred. Just as important is the fact that, depending upon the particulars of the hosting plan, you may be responsible for all the maintenance and security of the server. So you'll need to decide if you think you're better suited to handle server security than someone who does that full time and has likely been doing it for years. Also, the Web-hosting company will have people monitoring your server 24 hours per day, whereas you've got to sleep sometime.

 tip

When using dedicated or colocated hosting, make sure that the Web host will still provide some maintenance and security assistance.

CLOUD COMPUTING

There is another hosting option that's come up in the past couple of years: *cloud hosting*. Cloud computing sounds ethereal, but it's just moving some server functionality— processing of data, storing of data, handling emails, or whatever—to a different computer (or bank of computers), not under your control and on a different network. One benefit to cloud computing is that it can automatically scale to your needs without you needing to take extra steps. If, for some freak, benevolent reason, you go from processing an average of 100 sales per day to 10,000, the cloud will be able to handle the increased traffic, which might otherwise have crashed a basic hosting plan. But there are extra security concerns with cloud computing, and you'd need

to be prepared to pay the price. For example, if your site gets hit with a Denial of Service (DOS) attack (discussed in Chapter 2, "Security Fundamentals,") you'll have to foot the bill for the extra cloud computing, but the attack itself will have generated no extra revenue.

This book does not discuss cloud computing beyond what I've just said, as cloud hosting is appropriate for a comparatively small percentage of the market, and the technical particulars will depend upon whose cloud service you're using. But be aware of this potential avenue. You might want to look into vendors and pricing if you suspect that cloud computing could be a good fit for your site and situation.

My Hosting Recommendation

As a reader, you're probably looking for as many definitive answers as possible, so my recommendation is to select a quality shared or VPS hosting plan to begin, depending upon the project itself and your budget. You absolutely don't want to host the site on your personal computer; you absolutely don't want to use free hosting; and you most likely shouldn't go with dedicated hosting to start, unless you have money to burn. One important thing to know is that you're not permanently locked into a given hosting plan or even a Web host. A good Web host should be able to upgrade or expand your hosting plan with little or no downtime. So start with a plan that's reasonably basic, and, should you have the good fortune of profound success, you can scale up your plan to meet the increased demands over time.

It's possible to change Web hosts, as well, just not as easy. It's best to start with a great host that you'll be able to stick with for years and years. This means not only someone reliable, but also a host that's established in such a way to allow for your site's expansion. For example, a really cheap host probably does only shared hosting. You would never be able to move to a dedicated server with them, and you probably wouldn't want to. Conversely, the hosting company I use only provides VPS and dedicated hosting plans. The VPS works for me for now, and I can move to one or more dedicated servers with this same company when I have that need.

Finding a Good Host

The final question, then, is how do you know if a Web host is good? First, go online and search using terms like *web host review* or *best web host*. **In the search results, ignore every site whose sole purpose is to rate and review Web hosts.** Yes, that's right: ignore those. They're unreliable, built upon advertising, and you'll never know what kind of relationship they may have with the companies they're "ranking." Plus, in my experience, such sites are ranking Web hosts for the masses, for those that don't know any better. If you want to find a couple of recommendations this way, mostly as a basis of comparison, that's fine, but these rankings should not be used to make a decision.

The best way to find a good host is to get real-world feedback and comments from real people. One way to do so is by finding forums where people talk about their hosting experiences. In the past, I've also emailed people to ask them if they're happy with their host. You can also get recommendations through mailing lists and the like. If you want, you can ask for my recommendation, or ask in my support forums (**www.dmcinsights.com/phorum/**) to see what experiences other readers have had. You'll note that I haven't mentioned

 note

I found all the lousy Web hosts that I've used over the years by listening to "official" rankings of the best Web hosts!

who my host is, despite the fact that I'm quite pleased with them. I don't feel comfortable naming my Web host in this book, but you can find their name in my forums, newsletters, and blog.

Once you've got a few potential candidates, start by excluding those that are really cheap. You don't want to try to save money by skimping on Web hosting. It's not a good long-term plan. There are certainly cheaper hosting options than the one I've been using for a couple of years; but my site is always available; I've got peace of mind; and you can't put a price on that. Interestingly, my current host doesn't even offer a free month of hosting, as many companies do. Their argument, which I buy into, is that providing a free month invites malicious people to temporarily get a server just to send spam or do other harmful or annoying activities. You don't want to be part of a network where that's happening.

You should also rule out those companies that try to do too much: better to have a host that excels at one or two things than one that is average at several. One of the worst hosting experiences I ever had, if not the worst, was with a company whose primary function was as a domain registrar. They were fine as registrars but *terrible* as hosts.

As I already said, all Web hosts will offer tons of features and more disk space, bandwidth, and add-ons than you'll ever need. And it's almost impossible to compare performance from one host to the next. For me, then, I look at security and customer service. Great security minimizes the chances of a problem and great customer service provides a quick fix should a problem arise.

USING A PAYMENT SYSTEM

As with your choice of a Web-hosting company, the payment system you use for your e-commerce site will have a significant impact on the end result. This is not to say that the site will be married to a single payment system for eternity, but as with any divorce, ending a relationship with a payment system can be tedious and costly for your business.

The payment system is the differentiating element between a standard Web site and an e-commerce one. The whole point of a payment system is to transfer money between the customers and the business.

There are two broad types of payment systems, which are frequently known by a variety of names but can be described as either a *payment processor* or a *payment gateway*. In this book, I'll demonstrate an example of each type, but here, I'll outline the pros and cons of each.

 note

Some companies, like PayPal, offer both types of payment systems.

Payment Processors

A *payment processor* is a delayed payment system that normally goes through a third-party site (**Figure 1.1**). The best example is the *Website Payments Standard* option at PayPal (**www.paypal.com**). If you want to accept payment through PayPal using their basic service, you'll send the customer to PayPal's site along with your PayPal identification and some other information. The customer then uses PayPal to authorize the transfer of that amount of money. After which, PayPal returns the customer to your site, and at some later point in time PayPal will make the funds available to you, minus their fees.

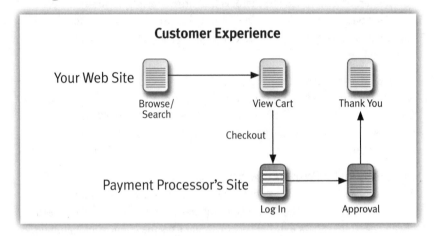

Figure 1.1

Using a payment processor like PayPal's Website Payments Standard or Google's Checkout is easy to establish, has low up-front costs, and uses a service that many customers will be familiar with (especially PayPal). On the other hand, these systems aren't as integrated into your site as the alternatives, and **sending customers away from your site is a risky e-commerce move, increasing the odds of losing the sale.** Also, the per-transaction costs tend to be a bit higher, and deposits may not be automatically made into your business's bank account (that is, you may need to go into the payment processor's system in order to accept and then transfer your credits).

In previewing this book with potential readers, many agreed with me that PayPal is a common enough option that it's worth using in an example in this book. Surprisingly, several others expressed a strong dislike for PayPal, both as a customer and as a developer. I've no objection to PayPal, and as I said, it's highly universal, so the first e-commerce example in this book, *Knowledge Is Power*, will use it.

Payment Gateways

A *payment gateway* is a real-time payment system that can be directly integrated into your own site, resulting in a process that's more professional and seamless. Instead of sending the user away, in the hopes they come back, transaction data will be transmitted behind the scenes and the customer won't leave your site at any point in the entire process (**Figure 1.2**). Also, a gateway will offer much better fraud prevention, among other extra features (more on fraud protection in the next section). The gateway will deposit your monies into a merchant account automatically, normally charging less per transaction than payment processors do.

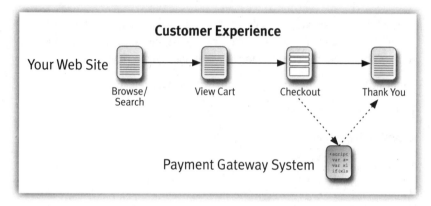

Figure 1.2

On the other side of the equation, a payment gateway may have higher setup costs and will require more programming to integrate the system into your site. They also require a merchant account, which is an account into which credit card charges can be deposited and refunded (for customer returns). You may or may not be able to use your business bank as your merchant account, depending upon your bank.

There are tons of payment gateways available; some gateway systems are actually resold through other vendors, giving you the ability to shop around for the best deal. Authorize.net (**www.authorize.net**) is perhaps the best-known payment gateway, and it will be used in the book's second example, *Coffee*.

tip

Payment systems will provide test accounts, dummy credit card numbers, and false processing systems through which you can test your site before going live.

tip

Make sure your payment solution provider is in full PCI compliance and can assist in guiding your site's compliance, too.

tip

Some gateways offer virtual terminals where the merchant can process credit card payments manually. These can be used to issue returns, for example.

Which Should You Use?

The short answer is that a payment gateway is more professional and ought to be your solution for all but the simplest e-commerce sites. But payment processors are quite commonly used and do make sense for some businesses, so don't dismiss them as an option entirely.

When selecting among payment providers, you should first determine if your business bank or Web-hosting company has an arrangement with any companies. By choosing a pre-approved vendor for this important service, you'll minimize some of the potential headaches and hopefully have an expert to turn to when you need technical support.

Another factor is geography: Different providers will work in your part of the world and will be limited as to what other regions they support. Also, you'll want to check that the currency the provider uses gels with your business.

There are many features to weigh when making your selection:

- Tools for fraud prevention
- Ability to perform recurring billing
- Acceptance of eChecks
- Automatic tax calculation
- Automatic shipping calculation and processing
- Digital content handling
- Integrated shopping cart

Clearly, many of these features can greatly simplify the development of your e-commerce site and result in a more professional Web application, but I would like to highlight fraud prevention. You may not have given much thought to the subject, but excellent fraud prevention is in the best long-term interest of your site. If someone can use a credit card at your site that isn't valid or isn't theirs, you'll have a false sale and later have some cleanup to perform to undo the transaction. Further, the person whose credit card was fraudulently used will think poorly of your business for allowing the fraud in the first place. For these reasons, using a gateway with sophisticated fraud-prevention tools is a must. The two most common techniques are to verify the billing address and the Card Verification Value (CVV)—those numbers on the back of the card.

A final, obvious factor that was not listed earlier is cost. You'll need to consider the initial setup costs, the monthly fees, plus the individual transaction expenses. If you require features that come at an extra cost, factor those in, too.

THE DEVELOPMENT PROCESS

After you've finalized your business plan, researched the laws, decided upon a hosting company, and selected a payment system, it's time to start putting down HTML tags, SQL commands, and **if-then** statements. The development process itself is really the point of this book, so let's take a look at that in detail (**Figure 1.3**).

 tip

If the price of your transactions will be small, like less than $10 on average, find a payment provider that supports *micropayments*, which have smaller transaction fees.

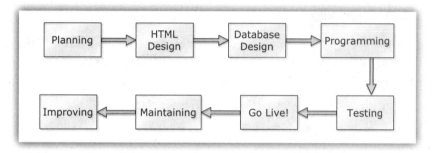

Figure 1.3

The development process occurs in phases. If each phase is approached deliberately and the end results are properly generated, you'll develop a great e-commerce site as efficiently as possible. If, on the other hand, you jump around, rush the process, skip steps, and make omissions, the whole procedure will take much longer, and the end result will be buggier.

At the end of the development process, you'll hopefully have created the best possible e-commerce site, but that site will undoubtedly need to be changed next week (as clients always want), next month, or next year. If the first goal is a smooth, optimal process, then the second is output—specifically PHP code and a MySQL database—that is flexible and scalable. When those inevitable changes need to be made, you should be able to do so without breaking or rewriting the entire system.

Site Planning

The first step in the development process is planning a generic site. This is much like establishing your business goals, but specifically with the site itself. What should the site do? What should it look like? Who are the target users? What browsers and/or devices should the site support? Use pen and paper, or any application in which you can make notes, and be as inclusive as you possibly can. It'll be much better, further down the road, if you considered an idea and ruled it out than if you never thought of it in the first place.

The best thing you can do at this point is look online. The Web is a rich tapestry of both the good and the bad, so look at the sites you like and use. What do they do well? What would you do differently? What fonts, colors, and designs appeal to you? There's an old adage about writing: *good writers plagiarize, great ones steal*. That's kind of true for the Web sites, too.

HTML Design

The next thing you should do in the development process is mock up the HTML designs for the site. I, for one, have absolutely no design skills whatsoever. If you could say the same, there are two simple solutions:

- Hire a qualified designer to create the HTML templates.

- Use an off-the-shelf design that you tweak a bit.

I've taken both approaches several times, which you use depends upon the site and your budget. If you're hiring someone, at a minimum, you'll want him or her to create a few templates:

- The home page

- An inner, basic content page

- A styled form

From these you can easily generate the looks of most of your site. If you're developing an e-commerce site that sells products, you'll also want *representative browsing* (that is, showing multiple products at once) and detailed listing pages.

If you don't have the budget or time to purchase a custom design, you can take an existing one and modify it to your needs. There are both free and commercial designs available, although you'll need to abide by the licensing where applicable. For example, some designs are free to use as long as you give credit to the designer in the footer. Other designs are free for noncommercial use but require licenses for commercial endeavors. In any case, you can take

tip

As a model for how to do e-commerce well, you can't do much better than examining Amazon.com.

tip

The HTML design process will, rightfully, include a few iterations of feedback, followed by updated designs.

tip

As I'm not a Web designer, I've relied upon freely available third-party templates for the two e-commerce sites in this book.

the existing template and then adjust the HTML and CSS to personalize the design for your or your client's tastes.

The goal at this point is to get the client (or you) to sign off on the look of the site. Moreover, the design also implies much of the functionality; getting approval of that is even more critical to the process. Think about: How will the look and function of the site be different if the user is logged in? How will navigation be handled? How are items added to the cart? How will the cart contents be shown? Also pay attention to the fundamentals of the user interface: simplicity, ease of use, proper navigation, breadcrumbs, obvious access to the cart, and so on.

tip

Your site's design should include obvious links for contacting the administrator, finding the site's return policy, and seeing the privacy policy.

Database Design

Designing the database is a key step, largely because changes to the database at a later date have far larger implications and potential complications than changing any other aspect of the site. Adding functionality through database changes is a steep challenge and fixing database flaws is excruciating, so **make every effort you can to get the database design right the first time.**

Good database design begins, naturally, with *normalizing* the database. If you aren't familiar with normalization, see any good resource on the subject, including my *MySQL: Visual QuickStart Guide, 2nd Edition* (Peachpit Press, 0-321-37573-4). Normalization and performance mean that you also:

note

This is absolutely the last reference I make to another book, I promise. Unless I think of another....

- Use the smallest possible column types.

- Avoid storing **NULL** values as much as possible.

- Use fixed-length columns when you can.

- Provide default values for columns, if applicable.

Performance is also greatly affected by using indexes properly. Declaring indexes is somewhat of an art, but some general rules are:

- Index columns that will be involved in **WHERE** and **ORDER BY** clauses.

- Avoid indexing columns that allow **NULL** values.

- Apply length restrictions to indexes on variable-length columns, such as indexing only the first 10 characters of a person's last name.

- Use **EXPLAIN** queries to confirm that indexes are being used.

- Revisit your indexes after some period of site activity to ensure they are still appropriate to the real-world data.

tip

The **--log-slow-queries** option in MySQL can be used to help you catch detrimental queries.

tip

A final consideration in your database design, which gets less attention, is the storage engine (or table type) in use. One of MySQL's strengths is its support for multiple storage engines, meaning you can select the one whose features best match your needs. For example, you can create MySQL tables in memory, which will perform exceptionally well but provide no data permanence. The two most common MySQL storage engines are *InnoDB* and *MyISAM*. The former is the default type for Windows computers and the latter is the default for all other operating systems. MyISAM is an excellent, all-purpose storage engine that also supports **FULLTEXT** indexes, useful in searches. The InnoDB engine doesn't support **FULLTEXT** but can handle transactions, an excellent fail-safe in sensitive situations.

If you have administrative-level control over your database, there are a number of configurations that impact MySQL's performance. To start, there is **back_log**, **key_buffer_size**, **max_connections**, and **thread_cache_size**. You can use a configuration file to change these settings from their defaults to values more appropriate to your server and site. See the MySQL manual for more information for the version of MySQL that your server is running—assuming that you have that kind of control over your server, of course.

Should you get to a point where your site is so active that multiple servers are appropriate, you can consider *replicating* the database. Database replication stores the same data on more than one server. By doing so you'll get improved security, reliability (should one server fail, the data still lives on elsewhere), and performance.

YOUR DEVELOPMENT TOOLS

What software you use on your computer to develop an e-commerce site is such a big and personal topic that I don't offer any recommendations on that front (at the very least because I primarily use a Mac and therefore couldn't recommended any development programs on Windows). If you don't already have a text editor or IDE that you like, again look online and get actual recommendations from people in order to select one. As with everything, your budget comes into play, although there are lots of excellent choices available at little to no cost.

Along with the programming software, you should consider project management tools, such as applications for organizing projects and taking notes. You may also need to use some accounting software, depending upon whether the e-commerce site is yours or not.

Programming

The primary focus of this book is really the PHP programming, where PHP acts as the glue between the user/browser and, well, pretty much everything else: the database, email, payment systems, and more. From a programming perspective, you'll want to create code that's not only functional, but also reusable, extendable, and secure.

To make reusable, extendable code, it must be well organized and thoroughly documented. **I cannot stress this enough: Document your code to the point of overkill.** As you program, begin with your comments and revisit them frequently. When you make any changes to your code, double-check that the comments remain accurate. You should also use flowcharts, UML diagrams (Unified Modeling Language), and other tools to outline and represent your site in graphical and noncode ways.

The security of your code is based upon so many factors that the next chapter will start discussing just this one subject. Secure programming is even more critical in e-commerce sites, however, so the topic will be reinforced time and again throughout the entire book.

Depending upon the circumstances, you may also want to look into version-control software such as subversion (**http://subversion.tigris.org**) or Git (**http://git-scm.com**). Version-control software makes site updates a smoother process, allowing you to accurately implement all site changes or roll back problems to previously sound states. If you're developing a site with a team of people, version control will help manage the shared files.

With PHP, unlike with many other languages, you have a choice of using an *object-oriented* or *procedural* approach. I'm perfectly comfortable doing either, and I don't believe one approach is clearly better than the next. I would advise against buying into the myth that OOP is more extendable or secure than procedural code. Poorly written OOP will cause you endless headaches and well-written procedural code won't hamper your site's long-term development in any way.

When asking for reader input on this book, there was a moderately heated discussion as to which approach I should use and to what extent. Some feel that OOP is the hallmark of professional programming; others don't know or care for it and wouldn't get much value out of an OOP-based book. In the end, I decided to use a mostly procedural approach, as it's the common denominator of all PHP programmers, and procedural code can more easily be turned into OOP than vice versa.

 tip

Formal PHP documentation can be achieved using PHPDoc (**www.phpdoc.org**).

 note

Because this book is really one giant comment on entire sites of PHP code, the scripts displayed in the book won't be as documented as yours should be.

 tip

MVC, short for Model, View, Controller, is a popular approach to designing Web sites. At the core, this design just implies good code organization.

Similarly, there was some discussion as to whether I should incorporate a framework or not. Again, my heart is not set one way or the other on frameworks. Sometimes I use them, sometimes I don't. In the end, I decided against using any framework in this book, because those chapters would inherently be more about the framework than the underlying example—an e-commerce site, the real focus of the book.

All that being said, when it comes to your own projects, you'll need to make the decision on procedural versus object-oriented, frameworks or not, and if using a framework, which one. Know upfront that these decisions will neither adversely affect nor guarantee the success of your e-commerce site. The only thing you don't want to do is start off on one path only to later change courses. That's a recipe for frustration and a likely guarantee of disaster.

Testing

Testing your Web site isn't a one-time, standalone step, but rather something you'll need to do often. **You cannot test your site too much!** Unfortunately, it's hard for the site developer to perform a truly good test of the site: He or she created it, so he or she knows how it should work and uses it accordingly. A better test is what happens when your family, coworkers, and annoying friends give the site a whirl. And I specify the *annoying* friends, because they're the ones who will attempt to do things you never would have imagined. When these people, who aren't Web developers themselves, purposefully or accidentally misuse the site, what happens? From these experiences you can improve the user interface and security of the whole application. Improving those two things will go a long way toward a successful e-commerce venture. Still, there are steps you can take to effectively test your site yourself.

Relatively new to PHP is the concept of *test-driven development* and *unit testing*: You define concrete and atomic tests of your code, and then run the tests to confirm the results. Each test should be concise and clear. As you write more code, you define more tests and continue to check each test to ensure that what you just did didn't break any other functionality. Test-driven development and unit testing are big enough subjects that I recommend you research both further on your own, when you're ready.

A different type of site testing you could address is *performance*. If you want to start with the big picture—how well the server copes with demand—software like ApacheBench (**http://httpd.apache.org**) and Siege (**www.joedog.org/index/siege-home**) will run benchmarks on your Web server, reporting on how many requests can be handled per second, which is the standard measuring tool for a site's performance. Once you start checking your site's performance, you will find that big, systemwide changes you make will have the greatest impact. These include:

- Changing the server hardware: increasing memory, installing faster hard drives, and using faster processors

- Changing the demands on the server: disabling unnecessary features, putting fewer users or sites on a single server, and balancing loads across multiple servers

- Caching the PHP output

- Caching the PHP execution

- Caching the database results

If you think about the process involved for handling the request of a PHP-MySQL based page, you'll see three areas where caching can be applied (**Figure 1.4**). First, if the database or PHP is caching the results of a database query, then that query will not need to be executed with each request. Second, by default, each request of a PHP script requires that the PHP code be executed as if it had never been run before. By applying an *opcode* cache such as the Alternative PHP Cache (APC, **www.php.net/apc**), the PHP code itself is cached by the system, making that execution faster. Finally, the end result is that HTML is sent to the Web browser. If you can cache the dynamically generated HTML, then no PHP code will be executed at all, no database queries are required, and the request itself becomes as fast as a request for a static HTML page.

 tip

Look online for specifics on implementing any of these caching techniques.

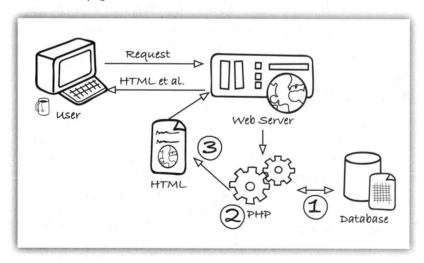

Figure 1.4

note

Performance testing and profiling are most useful in actual conditions. Testing the performance of your site under nonproduction situations is only theoretically meaningful.

You can also spend some time profiling your code, using tools like Xdebug (**www.xdebug.org**) or the Advanced PHP Debugger (APD, **www.php.net/apd**) to see where potential bottlenecks are in the PHP itself. Bottlenecks usually occur when PHP interacts with the file system, whether that means literal files on the server (like reading and writing text files or using sessions) or through the database application. I caution you against spending too much time worrying about profiling individual sections of code, because the improvements you can make that way will be relatively minor and possibly not worth your time. Better to learn good programming habits so that you don't have to worry about profiling after the fact.

Going Live

Once a site has been completely developed, tested, then updated to include the latest bug fixes and customer requests, it's time to go live. Before doing so, you should revisit all the legal and security issues to make sure the site is in full compliance. Second, have a plan in place for what should be done when something goes wrong (notice I said *when*, not *if*). Third, if any assumptions were made in the code, or any dummy processes installed, remove those. By "assumptions," I mean things such as using the test version of the payment system, not requiring real authentication to the administration pages, and so forth.

tip

Once your site is live, don't forget to submit it to all the top search engines.

Brick and mortar stores normally have what's called a *soft opening*. During this period the business is open and fully functioning, but not promoting itself actively. The hope is that the arrival of some traffic will catch issues and allow for improvements, without attempting to do so under the burden of a full user base. This is something you may want to consider as well, although in truth, pretty much every Web site that doesn't have millions of dollars of advertising behind it has a soft opening.

Maintaining

Depending upon the situation, going live may or may not be the end of your involvement with the project. If it's not, such as when it's your site, you'll need to have a plan in place for maintaining the project. **Site maintenance begins and ends with creating good, frequent backups of your site's data.** This is something the hosting company should be doing for you (check when you are researching hosts) and something you should be doing as well. Make sure that there are backups kept in multiple locations, too, so that a natural or man-made disaster doesn't wipe out both your server and your backups.

tip

For security purposes, safely store your backups, such as in a locked safe or a bank deposit box.

The maintenance of a site also requires that you keep an eye on the data itself. Check and optimize your database tables to improve their performance. Watch your database logs for slow and underperforming queries. Review your Web-server logs for *file not found* errors, high loads, and potential security problems. Analyze your data to find sales trends and places where you can make improvements. In short, collect and examine as much information as you can. And keep making backups!

Improving

The final step in the development process is improving what you've created. Improvements may stem from the client, from customer feedback, or changes in available technologies. Improving a site is really a subroutine of this entire development process: Think about what you want to change, plan its implementation, mock up the design, retool the database, write the code, test the end result, go live, and maintain the updated version of the site.

Although it's best to treat the development process as a linear progression of discrete steps, when you factor in repeated places for feedback, and the high potential for the process to be revisited for improvements, the real design process is best represented by **Figure 1.5**.

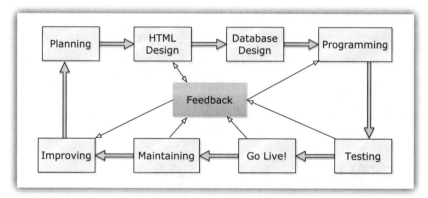

Figure 1.5

 note

The actual running of the site—dealing with customers, handling inventory, processing orders, reviewing customer feedback, and so on—is a whole separate way that a site has to be maintained.

2 | SECURITY FUNDAMENTALS

Although every chapter in the rest of the book will have some recommendations for improving the security of your Web site, security is such an important subject that this chapter focuses on it alone. There are three broad topics:

- Exploring general theory and background information

- Creating a secure environment

- Recognizing and combating common vulnerabilities

Some of the topics discussed here will be implemented in real-world code in subsequent chapters. A few of the other recommendations are steps to implement a single time. And a handful of tips will only apply if you have administrative-level influence over the server. Still, it's only by grasping the whole picture that you can implement security on a high level.

SECURITY THEORY

Before getting into actual security specifics, let's think about what it means to be secure. I want to start with two simple, but perhaps heretical, ideas:

- No Web site is secure.

- Maximum security isn't the goal.

These two statements probably sound so absurd that I've lost all credibility, but in no way am I saying that security isn't important. In fact, when it comes to e-commerce sites, security is the most important criteria. I'm just saying that you may need to think about security differently than you currently do. I'll explain...

No Web Site Is Secure

The first fact you have to accept about any type of security is that security is not a binary thing: where a site, application, or computer is either secure or not. Security is measured on a spectrum (**Figure 2.1**). The code, software, environment, people involved, and other factors move the security rating up and down that scale. No matter what you know or do, you'll never create a Web site that's *absolutely secure*; the only thing you can do is attempt to make it *more secure*.

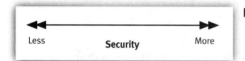

Figure 2.1

I've had people—well, one person—say this approach is wrong and danger-ous, but I think quite the contrary is true: When you begin to believe that your site is absolutely secure, that's when it's the most vulnerable because you've let your guard down. What you really should be doing is taking steps so that your site is *secure enough*.

 note

Accepting that you cannot create absolute security doesn't mean you shouldn't try but rather that you should never stop trying.

As an analogy, think about a car: If you drive somewhere, get out, but don't lock the car, it still may be relatively secure, depending upon the time of day, the type of car, the area in which it's parked, and the length of time you'll leave it there. Just leaving a car unlocked does not mean it's guaranteed to be broken into, just as locking it doesn't mean it won't be. It's certainly harder to break into a locked car, but not impossible. If you leave the car in your garage, it's much, much less likely to get broken into, until you leave the garage door open or someone breaks into the garage. And, of course, never taking a car out of the garage defeats the whole point of having a car.

The same is true for a Web site: Doing X, Y, and Z will make it harder to break into, but not impossible because there's always a potential flaw just around the corner. Even if the server isn't turned on and is sitting in a locked hosting cage somewhere, there are people who work for that hosting company who can still access the machine. Simply put, there is nothing you can do to guaran-tee absolute security.

I say that no Web site is secure for two reasons. First, to promote eternal vigilance when it comes to your site's security. **Complacency is dangerous.** The second reason is...

Maximum Security Isn't the Goal

Again, this may sound blasphemous, but it's really not. You have to first accept that security comes at a cost. Making something—pretty much anything—more secure requires more time and money. Also, anything that's more secure is inherently less usable and, in terms of computers, slower (**Figure 2.2**).

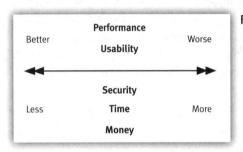

Figure 2.2

tip

The success of a site will increase its risks, as the extra attention will make it a bigger target for hackers.

Returning to my car analogy, if you live in a city, you likely lock the car when you drive it somewhere and park. But when you park it in your garage, you probably don't lock it. The same might be true if you live in a small town or if your car is a total beater. In some situations, maybe you use a secondary anti-theft device, like a steering wheel lock. What you're doing with your car, consciously or not, is adjusting the security measures in place based upon the perceived level of risk and the potential loss (for example, an expensive car versus a cheap one).

This is true of Web sites, as well: Different types of sites require different levels of security. A site that lists my favorite books is at a different point on the security spectrum than one that stores user information. Even that is on a less critical plateau than a site that handles credit cards. Even beyond that high-security level, there are sites for online banking, sensitive government and/or military data, and so forth (**Figure 2.3**).

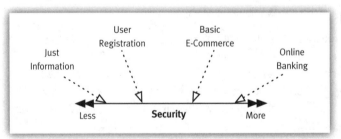

Figure 2.3

The goal, then, isn't to implement the highest level of security but rather the *highest level of security that's appropriate for the site*. Here are two concrete examples of what I mean:

You may already know that the Secure Sockets Layer (SSL) is an essential part of the e-commerce system. SSL provides the first line of defense for protecting user-submitted information; when the time comes to take the customer's credit card, SSL must be used. But this doesn't mean that SSL must be used for every page on your site. SSL puts a strain on the server, and only a fraction of SSL requests can be handled simultaneously compared to non-SSL requests. As a compromise between security and performance, you may choose to only use SSL for the checkout process, and use a non-SSL connection for the bulk of the site.

As another example, a shared host is going to be less secure than a dedicated host simply because more people have access to, and more software is running on, the server. On the other hand, a shared host will cost a tenth or less of what a dedicated host costs. You can increase the security by purchasing a more expensive hosting plan, but that may not be necessary, let alone prudent.

All this being said, I don't want you thinking that I'm cavalier about security or that you should be. In this chapter, you'll learn the fundamentals for creating a secure Web site, but it's not reasonable to think that your site has to be secure to the nth degree. There are many baseline recommendations—in terms of code and server environments—that you should ideally implement for any site. But you'll be presented with plenty of choices for which you must weigh all the pros and cons before coming to a decision. The goal is to hit the appropriate mark on the security spectrum for the given situation (as in Figure 2.3). Then, give your site a nudge just a wee bit to the right on that spectrum, just to be safe.

tip

When making security decisions, always err on the side of being too overprotective.

Security for Customers

E-commerce sites and Web sites in general have a client-server relationship: two parties equally participating in an event. There are two sides to security, as well: one you implement as the site developer and/or server administrator and one the customer is aware of. Now let's take a couple of pages to think about security from the customer's perspective.

There's an old expression that says cleanliness is next to godliness. My house wouldn't suggest that I live by that expression, but it leads me to an analogy I have for Web site security:

tip

The success of an e-commerce site partly depends upon a customer's comfort in spending money there.

Security is Next to Godliness.

Think of security the way you might think about cleanliness. Say you go to eat at a restaurant ... the restaurant may or may not *look* clean, and it may or may not *be* clean. But if the restaurant doesn't look clean, then it probably isn't actually clean, and you don't want to eat there. The same goes for a Web site's security: If it doesn't give the appearance of being secure, it probably isn't secure, and potential customers won't want to use the site (and shouldn't). So how does a site look secure to the lay user? It...

- Is professional in appearance

- Is honest and transparent with respect to what the business is, what its policies are, how customer information will be used, and so on

- Uses SSL

- Doesn't do anything that may make the customer feel the site isn't secure

This last quality is really the most important, as the common person may not really know the difference between a secure-looking and unsecure-looking site. A successful e-commerce site gives customers every reason to complete their sale and absolutely no reason not to. If a customer goes to a site and sees technical error messages, alerts from their browser (for example, because of poor JavaScript or improper use of SSL), and so forth, they'll likely take their business elsewhere. If the Web site does something that makes the customer say "Huh?" think of it like seeing a rodent scurry across the restaurant floor: It's time for the customer to go.

The second part of this analogy is that while it's important for a restaurant to *look* clean (so people will eat there), it's more important that it's *actually* clean (so that patrons don't get sick, so that the inspector doesn't shut it down, and so on). Your Web site must actually be secure, so that nothing bad can happen to the customers or your client.

The final reason I believe this analogy works is that it also supports the two maxims I already put forth. Security, like cleanliness, isn't an absolute and the amount of effort you put into it should depend upon the situation. The place where a restaurant keeps its garbage doesn't need to be that clean, but the kitchen sure does. Maybe you're the kind of person that would thoroughly clean monthly, weekly, or daily. Maybe you're the kind that will take cleaning to the disinfecting level. There's no right answer in these situations: There's better and there's worse, and there's what's right for you and your situation. The same goes for security. Most importantly, just because you cleaned today, doesn't mean it will stay clean forever. And the Web site that went live today without any issues could become vulnerable tomorrow, even if that's through no fault of your own.

tip

Having friends and family test your site is a good way to get feedback on potentially confusing or problematic parts.

tip

If you're creating a site for a client, put a plan in place so that someone continues to maintain the site's security after you're finished with the project.

PCI REQUIREMENTS

In Chapter 1, "Getting Started," I mention that you'll need to be aware of *PCI compliance*. Compliance means abiding by all twelve requirements outlined in the PCI DSS. Depending upon your level of involvement in the e-commerce project, some of these may not be applicable to you personally, but you should still be aware of them and pass them along to those that are responsible.

Taken verbatim from **www.pcisecuritystandards.org**, the requirements are:

Build and Maintain a Secure Network

Requirement 1: Install and maintain a firewall configuration to protect cardholder data.

Requirement 2: Do not use vendor-supplied defaults for system passwords and other security parameters.

Protect Cardholder Data

Requirement 3: Protect stored cardholder data.

Requirement 4: Encrypt transmission of cardholder data across open, public networks.

Maintain a Vulnerability Management Program

Requirement 5: Use and regularly update anti-virus software.

Requirement 6: Develop and maintain secure systems and applications.

Implement Strong Access Control Measures

Requirement 7: Restrict access to cardholder data by business need-to-know.

Requirement 8: Assign a unique ID to each person with computer access.

Requirement 9: Restrict physical access to cardholder data.

Regularly Monitor and Test Networks

Requirement 10: Track and monitor all access to network resources and cardholder data.

Requirement 11: Regularly test security systems and processes.

Maintain an Information Security Policy

Requirement 12: Maintain a policy that addresses information security.

If you go to the PCI Web site, you can download a 70-plus-page PDF that explains each of these regulations in more detail. The document also discusses how to test each condition and provides a worksheet to annotate your results. You should read this PDF at some point, but I want to add a few notes of my own here.

 note

Extra precautions apply if wireless technology will be used on your business's internal network.

 note

Depending upon the level of PCI compliance that applies to your business, you may be required to perform annual validation tests.

First, some of these rules, such as using a firewall and anti-virus software, may be beyond your role and server authority, but they still need to be done. In fact, you should use a firewall and anti-virus software on any server. Changing the default passwords is also a must, but the second requirement goes well beyond just changing passwords, into areas such as disabling unnecessary software.

As for requirements three and four, the best advice I can give is **not to store credit card information at all**, but if you do, ratchet your security up many, many levels. Also know that there are key pieces of data that you're not allowed to store, such as the card verification code or its PIN. Storing credit card information is not for the beginning developer or the small business, so please design your site and use payment gateways in such a way to relieve you of that burden.

Requirement number six—develop and maintain secure systems and applications—is really what this book is all about. That's a big topic whose bottom line is to program securely.

Requirements seven through nine are impacted by both the business and the hosting company. But one rule you can use in just the programming facet is number eight: providing unique identifiers to each administrator. Unless there will literally only be one person ever administrating a site, create a system and get in the habit of defining multiple users with appropriate permissions. In this book's first e-commerce example (paid access to content), one administrator type might only be able to manage the site's content. Another administrator might be able to do that and access the non-commercial customer data. The highest level of access might also allow for viewing payment data (in this case, a record of payments made, not the actual customer information charged for payments). Extra security can be achieved by forcing regular password changes, adding password requirements (length, use of capital and non-letters), and by disabling inactive accounts.

The remaining three requirements are ongoing tasks, necessary even if none of the site's code changes. I talk about this some in the first chapter: keeping a close eye on the server to catch something bad, and having a plan in place when it does.

These twelve requirements are excellent and appropriately encompassing. When you read the full PCI DSS document, you'll get tons of specific recommendations, each of which will improve your site's security that much more.

Some people feel that the PCI DSS is too demanding, although I think it's better to overdo security than to take risks. An opposite complaint about the PCI DSS is that it can fool people into thinking that their site or system is secure just because they've abided by these requirements. Remember that PCI DSS establishes a *baseline* for the *minimum* you must do toward improving security. If your situation warrants, there are always more steps you can take.

SERVER SECURITY

Most of the rest of the book will address security as affected by the PHP code you write, but let's first look at many of the server-based factors that play into the overall security of your e-commerce site. The approach to server security is simple:

1. Deny
2. Authorize
3. Record

You should first deny everybody and everything you can. Then allow limited capability only after proper authorization and authentication. Finally, record pretty much everything, so that you know what people might be trying to do (but failing) and what they did do.

Hosting Implications

The biggest question with respect to server security will be the hosting of the site. A shared host will be less secure than a VPS or dedicated hosting plan just by the virtue of having more people with access to the server itself. Further, any hosting that gives you some administrative-level control over the server *can* be more secure, as you'll be able to customize how the server runs and better lock it down. I would argue, however, that unless you're an expert in server administration, using a managed server is better than trying to do it all by yourself. Whatever your situation, do your best to limit the number of people that have physical and network access to the server.

Per the PCI DSS, the server should also be running a firewall and an anti-virus program. The anti-virus program has to be kept up to date if it's to be any good at all. But the same can be said for all the software on the server. Quite frequently, security holes are introduced when a design flaw (a bug) is found in common applications, like the Apache Web server, DNS, or an email system. Upgrading and patching these tools when new versions are released is a key component to your server's security.

And, of course, you should create very secure passwords for accessing the server and change them regularly.

 tip

A public Web page has an opposite security model: anyone and everyone is allowed to view it.

 note

An organization's own employees can be a weak security link. Be aware of the potential for "inside jobs."

 tip

Subscribe to software mailing lists so that you're contacted when new versions are released.

Finally, use the server's logs to track who accesses a site and when. This way you have a record of who could have done something bad. You may also want to be notified (via email or text message) when anyone logs in to the server at all.

PHP and Web Security

A secondary level of security is controlled by how the Web server (for example, Apache, IIS, and so on) and PHP are configured. First, keep both up to date, along with any related software. Specific security issues will depend upon the actual Web server in use, so research and stay up to date on security factors surrounding your particular Web server. By learning more about Apache, for example, you'll find that the **DocumentRoot** directive, which limits the Web server to working only with files found within that directory, can be a great security asset.

There are a number of adjustments you can make as to how PHP runs. The current settings can be seen by invoking the **phpinfo()** function (**Figure 2.4**). You'll find each setting listed with two columns: Local Value and Master Value. The local column indicates settings that are being overridden within the current directory.

Configuration		
PHP Core		
Directive	Local Value	Master Value
allow_call_time_pass_reference	On	On
allow_url_fopen	On	On
allow_url_include	Off	Off
always_populate_raw_post_data	Off	Off
arg_separator.input	&	&
arg_separator.output	&	&
asp_tags	Off	Off
auto_append_file	no value	no value

Figure 2.4

To change how PHP runs, edit the **php.ini** configuration file. The **phpinfo()** function also reveals its location. Some PHP settings can be set within a PHP script; although in terms of security, it's best to make the change on a global basis (otherwise, if you forget to make the change in any given script, you'd create a security hole).

You should start by using the **open_basedir** setting. It limits the directories from which PHP can open files. If you set this value to your Web directory, or the parent of the Web directory, malicious PHP code can't be used to read important system files located in other places.

On a similar note, you should, if you can, take advantage of non-Web directories as a place to store sensitive information. For example, your URL, **www.example.com**, might point to the actual server directory **/var/www/ username/htdocs**, so that loading **http://www.example.com/home.php**

tip

The PHP manual lists other security recommendations depending upon PHP's relationship to the Web server (CGI binary versus Apache module).

tip

The recommendation used to be to run PHP in safe mode, but that was never a great solution and has been deprecated.

tip

Don't leave a **phpinfo()** script publicly available on your server. It displays too much information about your server!

note

After making changes to the Web server or PHP configuration, restart the Web server to enact those changes.

executes (through the Web browser) **/var/www/username/htdocs/home.php** (**Figure 2.5** on the next page). In this case, the **htdocs** folder is called the *Web root directory*. Anything placed within that directory is theoretically accessible via the HTTP protocol. For example, the **image.png** file stored in the **images** subdirectory is available via **http://www.example.com/images/image.png**. Anything stored above the **htdocs** directory—**/var/www/username**, the parent of the Web directory—is not available via HTTP. Files and folders placed there can still be accessed by PHP running on the server, but cannot be directly accessed remotely via HTTP.

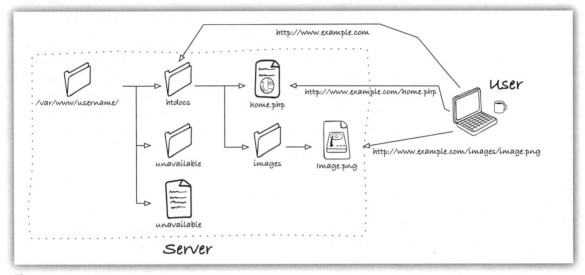

Figure 2.5

A second setting you can change is to disable **register_globals**. This setting makes global variables available in the local scope and is not inherently insecure: A properly written program will be just as safe, regardless of this setting. For that matter, disabling this setting does not mean your site will necessarily be secure. But disabling **register_globals** means not having to worry about someone's casual programming mistake creating a potential vulnerability. If you use third-party software, such as PHP-based forums and other add-ons, there's even more reason to disable **register_globals**.

 note

The **register_globals** directive, along with **safe_mode**, Magic Quotes, and others, has been deprecated and will disappear from future versions of PHP.

How errors are handled can often undermine the security, and the professionalism, of a Web site. A common attack is for hackers to supply problematic data in the hopes that generated errors will be revealing. To safeguard against this type of attack, start by developing your site under the error level of **E_ALL | E_STRICT**. By doing so, any potential problem will be reported to you via email or a log. Then, before the site goes live, disable **display_errors** so that no PHP problem will be shown to the user. Instead, use a custom error handler that displays appropriate messages to end users and reports detailed, technical messages only to you. You'll see specific code for doing this in the example chapters.

If you're using a shared host, another recommendation I'd make is to change the session directory. By default, PHP will write all session data to a common, temporary directory, such as **/tmp** on *nix systems. But this directory is readable and writable by anyone on the server, meaning that any user on the server—and a shared host may have dozens—can read the session data stored therein. A better alternative is to create a writable directory within your own, private area of the server that only your site will use for the sessions.

My final PHP recommendation isn't a setting, but involves practices you won't see me do elsewhere, so I want it to be clear now. You should absolutely avoid using functions that execute code on the server, such as **system()** and **exec()**. Also, be careful when using any function that manipulates server files and directories, whether that means creating, opening, reading, or writing. When you must manipulate server files and directories, be 100 percent certain that you're using thoroughly validated data in these function calls, not unvalidated user-supplied data.

Database Security

Even if your Web site will not be storing the most dangerous customer information—their credit card data—the database needs to be thoroughly protected, as the breach of any customer information is a huge business liability.

The front line of database defense is MySQL's access privileges system. MySQL allows you to create specific users that have limited permissions on only particular databases. Users are identified by the combination of their name, password, and host (that is, which computer the user is on). To start, create unique, secure usernames with unique, extremely secure passwords. And, as with pretty much everything, it's really best to change those passwords regularly. Also, be certain to change the root user's password on a new MySQL installation.

Next, every MySQL user should only be able to connect to MySQL from *localhost* or 127.0.0.1 (that is, from the same server). If MySQL is running on a machine separate from the Web server, you can create a MySQL user that has permission to connect only from that other server's IP address. An added benefit of restricting users to just 127.0.0.1 and specific IP addresses (if other IP addresses are absolutely necessary) is that you can then run MySQL with the **--skip-name-resolve** and **--skip-networking** options. This is more secure and will improve performance, because MySQL won't need to resolve host names.

tip

*nix is a common abbreviation for Unix and Unix-like operating systems, such as Linux.

tip

See the MySQL manual, or my book *MySQL: Visual QuickStart Guide, 2nd Edition* (Peachpit Press, 0-321-37573-4) for instructions on creating MySQL users.

note

Delete any databases whose name begins with "test," because MySQL allows any user to connect to them.

You should also create separate MySQL users for different types of activity. For example, the administrator user for the site will need **SELECT**, **INSERT**, and **UPDATE** permissions. They may also need **DELETE**, but it's best not to allow that unless absolutely necessary. Conversely, almost everything a customer will do on an e-commerce site will only require a MySQL user with **SELECT** privileges. Browsing and searching the catalog are simple **SELECT** queries. It may not be until the user starts to complete an order—actually check out— that an **INSERT** is required. An **UPDATE** would be needed if they can change their password or other personal information. **DELETE** permissions would never be appropriate. In theory, you could create three distinct types of MySQL users with specific permissions:

- Public: **SELECT**

- Customer: **SELECT, INSERT, UPDATE**

- Admin: **SELECT, INSERT, UPDATE, DELETE**

By taking this approach, any potential vulnerability that exists in the bulk of the site could not damage the database. The MySQL users with more privileges might only be connecting in areas that require customer or administrator login and an SSL connection, so there would be some added built-in safety there.

You should avoid giving **PROCESS, FILE, SHUTDOWN, GRANT, RELOAD, DROP, ALTER,** and **CREATE** privileges to any MySQL user that will be connecting from a Web site. If that site can be hacked, then the cracker will have too much database power. Instead, create a database administrator, for one or a limited number of databases, and only use that account to create and manage the database through a command-line interface, if at all possible.

In order to get data to and from the MySQL server in the most secure way possible, you can use SSL. This is only necessary when MySQL and PHP are running on separate machines, of course, and when the data is particularly sensitive. See the MySQL manual for instructions on setting up MySQL for your server's operating system and MySQL version. Understand that there will be performance degradation when using SSL with MySQL, due to the extra encryption and decryption work involved.

For the purposes of security, separation of site logic, and performance, you should consider putting as much functionality in the database as possible. This includes using view tables, stored procedures, triggers, and so forth. The *Coffee* site example in Part Three, "Selling Physical Products," of the book will demonstrate this point concretely.

 tip

Simplifying MySQL user permissions will also improve performance, because permissions have to be checked with each query.

As a final note, the MySQL server itself (the process known as **mysqld**) is a system process that is run by a specific operating system user (that is, the server process does not run as one of the MySQL database users). While it used to be common to run the **mysqld** process as the computer's root user, you should not do this. There are MySQL commands that manipulate the file system; if MySQL is running with ultimate authority, then it can manipulate any file on the server. Instead, run **mysqld** as a different, limited computer user.

SECURE TRANSACTIONS

Secure Sockets Layer (SSL) defines a protocol for protecting data transmitted over public networks. SSL is an absolute must for e-commerce sites and for many non-e-commerce sites, too. SSL provides encryption and decryption of data passed back and forth between the server and the client, making it safe from potentially prying eyes. If your site properly uses SSL, the user will see a closed lock icon in their browser (**Figure 2.6**). If the site improperly uses SSL, such as serving a mixture of SSL and non-SSL content, the user will see a broken lock icon (or one with a warning, **Figure 2.7**). Each browser behaves a bit differently, but for those users who pay attention to such things (and you do, don't you?), this visual indicator is a reassurance that it's safe to provide their most critical personal information.

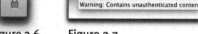

Warning: Contains unauthenticated content

Figure 2.6   **Figure 2.7**

The process works like this:

1. The browser makes an SSL request of a server.
2. The server sends a digital certificate to the browser.
3. The browser indicates what encryption it supports.
4. The server selects the best encryption possible.
5. Encryption keys are generated by the browser and server for the session.

These steps are required only the first time the browser makes an SSL request from that server; subsequent requests will use the encryption keys already created.

To use SSL, you must first buy a certificate. In terms of actual security, the digital certificate acts as the public key used for the encryption. In terms of perceived security, a certificate is intended to reassure the user that SSL is properly in place, that the underlying business is legitimate—that it's been

note

Transmitted data will pass through any number of computers between the client and the server, which is why SSL is necessary.

note

SSL should be used whenever it would be a problem if the data being transmitted could be seen by others.

note

In cases where sensitive form data is submitted, you should display AND handle the form using an SSL connection.

tip

Cookies can be restricted so that they're sent only over secure connections.

verified—and that the site is therefore safe to use. Browsers provide a way for users to view the certificate's details (**Figure 2.8** on the next page), although I don't know how commonly most people do this. If there's a mismatch between the certificate and how it's being used, or if you use a less secure certificate (like a self-signed one), the browser may even directly warn the user of the potential danger. **Figure 2.9**, which shows a Firefox response, is explicitly telling the user not to trust the site and the user has to take extra steps in order to proceed. If your site displayed this message to the user, it would be very bad for your business.

note

Failing to provide all the content on an HTTPS page—the HTML, the media, the JavaScript, the CSS, and so on—through the HTTPS protocol can create a broken lock icon in the browser.

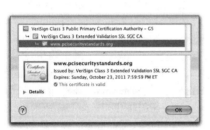

Figure 2.8

Figure 2.9

A certificate can be purchased from any number of Certifying Authorities (CA), from security specialists like Thawte (**www.thawte.com**) and VeriSign (**www.verisign.com**) to simple resellers such as GoDaddy (**www.godaddy.com**), to possibly your own hosting company. Built into all major browsers is a list of 50-plus major Certifying Authorities that are to be trusted. When you purchase a certificate from a major company, you're buying, in part, the assurance that the user's browser isn't going to warn them about the validity of the certificate (as in Figure 2.9). That's a legitimate reason to purchase a quality certificate instead of using a cheaper one. Each of these companies also sells levels of certificates at different prices, which is the next consideration.

tip

SSL can be used to secure lots of connection types, not just HTTP, but also FTP, SMTP, and so forth.

note

As already stated, because of the extra encryption work involved, servers can handle only a fraction—one-tenth is a reasonable rule of thumb— of SSL requests compared to non-SSL ones.

In terms of actual security (not perceived), one thing that may cost more is the maximum level of encryption used, from 40-bit to 256-bit. The higher the encryption, the better, although the maximum actual encryption level that will be used will depend upon the Web server and the browser involved in the transaction. A 128-bit security is fine for most sites; 256-bit is the online-banking level.

Next, some certificates come with warranties to reimburse you in case of a failure. The cheapest GoDaddy certificates might insure you for up to $2,000; expensive VeriSign ones cover up to $250,000. That's a big difference.

tip

Fairly active sites may only require one Web server but multiple database servers, in which case the one certificate might suffice.

tip

Certificates can be self-signed and cost nothing, but these aren't appropriate for e-commerce sites.

tip

If you spend more money on a certificate, you'll also get better technical support.

tip

The security measures you can take will also depend upon the versions of software in use—another reason to keep software up to date!

You'll also pay more to have a more flexible certificate. A valid certificate for a single domain is cheaper than one for all subdomains (**www.example.com**, **shop.example.com**, and **admin.example.com**); a single certificate valid for multiple domains (**example.com** and **example.net**) costs even more. Another consideration is the ability to use the same certificate on multiple servers or not. Only very active sites require multiple servers, but if you do, you'll need to buy the more expensive certificate.

Conversely, you should not use certificates tied to a given host or that are shared by multiple sites on the same server. These kinds of certificates may be free or cheap with your hosting, but they'll be a red flag to customers.

More expensive certificates also mean that the issuer has done more extensive checks into who the purchaser is. A cheap certificate basically says someone bought this certificate. An expensive certificate says someone bought this certificate for this domain that we've validated they own, and we've confirmed they're a valid company operating in X country, and we've spoken to them on the phone, and read a letter from their accountant, and so on (and I'm not making all that up). Finally, you can buy high-end certificates that enable the "green address bar" effect in some Web browsers, also called "extended validation" or EV). This is an obvious, visual cue to the user that they've got a really secure connection, and it's safe for them to do whatever they're about to do.

COMMON VULNERABILITIES

To wrap up this chapter, I want to talk about some of the common vulnerabilities Web sites are prone to and that you'll need to watch out for. You'll see some redundancies with the information already presented, but reinforcing good security approaches is never a bad thing.

Security is all about protecting data: protecting it from being seen, altered, or deleted by the wrong people. What most vulnerabilities have in common is they provide potential holes through which hackers can see or manipulate data to which they shouldn't have access. The following sections cover the most common security hacks and attacks, and what you need to do to prevent them.

Protecting Information

Dynamic Web sites deal with lots of information, from just content to user-supplied data to transaction histories. This data will be received by PHP scripts, passed to a MySQL database, and later retrieved from the database so it's again available in PHP. To strengthen this process, start by *taking* only the minimum amount of information needed: **You don't need to worry about protecting something you don't have.** Next, validate the user-supplied data to the utmost degree. PHP's *Filter* functions (**www.php.net/filter**), formerly found in PECL (PHP Extension Community Library, **http://pecl.php.net**) and part of the language core as of PHP 5.2, provide excellent tools for validating and sanitizing values. **Always assume that user input is wrong and then verify that it's right.**

Third, *store* only the minimum amount of data. For example, you may need to *take* twelve pieces of information about a customer, and then pass seven of those along to a payment gateway while *storing* only five in your own database. Fourth, if PHP and MySQL are on separate servers, use SSL to protect the data during transmission. Fifth, retrieve from the database only the information you actually need.

These just-mentioned techniques for handling data in PHP and MySQL can also be applied to the client-server relationship. Be very careful about what you store in the browser (in cookies), pass to the browser in HTML, or display as part of the URL. PayPal, with an amazing lack of foresight, used to accept the total price being charged in the URL, where it's available for anyone to easily — really easily — change! You also need to validate and/or sanctify cookie and URL data, treating it the same as any other user-supplied data (such as from a form), because cookies and URL parameters really are under the user's control.

For sensitive data being stored, but not stored in a database, change your sessions directory, and use the Web root directory's parent folder (see Figure 2.5). Make sure your server isn't giving away anything with error messages that are too revealing or lingering in **phpinfo()** scripts.

Finally, to protect all the server data, perform regular backups. If you use a RAID array of hard drives, you'll also be protected should a single drive fail.

Protecting the User

Protecting the user, aka the customer in an e-commerce site, is really the primary goal, because the trust of the customer is what makes your business thrive. Protecting their information is part of protecting them, but there's another way that your site may be of some harm: through *Cross-Site Scripting* (XSS) attacks. In an XSS attack, malicious person Alice injects JavaScript into your site. Most commonly this is done through components intended for user input, such as a comments or reviews area. When Bob loads your page in his Web browser (for example, when he looks at the product reviews), the

 tip

RAID drives or other fast hard drives can greatly improve the performance of your site.

malicious JavaScript is executed, to his detriment. The JavaScript might be used to read Bob's cookies or execute code found on Alice's site. Bob is the victim, and your site was an accomplice.

As scary as XSS may sound, preventing it is really quite simple. As always, you must validate user input. Admittedly, in a case like comments or reviews, you can't really come up with a strict model for what the submission should contain (compared to, say, an email address that has a precise format). However, you do know that it *shouldn't* contain JavaScript. By applying the **strip_tags()** function, which removes any HTML, JavaScript, or PHP from a string, to any user-provided input that will be redisplayed in the Web browser, you can prevent XSS attacks.

Another way to protect users is to educate them about common scams, potentially involving your site or not. The Web site associated with my personal bank does an excellent job of sending out emails indicating fake scams making the rounds. They also make it clear that they would never ask for certain types of personal information through email, stating that you should never send such information in any email reply.

Another recommendation for protecting users involves protecting their account. When people attempt to log in to your site, using a combination of a username or email address and a password, you have a choice as to how mistakes are reported. Indicating that just the password is wrong verifies that a submitted username or email address does exist in the database. This gives any potential hacker half of the equation; from there they can continue trying common passwords in order to access the user's actual account. Instead, just indicate that the combination does not match the database: Such a message doesn't confirm the validity of a given email address or username.

Protecting the Site

The Web site itself is the agent between the customer and the data, and it, too, has vulnerabilities. The first kind of attacks to be aware of are *Denial of Service* (DoS) attacks. These are brute force attacks where many zombie or slave servers, all around the world, attempt to connect to your site simultaneously. By doing so, your server will be so overwhelmed that it will not be able to handle legitimate requests. Unfortunately, there's not much you can do to prevent a DoS attack. Even if you have lots and lots and lots of servers, all around the world, service denial can still happen (it has happened to even the biggest sites). But by closing unused server ports, using a firewall, and monitoring network activity, you can minimize the potential. Fortunately, you have to be pretty successful to even be a target, so you could look at a DoS attack as a sign that you've made it (in a lemons-to-lemonade kind of way).

Whereas DoS attacks are relatively rare and hard to prevent, *SQL Injection* attacks are quite common and very easy to prevent. The premise behind an SQL Injection attack is that the user submits SQL to a site in the hope that a problematic SQL command will be executed, thereby either revealing sensitive information or damaging the database. For example, a login form might run a query like:

SELECT * FROM users WHERE email='$email' AND pass=SHA1('$pass')

The **$email** and **$pass** values presumably come from the login form. If the user were to submit *';DROP TABLE users;* as the password, and if steps weren't taken to prevent this, the resulting query would be:

SELECT * FROM users WHERE email='whatever@example.edu'
AND pass=SHA1('';DROP TABLE users;')

In theory, the one SQL command becomes three separate ones. First, there's an syntactically invalid **SELECT**, which would do nothing other than create an error, then the **DROP TABLE** command would be run, and then there's a third meaningless, syntactically invalid query. If these three queries were executed, that would be bad.

There are many ways of stopping these attacks from being productive. First, you should validate data to expected values as much as possible (that is, an email address has an exact format and certain values must be positive integers). Second, run all strings, even those you've validated, through a database-specific escaping function, such as **mysqli_real_escape_string()**:

$pass = mysqli_real_escape_string($dbc, $_POST['pass']);

Next, you should typecast all values that should be numeric to force them to be numbers:

$id = (int) $_GET['id'];

With that code, if the user manipulated **$_GET['id']** to be *';DROP TABLE users;*, that string would be typecasted to an integer with a value of zero. When used in a query, it will probably return no results, but it won't do any harm.

An alternative is to use *prepared statements*, in which specific values get separated from the query and are recombined on the database level. You must still validate data used in prepared statements—there's no purpose in running a query with data that's known to be bad, but the query will always be safe.

 tip

Prepared statements can also have a performance benefit, as you'll learn in Part Three.

Hackers will supply bad data to achieve three other goals:

- Remote File Inclusion
- Local File Inclusion
- System Calls

In a Remote File Inclusion (RFI) attack, the hacker attempts to get a site to include a file found on another server (probably theirs). PHP, when it calls **fopen()**, **require()**, **include()**, and the like, will execute any PHP code in the included file as if that code was part of the original file. So if Chuck can get your site to open and execute his code, he can start manipulating your server, with disastrous results. Again, prevention is simple: Don't use unvalidated user data in these function calls.

A Local File Inclusion (LFI) attack is similar, but the hopes are that a sensitive document on the same server, like a password file, will be read and displayed.

The same steps used to prevent RFI and LFI attacks apply if your site uses **exec()** and other functions that run commands on the server itself. It's best that your server not use these functions, but if they do, you absolutely cannot use unvalidated user data in them.

Moving on, if your site accepts file uploads from users, that system can be used to attempt a *Malicious File Execution* on your server. The hacker's hope is that he or she can upload, for example, his own PHP script to your system, and then execute that PHP script by loading it directly in their browser. Say your site allows users to upload images of themselves. You should validate that the upload is of a given type—gif, jpg, png—but that can easily be faked. If you were to store the uploaded files in the Web directory (for example, the **images** folder in Figure 2.5), then the hacker can later run the script by going to **http://www.yoursite.com/images/scriptname.php**. But if you store user submissions outside the Web directory (such as the **unavailable** folder in Figure 2.5), then uploaded files cannot be directly executed through the Web browser. Another prevention technique involves changing the name of the uploaded file: If the hacker doesn't know what it's called on the server, he or she can't invoke it.

The last type of attack you should know about is the *Cross-Site Request Forgery* (CSRF). This attack attempts to execute unauthorized commands from an authorized user. The success of these attacks is predicated upon the site trusting the user as they have previously been authenticated. For example, say your site has a page that adds credits to user accounts: There's a form for selecting a user and the number of credits; when the form is submitted, the

tip

Disabling the **register_globals** setting and using **open_basedir** can also help prevent RFI and LFI attacks.

tip

In Parts Two and Three of the book, you'll see techniques for securely handling file uploads.

credits are processed. Now say that Alice is an administrator who went to your site, was authenticated, and did whatever (it doesn't matter whether she used the add credit system or not). If Alice doesn't log out, there's still a cookie in her browser indicating that she's an authenticated user of your site. Next, Alice comes across some page in which hacker Bob has identified a PHP script as the source for an image tag:

```
<img src="http://www.yoursite.com/add_credits.php?user=12&credits=
➥100" />
```

This might be a public forum, or a review system, or any site that allows users to post images in some way.

When Alice loads the page with that image tag, her browser will make a request for the **add_credits.php** script on your site, passing along the user and credits numbers. This request will look, to the server, exactly the same as if Alice had consciously gone to the **add_scripts.php** page. That page will first confirm that the requesting user is authenticated, which Alice is. The page would then, in theory, perform whatever action is the result of receiving those two values in the URL.

This is a *blind attack* in that the original hacker Bob will never see the results of the request being made: He's just putting this out there in the hopes that, in this case, his account at your site gets credited when some authenticated user stumbles upon this code. Know that just authenticating the user will not prevent this kind of attack, because it's that trust that makes this kind of attack plausible.

To prevent a CSRF attack, start by teaching your administrators to log out. Then, restrict the lifetime of an authentication cookie so that it will expire some minutes after they've stopped being active on your site (online banks may only allow ten or fifteen minutes of user inactivity). This will narrow the window of CSRF danger to just that brief cookie lifetime.

Not making sensitive information (like a user ID value) public is also important, but just relying on a hacker not knowing about something isn't real security. Although it's possible to perform CSRF requests via POST, relying upon posted data for sensitive requests is more secure (and is in keeping with the approach that POST is to be used when a request will result in site changes).

The true CSRF prevention comes from guaranteeing that sensitive requests, like the transfer of credits, are actually prompted by your own site. You cannot reliably use a browser's "referrer" value (that is, what page the browser was on before this one), though. Instead, create your own tie between the HTML

note

CSRF attacks are more successful against very popular sites that use long-lasting cookies.

form and the page that handles its request. The tie itself will be a secret token, uniquely generated for each request. Here's what you'd do on the page that displays the form (with much of the code implied):

```php
<?php // form.php
...
$csrf_token = uniqid(); // or uniqid(rand(), true);
session_start();
$_SESSION['csrf_token'] = $csrf_token;
...
echo '<input type="hidden" name="csrf_token" value="' . $csrf_token . '"
⇒/>';
...
?>
```

On the page that handles the request, validate the token:

```php
<?php // handle_form.php
...
session_start();
if ( ($_SERVER['REQUEST_TYPE'] == 'POST') // only POST is allowed
&& (isset($_SESSION['csrf_token'], $_POST['csrf_token'])) // make sure
⇒the tokens exist
&& ($_SESSION['csrf_token'] == $_POST['csrf_token']) ) { // OK!
...
} else { // Invalid request!
}
...
?>
```

 tip

To prevent bots from trying to use a form, integrate a CAPTCHA (Completely Automated Public Turing test to tell Computers and Humans Apart) system.

Now the request will only be processed if Alice is still logged in (that is, her cookie is still live), if the request is via the POST method, if a *csrf_token* element exists in both **$_SESSION** and **$_POST**, and if the two values match. That's pretty good security!

PART TWO
SELLING VIRTUAL PRODUCTS

3 | FIRST SITE: STRUCTURE AND DESIGN

The first e-commerce site being developed in this book, *Knowledge is Power*, will provide content to paid subscribers. It will have these primary features:

- Straightforward use of HTML, PHP, and MySQL
- User accounts
- Ability for administrators to add HTML and PDF content
- PayPal for processing payments

This will be a relatively standard e-commerce example, applicable to most small- to medium-size businesses. By comparison, the more complex project, developed in Part Three, "Selling Physical Products," of the book, will use HTML, PHP, and MySQL in more advanced ways, won't require user accounts, will sell products that get shipped later (that is, the customer will not be billed immediately), and will integrate a different payment system. This is not to say that what you'll learn in this part of the book won't be applicable to real-world situations, quite the contrary.

The user account system will have several pieces: registering, logging in, logging out, retrieving forgotten passwords, and changing existing passwords. As a bonus, the user's password will be handled with extra security, in a way that you perhaps have not yet seen.

The available content that the customer is paying to see will be in two formats: HTML and PDF. For the former, you'll integrate a WYSIWYG editor into an HTML form so that administrators can easily create HTML without knowledge of

HTML. For the latter, you'll write a *proxy script* that serves protected files not available over HTTP or to non-validated users.

In this chapter, you'll set the stage for developing the site. This includes the database design, the organization of files on the server, the HTML template, plus a couple of necessary helper files that every other PHP script will use. The entire code for the site is also downloadable from **www.DMCInsights.com/ecom/**.

DATABASE DESIGN

The database I've designed for this example is simple, yet appropriate, with only five tables (**Figure 3.1**).

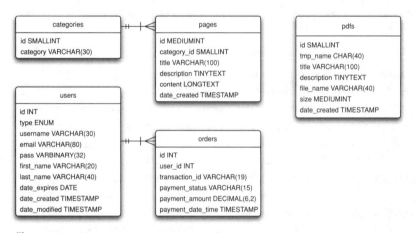

Figure 3.1

The **categories, pages,** and **pdfs** tables represent the "products" side of this e-commerce example. The **categories** table just lists the categories into which the HTML content will be organized. Each category will contain one or more pages, but each page will be in only one category.

The **pages** table stores the actual HTML content. For each HTML page, there are three important fields: **title, description**, and **content**. The **title** will be used as a link to each page and will also be used as the browser's title. The **description** is a short block of text that, um, describes the page's content. This value will be viewable to any user and to search engines. The **content** column stores the actual HTML content. You'll see all of this in action in Chapter 5, "Managing Site Content."

 tip

I'm a programmer, so I start designing the database and work my way to the HTML design. You might start with the user interface and work your way down to the database instead.

The **pdfs** table lists the particulars for each PDF file the site has, including a title for the PDF, like the HTML page title, a short description—viewable by anyone—the name of the actual PDF file, and its size in kilobytes. When a PDF file is uploaded to the site, it'll be given a non-obvious, temporary name (for example, *a0f07b9b15e38ca77219884a8bba9e57d01fae88*) that must also be stored; but when the PDF is served to the user, its original file name will be used instead. The PDFs are not being associated with information categories.

The **users** table stores a minimum amount of information about the customers. Each customer can create a username, and the system will also store their email address, a password, their first name, and their last name. The password will be stored as a *hash*, which is a representation of a value (as opposed to being an encrypted version that could be decrypted). Hashes always have exact lengths, so that column *could be* declared as a fixed **CHAR**. However, the password can take up less space if it's stored as binary data, which is how the column will be defined.

The site will have two types of users—members and administrators—so an **ENUM** column (that is, an enumerated list of options) will store the type, with the default value being *member*. Although administrators will never have to pay for access to the site, I thought it would make sense to use the same login system the non-administrators use, which means the administrators must be registered in the database, too. The **users** table also has a **date_expires** column that stores the date through which their account is active (that is, paid). When the user first subscribes and pays, the account will be set to expire in a year. When the user renews their membership, the account will be updated to one year later. Users whose accounts have expired will still be able to log in, but they won't be able to view any content and will be notified that they need to renew.

All payments will be handled through PayPal. Even though PayPal will provide detailed logs of every transaction, it's wise to record the basics of each transaction in this system as well. The **orders** table will store every transaction that goes through PayPal, associated with the ID of the user (as taken from the **users** table). Each order will be associated with exactly one user, but each user can have one or more records in the **orders** table. Three pieces of information from the PayPal transaction will be recorded, too: the **transaction_id**, which is a unique identifier; the **payment_status**, which is just a confirmation code; and the **payment_amount**. Storing this basic data will allow you to create a simple admin interface for viewing the total number of orders, amount of money taken in, and so on, without going to PayPal for that information. The **transaction_id** is the most sensitive piece of data stored in the database; through it, many details are accessible, but only to authorized PayPal users.

note

Most of the tables have a column that reflects when a record was added. The **users** table also has a field indicating when a record was last modified.

tip

With databases, it's much, much better to save more information than you end up needing than to later discover you haven't been storing something you do need.

I assume that you know how to create a database and its tables using a tool like phpMyAdmin, the command-line mysql client, and so forth. If you don't, see one of my MySQL-related books, search online, or just ask in my support forum. You can download the SQL commands from my Web site, but here they are as well:

```
CREATE TABLE `categories` (
    `id` SMALLINT NOT NULL AUTO_INCREMENT,
    `category` VARCHAR(30) NOT NULL,
    PRIMARY KEY (`id`),
    UNIQUE KEY `category` (`category`)
) ENGINE=MyISAM DEFAULT CHARSET=utf8;
CREATE TABLE `orders` (
    `id` INT UNSIGNED NOT NULL AUTO_INCREMENT,
    `user_id` INT UNSIGNED NOT NULL,
    `transaction_id` VARCHAR(19) NOT NULL,
    `payment_status` VARCHAR(15) NOT NULL,
    `payment_amount` DECIMAL(6,2) UNSIGNED NOT NULL,
    `payment_date_time` TIMESTAMP NOT NULL DEFAULT
    ➥CURRENT_TIMESTAMP,
    PRIMARY KEY (`id`),
    KEY `user_id` (`user_id`)
) ENGINE=MyISAM DEFAULT CHARSET=utf8;
CREATE TABLE `pages` (
    `id` MEDIUMINT UNSIGNED NOT NULL AUTO_INCREMENT,
    `category_id` SMALLINT UNSIGNED NOT NULL,
    `title` VARCHAR(100) NOT NULL,
    `description` TINYTEXT NOT NULL,
    `content` LONGTEXT NOT NULL,
    `date_created` TIMESTAMP NOT NULL DEFAULT CURRENT_TIMESTAMP,
    PRIMARY KEY (`id`),
    KEY `category_id` (`category_id`),
    KEY `creation_date` (`date_created`)
) ENGINE=MyISAM DEFAULT CHARSET=utf8;
CREATE TABLE `pdfs` (
    `id` SMALLINT UNSIGNED NOT NULL AUTO_INCREMENT,
    `tmp_name` CHAR(40) NOT NULL,
    `title` VARCHAR(100) NOT NULL,
    `description` TINYTEXT NOT NULL,
    `file_name` VARCHAR(40) NOT NULL,
    `size` MEDIUMINT UNSIGNED NOT NULL,
```

tip

Within SQL commands, wrapping table and column names in backticks isn't required but prevents possible conflicts with existing MySQL keywords.

tip

Because the cost of this site's service is only $10.00, the **payment_amount** column could be defined as a more restrictive **DECIMAL(4,2)**.

(continues on next page)

```
`date_created` TIMESTAMP NOT NULL DEFAULT CURRENT_TIMESTAMP,
  PRIMARY KEY (`id`),
  UNIQUE KEY `tmp_name` (`tmp_name`),
  KEY `date_created` (`date_created`)
) ENGINE=MyISAM DEFAULT CHARSET=utf8;
CREATE TABLE `users` (
  `id` INT UNSIGNED NOT NULL AUTO_INCREMENT,
  `type` ENUM('member','admin') NOT NULL,
  `username` VARCHAR(30) NOT NULL,
  `email` VARCHAR(80) NOT NULL,
  `pass` VARBINARY(32) NOT NULL,
  `first_name` VARCHAR(20) NOT NULL,
  `last_name` VARCHAR(40) NOT NULL,
  `date_expires` DATE NOT NULL,
  `date_created` TIMESTAMP NOT NULL DEFAULT CURRENT_TIMESTAMP,
  `date_modified` TIMESTAMP NOT NULL DEFAULT '0000-00-00 00:00:00',
  PRIMARY KEY (`id`),
  UNIQUE KEY `username` (`username`),
  UNIQUE KEY `email` (`email`)
) ENGINE=MyISAM DEFAULT CHARSET=utf8;
```

note

The database and the site as a whole will use the UTF-8 character set, allowing for any possible written language to be used.

You'll see that almost every column is defined as **NOT NULL**, which is ideal, in terms of performance and normalization standards. Default values are also set, as appropriate. Indexes, or keys, have been established on the primary keys, columns whose values must be unique, and columns that will be used in joins, **WHERE** clauses, and **ORDER BY** clauses, although you could certainly add a couple more indexes here and there.

SERVER ORGANIZATION

Before creating any HTML documents or PHP scripts, let's look at how the server should be organized. Unless your site is quite large (that is, it has so many separate files that creating subdirectories is appropriate), you'll normally place all the pages of the site within the Web root directory, which will be the case with this example. The Web root directory should also have folders for:

- Administration files
- CSS
- Images

- Media
- PHP includes
- JavaScript

This site will not place the administration pages—there are only two being developed in this book—in a separate directory, so you don't have to worry about that folder. Also, the initial version of the site won't need JavaScript or media folders. So the Web root directory needs just three subfolders to start, which I'll cleverly name **css**, **images**, and **includes**.

The **css** directory will contain one file, from the site template, named **styles.css** (more on the template later in the chapter). Eight images that come with the template will go into the **images** folder. The **includes** directory will store PHP scripts that will be included by other scripts. In other words, the **includes** directory is for files that won't be executed on their own. Over the next three chapters, you'll create six documents for the **includes** directory:

- **config.inc.php** is a script that defines the site's general behavior and various constants.

- **footer.html** is half of the HTML template.

- **form_functions.inc.php** defines a function used by every form.

- **header.html** is the other half of the HTML template.

- **login.inc.php** handles the login process.

- **login_form.inc.php** is the login form.

As you can tell, I'm breaking out much of the site functionality into separate files to make the site easy to maintain.

Along with all the PHP scripts that represent specific pages, such as registering, logging out, and so on, the site needs one more PHP script named **mysql.inc.php**. This script will connect to the database. Because that script defines sensitive information, it should ideally be stored outside the Web root directory.

The site also needs a folder to store PDFs that are available to paid subscribers. The PDFs will be placed in this folder by a script that handles the upload. In order to do that, the permissions on the folder must allow the Web server to write to it. Since this creates a potential security hole, it's best to place that folder outside the Web root. Additionally, the PDF scripts should be available to paid subscribers only, through a proxy script that validates the user. Keeping the PDF files from the Web directory prevents unpaid visitors from loading them.

 tip

For marginally improved security, give your includes and administration directories non-obvious names.

 note

In Chapter 7, "Second Site: Structure and Design," you'll learn other ways to protect your site's directories.

 note

A proxy script is a file that's used in place of something else, like a PHP script that presents a PDF instead of the user accessing the PDF directly.

note

Figures 3.2 and 3.3 together show every file and folder that will be created over the next four chapters.

 note

The **robots.txt** file shown in the figures won't be formally developed in this book but is available for viewing in the downloadable code.

Figure 3.2 shows the server organization, where the **html** folder is the Web root directory (**www.example.com** points there).

If you can't put anything below the Web root directory, which is common on shared hosts, you should use a structure like that shown in **Figure 3.3**.

Figure 3.2

Figure 3.3

As a precaution, use the Web server's tools to restrict access to the **includes** directory. Doing so will deny people access to it and the **pdfs** subfolder but won't interfere with a PHP script's ability to access its contents. Chapter 7 will discuss ways of doing this in detail.

FILE EXTENSIONS

When a user requests a page that uses a **.html** extension, the server will pass along the page's contents directly to the browser without any additional server processing. But when the user requests a page with a **.php** extension, the server will first run the page's content (that is, the code) through the PHP interpreter, which will then execute the code. (These are the standard settings; servers can be set up to treat extensions in other ways.) With this in mind, it's important that the site's primary pages—those that the user will directly access—use the **.php** extension in order for the code to be processed. Pages that are included by other PHP scripts and not run directly in the browser aren't handled by

the server directly, so you have your choice of what extension to use.

I use the **.html** extension for files that are primarily HTML, such as the header and footer. For pages that are primarily PHP, but are intended as included files, I use a combination: **.inc.php**. The **.inc** part indicates that it's a file to be included, but the **.php** prevents the code from being revealed should the file somehow be run directly in a Web browser. If you were to use just **.inc**, the server would probably not send the contents through the PHP interpreter, thereby sending potentially sensitive information to the browser. That's a security risk that's not worth taking.

CONNECTING TO THE DATABASE

Every PHP script in the site will require a connection to the database, so let's create a separate file in the **includes** directory for that purpose.

1. Create a new PHP script in your text editor or IDE to be named **mysql.inc.php.**

See Figures 3.2 and 3.3 for indications of where this file should be placed.

2. Define the constants for accessing the database:

```php
<?php
DEFINE ('DB_USER', 'username');
DEFINE ('DB_PASSWORD', 'password');
DEFINE ('DB_HOST', 'localhost');
DEFINE ('DB_NAME', 'ecommerce1');
```

You'll need to replace these values with those that are correct for your server. For my setup, I created a database called *ecommerce1* and created a MySQL user with **SELECT**, **INSERT**, and **UPDATE** privileges on that database. **You absolutely must use a more secure username and password than these!**

3. Connect to the database:

```php
$dbc = mysqli_connect (DB_HOST, DB_USER, DB_PASSWORD, DB_
➥NAME);
```

The **mysqli_connect()** function is used to connect to the database. The connection is assigned to the **$dbc** variable, which will be used by many functions in other scripts.

4. Establish the character set:

```php
mysqli_set_charset($dbc, 'utf8');
```

This function indicates what character set should be used for communications between PHP and the database. The database tables, the HTML pages, and the PHP-MySQL connection must all use the same character set.

5. Begin defining a function for making data safe to use in queries:

```php
function escape_data ($data) {
    global $dbc;
```

 note

Since the site will be using the UTF-8 character set, your text editor or IDE must be set to encode each page also using UTF-8.

 note

If your PHP-MySQL setup does not support the MySQL Improved extension, which I'll be using, you'll need to use the older MySQL functions, which have slightly different syntax. See the PHP manual for details.

 note

Any connection errors that occur will be handled by the custom error handler defined in the configuration file (in just a couple of pages).

This function will take a piece of data as its lone argument and make it safe to use in database queries. In other words, this function will prevent SQL Injection attacks from succeeding (see Chapter 2, "Security Fundamentals"). The function does three things:

- Removes extra slashes if Magic Quotes is enabled
- Trims extra spaces from the data
- Runs the data through the **mysqli_real_escape_string()** function

This last task is the most important, because the **mysqli_real_escape_string()** function will make a value safe to use in a query, keeping in mind the database's configuration and character set in use. The function needs the database connection, which is made available through the **global** command.

6. Strip the extra slashes if Magic Quotes is on:

if (get_magic_quotes_gpc()) $data = stripslashes($data);

Magic Quotes was created to provide a blanket level of security on incoming data, but it's not as secure as using **mysqli_real_escape_string()**. Hopefully, Magic Quotes is disabled on your server; but if Magic Quotes is enabled, then incoming data will already have slashes applied to potentially problematic characters that might break a query. Those slashes would be a problem, because **mysqli_real_escape_string()** will also apply slashes, thereby creating two slashes when there should be only one. To prevent that from happening, this line of code checks the Magic Quotes setting and calls the **stripslashes()** function if Magic Quotes is on.

7. Return a trimmed, secure version of the data:

return mysqli_real_escape_string (trim ($data), $dbc);

The difference between **mysqli_real_escape_string()** and something like Magic Quotes or **addslashes()** is that **mysqli_real_escape_string()** identifies what characters could be problematic based upon the database, the character set in use, and so forth.

8. Complete the **escape_data()** function:

} // End of the escape_data() function.

9. Save the file.

You may notice that you're not being instructed to include the closing PHP tag here. This is acceptable and, in some situations, actually better. If you were to use the closing tag and then inadvertently leave an extra space or blank line after that tag, the inclusion of this file by other scripts will result

note

Magic Quotes as a feature has been deprecated and will disappear from future versions of PHP.

note

The **mysql.inc.php** file found in the downloadable source code for this book contains additional code discussed in later chapters.

note

All included PHP files will omit the closing PHP tag to prevent "headers already sent" errors.

in headers being sent to the Web browser. If the including (that is, parent) script later attempts to send a cookie, start a session, or redirect the browser, you'll get a "headers already sent" error message (**Figure 3.4**). By omitting the closing tag, that cannot happen (at least not when this script is included).

An error occurred in script '/Users/larryullman/Sites/ecom_book/ex1/html/index.php' on line 26: session_start() [function.session-start]: Cannot send session cookie - headers already sent by (output started at /Users/larryullman/Sites/ecom_book/ex1/html/includes/header.html:5)

Figure 3.4

THE CONFIG FILE

The next PHP script to be created is a configuration file. Like the **mysql.inc.php** script, this one will be used by every script in the site (although some sites will have pages that don't require a database connection, every PHP script in every site should always use the configuration file). The configuration file has four purposes:

- Define systemwide settings so they may be changed easily
- Define useful constants that may be used by multiple scripts
- Start the session
- Establish how errors will be handled

Let's start defining the configuration file now, and in Chapter 4, "User Accounts," more code will be added to it.

1. Create a new PHP script in your text editor or IDE to be named **config.inc.php** and stored in your **includes** directory, as in Figures 3.2 and 3.3.

2. Define the **$live** and **$contact_email** variables:

```
<?php
$live = false;
$contact_email = 'you@example.com';
```

The **$live** variable is really the most important variable because it'll dictate how errors will be handled. Depending upon the payment gateway, this variable could also be used to switch from just testing the payment processing to actually using it. However, PayPal is a bit different, so that won't be the case in this example.

 tip

In the downloaded version of **config.inc.php** you'll see a bit of extra code, which you'll add in Chapter 4.

The **$contact_email** variable is for the email address to which error messages will be sent when the site goes live. It could also be used for contact forms, or you could define different email addresses for different purposes.

3. Define the constants:

define ('BASE_URI', '/*path*/*to*/*Web*/*parent*/folder/');
define ('BASE_URL', 'www.example.com/');
define ('MYSQL', '/*path*/*to*/mysql.inc.php');

These are the first three constants the site will use, and you'll need to change the values accordingly. The first constant should point to the parent of the Web root directory, if your site can use it. So, in Figure 3.2, **BASE_URI . pdfs** will be where the PDFs are stored and **BASE_URI . mysql.inc.php** will be the location of the MySQL connection script. If you can't access above the Web root directory, then assign to **BASE_URI** the Web root directory itself. So, in Figure 3.3, **BASE_URI . 'includes/pdfs'** will be where the PDFs are stored.

The second constant is the base URL of the site, without the protocol, such as **www.example.com/**. I've specifically left off the *http://*part, because some pages will use *https://*.

The third constant points to the MySQL connection script just created. You can use **BASE_URI** to help create this full path.

Constants like these are used for a couple of reasons. First, if you reference certain values in multiple scripts in multiple directories, it can be hard getting the references consistently correct. By using absolute references, they'll always be right. Second, if you change anything big about the site—its domain name or its hosting—just changing these values is all you will need to do.

4. Start the session:

session_start();

The site will use sessions to track logged-in users. Since every page will require the configuration file, starting the session here will make sure that every page has access to the session data. Plus, if you want to customize the session, like its name or how long it lasts, you can do that in one place.

On the other hand, this also means that sessions will be started in some situations where they're not actually necessary, like when someone views the home page or a content listing page, without going further.

 note

Both the **BASE_URI** and **BASE_URL** values end with a slash.

5. Begin defining an error-handling function:

function my_error_handler ($e_number, $e_message, $e_file, $e_line,
⇢$e_vars) {
  global $live, $contact_email;

PHP allows you to define your own functions for handling errors. By doing so, you can precisely control what errors get reported, how, and in what detail. Every time a PHP error occurs, or one is triggered using **trigger_error()**, this function will be called by a script that will be created shortly. The only exceptions are parse and other serious PHP errors that would prevent this script from being executed in the first place.

An error-handling function can be defined to take anywhere from two to five arguments. Here I'm using all five. The first is a numeric error identifier that might be assigned a value such as 2, which represents an **E_WARNING**. The second argument is the received error message. The next argument is the name of the file in which the error occurred, and the fourth is on which line. The fifth argument is an array of every variable that existed when the error occurred. This can be useful debugging information (and when it comes to debugging, more information is almost always better than less).

6. Begin creating a detailed error message:

$message = "An error occurred in script '$e_file' on line $e_line:
⇢\n$e_message\n";

The detailed error message will start with the name of the file in question, the line number, and the message string.

7. Add the backtrace information:

$message .= "<pre>" .print_r(debug_backtrace(), 1) . "</pre>\n";

A *backtrace* is essentially everything that happened up until the point of the error. This will include files that were executed, functions that were called, arguments passed to the functions, and variables that existed. You can get the backtrace information by calling the **debug_backtrace()** function, which returns an array. To add that array to the error message, pass it (or the function call that creates the array) as the first argument to **print_r()** and use **1** or **true** as the second value in **print_r()**. Providing a positive second argument to **print_r()** tells the function to return the value, instead of printing it. I'm wrapping this code in HTML preformatted tags, **<pre>...</pre>**, to make it easier to read.

If you don't want the detailed backtrace, you could just append the list of variables and values to the message, like so:

$message .= "<pre>" . print_r ($e_vars, 1) . "</pre>\n";

8. If the site isn't live, show the error message in the browser:

if (!$live) {
    echo '<div class="error">' . nl2br($message) . '</div>';

For a nonlive site, it's best to immediately be notified of any problems. Here, the error message will be printed within a **<DIV>** that's been assigned a class of *error*. To turn the newlines (the **\n**) into HTML break tags, the **nl2br()** function is applied. **Figure 3.5** shows a sample detailed error message in the browser.

```
An error occurred in script '/Users/larryullman/Sites/ecom_book/ex1/html/index.php' on line 26:
Undefined variable: var
Array
(
    [0] => Array
        (
            [file] => /Users/larryullman/Sites/ecom_book/ex1/html/index.php
            [line] => 26
            [function] => my_error_handler
            [args] => Array
                (
                    [0] => 8
                    [1] => Undefined variable: var
                    [2] => /Users/larryullman/Sites/ecom_book/ex1/html/index.php
```

Figure 3.5

9. If the site is live, send the error in an email:

} else {
    error_log ($message, 1, $contact_email, 'From:admin@example.
    ⟿com');

The **error_log()** function can log errors in different ways. Its first argument is the error message. The second is a destination type, with 1 meaning email (the default of zero would send the message to the operating system's log). The third argument is the destination itself; with an email, this is the "to" email address. The fourth argument is only for sending emails and is for adding any additional headers, such as the "from" email address.

10. If the site is live, show a generic message, if the error isn't a notice:

if ($e_number != E_NOTICE) {
    echo '<div class="error">A system error occurred. We apologize for
    ⟿the inconvenience.</div>';
}

If the site is live, the user should not see the detailed error message (that would be a terrible security violation); instead they'll get a nondescript

note

Hopefully, in a fully tested, live site, customers will never see even the generic error message, because all the bugs will have been squashed already.

response. But some errors that occur may not be actual problems, just technical oversights that have no impact on the functionality. Such errors are raised as notices, so an error will only be reported if it's not on the notice level. In fact, the error indicated in Figure 3.5 would not be reported if the site were live. **Figure 3.6** shows what the user might see with a different type of error.

A system error occurred. We apologize for the inconvenience. **Figure 3.6**

11. Complete the **my_error_handler()** function:

```
} // End of $live IF-ELSE.
    return true;
} // End of my_error_handler() definition.
```

The error-handling function should return a nonfalse value to indicate the error has been handled. If the function returns **false**, then PHP's default error handler will also be invoked (which would be bad on a live site).

12. Apply the error handler:

```
set_error_handler ('my_error_handler');
```

This line actually tells PHP to use the custom function for handling errors. If you don't execute this function call, then PHP will still use its default handler. This is also why a parse error won't go through your own error handler, because the parse error prevents the PHP script from being executed.

13. Save the file.

THE HTML TEMPLATE

To create the browser side of the site, you should start by designing one or more HTML templates that portray what the final, dynamic site should look like. For this site, I wanted to use an elegant design that wouldn't detract from what the site is selling: its content. I am incapable of creating such a design. Looking around online for available Web templates, I settled upon the free Kilo theme, created by spyka Webmaster (**www.spyka.net**). To customize that template to this site, I updated the header for this site's theoretical name and byline, changed the top navigation items, altered the side content bar, tweaked the footer, and played with the CSS a bit. You can find the end result by downloading the code from my Web site.

 tip

Feel free to use your own design or tweak the Kilo theme to your tastes instead.

On the right side of the screen, I wanted the site to show a login form if the user is not logged in (**Figure 3.7**), but display some account management links if they are (**Figure 3.8**). If the logged-in user is an administrator, they'll see an additional group of options (**Figure 3.9**).

The site's content will be organized in categories, listed on the right as well. Visitors that aren't paid subscribers will just be able to see what content is available (titles and short descriptions); paid subscribers will be able to see the content itself.

Figure 3.7

Figure 3.8

Figure 3.9

To incorporate this HTML design into every page in the site, I'll use a standard technique whereby the template is broken down into a header file and a footer file. Each page will include the header, then display the page-specific content, and then include the footer. Once you've finalized the basic template (or templates), you can start creating the individual files.

Creating the Header

The header needs to begin the HTML page, include any necessary CSS and JavaScript, and code the body of the page up until the point where the page-specific content begins.

1. Open your designed template file in your text editor or IDE, if it is not already.

2. Copy all the HTML from the template file, up to the page-specific content:

```
<!DOCTYPE html PUBLIC "-//W3C//DTD XHTML 1.0 Strict//EN"
➥"http://www.w3.org/TR/xhtml1/DTD/xhtml1-strict.dtd">
<html xmlns="http://www.w3.org/1999/xhtml">
<head>
    <meta http-equiv="Content-Type" content="text/html;
    ➥charset=utf-8" />
    <title>Knowledge is Power: And It Pays to Know</title>
    <link rel="stylesheet" href="css/styles.css" type="text/css" />
</head>
<body>
<div id="wrap">
    <div class="header">
        <!-- TITLE -->
        <h1><a href="index.php">Knowledge is Power</a></h1>
        <h2>and it pays to know</h2>
        <!-- END TITLE -->
    </div>
    <div id="nav">
        <ul>
        <!-- MENU -->
            <li class="selected"><a href="index.php"><span>Home
            ➥</span></a></li>
            <li><a href="about.php"><span>About</span></a></li>
            <li><a href="contact.php"><span>Contact</span></a></li>
            <li><a href="register.php"><span>Register</span></a></li>
        <!-- END MENU -->
```
(continues on next page)

tip

If your site uses more than one template, just create multiple header and footer files and then include the proper ones for each specific page.

```
    </ul>
  </div>
  <div class="page">
    <div class="content">
```

3. Create a new file to be named **header.html** and stored in the **includes** directory.

4. Paste in the copied code.

5. Save the file.

Adding Dynamic Functionality to the Header

The next series of steps add dynamic functionality to the HTML template by incorporating PHP within the HTML. You'll want to do this for anything that might change on a page-by-page basis or otherwise won't be static. For the header file, there are two areas that should be dynamic: the page title and the highlighting of the top navigation link (see the first tab in Figure 3.7).

1. In **header.html**, use an **if-else** clause to define the page title:

```php
<title><?php if (isset($page_title)) {
    echo $page_title;
} else {
    echo 'Knowledge is Power: And It Pays to Know';
}
?></title>
```

The page's title shows at the top of the browser window, in bookmarks, and in the browser's history; it should be different from one page to the next. The aptly named **$page_title** variable will be available to the header file to represent that value. However, proper programming says that you shouldn't assume that the variable exists. So this code first checks if that variable is set (that is, has a value). If it is, that value will be printed as the page's title. If **$page_title** is not set, a default title will be used.

2. Remove the list items (between the opening and closing **MENU** comments) that constitute the top navigation tabs.

The navigation tab for the currently viewed page has a specific CSS class applied to it, which changes how it appears. You could use JavaScript to create this effect, but for easy, all-browser compatibility, I'll make this happen in PHP.

3. In place of the list items, begin a PHP code block:

<?php

4. Create an array of pages:

$pages = array (
   'Home' => 'index.php',
   'About' => 'about.php',
   'Contact' => 'contact.php',
   'Register' => 'register.php'
);

This array represents the main navigation items. The key for each element is the text to be displayed on the tab. The value for each element is the corresponding page (that is, what page that tab will be linked to).

5. Determine which page is currently being viewed:

$this_page = basename($_SERVER['PHP_SELF']);

In order to dynamically apply a class to the current page, the script needs to know what the current page is, which happens to be the value PHP assigns to **$_SERVER['PHP_SELF']**. If the user is viewing **http://www.example.com/dir/file.php**, then **$_SERVER['PHP_SELF']** will have a value of **/dir/file.php**. To get just the **file.php** part of that, the **basename()** function is applied.

6. Loop through each page:

foreach ($pages as $k => $v) {

   echo '<li';

This loop will run once for each item in the array. Within the loop, the **$k** and **$v** values can be used to create the navigation tabs. The first line of code within the loop begins a new HTML list item.

7. Add the class if it's the current page:

if ($this_page == $k) echo ' class="selected"';

The current page needs to use the HTML: **<li class="selected">**. This code will do that.

8. Complete the list item started in Step 6:

echo '><a href="' . $v . '"><span>' . $k . '</span></a></li>
';

First the opening **<li>** tag is closed. Then a link is created to the specific page, represented by **$v**. Next, the displayed text is written within **<span>** tags, and the link and list item tags are completed. The **echo** statement

note

A few of the pages linked in the header and footer won't actually be created in this book but will be quite easy for you to create, when necessary.

note

I generally recommend that programmers use curly brackets for all conditionals. When you don't, like when I'm saving space in this book, place the entire construct on one line to be clear, as in Step 7.

tip

Have your PHP code create tidy HTML output in case you need to examine it.

concludes on the next line so that a newline is added to the HTML source of the page (**Figure 3.10**).

```
<!-- MENU -->
<li class="selected"><a href="index.php"><span>Home</span></a></li>
        <li><a href="about.php"><span>About</span></a></li>
        <li><a href="contact.php"><span>Contact</span></a></li>
        <li><a href="register.php"><span>Register</span></a></li>
                        <!-- END MENU -->
```

Figure 3.10

9. Complete the **foreach** loop and the PHP code block:

} // End of FOREACH loop.

?>

To be clear, this closing PHP tag is required, because this closes a PHP block dropped within a larger body of HTML.

10. Save the file.

That's it for the header.

Creating the Footer

The footer takes over after the page-specific content. It creates the sidebar items, and the page footer (such as the copyright and other tertiary links), and completes the HTML page.

1. Open the designed template file in your text editor or IDE, if it is not already.

2. Copy all the HTML from the template file, from the page-specific content to the end, like so:

</div>
<div class="sidebar">
<!-- SIDEBAR -->
<div class="title">
　　<h4>Manage Your Account</h4>
</div>
<ul>
　　<li><a href="renew.php" title="Renew Your Account">Renew
　　⇨Account</a></li>
　　<li><a href="change_password.php" title="Change Your
　　⇨Password">Change Password</a></li>
　　<li><a href="favorites.php" title="View Your Favorite
　　⇨Pages">Favorites</a></li>

```
<li><a href="recommendations.php" title="View Your
➥Recommendations">Recommendations</a></li>
<li><a href="logout.php" title="Logout">Logout</a></li>
</ul>
<div class="title">
    <h4>Content</h4>
</div>
<ul>
    <li><a href="category.php?id=3" title="Common Attacks">
    ➥Common Attacks</a></li>
    <li><a href="category.php?id=5" title="Database Security">
    ➥Database Security</a></li>
    <li><a href="category.php?id=1" title="General Web
    ➥Security">General Web Security</a></li>
    <li><a href="category.php?id=4" title="JavaScript Security">
    ➥JavaScript Security</a></li>
    <li><a href="category.php?id=2" title="PHP Security">PHP
    ➥Security</a></li>
    <li><a href="pdfs.php" title="PDF Guides">PDF Guides</a>
    ➥</li>
</ul>
<!-- END SIDEBAR -->
</div>
<div class="footer">
<p><a href="site_map.php" title="Site Map">Site Map</a> |
➥<a href="policies.php" title="Site Policies">Policies</a>
➥   &copy; Knowledge is Power | Design by
➥<a href="http://www.spyka.net">spyka webmaster</a></p>
</div>
</div> <!-- END PAGE -->
</div>
</body>
</html>
```

That's the footer code for a logged-in, non-administrative user. In the next series of steps, the code for the other two possible situations (a visitor who is not logged in and an administrator who is logged in) are changed.

3. Create a new file to be named **footer.html** and stored in the **includes** directory.

4. Paste in the copied code.

5. Save the file.

Adding Dynamic Functionality to the Footer

Now you need to do to the footer file what you did to the header: Use PHP to dynamically generate some HTML. There are two alterations to make. First, the sidebar should show the login form if the user is not logged in, account links if they are, and also administrative links if they're logged in and are an administrator. Second, you can dynamically pull the list of categories from the database.

1. In **footer.html**, in lieu of the *Manage Your Account* links, begin an **if-else** conditional:

```
<?php
if (isset($_SESSION['user_id'])) {
```

The page will know that the user is logged in if **$_SESSION['user_id']** is set.

2. Recreate the *Manage Your Account* links using PHP:

```
echo '<div class="title">
    <h4>Manage Your Account</h4>
</div>
<ul>
    <li><a href="renew.php" title="Renew Your Account">Renew
    ⇒Account</a></li>
    <li><a href="change_password.php" title="Change Your Password">
    ⇒Change Password</a></li>
    <li><a href="favorites.php" title="View Your Favorite Pages">
    ⇒Favorites</a></li>
    <li><a href="recommendations.php" title="View Your
    ⇒Recommendations">Recommendations</a></li>
    <li><a href="logout.php " title="Logout">Logout</a></li>
</ul>
';
```

This PHP code creates the same links as in the original template. Two of these linked pages will be created in subsequent chapters. The closing single quote ends on its own line in order to create a newline in the HTML source.

3. Display administration options, if the user is also an administrator:

```
if (isset($_SESSION['user_admin'])) {
    echo '<div class="title">
    <h4>Administration</h4>
</div>
<ul>
    <li><a href="add_page.php" title="Add a Page">Add Page</a></li>
    <li><a href="add_pdf.php" title="Add a PDF">Add PDF</a></li>
    <li><a href="#" title="Blah">Blah</a></li>
</ul>
';
}
```

If the user is logged in and is of type *admin*, they should get extra options. This code will create a secondary panel of links in the sidebar. You'll develop the **add_page.php** and **add_pdf.php** scripts in Chapter 5.

4. Complete the primary conditional:

```
} else {
    require ('includes/login_form.inc.php');
}
?>
```

The **else** clause applies if the user's not logged in. In that case, the login form should be displayed instead of any account links. To keep the code tidy, the login form will be written in a separate file that you'll develop in the next chapter.

5. In place of the static HTML category links, dynamically generate them:

```
<?php
$q = 'SELECT * FROM categories ORDER BY category';
$r = mysqli_query($dbc, $q);
while (list($id, $category) = mysqli_fetch_array($r, MYSQLI_NUM)) {
    echo '<li><a href="category.php?id=' . $id . '" title="' . $category .
    '">' . $category . '</a></li>';
}
?>
```

This is basic PHP and MySQL: A query is run, its results are fetched, and one list item is created for each returned record. The links pass along the category ID in the URL that will be used by **category.php**, which you'll write in Chapter 5.

 tip

If you want to test how the site comes together, prior to creating the login form file, just comment out the line that includes it (in Step 4).

 note

If your content categories aren't likely to change often, it'd be better to hardcode the category links as HTML and save yourself the overhead of the extra database query.

The link to the PDFs page is separate because that's not a content category in the database.

6. Save the file.

And that's it for the footer.

Creating the Home Page

To put it all together, you'll create the home page, which will combine the four files—configuration, header, MySQL connection, and footer—into one complete page.

1. Create a new PHP script in your text editor or IDE to be named **index.php** and stored in the Web root directory.

2. Include the configuration file:

**<?php
require ('./includes/config.inc.php');**

The config file defines system settings, handles errors, and starts the session, so it should always be the first (noncomment) code in your pages.

3. Include the header file:

include ('./includes/header.html');

4. Require the database connection:

require (MYSQL);

The database connection script can be included by referring to the MYSQL constant, defined in the configuration file. This means that even if you change the name or location of **mysql.inc.php,** you have to change only one line in the configuration file and all your pages will still include that script properly.

In this particular version of the home page, the database connection isn't needed until the footer, but most pages will need it before the page-specific content.

5. Create the page-specific content:

**?><h3>Welcome</h3>
<p>Welcome to Knowledge is Power, a site dedicated to keeping you up
➥to date on the Web security and programming information you need to
➥know. Blah, blah, blah. Yadda, yadda, yadda.</p>**

note

The parentheses with **require** and **include** aren't required, but you'll see me use them in this book.

note

In the downloadable version of **index.php,** you'll see a bit of extra code, which you'll add in Chapter 4.

6. Include the footer file:

```php
<?php
include ('./includes/footer.html');
?>
```

7. Save the file.

8. Load the file in your Web browser to test the result.

Since this is PHP, you must run **index.php** through a URL (such as **http://**_something_), not through **file://**.

9. To test what it looks like when logged in, add this line after including the configuration file:

```php
$_SESSION['user_id'] = 1;
```

10. To test what the page looks like when logged in as an administrator, add the following line of code after including the configuration file:

```php
$_SESSION['user_type'] = 'admin';
```

REQUIRE AND INCLUDE

In the home page, I use both **require** and **include** to bring in the four scripts. These two control structures (they're not technically functions) serve the same purpose but differ in how they fail. Failure to _include_ a file results in a warning; failure to _require_ a file results in a fatal error. Because the configuration and MySQL files are critical to the site's functionality, failure to incorporate them should be fatal. Conversely, failure to incorporate the header or footer is just a cosmetic issue, not that you'd want that to happen either.

You may notice that I did not use **require_once** or **include_once**. These two control structures run checks to ensure that the same file isn't incorporated multiple times by the same script. Because of those repeated checks, using them has an adverse effect on the site's performance. In this site, which is straightforward, a repeated inclusion of a file is highly unlikely, so it's best to go with the more direct **require** and **include**. If you have a very complex site, with lots of included files that include other files, using the _once variants may be necessary. You will see a couple of appropriate uses of **include_once** in later chapters.

4 | USER ACCOUNTS

The next step in the evolution of the *Knowledge is Power* e-commerce site is to create a system of user accounts. When the site is complete, PayPal will be the crucial part in the registration process, but just to understand the user account system on its own, as well as to be able to create an administrative user for the next chapter, let's look at user accounts as a separate entity first.

There are four primary facets to the implementation of user accounts in this chapter. First, a new user registers. Second, a registered user logs in. Third, the logged-in user logs out (in theory, many people, including me, don't always do so). Fourth, users need to be able to retrieve a forgotten password and change an existing password.

Although this example won't be storing any sensitive e-commerce data, security will still be taken seriously, for the benefit of the customers and the site itself. In a few places, I'll make recommendations as to how you can increase security even further, and the chapter ends with even more suggestions.

DEFINING HELPER FUNCTIONS

Before getting into the primary scripts, there are three helper functions that you should define. The first will greatly facilitate handling some of the site's forms. The second will transform a user-supplied password into a format that's more secure to store. And the third will redirect the browser should the user not meet the requirements for accessing a particular page.

There are a few benefits to using these custom functions:

- Keeps complex logic from cluttering up other code

- Allows the same logic to be used in multiple scripts

- Makes changes to the logic a snap

The last two are really the key points: If you separate out processes, they can be used by different parts of a site without having to repeat the code. And if you later decide you need to tweak the process, you can do so in one place.

Creating Form Inputs

The functionality provided by the scripts in this chapter is almost entirely form-based: The user must complete a registration, login, change password, or forgot password form. All these forms use just two types of form inputs— text and password (not counting the submit buttons). An input starts off with this simple HTML:

```
<input type="type" name="name" id="name" />
```

For example:

```
<input type="text" name="username" id="username" />
```

In cases where the form was submitted but not properly completed, the user will be presented with the form again. As a convenience, the form should remember the entered values (that is, it should be *sticky*). To achieve that effect, you need to add **value="whatever value"** to each input. In PHP code, that would be:

```
<input type="text" name="username" id="username"
value="<?php echo $_POST['username']; ?>" />
```

However, the first time the form is loaded, **$_POST['username']** won't be set, so the code should really be:

```
<input type="text" name="username" id="username" value=
"<?php if (isset($_POST['username'])) echo $_POST['username']; ?>" />
```

 tip

You can add sizes to the inputs, if you want. I chose not to size them, so they would all be equally sized to the browser's default.

Figure 4.1

Figure 4.2

If the user, for whatever reason, used quotation marks in their value, the quotation marks will mess up the HTML. **Figure 4.1** shows the result if the user enters *Jeff "The Dude" Lebowski* as the username. To protect against that, you can use the **htmlspecialchars()** function (**Figures 4.2** and **4.3**):

```
\<input type="text" name="username" id="username" value=
➥"<?php if (isset($_POST['username'])) echo htmlspecialchars(
➥$_POST['username']); ?>" />
```

```
<input type="text" name="username" id="username" value="Jeff &quot;The Dude&quot; Lebowski"
```

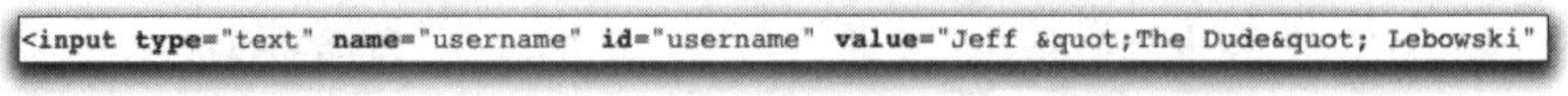

Figure 4.3

And, if Magic Quotes is enabled, the **stripslashes()** function should be applied to the value. You'll add that code shortly, but first, there's one more complication: If the form isn't completed properly, it'd be nice to add a CSS class to the input so that it's displayed with a red border:

```
<input type="text" name="username" id="username" value=
➥"<?php if (isset($_POST['username'])) echo htmlspecialchars(
➥$_POST['username']); ?>" <?php if (/* error on this input */)
➥echo ' class="error"'; ?> />
```

Also, in that case, the error message should be added after the input (**Figure 4.4**):

```
Username  Jeff "The Dude" Lebowski   Letters and numbers only!
```

Figure 4.4

```
<input type="text" name="username" id="username" value=
➥"<?php if (isset($_POST['username'])) echo htmlspecialchars(
➥$_POST['username']); ?>" <?php if (/* error on this input */)
➥echo ' class="error"'; ?> /> <?php if (/* error on this input */)
➥echo '<span class="error">' . /* error message */ . '</span>'; ?>
```

As you can tell, there's a lot of logic going into these inputs and their error handling, and they haven't even addressed Magic Quotes yet. The code above is just a mess to look at; it'll need to be used a dozen times; and if you later decide to handle things differently, you'll be editing code all day. So instead, let's write one function that does all this automatically. In Chapter 5, "Managing Site Content," forms will also contain textareas, so this function will be flexible enough to handle those, too.

1. Create a new PHP file in your text editor or IDE to be named **form_functions.inc.php**.

   This file should be stored in the **includes** directory.

2. Begin defining the function:

   ```php
   <?php
   function create_form_input($name, $type, $errors) {
   ```

   The function takes three arguments. The first is the name that will be given to the element. The second is the element type, which will be either *text* or *password* in this chapter, and *textarea* in the next. The third argument will be an array of errors.

3. Check for and process the value:

   ```php
   $value = false;
   if (isset($_POST[$name])) $value = $_POST[$name];
   if ($value && get_magic_quotes_gpc()) $value = stripslashes($value);
   ```

   First, the function assumes that no value exists. Then, if a value does exist for this input in **$_POST**, that value is assigned to **$value**. The third step strips extraneous slashes from the value, but only if Magic Quotes is enabled.

   This function assumes that the form uses the POST action. You could create another argument that accepts POST or GET and checks the corresponding superglobal for the value, if you want to make the function even more flexible.

4. Check the input type:

   ```php
   if ( ($type == 'text') || ($type == 'password') ) {
   ```

   This function will create text inputs, password inputs, and textareas. The first two are virtually the same in syntax, except for the **type** value used in the HTML. The function starts by handling those two types.

5. Begin creating the input:

   ```php
   echo '<input type="' . $type . '" name="' . $name . '" id="' . $name . '"';
   ```

   This is the initial shell of the HTML input, with its **type**, **name**, and **id** properties.

6. Add the input's value, if applicable:

   ```php
   if ($value) echo ' value="' . htmlspecialchars($value) . '"';
   ```

   If the **$value** variable has a value, then it should be added to the input, after running it through **htmlspecialchars()**.

 note

I'm using the plural *functions* in the file name even though only one function is being defined. Other functions might be added to it later (in theory).

 note

If you're new to programming, I recommend writing conditionals over multiple lines and always using curly brackets, but this book will have some single-line conditionals to save space.

7. Check for an error:

```
if (array_key_exists($name, $errors)) {
    echo 'class="error" /> <span class="error">' . $errors[$name] .
    ➥'</span>';
} else {
    echo ' />';
}
```

The **$errors** variable will be assigned to an array when the function is called. That array will contain every form error that occurred, indexed by the input's name (you'll see this in the scripts that handle the forms). So if the array has a key with the same name as this input, the *error* class is added to the input and then the error message is added after the input (see Figure 4.4).

If no such array element exists, then the input is completed without any additional class styling.

8. Check if the input type is a textarea:

```
} elseif ($type == 'textarea') {
```

9. Display the error first:

```
if (array_key_exists($name, $errors)) echo ' <span class="error">' .
➥$errors[$name] . '</span>';
```

Unlike with the text and password inputs, where the error message will be displayed to the right of the input itself, for textareas, I want to display the error message above the textarea, so that it's most obvious (**Figure 4.5**).

10. Start creating the textarea:

```
echo '<textarea name="' . $name . '" id="' . $name . '" rows="5"
➥cols="75"';
```

Here, the textarea's opening tag is created, providing dynamic **name** and **id** values. I've chosen to hardcode the textarea's size into this function to make the default scale a bit bigger than what the browser would otherwise create.

11. Add the *error* class, if applicable:

```
if (array_key_exists($name, $errors)) {
    echo ' class="error">';
} else {
    echo '>';
}
```

The *error* class must be added to the opening textarea tag, if an error exists with this element.

Figure 4.5

12. Add the value to the textarea:

if ($value) echo $value;

The value for textareas is written between opening and closing textarea tags. Step 11 closed the opening tag and Step 13 will create the closing one, so the value should just be printed here.

13. Complete the textarea:

echo '</textarea>';

14. Complete the function:

} // End of primary IF-ELSE.
} // End of the create_form_input() function.

15. Save the file.

Again, I'm not using a closing PHP tag, the reason for which I discussed in Chapter 3, "First Site: Structure and Design."

Protecting Passwords

The next helper function will turn the user-supplied password into a more secure format to be stored in the database. Passwords can be represented in three ways:

- In plain text, which is a terrible thing to do

- In an encrypted format, which *can* be decrypted

- In a hashed format, which *cannot* be decrypted

If you store passwords in an encrypted format, it's safe from prying eyes and can be retrieved when necessary. But if someone gets onto your server and can find your code for performing the decryption, they'll be able to view every user's password. And it turns out that you don't really need passwords to be decryptable: It doesn't matter whether anyone can ever see the plain text in its original form again or not.

An alternative is to create a *hash* of the password, a hash being a representation of data. For example, MD5 is a hashing algorithm that's been around for years. The MD5 hash of the word *password* is *5f4dcc3b5aa765d61d8327deb 882cf99*; the MD5 hash of the word *omnivore* is *04f7696e917f292f99925f80fc db1db1*. You can create a hash out of any piece of data, and, in theory, no two pieces of data have the same hash.

Storing the hash version of a password is more secure in that it cannot be decrypted. If a hacker gets your data, the best she or he can do is create

 note

The discovery of a user's password is a huge security violation as many people use the same email and password combination at many sites.

hashes of common words in the hope that she or he finds the matching hash (this is called a "dictionary attack"). But storing a hash still makes logging in possible: When a user logs in, the hashed version of their login password just needs to equal the already stored hashed version. If the two hashes equate, the submitted password is correct.

Once you've decided to hash the passwords, you'll need to choose what hashing *algorithm* (or, formula) to use and where the hashing should take place. By the latter I mean that you can hash the password in either the database or in your PHP code. Normally, I recommend having the database do as much as possible, but PHP has more sophisticated hashing functions available than MySQL, and if you perform the hash in PHP, you no longer have the risk of sending a plain text password to the database.

MD5 is a common, legacy, hashing algorithm, but not very secure. An improvement is SHA or SHA1, which is fine for many applications. For improved security, I'm going to turn to PHP's relatively new **hash_hmac()** function. This function is part of PHP's Hash extension, enabled by default as of PHP 5.1.2.

Hashing algorithms create hexadecimal representations: fixed strings containing only numbers and letters (as in the *password* and *omnivore* examples). You can store a hash in a database in that format. But as an improvement, it's more efficient to store binary data in the database instead of character data, so let's tell the hashing function to return binary data. Since binary data can contain characters that will break queries (such as a single quotation mark or a backslash), the output should still be run through the **mysqli_real_escape_string()** function. The resulting password generating function is defined like so:

```
function get_password_hash($password) {
    global $dbc;
    return mysqli_real_escape_string ($dbc, hash_hmac('sha256',
    ⇒$password, 'c#haRl891', true));
}
```

The **hash_hmac()** function takes up to four arguments. The first is the algorithm to use, *SHA256* in this case. This is an improved version of SHA1.

The second argument is the data to be hashed. This will be the value assigned to **$password** when the **get_password_hash()** function is called.

The third argument is a hash *key*, which makes the generated hash unique. The same key must be used when comparing two hashes.

The fourth argument is optional. If you use **true**, the output will be in raw, binary format. Otherwise, the output will be hexadecimal characters.

note

If you use an SSL connection between PHP and MySQL, sending plain text data back and forth is less dangerous.

note

You cannot later change the algorithm for processing passwords without resetting every existing user's password.

tip

Use the **hash_algos()** function to see what algorithms your server supports.

tip

Search online for more information on hashing, algorithms, and keys.

The output of the **hash_hmac()** function is then run through **mysqli_real_escape_string()** before being returned.

If your server doesn't support **hash_hmac()**, you could use this syntax instead:

return mysqli_real_escape_string ($dbc, sha1($password, true));

Just using **sha1()**, instead of the SHA256 algorithm, isn't as secure, but SHA256 level of security may not be warranted in your situation.

Because this function will be used with database queries, and because it requires the database connection, it should be defined in the **mysql.inc.php** script.

Redirecting the Browser

The third helper function will be used to limit access to pages to proper users. For example, a couple of public pages should only be viewable by current users, and the two administrative pages should be viewable by administrators only. If the current user doesn't meet the page's criteria, the browser should be redirected elsewhere, and the current page should be terminated (**Figure 4.6**). By writing this process in a function, any page that requires authorization will need to invoke only this function, without any additional logic.

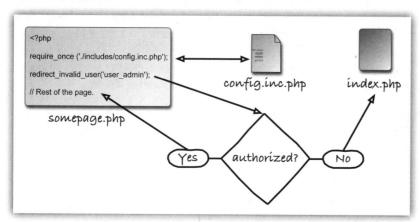

Figure 4.6

Since the configuration file, **config.inc.php**, will be included by every script in the site, it makes sense to define this function there:

function redirect_invalid_user($check = 'user_id', $destination =
➥'index.php', $protocol = 'http://') { *(continues on next page)*

```
if (!isset($_SESSION[$check])) {
    $url = $protocol . BASE_URL . $destination;
    header("Location: $url");
    exit();
}
}
```

The function takes three arguments, all of which are optional. The first is the session array element to validate against, the default being *user_id*. In other words, if **$_SESSION['user_id']** is not set, the user hasn't logged in and shouldn't be looking at this page. In Chapter 5, this same function will be used to restrict access to administrators or to users whose accounts have not expired.

The second argument to the function is the page to which the user should be redirected. By default, this will be the home page, but you could send them to the registration page or anywhere by changing the value passed to this function.

The third argument is the protocol to use, with the default being *http://*. I've included this option so that users can be redirected to SSL or non-SSL pages.

Within the function, a conditional checks the session variable. If it's not set, a redirection URL is defined by concatenating the protocol and destination to the **BASE_URL** constant (also defined in the configuration file). Then a **header()** call performs the actual redirection. Finally, the **exit()** function (language construct, technically) will terminate the script (the one that called this function). This is necessary because PHP will continue to execute a script after a **header()** call, even if the browser has already moved on.

When creating the login script later in this chapter, you'll have to keep in mind how this redirection function works. Specifically, authorization is based upon a value being set, not based upon what that value is. For example, a logged-in user just has any *user_id* value and an administrator will also have any *user_admin* value. But non-administrators should not be assigned a *user_admin* value, even if that value is *false* or *no*.

I imagine this function only being called immediately after including the configuration file (see Figure 4.6), so the function does not check that headers haven't already been sent, which would prevent the browser from being redirected. If you want to account for that possibility, just use the **headers_sent()** function in a conditional. If it returns **false**, redirect the user; if it returns **true**, include the header and footer and display an error message:

```
if (!headers_sent()) {
    // Redirect code.
} else {
    include_once('./includes/header.html');
    trigger_error('You do not have permission to access this page. Please log
    ⮑in and try again.');
    include_once('./includes/footer.html');
}
```

tip

I use **include_once()** instead of **include()** in this block of code because if the headers have been sent already, that's possibly because the header file was included prior to calling this function.

REGISTRATION

Now that the helper functions have been defined, let's make the actual scripts that perform the account services, starting with registration. The registration form needs to present fields for everything being stored in the database. Plus, it's standard to have the user confirm their password, just to make sure they know what it is (as password inputs don't display the entered text, it's easy to unknowingly make a mistake). The same PHP script will display the form and handle its results. Therefore, if the registration form is incomplete, it can be shown again, with the existing values in place, along with detailed error messages (**Figure 4.7**).

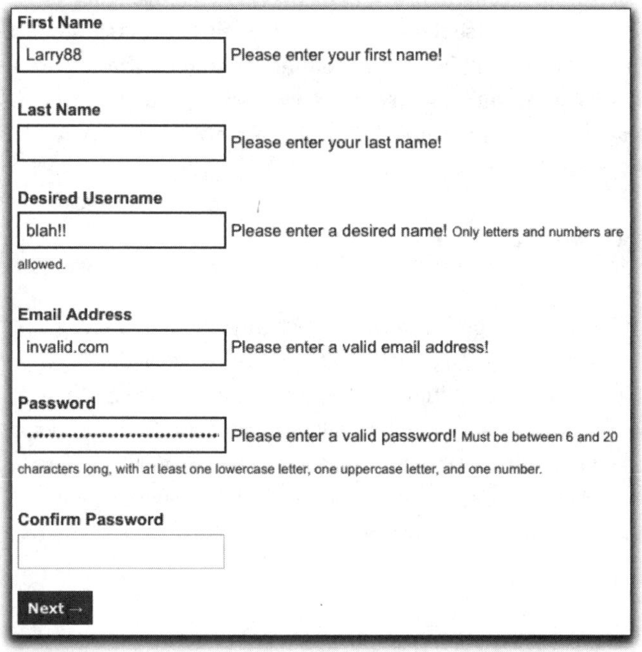

Figure 4.7

The registration script I came up with, which you can download from **www.DMCInsights.com/ecom/**, is about 160 lines total, including comments. Rather than walk you through the entire script in one long series of steps, let's look at this script as its three distinct parts.

Creating the Basic Shell

Every PHP page in the site—every script that a user will access directly and that won't be included by other PHP scripts—has the same basic structure. First, it includes the configuration file, then the HTML header (likely setting the page title beforehand), and then the MySQL connection script. Next comes the page-specific content and, finally, the footer is included. Here then, is what you can start with for **register.php**:

register.php

```
1   <?php
2   require ('./includes/config.inc.php');
3   $page_title = 'Register';
4   include ('./includes/header.html');
5   require (MYSQL);
6   ?><h3>Register</h3>
7   <p>Access to the site's content is available to registered users at a cost
    ➥of $10.00 (US) per year. Use the form below to begin the registration
    ➥process. <strong>Note: All fields are required.</strong> After
    ➥completing this form, you'll be presented with the opportunity to
    ➥securely pay for your yearly subscription via <a href="http://www.
    ➥paypal.com">PayPal</a>.</p>
8   <?php
9   include ('./includes/footer.html');
10  ?>
```

For the registration page, it's important that you give the customer a sense of the process. You may want to graphically indicate the steps involved using a progress bar (or progress meter), although this particular process really only has two steps. Also indicate how all the data will be used (for example, explain that they won't be spammed), and maybe refer them to whatever site policies exist (I've created a link to a policy file in the footer). Just do everything you can to reassure the user that it's safe to proceed.

Creating the Form

The registration form contains six inputs: four text and two password (plus the submit button). We've already defined a function for creating these inputs, so the first thing the registration form needs to do is include the **form_functions.inc.php** file. I did this just before the page-specific content:

```
require ('./includes/form_functions.inc.php');
?><h3>Register</h3>
```

The form itself looks like:

```
<form action="register.php" method="post" accept-charset="utf-8"
style="padding-left:100px">
    <p><label for="first_name"><strong>First Name</strong></label>
    <br /><?php create_form_input('first_name', 'text', $reg_errors); ?>
    </p>
    <p><label for="last_name"><strong>Last Name</strong></label>
    <br /><?php create_form_input('last_name', 'text', $reg_errors); ?>
    </p>
    <p><label for="username"><strong>Desired Username</strong>
    </label><br /><?php create_form_input('username', 'text',
    $reg_errors); ?> <small>Only letters and numbers are allowed.
    </small></p>
    <p><label for="email"><strong>Email Address</strong></label>
    <br /><?php create_form_input('email', 'text', $reg_errors); ?></p>
    <p><label for="pass1"><strong>Password</strong></label><br />
    <?php create_form_input('pass1', 'password', $reg_errors); ?>
    <small>Must be between 6 and 20 characters long, with at least one
    lowercase letter, one uppercase letter, and one number.</small></p>
    <p><label for="pass2"><strong>Confirm Password</strong>
    </label><br /><?php create_form_input('pass2', 'password',
    $reg_errors); ?></p>
    <input type="submit" name="submit_button" value="Next &rarr;"
    id="submit_button" class="formbutton" />
</form>
```

You'll see that with the aid of the **create_form_input()** function, all the code for creating each input plus handling all the errors is extremely simple. As an example, for the first-name input, the function is called indicating that the input should have **name** and **id** values of *first_name* and should be of *text* type. The third argument to the function is an array of errors named **$reg_errors**. In a few pages, this array will be added to the registration script,

 tip

In theory, the user's name may be used to greet them personally on the site or in emails sent to them.

so that it's already defined prior to this point. This same function is called for all six inputs, changing the arguments accordingly.

For the username and passwords, note that the user is being presented with a clear indication of what's expected of them. It drives me crazy when sites complain that I did not complete a form properly (such as by not using at least one number or capital letter in a password) when no such instructions were included.

Processing the Form

The bulk of the **register.php** script is the validation of the form and the insertion of the new record into the database. That part of the script is over 100 lines of code, so I'll walk through it more deliberately. **Figure 4.8** shows a flowchart of how this entire page will be used and may help you understand what's going on with the code. Note that all the code in the steps that follow gets placed after the MySQL connection script is included—because you'll need access to the database—but before the **form_functions.inc.php** include and the page-specific content. Again, see the downloadable scripts if you're confused about the order of things.

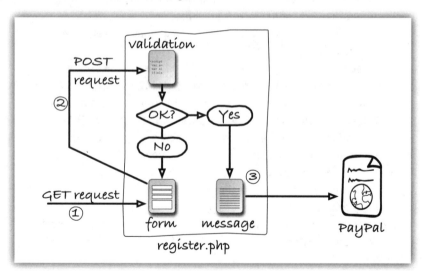

Figure 4.8

1. Create an empty array for storing errors:

   $reg_errors = array();

   This array will be used to store any errors that occur during the validation process. Normally, I might include this line within the section that begins the validation process (see Step 2), but because the **create_form_input()**

function calls are going to use **$reg_errors** the very first time the page is loaded, you need to create this empty array at this point.

2. Check for a form submission:

if ($_SERVER['REQUEST_METHOD'] == 'POST') {

The first time the user goes to **register.php**, it will be a GET request, so this conditional and all the code to follow won't apply. When the user clicks submit, a POST request will be made of **register.php,** and this code will be executed.

3. Check for a first name:

if (preg_match ('/^[A-Z \'.-]{2,20}$/i', $_POST['first_name'])) {
    $fn = mysqli_real_escape_string ($dbc, $_POST['first_name']);
} else {
    $reg_errors['first_name'] = 'Please enter your first name!';
}

Names are difficult to validate, so I'm using a *regular expression* that's neither too strict nor too lenient. The pattern insists that the submitted value be between 2 and 20 characters long and only contain a combination of letters (case-insensitive), the space, a period, an apostrophe, and a hyphen. If the value passes this test, then the escaped version of that value is assigned to the **$fn** variable. If the value does not pass this test, then a new element is added to the **$reg_errors** array. The element uses the same key as the form input, so that the **create_form_input()** function can properly display the error.

4. Check for a last name:

if (preg_match ('/^[A-Z \'.-]{2,40}$/i', $_POST['last_name'])) {
    $ln = mysqli_real_escape_string ($dbc, $_POST['last_name']);
} else {
    $reg_errors['last_name'] = 'Please enter your last name!';
}

This is pretty much the same code as for the first name, but with a longer maximum length.

5. Check for a username:

if (preg_match ('/^[A-Z0-9]{2,30}$/i', $_POST['username'])) {
    $u = mysqli_real_escape_string ($dbc, $_POST['username']);
} else {
    $reg_errors['username'] = 'Please enter a desired name!';
}

 tip

If you're not comfortable with Perl-Compatible Regular Expressions (PCRE), search online for tutorials or see my book *PHP and MySQL for Dynamic Web Sites: Visual QuickPro Guide.*

note

Size restrictions in regular expressions should match the restrictions on those same values in the database columns.

The username, per the instructions indicated in the form, is restricted to just letters and numbers. The username has to be between 2 and 30 characters long.

6. Check for an email address:

```
if (filter_var($_POST['email'], FILTER_VALIDATE_EMAIL)) {
    $e = mysqli_real_escape_string ($dbc, $_POST['email']);
} else {
    $reg_errors['email'] = 'Please enter a valid email address!';
}
```

Unlike names, email addresses have to adhere to a fairly strict syntax. The simplest and most fail-safe way to validate an email address is to use PHP's **filter_var()** function, part of the Filter extension added in PHP 5.2. Its first argument is the variable to be tested and its second is a constant representing a validation model.

If you're not using a version of PHP that supports the Filter extension, you'll need to use a regular expression instead (you can find good patterns online and in my books).

7. Check for a password and match against the confirmed password:

```
if (preg_match ('/^(\w*(?=\w*\d)(?=\w*[a-z])(?=\w*[A-Z])\w*)
➥{6,20}$/', $_POST['pass1'])) ) {
    if ($_POST['pass1'] == $_POST['pass2']) {
        $p = mysqli_real_escape_string ($dbc, $_POST['pass1']);
    } else {
        $reg_errors['pass2'] = 'Your password did not match the confirmed
        ➥password!';
    }
} else {
    $reg_errors['pass1'] = 'Please enter a valid password!';
}
```

Okay, so, um, here's a little magic for you. Good validation normally uses regular expressions, with which not everyone is entirely comfortable. And, admittedly, even I often have to look up the proper syntax for patterns, but this one requires a high level of regular expression expertise. For the password to be relatively secure, it needs to contain at least one uppercase letter, one lowercase letter, and one number. In other words, it can't just be a word out of the dictionary, all in one case. Creating a regular expression that confirms that these characters exist in the password, but in any posi-

note

Technically, a valid email address would not contain any characters that could be used in an SQL Injection attack, but it's still best to run the email address through the escaping function.

note

The strength of a user account system will depend upon how secure you require your users' passwords to be.

tip

The Cracklib PECL extension can be used to test the strength of a password.

tion in the string, requires what's called a *zero-width positive lookahead assertion*, represented by the *?=*. The positive lookahead makes matches based upon what follows a character. Rather than reading a page of explanation as to how this pattern works beyond that simple definition, you can test it for yourself to confirm that it does and research zero-width positive lookahead assertions online if you're really curious.

8. If there are no errors, check the availability of the email address and username:

if (empty($reg_errors)) {
    $q = "SELECT email, username FROM users WHERE email='$e' OR
    ➥username='$u'";
    $r = mysqli_query ($dbc, $q);
    $rows = mysqli_num_rows($r);
    if ($rows == 0) { // No problems!

If the **$reg_errors** array is still empty, then no errors occurred (because even one error would add an element to this array, making it no longer empty). Next, a query looks for any existing record that has the submitted email address or username. In theory, this query could return up to 2 records (one for the email address and one for the username); if it returns no records, it's safe to proceed.

note

In truth, I just added the username field to demonstrate how to guarantee both unique email addresses and usernames.

9. Add the user to the database:

$q = "INSERT INTO users (username, email, pass, first_name,
➥last_name, date_expires) VALUES ('$u', '$e', '"
➥. create_password_hash($p) . "', '$fn', '$ln', ADDDATE(NOW(),
➥INTERVAL 1 MONTH))";
$r = mysqli_query ($dbc, $q);

The query uses the submitted values to create a new record in the database. Note that for the password value, the **get_password_hash()** function is called. The user's type does not need to be set because if no value is provided for an **ENUM** column, the first enumerated value—here, *member*—will be used.

note

As a security measure, the user's type can only ever be *member* after going through the registration process. You must go into the database and change a user's type manually in order to create an administrator.

Until PayPal is integrated in Chapter 6, "Using PayPal," I'm setting the account expiration date to a month from now. Once PayPal has been integrated, the expiration will be set to yesterday. In that case, when PayPal returns an indication of successful payment, the user's account will be set to expire in a year.

10. If the query created one row, thank the new customer and send out an email:

```
if (mysqli_affected_rows($dbc) == 1) {
    echo '<h3>Thanks!</h3><p>Thank you for registering! You may now
    ➥log in and access the site\'s content.</p>';
    $body = "Thank you for registering at <whatever site>. Blah. Blah.
    ➥Blah.\n\n";
    mail($_POST['email'], 'Registration Confirmation', $body, 'From:
    ➥admin@example.com');
    include ('./includes/footer.html');
    exit();
```

First, a Thanks! page is displayed (**Figure 4.9**). The next step would be to send them off to PayPal, which we'll add in Chapter 6. Also, an email can be sent to the user saying whatever you want, although do not include the user's password in that email. Finally, the footer is included and a call to **exit()** stops the page. This is necessary so that the registration form isn't shown again, thereby confusing the user.

Figure 4.9

11. If the query didn't work, create an error:

```
} else {
    trigger_error('You could not be registered due to a system error. We
    ➥apologize for any inconvenience.');
}
```

At this point, if the query didn't create a new row, there was a database or query error. In that case, the **trigger_error()** function is used to generate an error that will be managed by the error handler in the configuration file. On a live, already tested site, this would likely occur only if the database server is down or overloaded.

12. If the email address or username is unavailable, create errors:

```
} else {
    if ($rows == 2) { // Both are taken.
        $reg_errors['email'] = 'This email address has already been
        ➥registered. If you have forgotten your password, use the link at
        ➥right to have your password sent to you.';
        $reg_errors['username'] = 'This username has already been
        ➥registered. Please try another.';
```

The **else** clause applies if the **SELECT** query returns any records. This means that the email address and/or the username have already been registered. Now we need to determine which of the two values is the culprit. If two rows were returned, then both have already been registered. The assumption then is that the same customer already registered (because their email address is in the system) and another customer already has that username (because it's associated with a different email address). The error messages are added to the **$reg_errors** array, indexed at *email* and *username*, so that they'll appear beside the appropriate form input when the form is redisplayed.

13. Confirm which item has been registered:

```
} else { // One or both may be taken.
    $row = mysqli_fetch_array($r, MYSQLI_NUM);
    if( ($row[0] == $_POST['email']) && ($row[1] == $_POST
    ➥['username'])) { // Both match.
        $reg_errors['email'] = 'This email address has already been
        ➥registered. If you have forgotten your password, use the link at
        ➥right to have your password sent to you.';
        $reg_errors['username'] = 'This username has already been
        ➥registered with this email address. If you have forgotten your
        ➥password, use the link at right to have your password sent to
        ➥you.';
    } elseif ($row[0] == $_POST['email']) { // Email match.
        $reg_errors['email'] = 'This email address has already been
        ➥registered. If you have forgotten your password, use the link at
        ➥right to have your password sent to you.';
    } elseif ($row[1] == $_POST['username']) { // Username match.
        $reg_errors['username'] = 'This username has already been
        ➥registered. Please try another.';
    }
} // End of $rows == 2 ELSE.
```

If only one row was returned, then the code needs to figure out if the user-name matched, the email address matched, or both matched in the same record. Three conditionals test for each possibility, with appropriate error messages assigned (**Figures 4.10** and **4.11**).

Figure 4.10

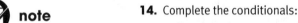

Figure 4.11

14. Complete the conditionals:

> **} // End of $rows == 0 IF.**
> **} // End of empty($reg_errors) IF.**
> **} // End of the main form submission conditional.**

15. Save and test the registration script.

ACTIVATING ACCOUNTS

On a site that doesn't require payment, I would normally include an activation process:

1. When the user registers, a random code is stored in the **users** table.

2. An email is sent to the registered email address, which includes a link to an activation page on the site. The link passes the user's email address and the specific code to the PHP page: **https://www.example.com/activate. php?x=email@example.com&y=*CODE***

3. The PHP page confirms that there is a record in the table with that combination of email address and code, then activates that account (normally by setting the code column to **NULL**).

4. When the user logs in, the query must confirm that the email and password combination is correct, and that the code column in the table has a **NULL** value.

This is called a "closed-loop" confirmation process and prevents fake registrations. In this *Knowledge is Power* site, using PayPal will prevent fake registrations, because hackers don't normally spend money in their hack attempts.

LOGGING IN

Logging in to the site is a two-step process: completing the form and validating the submitted values against the database. The login form is not its own page—it's shown in the sidebar to all non-logged-in users, so it cannot use the same single-script approach as in **register.php**. The question, then, was where the user should end up when they do successfully log in and when they don't. In both cases, I decided they should end up back on the home page; for this reason, the login form gets submitted to **index.php**. Therefore, the index page needs to be updated with the code for handling the form. Rather than write that code directly into the home page, it's best included as a separate file, just after the database connection but prior to the inclusion of the header file:

```
if ($_SERVER['REQUEST_METHOD'] == 'POST') {
    include ('./includes/login.php');
}
```

This works because normally **index.php** will be requested via GET. If it's a POST request, the login form has been submitted, so this script includes the file that will test the login credentials.

Processing the Form

I think it will actually be easier to follow the login process if I talk about the form last, so let's look at the code that handles the login form first. That process needs to:

1. Validate the submitted email address and password.
2. Compare the submitted values with those in the database.
3. Create errors if the values are incorrect.
4. Store data in a session if the values are correct.

Here's how all of that works in actual code:

1. Create a new PHP script in your text editor or IDE to be named **login.inc.php**.

This will be stored in the **includes** directory.

2. Create an empty array for recording errors:

```
<?php
$login_errors = array();
```

This errors array will be used just like **$reg_errors** in the registration script.

 tip

By including the login processing code, instead of writing it to the **index.php** file, I'm maintaining better separation of code.

 tip

It's best to give variables in included files unique names so they don't overwrite any variables created by the parent script.

3. Validate the email address:

```
if (filter_var($_POST['email'], FILTER_VALIDATE_EMAIL)) {
    $e = mysqli_real_escape_string ($dbc, $_POST['email']);
} else {
    $login_errors['email'] = 'Please enter a valid email address!';
}
```

This code replicates that in the registration process, using PHP's Filter extension to validate the email address.

4. Validate the password:

```
if (!empty($_POST['pass']) ) {
    $p = mysqli_real_escape_string ($dbc, $_POST['pass']);
} else {
    $login_errors['pass'] = 'Please enter your password!';
}
```

To validate the password, I'm just making sure it's not empty. Part of the reason is performance—this will be faster than the zero-width positive lookahead regular expression used in the registration process—and part of the reason will be explained later in the chapter.

In theory, you don't need to validate the submitted values because the database query will be confirming whether the submitted values are correct or not, but database queries are expensive (in terms of server resources and performance), so it's best not to run one unless necessary.

5. If there are no errors, query the database:

```
if (empty($login_errors)) {
    $q = "SELECT id, username, type, IF(date_expires > NOW(), true,
    false) FROM users WHERE (email='$e' AND pass='" .
    ⇒get_password_hash($p) . "')";
    $r = mysqli_query ($dbc, $q);
```

The basic query selects four values from the **users** table: their ID, username, type, and account expiration. The **WHERE** clause checks that the email address matches the submitted email address and that the password matches the hashed version of the password.

For the account expiration, I'm doing something that may be new to you. I don't really care *when* the user's account expires, only if it's valid right now. One way of accomplishing this would be to select the expiration value, which is a date, and then use PHP to convert it into a timestamp and compare it to the current timestamp. That's a lot of code and logic to put onto PHP. Instead, I'm doing an **IF** conditional within my MySQL query. That syntax is just:

IF(date_expires >= NOW(), true, false)

The first expression is the condition being tested; the second is what's returned if the condition is true; the third value is what's returned if the condition is false. Thus, if the expiration date is greater than or equal to this moment, the value **true** will be selected.

6. If one row was returned by the database query, fetch the data and store it in a session:

```
if (mysqli_num_rows($r) == 1) {
    $row = mysqli_fetch_array ($r, MYSQLI_NUM);
    $_SESSION['user_id'] = $row[0];
    $_SESSION['username'] = $row[1];
    if ($row[2] == 'admin') $_SESSION['user_admin'] = true;
    if ($row[3] == 1) $_SESSION['user_not_expired'] = true;
```

First, the user's ID and name are stored in the session, but given **user<*something*>** names, so that they won't possibly conflict later on with anything else I might store in the session.

To indicate that the user is an administrator, I only want to create a **$_SESSION['user_admin']** element if the user's type equals *admin*. I don't want to create a **$_SESSION['user_admin']** element equal to **false** if their type is *member*. This is because the function that will validate a user's access to pages—**redirect_invalid_user()** in **config.inc.php**—will check only if a session variable is set, not what its actual value is.

For the expiration, I only want to store a value indicating that the account hasn't expired. MySQL will return the number **1** for the Boolean value **true**, so if **$row[3]** (which is the value in the array for the expiration status) equals that, I create a new element in **$_SESSION**. Again, I'm not assigning a value if the account has expired.

7. If no row was returned, create an error message:

```
} else {
    $login_errors['login'] = 'The email address and password do not
    ↩match those on file.';
}
```

This error message will apply if the user supplied a valid email address and a password but the values didn't match those stored in the database. For security purposes, the script doesn't indicate which of the two values is incorrect, or if the email address has been registered at all.

8. Complete the script:

} // End of $login_errors IF.

As with all other scripts that will be included by other scripts, I'm omitting the closing PHP tag.

9. Save the file.

Creating the Form

The last script to discuss, **login_form.inc.php**, is actually the first step in the process. It needs to do just two things: present a form and report any errors that occurred when the form was submitted. The form contains two inputs: one for the email address and one for the password. Both are created using the same **create_form_input()** function, which means that the **form_functions.inc.php** script must be included. The function needs to take an array of errors—**$login_errors**—as its third argument. That array is created in **login.inc.php**. However, if the user is just loading the login form for the first time, **$login_errors** won't exist, so this script should initialize an empty array in that case. As a second complication, on the **register.php** and **forgot_password.php** pages, the **form_functions.inc.php** script will already have been included, making **require_once()** the appropriate way to include that file here.

Here's the complete **login_form.inc.php**:

includes/login_form.inc.php

```
1   <?php
2   if (!isset($login_errors)) $login_errors = array();
3   require_once ('./includes/form_functions.inc.php');
4   ?><div class="title">
5       <h4>Login</h4>
6   </div>
7   <form action="index.php" method="post" accept-charset="utf-8">
8   <p><?php if (array_key_exists('login', $login_errors)) {
9       echo '<span class="error">' . $login_errors['login'] . '</span><br />';
10  }?><label for="email"><strong>Email Address</strong></label>
    ➥<br /><?php create_form_input('email', 'text', $login_errors); ?>
    ➥<br /><label for="pass"><strong>Password</strong></label>
    ➥<br /><?php create_form_input('pass', 'password', $login_errors); ?>
    ➥<a href="forgot_password.php" align="right">Forgot?</a><br />
    ➥<input type="submit" value="Login &rarr;"></p>
11  </form>
```

Just before the email address label, you'll see this code:

```
<?php if (array_key_exists('login', $login_errors)) {
    echo '<span class="error">' . $login_errors['login'] . '</span><br />';
}?>
```

By default, all errors are reported via the **create_form_input()** function. However, this form is a bit different in that **login.inc.php** could create an error (that is, an element in the **$login_errors** array) not associated with a particular form input. That error occurs when both fields are properly filled out but the values don't, together, match a record in the database. In that case, the **$login_errors['login']** element is assigned an error message. Therefore, the form first checks if that array element exists in **$login_errors**, in which case the error message will be displayed just before the two inputs (**Figure 4.12**). Other error messages are associated with the offending form input (**Figure 4.13**).

Figure 4.12

Figure 4.13

 tip

You could also change the header file so that the register tab is not shown to users that are logged in.

After you've done all this, you can now test the login process.

LOGGING OUT

Logging out is the simplest part of the process. The **logout.php** page starts off as a standard script, including the configuration file, the header, the MySQL connection, and the footer. Only logged-in users should be able to access this page, though, so a call to **redirect_invalid_user()** is included just after the configuration file is defined.

To wipe out the session, three steps are required. First, clear out the **$_SESSION** array that represents the variables available to this script:

$_SESSION = array();

Next, the **session_destroy()** function actually removes the data stored on the server:

session_destroy();

Finally, modify the session cookie in the user's browser so it no longer has a record of the session ID:

setcookie (session_name(), '', time()-300);

That line sends a cookie with the same session name, but no value (no session ID) and an expiration of five minutes ago.

> **tip**
>
> At **www.php.net/session_destroy**, you can see code to dynamically match all the **setcookie()** parameters to those used to create the cookie.

The complete **logout.php** is:

logout.php

```
<?php
require ('./includes/config.inc.php');
redirect_invalid_user();
$_SESSION = array();
session_destroy();
setcookie (session_name(), '', time()-300);
$page_title = 'Logout';
include ('./includes/header.html');
echo '<h3>Logged Out</h3><p>Thank you for visiting. You are now logged out. Please come back soon!</p>';
require (MYSQL);
include ('./includes/footer.html');
?>
```

Figure 4.14 shows the result.

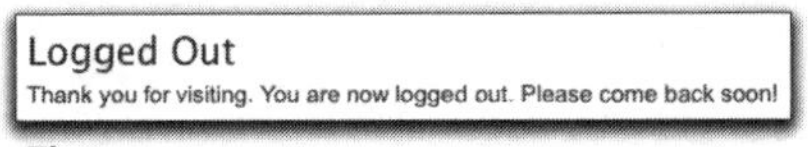

Figure 4.14

MANAGING PASSWORDS

The site will have two pages for managing user passwords. One will be used to recover a forgotten password and the other will change an existing password. Both pages are simple forms, but a user must be logged in to change their password and wouldn't be logged in to recover a forgotten one.

Recovering Passwords

Because the user passwords are not being stored in an encrypted format, they cannot be decrypted and recovered. When the user forgets or loses their password, the only option then is to create a new password and send it to them in an email. The form to start this process is simple: it just takes an email address (**Figure 4.15**).

Figure 4.15

1. Create a new PHP script in your text editor or ID to be named **forgot_password.php** and stored in the Web root directory.

2. Include the standard stuff:

```php
<?php
require ('./includes/config.inc.php');
$page_title = 'Forgot Your Password?';
include ('./includes/header.html');
require (MYSQL);
```

3. Create an array for storing errors:

```php
$pass_errors = array();
```

4. Validate the email address:

```php
if ($_SERVER['REQUEST_METHOD'] == 'POST') {
    if (filter_var($_POST['email'], FILTER_VALIDATE_EMAIL)) {
        $q = 'SELECT id FROM users WHERE email="'. mysqli_real_
        ➥escape_string ($dbc, $_POST['email']) . '"';
        $r = mysqli_query ($dbc, $q);
        if (mysqli_num_rows($r) == 1) { // Retrieve the user ID.
            list($uid) = mysqli_fetch_array ($r, MYSQLI_NUM);
        } else { // No database match made.
            $pass_errors['email'] = 'The submitted email address does not
            ➥match those on file!';
        }
```

If the page is accessed via a POST request, then the form has been submitted. The first thing it should do is validate that a proper email address was provided. This is a two-step process. First, the **filter_var()** function confirms that the submitted value adheres to the email syntax. Then a query specifically confirms that this email address exists in the database. If it does, then the user ID value is retrieved. If it doesn't exist in the database, an error message is assigned to the array.

note

Because the random, generated password won't meet the criteria of the user-generated password, neither the login form nor the change-password form applies the zero-width positive lookahead expression to the current password.

tip

To make the generated password more secure, insert one or more random capital letters into it.

5. Complete the **filter_vars()** conditional:

} else { // No valid address submitted.
    $pass_errors['email'] = 'Please enter a valid email address!';
} // End of $_POST['email'] IF.

This error applies if the user doesn't provide a syntactically valid email address.

6. Generate a new password:

if (empty($pass_errors)) { // If everything's OK.
        $p = substr(md5(uniqid(rand(), true)), 10, 15);

To generate the password, call the **uniqid()** function, which returns a unique ID. If it's passed some value as its first argument, that will be used as the prefix, thereby expanding the returned string. For the prefix value, invoke the **rand()** function. When a second argument of true is passed to **uniqid()**, a more random unique ID will be returned. This value will be sent through **md5()**, which will create a string 32 characters long, consisting of letters and numbers. From that string, take a substring starting with the eleventh character (because indexes start at zero) and going for fifteen characters. The end result will be a completely random and unique password like *6e968eff0833110*.

7. Add the new password to the database:

$q = "UPDATE users SET pass='" . get_password_hash($p) . "' WHERE
➥id=$uid LIMIT 1";
$r = mysqli_query ($dbc, $q);
if (mysqli_affected_rows($dbc) == 1) { // If it ran OK.

The query uses the user ID value just fetched from the database to know which record to update. The generated password must also be run through the **get_password_hash()** function.

8. Send the new password to the user:

$body = "Your password to log into <whatever site> has been
➥temporarily changed to '$p'. Please log in using that password and this
➥email address. Then you may change your password to something more
➥familiar.";
mail ($_POST['email'], 'Your temporary password.', $body, 'From:
➥admin@example.com');

This is a very simple email message (**Figure 4.16**). You should make it more interesting.

Figure 4.16

9. Print a message and wrap up:

echo '<h3>Your password has been changed.</h3><p>You will receive
➡the new, temporary password via email. Once you have logged in
➡with this new password, you may change it by clicking on the "Change
➡Password" link.</p>';
include ('./includes/footer.html');
exit();

As with any process, you want to indicate to the user what should happen next (**Figure 4.17**). The **exit()** line terminates the script so that the form is not shown again.

> **Your password has been changed.**
> You will receive the new, temporary password via email. Once you have logged in with this new password, you may change it by clicking on the "Change Password" link.

Figure 4.17

10. If the database update couldn't run, generate an error:

} else { // If it did not run OK.
    trigger_error('Your password could not be changed due to a system
    ➡error. We apologize for any inconvenience.');
}

This **else** clause applies if the database query didn't work, indicating a system error.

11. Complete the processing section of the script:

    } // End of $uid IF.
} // End of the main Submit conditional.

12. Create the form:

```
require ('./includes/form_functions.inc.php');
?><h3>Reset Your Password</h3>
<p>Enter your email address below to reset your password.</p>
<form action="forgot_password.php" method="post" accept-charset=
↩"utf-8">
    <p><label for="email"><strong>Email Address</strong></label>
    ↩<br /><?php create_form_input('email', 'text', $pass_errors); ?>
    ↩</p>
    <input type="submit" name="submit_button" value="Reset &rarr;"
↩id="submit_button" class="formbutton" />
</form>
```

The form uses the same **create_form_input()** function to generate the single text input.

13. Complete the page:

```
<?php
include ('./includes/footer.html');
?>
```

14. Save and test the forgotten password script.

Changing Passwords

Changing a password is kind of like a combination of the login and registration processes. The user should enter their current password as an extra precaution, plus their new password, and a confirmation of their new password (**Figure 4.18**). The user must be logged in to perform this task.

tip

An alternative approach is to send an email to the user with a link they have to click in order to reset their password.

Change Your Password
Use the form below to change your password.

Current Password

[   ]

New Password

[   ] Must be between 6 and 20 characters long,
with at least one lowercase letter, one uppercase letter, and one number.

Confirm New Password

[   ]

Change →

Figure 4.18

1. Create a new PHP script in your text editor or IDE to be named **change_password.php** and stored in the Web root directory.

2. Include the standard stuff:

```php
<?php
require ('./includes/config.inc.php');
redirect_invalid_user();
$page_title = 'Change Your Password';
include ('./includes/header.html');
require (MYSQL);
```

You'll notice that just before the header is included, the script invokes the **redirect_invalid_user()** function so that only logged-in users can access the page.

3. Create an array for storing errors:

```php
$pass_errors = array();
```

4. Validate the current password:

```php
if ($_SERVER['REQUEST_METHOD'] == 'POST') {
    if (!empty($_POST['current'])) {
        $current = mysqli_real_escape_string ($dbc, $_POST['current']);
    } else {
        $pass_errors['current'] = 'Please enter your current password!';
    }
```

As with the login form, this conditional only checks that there's a password value. If the user is changing their password from a legitimate system-generated one, the current password wouldn't pass the more strict regular expression.

5. Validate the new password:

```php
if (preg_match ('/^(\w*(?=\w*\d)(?=\w*[a-z])(?=\w*[A-Z])\w*)
{6,20}$/', $_POST['pass1']) ) {
    if ($_POST['pass1'] == $_POST['pass2']) {
        $p = mysqli_real_escape_string ($dbc, $_POST['pass1']);
    } else {
        $pass_errors['pass2'] = 'Your password did not match the
        confirmed password!';
    }
} else {
    $pass_errors['pass1'] = 'Please enter a valid password!';
}
```

This code is almost exactly like that in the registration script, except that errors are assigned to the **$pass_errors** array.

6. If everything is fine, validate the current password against the database:

if (empty($pass_errors)) { // If everything's OK.
   $q = "SELECT id FROM users WHERE pass='" . get_password_
   ⇒hash($current) . "' AND id={$_SESSION['user_id']}";
   $r = mysqli_query ($dbc, $q);
   if (mysqli_num_rows($r) == 1) { // Correct

To confirm that the current password is correct, a database query is run, similar to the login query except that it uses the user's ID (from the session), instead of their email address.

7. Update the database with the new password:

$q = "UPDATE users SET pass='" . get_password_hash($p) . "' WHERE
⇒id={$_SESSION['user_id']} LIMIT 1";
if ($r = mysqli_query ($dbc, $q)) { // If it ran OK.

This query is almost exactly like that in **forgot_password.php**.

8. Indicate to the user the successful change:

echo '<h3>Your password has been changed.</h3>';
include ('./includes/footer.html');
exit();

The message is printed, the footer is included, and then the script is terminated using **exit()** so that the form isn't shown again (**Figure 4.19**). You may also want to email the user to indicate the password change (without actually emailing the new password to them).

Your password has been changed.

Figure 4.19

9. If there was a problem, trigger an error:

} else { // If it did not run OK.
   trigger_error('Your password could not be changed due to a system
   ⇒error. We apologize for any inconvenience.');
}

This **else** clause applies if the database update failed, which really shouldn't happen on a live, tested site.

10. Complete the processing section of the script:

```
    } else {
        $pass_errors['current'] = 'Your current password is incorrect!';
    } // End of current password ELSE.
  } // End of $p IF.
} // End of the form submission conditional.
```

This **else** clause applies if the supplied current password doesn't match the one in the database for the current user. In that case, an error is added that will be displayed next to the current password input.

11. Display the form:

```
require ('./includes/form_functions.inc.php');
?><h3>Change Your Password</h3>
<p>Use the form below to change your password.</p>
<form action="change_password.php" method="post"
➥accept-charset="utf-8">
    <p><label for="pass1"><strong>Current Password</strong>
    ➥</label><br /><?php create_form_input('current', 'password',
    ➥$pass_errors); ?></p>
    <p><label for="pass1"><strong>New Password</strong></label>
    ➥<br /><?php create_form_input('pass1', 'password',
    ➥$pass_errors); ?> <small>Must be between 6 and 20 characters
    ➥long, with at least one lowercase letter, one uppercase letter, and
    ➥one number.</small></p>
    <p><label for="pass2"><strong>Confirm New Password</strong>
    ➥</label><br /><?php create_form_input('pass2', 'password',
    ➥$pass_errors); ?></p>
    <input type="submit" name="submit_button" value="Change
    ➥&rarr;" id="submit_button" class="formbutton" />
</form>
```

The form has three password inputs. Each is generated using the **create_form_input()** function.

12. Complete the page:

```
<?php
include ('./includes/footer.html');
?>
```

13. Save and test the change password script.

IMPROVING THE SECURITY

The user accounts system in this example demonstrates a good approach to security. For starters, users are forced to use both letters and numbers in their password and at least one letter in each case. You could improve the security by requiring at least one nonalphanumeric character and by increasing the minimum length. Security is inversely proportional to convenience, so you would only make these changes knowing that you'll annoy some of your potential customers. I also chose not to implement a "remember me" option because requiring that users log in each time they visit the site makes for better security (although, again, doing so is an inconvenience).

As another safeguard, the passwords are securely hashed before being sent to the database, where they're stored in binary format. And the only user account type that can be created through the registration process is the standard member; there's no way to trick the system into creating an administrative account.

Another, obvious and relatively easy way you can improve the security of the site is to implement SSL for the registration and login processes. To do so, change the link to the registration page to: **'https://' . BASE_URL . 'register.php'**. That form will be loaded via HTTPS, and the form data will be posted back to the server via HTTPS, too. In fact, with nothing but relative links in the site, everything will be HTTPS until you create a link that returns to an HTTP connection.

Serving the login form over HTTPS is trickier, because the form is included by other pages. Your options are to serve every page over HTTPS, which isn't ideal, or to create a separate login page.

As mentioned before, you could implement an activation process as part of the registration, in which case the customer would be sent to PayPal after activating the account, not after first registering. You could also send an email when a password change is requested and only by clicking the link in that email would the user have their password reset. Right now, anyone can reset other users' passwords, which is a bother, even if it doesn't adversely affect the security.

Because this system relies upon a login to authenticate the user, much of its security depends upon using sessions and a cookie (for storing the session ID in the browser). Limiting the life of the cookie, changing the session name (which is also the cookie's name), and tweaking the other cookie parameters can all increase the site's security. You can even send the cookie only over SSL, but that would require using SSL for every page once the user logged in.

tip

Part Three, "Selling Physical Products," of the book will demonstrate switching the use of SSL as appropriate.

tip

Storing session IDs in cookies is preferred, security-wise, to storing it in links and forms.

For the session itself, one recommendation that I made in Chapter 2, "Security Fundamentals," was to change the session storage directory if using a shared host. You can also shorten how quickly the session expires, as well as how quickly the session cookie expires.

These are all *potential* alterations you could make. One recommendation you should implement is changing the session ID for administrative users. By doing so, you can prevent a *session fixation attack*.

A *session fixation attack* is when a malicious user, Alice, starts her own session on your site, quite legitimately. She then gets administrator Bob to visit the site using that same session ID, normally by getting Bob to click a link with the session ID embedded. When Bob logs in to the site, that same session will now be associated with an administrative account, giving Alice administrative access through her browser and existing session. Preventing this is quite simple: Change the session ID using the **session_regenerate_id()** function. By doing so, when Bob logs in, his session ID will change, meaning Alice's legitimate session won't be updated to reflect Bob's administrative status.

To add this technique to the **login.inc.php** script, change the storing of data in the session to:

```
if ($row[2] == 'admin') {
    session_regenerate_id(true);
    $_SESSION['user_admin'] = true;
}
$_SESSION['user_id'] = $row[0];
$_SESSION['username'] = $row[1];
if ($row[3] == 1) $_SESSION['user_not_expired'] = true;
```

You'll need to call **session_regenerate_id()** before storing any session data, because by passing a value of **true** as the first argument to the function, any existing session data is also destroyed.

Finally, access to site content in this example will be determined by dates without times. With the sessions as written, the worst thing that could happen would be that a user whose account expires today is allowed to continue accessing site content for some minutes or hours into tomorrow. But even that is only true if the user keeps their session active. Not a huge concern, in my opinion.

 tip

An even more secure way to store session data is to put it into the database.

5 | MANAGING SITE CONTENT

If you're reading this book in order—and I certainly hope you are—then you've got a site where users can register, log in, change their password, and log out, but there's nothing for them to look at! On the other hand, they haven't paid anything yet either, so...

In this chapter, you'll create the content management side of the equation, with two kinds of content: HTML pages and PDFs. I'll tell you how to write the code for creating and displaying the content.

But first, you'll need to create an administrative user.

CREATING AN ADMINISTRATOR

Even though administrators will use the same login system and the same underlying **users** table as regular users, for security reasons, you cannot create an administrator through the site itself. By making that decision, no possible flaw in the site could result in administrators being created. And since administration accounts won't be created often, it makes sense not to implement that feature anyway. But you still need at least one administrator, so let's do that now.

1. Register the administrator using the same registration page.

This would likely be the first user that gets registered anyway, just to test the system. Enter the administrator's email address and give the administrator a logical username, such as *admin*.

2. Access your database using a third-party interface.

On a hosted server, you most likely have a phpMyAdmin interface for manipulating your database, accessible only after logging in to a control panel. Or you could use the command-line MySQL client, if you prefer.

3. Change the user's type value.

You can change the type by running a query such as:

UPDATE users SET type='admin' WHERE email='*theEmailAddress*'

Or, if you're using phpMyAdmin:

A. Browse the **users** table.

B. Click the pencil icon next to the record you want to change (**Figure 5.1**).

tip

The system, as written, allows for any number of administrators, all with the same powers (which is not many).

Figure 5.1

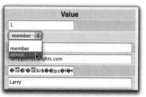

Figure 5.2

C. Use the editor form to change the user type (**Figure 5.2**).

D. Click Go.

ADDING PAGES

As I've said (several times over by now), the site will have two kinds of content. The first kind will be HTML, but the site's not going to assume that the administrator knows how to create an HTML page. Instead, there will be an interface for doing so. The administrator will use a simple, single page that displays and handles an HTML form. To create the HTML content, a *What You See Is What You Get* (WYSIWYG) editor will be incorporated into the form (**Figure 5.3**).

Add a Site Content Page

Fill out the form to add a page of content:

Title

Category
Select One

Description

Content

Path: p   Words: 0

Add This Page

Figure 5.3

Creating the Basic Script

To start, you'll create the PHP script, which displays and handles the form. Then you'll integrate the WYSIWYG editor in a separate series of steps.

1. Create a new PHP script in your text editor or IDE to be named **add_page.php** and stored in the Web root directory.

2. Include the configuration file:

   <?php
   require_once ('./includes/config.inc.php');

3. Redirect non-administrators:

   redirect_invalid_user('user_admin');

   The **redirect_invalid_user()** function, defined in **config.inc.php** (in Chapter 4, "User Accounts"), will redirect invalid users to another page. That function's first argument is the session variable to check for. In this case, it'll be *user_admin*, because **$_SESSION['user_admin']** is set only if the user is an administrator.

4. Include the header file:

   $page_title = 'Add a Site Content Page';
   include ('./includes/header.html');

   It's important that the redirection take place before you include the header file.

5. Require the database connection:

   require(MYSQL);

6. Create an array for storing errors:

   $add_page_errors = array();

   Just like the registration, login, and password forms, this script will use one array for storing any problems with the user-supplied form data.

7. Validate the page title:

   if ($_SERVER['REQUEST_METHOD'] == 'POST') {
   ** if (!empty($_POST['title'])) {**
   ** $t = mysqli_real_escape_string($dbc, strip_tags($_POST['title']));**
   ** } else {**
   ** $add_page_errors['title'] = 'Please enter the title!';**
   ** }**

   Simply by restricting access to this page to administrative users, there's less risk of it being abused, so the validation routines do not need to be

tip

Validation of administrator-generated content does not need to be as strict as public content as long as there is restricted access to the admin pages.

quite as strict as those on the public pages. For the page's title, you're confirming only that it isn't empty, as opposed to validating it using a regular expression. The **strip_tags()** function is still applied to the title, because no HTML should be there when the content is listed or displayed (as you'll shortly see).

8. Validate the category:

```
if (filter_var($_POST['category'], FILTER_VALIDATE_INT, array(
➥'min_range' => 1))) {
    $cat = $_POST['category'];
} else {
    $add_page_errors['category'] = 'Please select a category!';
}
```

Each HTML page is in a single category, which should be a foreign key to the values in the **categories** table. To confirm that the category value is an integer greater than, or equal to, 1, I'm again turning to PHP's Filter extension. If you don't have that extension enabled, you could do this:

```
if (isset($_POST['category']) && ( (int) $_POST['category'] >= 1 )) {
```

9. Validate the description:

```
if (!empty($_POST['description'])) {
    $d = mysqli_real_escape_string($dbc, strip_tags(
    ➥$_POST['description']));
} else {
    $add_page_errors['description'] = 'Please enter the description!';
}
```

The description is being treated in the same manner as the title. I'm again stripping out any HTML or PHP tags.

For all these validation routines, failures result in messages being added to the errors array.

10. Validate the content:

```
if (!empty($_POST['content'])) {
    $allowed = '<div><p><span><br><a><img><h1><h2><h3><h4>
    ➥<ul><ol><li><blockquote>';
    $c = mysqli_real_escape_string($dbc, strip_tags($_POST['content'],
    ➥$allowed));
} else {
    $add_page_errors['content'] = 'Please enter the content!';
}
```

The content is the heart of the page and is expected to contain *some* HTML. However, you probably don't want to allow just *any* HTML. For example, allowing the **<SCRIPT>** tag opens the door for Cross-Site Scripting (XSS) attacks and allowing the **<TABLE>** tag lets the administrator potentially mess up the layout of the page. The **strip_tags()** function takes an optional second argument, which is a string of allowed tags. I've defined several allowed tags, but you might want to expand the list.

11. If there are no errors, add the record to the database:

if (empty($add_page_errors)) { // If everything's OK.
  $q = "INSERT INTO pages (category_id, title, description, content)
  ➥**VALUES ($cat, '$t', '$d', '$c')";**
  $r = mysqli_query ($dbc, $q);
  if (mysqli_affected_rows($dbc) == 1) { // If it ran OK.
    echo '<h4>The page has been added!</h4>';
    $_POST = array();

Figure 5.4

Most of this should be fairly standard stuff for you. The last line, though, clears the **$_POST** array so that the already-inserted values aren't redisplayed in the sticky HTML form (**Figure 5.4**).

12. Trigger an error if the query failed:

    } else { // If it did not run OK.
      trigger_error('The page could not be added due to a system
      ➥**error. We apologize for any inconvenience.');**
    }
  } // End of $add_page_errors IF.
} // End of the main form submission conditional.

13. Include the **form_functions.inc.php** script:

require ('includes/form_functions.inc.php');
?>

As with the public forms, this form and **add_pdf.php** will use the helper function defined in **form_functions.inc.php**.

 tip

Depending upon the experience of the site administrator, you may want to add better instructions to this page.

14. Begin the form:

<h3>Add a Site Content Page</h3>
<form action="add_page.php" method="post" accept-charset=
➥**"utf-8">**
  <fieldset><legend>Fill out the form to add a page of content:</legend>
    <p><label for="first_name"><strong>Title</strong>
    ➥**</label>
<?php create_form_input('title', 'text',**
    ➥**$add_page_errors); ?></p>**

The form contains one text input, one drop-down menu, and two textareas. The text input and textareas will be created using the **create_form_input()** function.

15. Add the category menu:

```
<p><label for="category"><strong>Category</strong></label><br />
<select name="category"<?php if (array_key_exists('category',
➥$add_page_errors)) echo ' class="error"'; ?>>
<option>Select One</option>
<?php // Retrieve all the categories and add to the pull-down menu:
$q = "SELECT id, category FROM categories ORDER BY category ASC";
$r = mysqli_query ($dbc, $q);
while ($row = mysqli_fetch_array ($r, MYSQLI_NUM)) {
    echo "<option value=\"$row[0]\"";
    // Check for stickyness:
    if (isset($_POST['category']) && ($_POST['category'] == $row[0]) )
    ➥echo ' selected="selected"';
        echo ">$row[1]</option>\n";
}
?>
</select><?php if (array_key_exists('category', $add_page_errors))
➥echo ' <span class="error">' . $add_page_errors['category'] .
➥'</span>'; ?></p>
```

The **create_form_input()** function wasn't written to handle select menus. In part, this is because they're too different from inputs and textareas, and in part because there's only one select menu on the site. So this code has to replicate all that function's logic, including making the form sticky and displaying errors (**Figure 5.5**).

16. Complete the form:

```
<p><label for="description"><strong>Description</strong>
➥</label><br /><?php create_form_input('description', 'textarea',
➥$add_page_errors); ?></p>
<p><label for="content"><strong>Content</strong></label>
➥<br /><?php create_form_input('content', 'textarea',
➥$add_page_errors); ?></p>
<p><input type="submit" name="submit_button" value="Add This
➥Page" id="submit_button" class="formbutton" /></p>
</fieldset>
</form>
```

tip

For the query and query result, I prefer short variables names— **$q** and **$r**, accordingly, but you may want to use something more verbose, such as **$query** and **$result**.

Figure 5.5

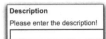

Figure 5.6

The two textareas are also generated by the **create_form_input()** function, although textareas will display their errors before the textarea box (**Figure 5.6**), not after, as with the text inputs.

17. Complete the page:

```php
<?php
include('./includes/footer.html');
?>
```

18. Save the file and load it in your Web browser.

At this point, the form will look like that in Figure 5.3, except the content textarea will look like the description's textarea.

Adding a WYSIWYG Editor

Web-based WYSIWYG editors are so common these days that you have many to choose from. To create a WYSIWYG editor, you install the editor code on your site, create a textarea in a form, and then indicate that the editor should be used for that textarea. The two most common WYSIWYG editors are probably CKEditor (**www.ckeditor.com**, formerly FCKEditor, although FCKEditor is still available) and TinyMCE (**http://tinymce.moxiecode.com**). I've used these in different projects and they're more similar than not. All are written in JavaScript, are open source, and have a slew of plug-ins for adding features such as spell check or fancy lists. The documentation for these projects is fair, and if you can follow the right syntax outlined therein, you should have no trouble installing and customizing these tools.

For no particular reason, I choose to use TinyMCE for this project. I'll walk you through the steps for integrating TinyMCE here. But first, there's one thing you should know...

 tip

There are free third-party file management plug-ins available, but I have not found them to be as good as the commercial ones.

A WYSIWYG editor can make it easy to create styled and formatted HTML, containing any valid tag, from lists to links to font-related elements. A WYSIWYG editor can also make it easy to add any kind of media, most commonly images and video. However, TinyMCE and CKEditor require a plug-in to manage file uploads and, in both cases, the plug-ins are created by the same companies and are commercial products. For this reason, I'm not integrating that functionality into this example. When the time comes that you need this functionality, just check out the corresponding documentation for the WYSIWYG editor of your choice.

1. Download the latest version of TinyMCE from **http://tinymce.moxiecode.com**.

2. Extract the files from the download.

3. Copy the **tiny_mce** folder from the extracted files to your Web root directory.

When you extract the files in Step 2, the result will be a folder called **tinymce**. Within that are **examples** and **jscripts** folders. Within **jscripts** is the **tiny_mce** folder that contains the files you actually need.

4. Open **add_page.php** in your text editor or IDE, if it is not already.

5. After the closing form tag, add:

```
<script type="text/javascript" src="/tiny_mce/tiny_mce.js"></script>
```

The first thing you'll need to do is include the main **tiny_mce.js** file, which is what this line does.

6. On the next line, begin customizing TinyMCE:

```
<script type="text/javascript">
    tinyMCE.init({
        // General options
        mode : "exact",
        elements : "content",
        theme : "advanced",
        width : 800,
        height : 400,
```

This JavaScript code will turn a textarea into a WYSIWYG editor. To do so, the **tinyMCE** class's **init()** function is called, sending it several name-value pairs. You can find these all detailed in the TinyMCE documentation, of course, but I'll highlight the most important. A **mode** of *exact* means that only specific textareas should be converted, as opposed to all of them on that page. The **elements** value, *content*, indicates that the textarea with an **id** value of *content* should be converted. This matches the **name** and **id** values already given to the content textarea. The **theme** dictates what buttons and other configuration is used. You can see different themes in the documentation and in the examples folder; this page will use the advanced theme. The **width** and **height** properties change the size of the editor.

7. Identify the plug-ins to use:

```
plugins : "advlink,advlist,autoresize,autosave,contextmenu,fullscreen,
➡iespell,inlinepopups,media,paste,preview,safari,searchreplace,
➡visualchars,wordcount,xhtmlxtras",
```

TinyMCE has a slew of plug-ins. Here I'm choosing to enable 16 of them.

 tip

Web pages will load more quickly if JavaScript is placed at the end of the document.

 tip

You cannot use the same **<SCRIPT>** tag to include a separate JavaScript file and to write inline JavaScript code.

 tip

You can customize how TinyMCE behaves using a global configuration file or individually when you use it in a particular script.

tip

Match the allowed tags in the **strip_tags()** function to the buttons in the editor.

tip

By restricting what's possible in a WYSIWYG editor, you can keep administrators from making ugly, unruly content.

tip

If the editor doesn't show or doesn't reflect your customizations, make sure you refresh the browser. If there's still a problem, the cause is probably a syntax error in your JavaScript.

8. Customize the editor's buttons:

theme_advanced_buttons1 : "cut,copy,paste,pastetext,pasteword,l,
⮑undo,redo,removeformat,l,search,replace,l,cleanup,help,code,
⮑preview,visualaid,fullscreen",
theme_advanced_buttons2 : "bold,italic,underline,strikethrough,l,
⮑justifyleft,justifycenter,justifyright,justifyfull,l,formatselect,l,bullist,
⮑numlist,l,outdent,indent,blockquote,l,sub,sup,cite,abbr",
theme_advanced_buttons3 : "hr,l,link,unlink,anchor,image,l,charmap,
⮑emotions,iespell,media",

Each line indicates a row of buttons to create in the editor (**Figure 5.7**). TinyMCE uses specific names to create specific buttons, most of which are obvious. Using the pipe character (**l**) creates separators within a line so that you may group related buttons.

Figure 5.7

9. Complete the customization:

theme_advanced_toolbar_location : "top",
theme_advanced_toolbar_align : "left",
theme_advanced_statusbar_location : "bottom",
theme_advanced_resizing : true,

The first three settings dictate where the toolbar and status bar are placed and aligned. The fourth says that the editor should be resized as the content grows, which is a nice touch.

10. Complete the script block:

content_css : "/css/style.css",
});
</script>

You can associate your site's CSS file with the editor so that content created within it will look the same as it will within a site page. That's what this line here does. The reference to the CSS file can be absolute, as in this case, or relative to the page that uses TinyMCE (not relative to the TinyMCE folder).

11. Save the file.

12. Reload the Web page in your browser to see the result (see Figure 5.3).

13. Create several pages of content.

Or, if you'd rather, you can use the SQL commands from my Web site (**www.DMCInsights.com/ecom/**) to populate the database for you.

DISPLAYING PAGE CONTENT

Now that you have several pages of pretend content in the database, it's time to create the scripts to display that content. There are two:

- **category.php** lists the specific pages under a category.

- **page.php** shows the actual content.

For marketing purposes, **category.php** will be available to any user. The **page.php** script will also be available to any user, but if they're not logged in with a valid account, they'll only see the same description of the content that's displayed on the category page. Only current customers can see the full content.

Creating category.php

The **category.php** script receives an ID value in the URL (from the links in the footer). The script should validate the ID value, then select the category's information from the database. By doing so, the category's name can be used as the browser's title. Next, the script retrieves and lists all the pages that exist within that category (**Figure 5.8**).

Figure 5.8

1. Create a new PHP script in your text editor or IDE to be named **category.php** and stored in the Web root directory.

2. Include the configuration file:

<?php
require('./includes/config.inc.php');

3. Require the database connection:

require(MYSQL);

4. Validate the category ID:

if (isset($_GET['id']) && filter_var($_GET['id'], FILTER_VALIDATE_INT,
➥array('min_range' => 1))) {

The **filter_var()** function is being used to validate the category ID, the same as in the **add_page.php** script.

5. Get the category title:

$q = 'SELECT category FROM categories WHERE id=' . $_GET['id'];
$r = mysqli_query($dbc, $q);

This query serves two purposes. First, it confirms that the supplied ID value is not only a valid integer, but that it also corresponds to a value from the database. Second, it will retrieve the category's name to use as the browser's title and as a page heading (see Figure 5.8).

6. If one row was not returned, report the problem:

```
if (mysqli_num_rows($r) != 1) {
    $page_title = 'Error!';
    include ('./includes/header.html');
    echo '<p class="error">This page has been accessed in error.</p>';
    include ('./includes/footer.html');
    exit();
}
```

If the query doesn't return exactly one row, then an invalid category ID was provided. In that case, a default page title is created, the header is included, an error message is displayed, the footer is included, and the script is terminated. **Figure 5.9** shows the end result.

 note

The results shown in Figure 5.9 will only be seen by users attempting things they shouldn't.

Figure 5.9

7. Fetch the category title and use it as the page title:

```
list ($page_title) = mysqli_fetch_array($r, MYSQLI_NUM);
include ('./includes/header.html');
echo "<h3>$page_title</h3>";
```

If the previous query did return one record, the selected column is fetched directly into the **$page_title** variable, then the header is included and a page header is displayed.

8. Print a message if they're not an active user:

```
if (isset($_SESSION['user_id']) && !isset($_SESSION[
➥'user_not_expired'])) {
    echo '<p class="error">Thank you for your interest in this content.
    ➥Unfortunately your account has expired. Please <a href="renew.php">
    ➥renew your account</a> in order to access site content.</p>';
} elseif (!isset($_SESSION['user_id'])) {
    echo '<p class="error">Thank you for your interest in this content. You
    ➥must be logged in as a registered user to view site content.</p>';
}
```

Three types of users could be looking at this page: guests (people not logged in), logged-in users whose accounts have expired, and logged-in users whose accounts have not expired. In the last case, no error messages need to be displayed.

In the second case, **$_SESSION['user_id']** will be set, but **$_SESSION['user_not_expired']** won't be. This latter element would have been assigned a value of **true** if their account was still good when the user logged in. In this situation, the user is told that they need to renew their account.

If the user isn't logged in at all, a message says that they need to be registered and logged in to view the content.

9. Get the pages associated with this category:

```
$q = 'SELECT id, title, description FROM pages WHERE category_id='
➥. $_GET['id'] . ' ORDER BY date_created DESC';
$r = mysqli_query($dbc, $q);
if (mysqli_num_rows($r) > 0) {
    while ($row = mysqli_fetch_array ($r, MYSQLI_ASSOC)) {
        echo "<div><h4><a href=\"page.php?id={$row['id']}\">
        ➥{$row['title']}</a></h4><p>{$row['description']}</p>
        ➥</div>\n";
    }
```

tip

The **list()** function assigns parts of an array to individual variables.

tip

Because the PHP script finished using the results of the first query, it's safe to use the same **$q** and **$r** variables here.

Each returned record will be displayed on the page as its own **<DIV>**. The page title will be put within **<H4>** tags and linked to **page.php**, passing along the page ID in the URL. After the title, the page's description is added.

10. Print a message if no pages are available:

} else {
    echo '<p>There are currently no pages of content associated with ⇒this category. Please check back again!</p>';
}

On a live site, hopefully there won't be any categories in the database that don't have content. But, so as not to make any assumptions, if the **pages SELECT** query doesn't return any rows, a message will be shown to the user to check back again (**Figure 5.10**).

> **PHP Security**
> There are currently no pages of content associated with this category. Please check back again!

Figure 5.10

11. If no valid ID was received by the page, display an error:

} else { // No valid ID.
    $page_title = 'Error!';
    include ('./includes/header.html');
    echo '<p class="error">This page has been accessed in error.</p>';
} // End of primary IF.

This is a replication of the code executed if the category **SELECT** does not return one record.

12. Include the HTML footer and complete the page:

include ('./includes/footer.html');
?>

13. Save and test the category script.

Creating page.php

Like **category.php**, the **page.php** script also receives an ID value in the URL (from the links in **category.php**). The script should validate the ID value, then select the page's information from the database. The page's title will be used as the browser's title and displayed as a page header. What comes next will depend upon the person viewing the page:

tip

The script as written does not paginate the page listings. If a category might have more than, say, 15 or 20 pages associated with it, you may want to add pagination, which is discussed in my book, *PHP and MySQL for Dynamic Web Sites: Visual QuickPro Guide*.

- Logged-in users with current accounts will see the content (**Figure 5.11**).

- Logged-in users with expired accounts will see the content's description, along with a recommendation to renew their account.

- Guests will see the content's description, along with a recommendation to register (**Figure 5.12**).

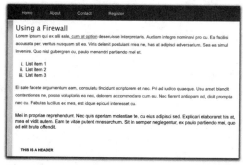

Figure 5.11

Figure 5.12

As you would expect, much of this functionality will be like the **category.php** script.

1. Create a new PHP script in your text editor or IDE to be named **page.php** and stored in the Web root directory.

2. Include the configuration file:

```
<?php
require('./includes/config.inc.php');
```

3. Require the database connection:

```
require(MYSQL);
```

4. Validate the page ID:

```
if (isset($_GET['id']) && filter_var($_GET['id'], FILTER_VALIDATE_INT,
➥array('min_range' => 1))) {
```

This is the same validation used with the category ID. If your version of PHP does not support the Filter extension, you could use:

```
if (isset($_GET['id']) && ( (int) $_GET['id'] >= 1 )) {
```

5. Get the page info:

```
$q = 'SELECT title, description, content FROM pages WHERE id='
➥. $_GET['id'];
$r = mysqli_query($dbc, $q);
```

A simple query retrieves three fields from the **pages** table for one record.

6. If no rows were returned, print an error:

```
if (mysqli_num_rows($r) != 1) {
    $page_title = 'Error!';
    include ('./includes/header.html');
    echo '<p class="error">This page has been accessed in error.</p>';
    include ('./includes/footer.html');
    exit();
}
```

Again, as with **category.php**, if the supplied ID value is an integer but doesn't correlate to any database record, a complete page is created that indicates a problem (similar to Figure 5.9).

7. Fetch the page info:

```
$row = mysqli_fetch_array($r, MYSQLI_ASSOC);
$page_title = $row['title'];
include ('includes/header.html');
echo "<h3>$page_title</h3>";
```

The page's title will be used as the browser's title and as a header on the page.

8. Display the content if the user's account is current:

```
if (isset($_SESSION['user_not_expired'])) {
    echo "<div>{$row['content']}</div>";
} elseif (isset($_SESSION['user_id'])) { // Logged in but not current.
    echo '<p class="error">Thank you for your interest in this content, but
    ↪your account is no longer current. Please <a href="renew.php">renew
    ↪your account</a> in order to view this page in its entirety</p>';
    echo "<div>{$row['description']}</div>";
} else { // Not logged in.
    echo '<p class="error">Thank you for your interest in this content.
    ↪You must be logged in as a registered user to view this page in its
    ↪entirety.</p>';
    echo "<div>{$row['description']}</div>";
}
```

This conditional dictates what is shown on the page, based upon the user viewing it. Only logged-in users with current accounts—those who have a **$_SESSION['user_not_expired']** value—can see the content itself. The other user types see only the description, along with a message appropriate to their situation.

9. Complete the ID conditional:

```
} else { // No valid ID.
   $page_title = 'Error!';
   include ('includes/header.html');
   echo '<p class="error">This page has been accessed in error.</p>';
} // End of primary IF.
```

If no valid ID value was received by this page, the user will see this error message.

10. Complete the page:

```
include ('./includes/footer.html');
?>
```

11. Save and test the **page.php** script.

To test it, you'll need to click a link on **category.php**. You should also test it as three different user types—guest, expired member, and active member—to get the full effect.

ADDING PDFS

The second administrative page for this example will handle uploading PDF files to the site. Although the administrator needs to provide only three pieces of information—a title, a description, and the PDF file itself—the process for handling the form is tricky, largely because I wanted to make the form *sticky*, like the others in the site. As you may know, the file form input can't be made sticky in the same way that a text input can, so I had to use some logic to fake the concept (**Figure 5.13**).

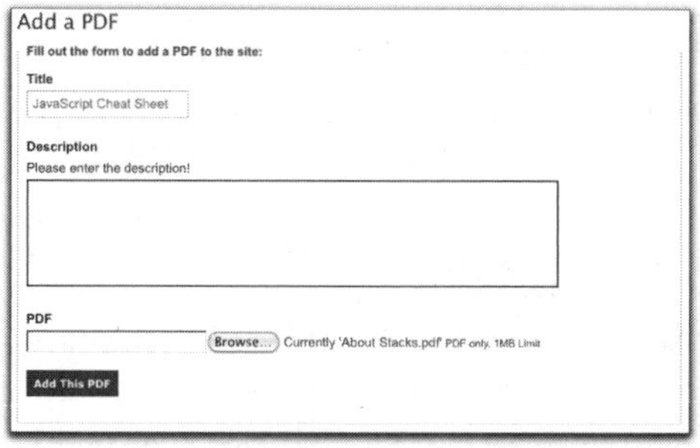

Figure 5.13

Also, allowing users—even administrators—to upload files to your server is a potential security hole, so several techniques need to be applied to make this process as safe as possible. But first, the server needs to be set up to allow for file uploads.

Setting Up the Server

Server permissions on files and directories comes down to *who* can do *what*. As for the *what*, the options are: read, write, and execute. The *who* is either the specific server user or groups of users.

Before a PHP script can put files onto the server, there must be a folder on the server to which the PHP script can *write*, which is to say alter the directory's contents. As PHP is run through the Web server, the *who* is the Web server user. So the goal is to create a folder that the Web server user can write to.

Figure 5.14

How you go about actually doing this will depend upon how your server is set up, the operating system in use, and how PHP is running with respect to the Web server. At the end of the day, what this normally means is that you'll create a directory and give "everyone" permission to write to it. In Unix terms, this is represented by the number 777. Normally, your Web host provides a control panel through which you can change a folder's permissions, or you may be able to do it through your FTP application (**Figure 5.14**).

Although allowing everyone to do everything with a directory may sound extremely dangerous, it's not. What is meant by "everyone" is every user on the server. By "user" I mean a user account registered with the server. For example, there may be a *mysql* user that runs the database and the Web server may run as the user *nobody*. With *open* permissions, both of these users, as well anyone with FTP or SSH access to the server, can read from, write to, or execute the files in the directory. That's not insignificant, but being available to everyone does not mean that anyone on the Internet can write files to that directory: a recognized server user is still required.

All that being said, it doesn't mean that you should be blasé about creating an open directory like this. If you're on a shared server, everyone with a user account on that server can manipulate this directory—assuming they know it exists, of course, which is a big if. And, if there's a security hole in a Web site, that vulnerability could be used to manipulate the directory—in this case, by users over the Internet—as the Web server user would be the active agent.

There are many instances in which an open directory is necessary for the functioning of a site. The question becomes how to make the system as secure as possible. The answer is found by thinking like a hacker. If a hacker can't break into a server, the next goal will be to have the server execute some dangerous code for her or him. One way of doing so is trying to get PHP (or whatever) to open, require, or include—thereby executing—some dangerous code found on another server. I talk about this in Chapter 2, "Security Fundamentals." A second route is to get the dangerous code onto the server somehow and then execute it directly. That's a two-step process. Protecting against such an attempt is also, therefore, a two-step process:

1. Do everything you can to prevent dangerous code from being placed on the server.

2. Make it difficult, if not impossible, to directly execute dynamically added content.

For the first step, it's largely a matter of validating uploaded content: making sure it's of an acceptable type. For the second step, the best solution is to store uploaded content in a directory outside the Web root directory. In such a case, if bad person Bob (on the Internet, not on your server) can trick your system into uploading some dangerous script, he still could not execute that script, as there would be no way to invoke it if it's not in the Web root directory.

If that's not possible (for example, some shared hosts don't allow you to put content above the Web directory), you should create a non-obvious folder within the Web directory. This folder will still require the open permissions, but you should password-protect the directory so that it's only available (over HTTP) to authorized users. You can do this using your Web host's control panel.

Once you've created the **pdfs** directory with open permissions, and protected it appropriately if you had to place it in the Web root directory, you can create the PHP script that will upload a PDF file to that folder. But first, I would recommend creating another constant in the configuration file that is an absolute path to this folder:

```
// In config.inc.php:
define ('PDFS_DIR', BASE_URI . 'pdfs/');
```

Creating the PHP Script

This PHP script has the same basic structure as all the other forms: The form is first displayed; the data is validated after the user submits the form; and the form is displayed again with its current values indicated should there be any errors. But this particular process will be trickier than the other forms in that it's also dealing with an uploaded file. The file input cannot be made sticky and, more importantly, the actual file on the server must be addressed when the form is being redisplayed because of other errors. I'll explain all the corresponding logic in the following steps.

1. Create a new PHP script in your text editor or IDE to be named **add_pdf.php** and stored in the Web root directory.

tip

Ways to use the Web server to protect directories are discussed in Chapter 7, "Second Site: Structure and Design."

tip

In Chapter 3, "First Site: Structure and Design," I talked about the server's organization and where the **pdfs** directory should ideally go.

tip

Change the value of **PDFS_DIR** so that it's correct for your server.

2. Include the configuration file:

```php
<?php
require_once ('./includes/config.inc.php');
```

3. Redirect non-administrators:

```php
redirect_invalid_user('user_admin');
```

4. Include the header file:

```php
$page_title = 'Add a PDF';
include('./includes/header.html');
```

5. Require the database connection:

```php
require(MYSQL);
```

6. Create an array for storing errors:

```php
$add_pdf_errors = array();
```

7. If the form was submitted, validate the title and description:

```php
if ($_SERVER['REQUEST_METHOD'] == 'POST') {
    if (!empty($_POST['title'])) {
        $t = mysqli_real_escape_string($dbc, strip_tags($_POST['title']));
    } else {
        $add_pdf_errors['title'] = 'Please enter the title!';
    }
    if (!empty($_POST['description'])) {
        $d = mysqli_real_escape_string($dbc, strip_tags(
        ➥$_POST['description']));
    } else {
        $add_pdf_errors['description'] = 'Please enter the description!';
    }
```

The validation routines just check for any value for both of these inputs. If they're not empty, the values are run through the **strip_tags()** function, and then **mysqli_real_escape_string()**. If either value is empty, an error message is added to the array.

8. Check for a PDF:

```php
if (is_uploaded_file ($_FILES['pdf']['tmp_name']) && ($_FILES['pdf']
➥['error'] == UPLOAD_ERR_OK)) {
    $file = $_FILES['pdf'];
```

The first time the form is submitted, there should be data in the special **$_FILES** array, thanks to the file input whose name is *pdf*. This conditional checks that there is an uploaded file and that there is no error (because you can have an uploaded file but also an error). If both conditions are true, the **$file** variable is turned into a shorthand version of **$_FILES['pdf']**, for later use.

9. Validate the file information:

$size = ROUND($file['size']/1024);
if ($size > 1024) {
    $add_pdf_errors['pdf'] = 'The uploaded file was too large.';
}
if (($file['type'] != 'application/pdf') && (substr($file['name'], -4) !=
➥ '.pdf')) {
    $add_pdf_errors['pdf'] = 'The uploaded file was not a PDF.';
}

First, the file's size is calculated in kilobytes. This value will first be used to make sure the file isn't too large. On the public side, this value will be displayed to the end user indicating how big the PDF is (a nice feature). If the file is larger than a megabyte (or 1,024 kilobytes), an error message is created. Since the **MAX_FILE_SIZE** hidden form input is a recommendation that's easy to circumvent, it's best to check the file's size using PHP, too.

Next, the file's type is validated. The first part of the conditional checks if the type is not equal to *application/pdf*, which is the MIME type the browser will associate with an uploaded PDF. But a MIME type is easy to fake, so you can't rely upon just that. The second part of the conditional checks that the file's name concludes with *.pdf*. Since any file's extension dictates how the file is treated by computers, this is another good security check (although not 100 percent foolproof).

From a security perspective, by this point, reasonable steps have been taken to ensure that the uploaded file is not too large and is a PDF.

10. If there were no errors, create the file's new name and destination:

if (!array_key_exists('pdf', $add_pdf_errors)) {
    $tmp_name = sha1($file['name'] . uniqid('',true));
    $dest = PDFS_DIR . $tmp_name . '_tmp';

For security purposes, the uploaded file should be renamed to something random and unpredictable. To do so, the **sha1()** function will create a 40-character hash from some data. The data to be hashed is the file's original name plus a unique identifier.

The destination value is the absolute path to where the file will be stored on the server—its final resting place, including the file's new name. The

tip

As written, only one error will be associated with the file input, so if the uploaded file is both too large and not a PDF, the user will see only the second error.

tip

A stricter way of validating a PDF's type is to read in the file's binary data and make sure it matches the PDF specification.

tip

Renaming uploaded files is generally recommended so that hackers won't know what an uploaded file is called on the server.

PDFS_DIR constant added to **config.inc.php** earlier in the chapter is used for part of that destination. At this point, I'm also adding _tmp to the file's name to indicate that the file is on the server but not associated with a database record as of yet.

11. Move the file:

```
if (move_uploaded_file($file['tmp_name'], $dest)) {
    $_SESSION['pdf']['tmp_name'] = $tmp_name;
    $_SESSION['pdf']['size'] = $size;
    $_SESSION['pdf']['file_name'] = $file['name'];
    echo '<h4>The file has been uploaded!</h4>';
} else {
    trigger_error('The file could not be moved.');
    unlink ($file['tmp_name']);
}
```

The **move_uploaded_file()** function will transfer only files uploaded via HTTP POST, so it can't be manipulated to move other files around on the server. Its first argument is the file to move, which is represented by the file's temporary name (something like /tmp/php4902). The second argument is the file's destination, which includes both the directory and file name.

Next, three pieces of information about the file are stored in the session for later reference. This includes the file's new name, its size, and its original name. Then a message is displayed indicating that the file has been handled.

If the file could not be moved, an error message is triggered and the uploaded file is removed (so it's not cluttering up the temporary directory).

12. If there was no uploaded file, look for an error:

```
    } // End of array_key_exists() IF.
} else { // No uploaded file.
    switch ($_FILES['pdf']['error']) {
        case 1:
        case 2:
            $add_pdf_errors['pdf'] = 'The uploaded file was too large.';
            break;
        case 3:
            $add_pdf_errors['pdf'] = 'The file was only partially uploaded.';
            break;
        case 6:
        case 7:
```

 tip

There is no error code 5 (that's not a typo in the book).

```
    case 8:
        $add_pdf_errors['pdf'] = 'The file could not be uploaded due to
        ⇒a system error.';
        break;
    case 4:
    default:
        $add_pdf_errors['pdf'] = 'No file was uploaded.';
        break;
    } // End of SWITCH.
} // End of $_FILES IF-ELSEIF-ELSE.
```

The PHP manual lists all the file upload-related error codes. This script should not be too descriptive in its error reporting to the user, so each code is turned into a more generic message. Some codes, such as 1 and 2 or 6, 7, and 8, have the same net meaning, so I'm using a *fall-through* in the **switch**, where multiple cases have the same effect.

13. Add the PDF to the database:

```
if (empty($add_pdf_errors)) { // If everything's OK.
    $fn = mysqli_real_escape_string($dbc, $_SESSION['pdf']
    ⇒['file_name']);
    $tmp_name = mysqli_real_escape_string($dbc, $_SESSION['pdf']
    ⇒['tmp_name']);
    $size = (int) $_SESSION['pdf']['size'];
    $q = "INSERT INTO pdfs (tmp_name, title, description, file_name,
    ⇒size) VALUES ('$tmp_name', '$t', '$d', '$fn', $size)";
    $r = mysqli_query ($dbc, $q);
```

If there were no errors, the next step is to insert the PDF data into the database. To do so, the three pieces of information about the file, already stored in the session, are made safe to use in the query (the title and description were already run through **mysqli_real_escape_string()** by this point).

14. If the query worked, rename the file:

```
if (mysqli_affected_rows($dbc) == 1) { // If it ran OK.
    $original = PDFS_DIR . $_SESSION['pdf']['tmp_name'] . '_tmp';
    $dest = PDFS_DIR . $_SESSION['pdf']['tmp_name'];
    rename($original, $dest);
```

To make the upload permanent, the file will have the _tmp removed from its name.

15. Indicate the success to the user and clear the values:

```
echo '<h4>The PDF has been added!</h4>';
$_POST = array();
$_FILES = array();
unset($file, $_SESSION['pdf']);
```

All these values need to be cleared so that the form doesn't display any existing values.

16. If there was a problem with the query, trigger an error:

```
} else { // If it did not run OK.
    trigger_error('The PDF could not be added due to a system error.
    ➥We apologize for any inconvenience.');
    unlink ($dest);
}
```

There should not be a database query error on a live, tested site, but just in case, an error will be triggered and the file will be deleted (so that there's no file on the server without a corresponding database reference).

17. Complete the processing part of the script:

```
    } // End of $errors IF.
} else { // Clear out the session on a GET request:
    unset($_SESSION['pdf']);
} // End of the submission IF.
```

The **else** clause applies if this is a GET request. In that case, the script should clear any potential value that might be in **$_SESSION['pdf']**. This is really only necessary in cases where the administrator uploaded a file but had other errors, then clicked the *Add PDF* link again.

18. Begin the form:

```
require ('includes/form_functions.inc.php');
?><h3>Add a PDF</h3>
<form enctype="multipart/form-data" action="add_pdf.php"
➥method="post" accept-charset="utf-8">
    <input type="hidden" name="MAX_FILE_SIZE" value="1048576"
/>
```

This form will use the same **create_form_input()** function for the title and the description. The form must use the **enctype** property and the POST method in order to handle the file data. The **MAX_FILE_SIZE** value is a suggestion to the browser, which may or may not be ignored.

19. Create the first two elements:

```
<fieldset><legend>Fill out the form to add a PDF to the site:</legend>
   <p><label for="title"><strong>Title</strong></label><br />
   ↪<?php create_form_input('title', 'text', $add_pdf_errors); ?></p>
   <p><label for="description"><strong>Description</strong>
   ↪</label><br /><?php create_form_input('description', 'textarea',
   ↪$add_pdf_errors); ?></p>
```

20. Start creating the file input:

```
<p><label for="pdf"><strong>PDF</strong></label><br />
<?php echo '<input type="file" name="pdf" id="pdf"';
```

There's no file input generation in the **create_form_input()** function because there's only one file input in the entire site (and because file inputs are quite different than text, password, or textareas). Because a fair amount of PHP logic will be required to properly handle the file input, the input code itself is begun by a PHP **echo** statement. The statement does not close the input element yet so that an *error* class may be added (in the next step).

21. Check for an error:

```
if (array_key_exists('pdf', $add_pdf_errors)) {
   echo ' class="error" /> <span class="error">'
   ↪. $add_pdf_errors['pdf'] . '</span>';
} else { // No error.
   echo ' />';
```

If there was an error, the *error* class is added to the input—so that it'll be outlined in red—and the error message is added after the input. If there was no error, then the input is closed.

22. If the file already exists, indicate that to the user:

```
if (isset($_SESSION['pdf'])) {
   echo " Currently '{$_SESSION['pdf']['file_name']}'";
}
```

This is still part of the **else** indicating there's no error with this input. That would be the case if the form was loaded for the first time or if it has been submitted, but there were errors with the other form elements. In this latter case, a file has been uploaded already and the form should indicate the existence of that file to the user (see Figure 5.13).

23. Complete the file input:

```
} // end of errors IF-ELSE.
?> <small>PDF only, 1MB Limit</small></p>
```

 tip

If the user sees the form again because of an error and then completes the form while submitting a new PDF, the new PDF file will be used in place of the old one.

note

Through incomplete use of this script, it is possible to end up with extraneous files on the server, but their names will end with *_tmp* and can be deleted manually.

Figure 5.15

24. Complete the form and the page:

```
<p><input type="submit" name="submit_button" value="Add This
➥PDf" id="submit_button" class="formbutton" /></p>
</fieldset>
</form>
<?php
include ('./includes/footer.html');
?>
```

25. Save the script and test the PDF upload process.

Figure 5.15 shows the result of successfully adding a new PDF.

DISPLAYING PDF CONTENT

Just like the HTML content, displaying the PDF content on the site requires two scripts. The first, **pdfs.php**, just lists every PDF in the catalog, along with a link to view the PDF itself. The second, **view_pdf.php**, retrieves and displays a specific PDF, but only after validating the user.

Creating pdfs.php

The **pdfs.php** page works much like **category.php**, except that it does not receive an ID value in the URL. It just displays every PDF (**Figure 5.16**).

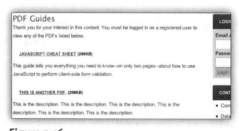

Figure 5.16

1. Create a new PHP script in your text editor or IDE to be named **pdfs.php** and stored in the Web root directory.

2. Include the configuration file:

```
<?php
require ('./includes/config.inc.php');
```

3. Require the database connection:

```
require(MYSQL);
```

4. Include the header file and display a page header:

```
$page_title = 'PDFs';
include ('./includes/header.html');
echo '<h3>PDF Guides</h3>';
```

5. Print a message if the user is not active:

```
if (isset($_SESSION['user_id']) && !isset($_SESSION['user_not_
➥expired'])) {
    echo '<p class="error">Thank you for your interest in this content.
    ➥Unfortunately your account has expired. Please <a href="renew.php">
    ➥renew your account</a> in order to view any of the PDFs listed
    ➥below.</p>';
} elseif (!isset($_SESSION['user_id'])) {
    echo '<p class="error">Thank you for your interest in this content.
    ➥You must be logged in as a registered user to view any of the PDFs
    ➥listed below.</p>';
}
```

The messages differ slightly from those in **category.php**, but the checks on the user's status are the same.

6. Get the PDFs:

```
$q = 'SELECT tmp_name, title, description, size FROM pdfs ORDER BY
➥date_created DESC';
$r = mysqli_query($dbc, $q);
if (mysqli_num_rows($r) > 0) {
```

The query returns the temporary name, title, and description for each PDF in the database, in order from newest to oldest.

7. Fetch and display every PDF:

```
while ($row = mysqli_fetch_array ($r, MYSQLI_ASSOC)) {
    echo "<div><h4><a href=\"view_pdf.php?id={$row['tmp_name']}\">
    ➥{$row['title']}</a> ({$row['size']}kb)</h4><p>{$row['description']}
    ➥</p></div>\n";
} // End of WHILE loop.
```

Each record is displayed as its own **<DIV>**, with the title as a linked **<H4>**, followed by the size of the file. The file's description comes next. Each link points to **view_pdf.php,** passing along the temporary name—the 40-character hash—in the URL.

8. Complete the page:

```
} else { // No PDFs!
    echo '<p>There are currently no PDFs available to view. Please check
    ➡back again!</p>';
}
include ('./includes/footer.html');
?>
```

This message will be shown if there are no PDFs in the database, which will hopefully never be the case.

9. Save the script and test **pdfs.php** in your Web browser.

You obviously can't test any of the links until you create **view_pdf.php** first.

Creating view_pdf.php

The user arrives at this final script after clicking a link in **pdfs.php**. This page's sole purpose is to display the PDF to the user, provided that their account is active.

1. Create a new PHP script in your text editor or IDE to be named **pdf.php** and stored in the Web root directory.

2. Include the configuration file and the database connection:

```
<?php
require ('./includes/config.inc.php');
require(MYSQL);
```

3. Create a flag variable:

```
$valid = false;
```

This script will have many tests before getting to the point of actually displaying the PDF, so it will start by assuming that something's wrong.

4. Validate the PDF ID:

```
if (isset($_GET['id']) && (strlen($_GET['id']) == 40) &&
➡(substr($_GET['id'], 0, 1) != '.') ) {
    $file = PDFS_DIR . $_GET['id'];
    if (file_exists ($file) && (is_file($file)) ) {
```

The PDF identifier should come into this script through the URL. The ID won't be an integer, but it must be exactly 40 characters long, so that's a good first thing to look at. A common way to hack a system such as this would be for the malicious user to submit *../**path**/**to**/**something**/**useful*** as the value, where the **..** moves up a directory. The intention would be to have the PHP script grab and display a sensitive document, such as a server password file. To prevent that from happening, the third part of the conditional checks that the first character isn't a period.

If all three conditions are true, then an absolute path to the file is defined. Next, the file is tested to confirm that it exists and is a file (as opposed to a directory).

5. Get the PDF information from the database:

```
$q = 'SELECT title, description, file_name FROM pdfs WHERE
⟿tmp_name="' . mysqli_real_escape_string($dbc, $_GET['id']) . '"';
$r = mysqli_query($dbc, $q);
if (mysqli_num_rows($r) == 1) { // Ok!
    $row = mysqli_fetch_array($r, MYSQLI_ASSOC);
    $valid = true;
```

The query fetches the PDF's title, description, and original file name. The first two pieces of information will be used if the current viewer doesn't have permission to see the PDF itself. If one row was returned, the data is retrieved and the **$valid** variable is changed to **true**.

6. Only display the PDF to a user whose account is active:

```
if (isset($_SESSION['user_not_expired'])) {
    header('Content-type:application/pdf');
    header('Content-Disposition:inline;filename="' . $row['file_name']
⟿. '"');
    $fs = filesize($file);
    header ("Content-Length:$fs\n");
    readfile ($file);
    exit();
```

If the user's account is active, the PDF should be loaded in the browser. To do that in PHP, start by sending a header indicating the content type. Then indicate the content's disposition—*inline*, meaning show the file in the browser—and what its filename is. For the file's name, the original file name is provided. Next, the size of the file is indicated, using the actual file's size, not the database-stored approximation. Finally, the **readfile()** function reads in all the binary data and sends it to the browser. The script is then terminated.

 note

Different browsers will use the filename disposition differently.

7. For inactive users, show the content's description:

```
} else { // Inactive account!
    $page_title = $row['title'];
    include ('./includes/header.html');
    echo "<h3>$page_title</h3>";
```

(continues on next page)

```
if (isset($_SESSION['user_id'])) {
    echo '<p class="error">Thank you for your interest in this
    ➥content. Unfortunately your account has expired. Please
    ➥<a href="renew.php">renew your account</a> in order to
    ➥access this file.</p>';
} else {
    echo '<p class="error">Thank you for your interest in this
    ➥content. You must be logged in as a registered user to view this
    ➥file.</p>';
}
echo "<div>{$row['description']}</div>";
include ('./includes/footer.html');
} // End of user IF-ELSE.
```

If the user is logged in but inactive (that is, their account has expired), they'll be asked to renew their account (**Figure 5.17**). If the user is not logged in, they'll be asked to log in (**Figure 5.18**).

Figure 5.17   **Figure 5.18**

8. Complete the conditionals:

```
        } // End of mysqli_num_rows() IF.
    } // End of file_exists() IF.
} // End of $_GET['id'] IF.
```

9. Indicate a problem and complete the page:

```
if (!$valid) {
    $page_title = 'Error!';
    include ('./includes/header.html');
    echo '<p class="error">This page has been accessed in error.</p>';
    include ('./includes/footer.html');
}
?>
```

If the page did not receive an ID value corresponding to a database record and an actual file on the server, the user will see an error message like that in Figure 5.9.

10. Save the file and test it by clicking a link on **pdfs.php**.

6 | USING PAYPAL

The final, yet most important step in the *Knowledge is Power* site is to integrate PayPal so that the site may actually make money. It's not hard to use PayPal, but it's such a critical step that I want to give it extra attention. And, as with many technologies, wading through all the documentation and possible uses can be the hardest part.

In this chapter, you'll learn about the current state of PayPal and what payment options PayPal offers. The next step is to sign up for PayPal's Sandbox feature, so that you can create dummy PayPal accounts for testing purposes. After that, you can complete the PHP scripts required by the site and completely test the end result. Once you're satisfied that everything is working properly with your test accounts, you will repeat some of these steps for a live PayPal account, quickly update a couple of pages, and you're good to go!

ABOUT PAYPAL

PayPal is perhaps the biggest payment solution provider around, and there's good reason to consider using it with your e-commerce sites. From a development standpoint, it's quite simple to integrate PayPal. From the customer's point of view, PayPal is a trusted name, which makes a big difference in a user's willingness to part with their money. With other providers, you may be able to create a more professional experience or save money on transaction fees, but don't dismiss PayPal, just because it may be the "lowest common denominator" of solutions.

One frequent misconception about PayPal is that customers must also have a PayPal account. If a customer does have a PayPal account, they can make a payment using it. But both PayPal users and non-PayPal users can also pay with their credit cards through PayPal's system. A second misconception is that PayPal transactions always go through the PayPal site. This used to be the case, but PayPal has two primary payment solutions now, one of which allows you to handle customer transactions without the user leaving your site.

PayPal offers:

- No setup fees

- No monthly costs for the basic payment option

- Fraud protections

- Shipping calculators and shipping label service

- Tax calculators

- Availability in 190 countries and with 21 currencies

- Currency conversions

- International tax and shipping calculators

- Ability to send invoices

- Inventory management

- A virtual terminal to manually process transactions

- Integration with popular third-party e-commerce systems, such as osCommerce and ZenCart

What PayPal doesn't do, however, is transfer money directly into your bank account. The funds received from transactions get applied to **your PayPal account**. You can then go into your PayPal account and transfer money to your registered bank account, which will probably take a couple of days to go through. At the PayPal Web site, you can also view monthly reports, search through your transaction history, and even allow different types of users to access the PayPal account (for example, a low-level user may only be allowed to print shipping labels without seeing any payment details).

 tip

PayPal has tons of documentation and videos explaining the various programs, features, and fees. Almost too much, really...

 tip

You must have a Premiere or Business PayPal account in order to receive money.

 note

All the information about PayPal in this chapter is current as of this writing and is subject to change.

Payment Solutions

PayPal offers two base payment solutions, named *Website Payments Standard* and *Website Payments Pro*. Both solutions allow you to accept payment from PayPal users or via credit cards. Both solutions also allow you to use a shopping cart, whether a custom one of your own devising or a third-party system.

The Standard option is pretty much what people historically think of as PayPal: The customer starts off on your site and then heads to the PayPal site to complete the transaction, after which they can return to your site. There is no monthly fee for this option, and it's easy to set up: You just need your own PayPal account. Although you can customize the PayPal experience to some degree, it will be clear to the customer that they are no longer on your site, and the charge on the customer's credit card statement will use a combination of PayPal and your business's name.

The Pro payment solution is like other payment gateways in that the customer does not need to leave your site to complete the transaction (that is, to pay you). The Pro system is $30 per month and you have to complete a credit application to qualify (you'll need your own PayPal account as well, of course). The Pro system will also let you customize the fraud protection, but you will need to take extra steps to protect the credit card data because it'll be temporarily handled on your system (stricter PCI compliance will be necessary).

The transaction fees, regardless of the solution type, are 30 cents per transaction. You'll also pay a percentage of the transaction total, depending upon how much business you do per month (**Table 6.1**).

Table 6.1 PayPal Fees

Monthly Sales	Per Transaction Fee
$0 to $3,000	2.9% + $0.30
$3,000.01 to $10,000	2.5% + $0.30
$10,000.01 to $100,000	2.2% + $0.30
over $100,000	1.9% + $0.30

In this chapter, you'll use the Website Payments Standard solution. You can assume that most of what I say and do throughout the rest of this chapter applies only to it. The next e-commerce site, *Coffee* (in Chapter 7, "Second Site: Structure and Design"), will use another payment gateway. That process and code is comparable to using PayPal's Website Payments Pro solution.

note

There's no guarantee a user will immediately return to your site after completing the PayPal process.

note

All prices in this chapter and book are in United States dollars.

tip

If your transactions normally average less than $10 each, you can save money by using PayPal's *micropayments* rates.

note

Currency conversions and payments from other countries have extra fees.

Payment Buttons

The Website Payments Standard system relies upon using PayPal's tools to generate HTML code specific for your e-commerce situation. By filling out a form and answering a few questions, PayPal will create some HTML that you can drop into the right spot on your Web site. The code itself creates an HTML button that, when clicked, takes the user to PayPal.

There are different types of default buttons for different situations:

- *Buy Now*, for selling single items

- *Add to Cart*, for selling multiple items

- *Subscribe*, for selling subscriptions

- *Donate*, for accepting donations

You've no doubt seen examples of these buttons many times over (**Figure 6.1**). The Buy Now and Add to Cart buttons also let you set different attributes for products and adjust the price based upon the selected attributes. For example, if you sell software through your site, the customer might be allowed to select the number or type of licenses to purchase.

You can start with one of these default buttons, customize it to your situation, and even use a different image for the button itself. As a security feature, the button only passes identifiers—an indicator of your account and a button ID—to the PayPal Web site. All the particulars, such as the price to be charged, are stored within PayPal's system, meaning that a hacker can't manipulate those values.

For this project, you'll use the subscribe option, because the site is selling subscriptions to its content. The subscribe feature comes in two formats:

- Recurring payments via a PayPal account

- Recurring payments without a PayPal account

The latter allows anyone to use a credit card to make the purchase; there is a $19.99/month fee (to you, the merchant) for this service.

Once the user subscribes via PayPal, they'll automatically be billed again when the time period you establish is up. From a business perspective, a recurring payment is great, because you continue to get your money until the customer cancels the recurring payment. You should indicate this to the user, though, and perhaps let them know their account is about to expire and that they'll be billed again prior to that occurring (or else you'll have to be prepared to process some refunds).

 tip

Buttons you've created can be customized later, like to change the price charged for an item.

Figure 6.1

 tip

You can even offer trial periods as part of a subscription, although you won't in this site.

 tip

You could create a script that emails any user whose account is about to expire within the next week. Then execute the script once or twice a week.

 tip

Users can see what automatic billings they have agreed to under the *My preapproved payments* section of their PayPal Profile page.

TESTING PAYPAL

As part of the process of testing a new Web site, you most certainly want to test the payment-handling system. PayPal, like most payment solutions, offers a playground environment that can pretend to handle transactions without any real money changing hands. With PayPal, you test transactions using the PayPal Sandbox. So let's start by setting that up.

THE MANY FACES OF PAYPAL

There are three different PayPal-related sites that you'll deal with. The first and most obvious is the real PayPal, at **www.paypal.com**. Before the site goes live, you'll need a PayPal account there, representing the site. You'll recreate your button there, and you'll see your transactions there.

There are two sites used as part of the testing process. The first is the Sandbox, at **http://developer.paypal.com**. To create and use test accounts, you'll register at the Sandbox with a real email address, and then log in. To use those sample accounts to test your site, you'll need to remain logged in to the Sandbox (in the same browser).

The last site you'll use is the Sandbox Test Site at **www.sandbox.paypal.com**. This site looks and functions exactly like the real PayPal, except that it says "Test Site" and "Sandbox" here and there.

As you read the rest of this chapter, pay close attention to which PayPal site I reference at each step. Make sure that the URL in your browser matches each instruction appropriately.

Registering at the PayPal Sandbox

The PayPal Sandbox is a replication of the real PayPal, but you create and control the cast of characters. To use it, you'll need to register with a real email address and password to create a Sandbox account, then you can use that account to create fake buyers and sellers.

1. Go to **https://developer.paypal.com**.

2. If you do not already have a PayPal Sandbox account (which is not the same as a PayPal account), create one by clicking Sign Up Now.

3. Complete the simple registration form (**Figure 6.2**).

PayPal recommends that you use a different email address and password than your actual PayPal account, for security sake.

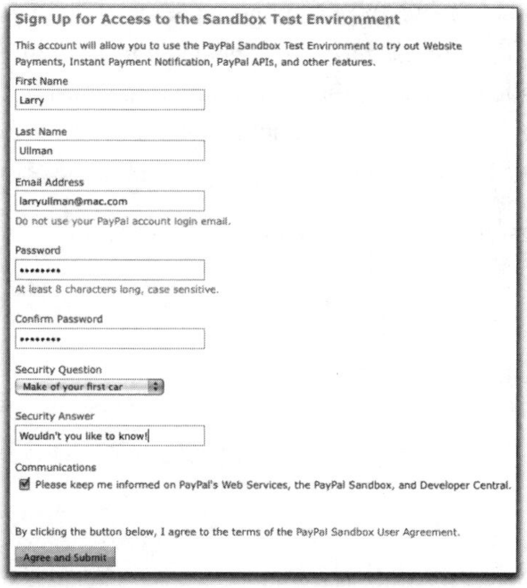

Figure 6.2

4. Check your email.

After registering, you'll receive an email with a link that you must click to activate your account.

5. Click the link in the email to activate the account.

6. Log in to the PayPal Sandbox using your email address and password.

Creating Test Accounts

Once you've registered and logged in to the Sandbox, the next step is to create at least two accounts: one merchant (the business) and one personal (the customer).

1. Log in to the PayPal Sandbox, if you have not already.

2. Click the *Test Accounts* link.

At the time of this writing, there are only four main areas of the Sandbox, aside from the home page.

3. Click the *Preconfigured* link beside the Create Account label (**Figure 6.3**).

Test Accounts

Create a test business account to represent a merchant and a test personal account to represent a buyer.

Create Account: Preconfigured | Create Manually
Website Payments Pro (US, UK)

Figure 6.3

 tip

You can ignore the fact that Figure 6.3, and perhaps your own experience, has PayPal showing *Website Payments Pro*.

You can create test accounts in two ways: preconfigured or manually. If you choose preconfigured, then the site will generate almost all the account information for you automatically, such as the email address, password, physical address, and more. If you choose the manual option, you'll need to provide all this information.

4. On the Create a Sandbox Test Account page, create a Seller account (**Figure 6.4**).

Figure 6.4

You'll need to indicate the seller's country and the account type first. For the login email, use any meaningful six characters, and please note that this is not an actual email address; a temporary one will be created by the Sandbox using this value. You may want to use just "seller." The password will be generated for you automatically, and you can leave it as is.

It's up to you whether to add a credit card and/or a bank account balance or not. For the merchant, neither is required, although by adding one or both, the account will be marked automatically as verified (in the PayPal Sandbox world).

5. Click the Create Account button.

6. Repeat Steps 3-5 for one or more buyer accounts.

For the buyers, you'll need to create one or more with a positive bank account balance and/or a credit card. For full testing, you can create a buyer with insufficient funds, too, or buyers from other countries.

tip

Write down every password, because you will need them for the test account.

tip

If you create a buyer account without a credit card or bank account or with insufficient funds, that buyer account will pay using pretend e-checks.

Each account you create will be listed on the Test Accounts page (**Figure 6.5**).

Figure 6.5

tip

Once created, an account's details can be updated after logging in to the Sandbox Test Site (using that account), as if it were a real PayPal account.

tip

In the PayPal Sandbox, all payments succeed without being reviewed unless you enable payment review for an account.

Creating a Button

Once you've created two or more accounts, you can add a fake PayPal button to your Web site to simulate the e-commerce transactions. This is arguably the most important sequence of steps, because you'll perform these same actions for real when you take your site live.

1. On the Sandbox Test Accounts page (see Figure 6.5), select the seller account and click the Enter Sandbox Test Site button.

By taking this step, you'll be able to enter fake PayPal as one of the test users. Using the PayPal Sandbox Test Site, you can perform the same tasks that real PayPal users perform: check account balances, review transactions, update account details, and, for merchants, create buttons for selling products and services.

2. In the pop-up window that appears, log in using the seller account.

The results of Step 1 will create a pop-up window that looks like the regular PayPal site, plus the words "Sandbox" and "Test Site" scattered about. You'll also see that the email address associated with the account selected in Step 1 will be entered automatically into the login form.

3. Click the Merchant Services tab.

4. Under Create Buttons, click Subscribe.

5. On the Create PayPal payment button page, enter an item name (**Figure 6.6** on the next page).

tip

In this first part of the form, you can also change the text and look of the button.

Figure 6.6

The button type should be selected automatically (as a subscription). You may or may not want to change the currency, too.

6. Further down under Step 1 of the form, enter a billing amount and cycle period (**Figure 6.7**).

The billing amount is obviously the most important consideration. The billing cycle is for how long that billing amount covers. You can choose to have automatic billing stop after two or more cycles, or never.

7. Opt to use your secure merchant account ID (see Figure 6.7).

8. Under Step 2 of the form, make sure that the Save button at PayPal option is selected (**Figure 6.8**).

Figure 6.7

tip

If you save your button with your PayPal account, it'll be more secure and easier to update.

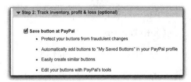

Figure 6.8

9. Under Step 3 of the form, indicate that you don't need the customer's shipping address.

If you were selling a physical product, you'd want the user to confirm the shipping address in PayPal. You could then use PayPal to generate the shipping label for you, taking the cost out of the money already transferred to your account.

10. Also under Step 3 of the form, supply the "cancel" and "finish" URLs, and select the corresponding check boxes (**Figure 6.9**).

These two values must point to pages on your server, available via HTTPS. The two scripts will be created later in this chapter to be named **cancel.php** and **thanks.php**.

11. Click Create Button.

Figure 6.9

12. On the next page, copy the generated code (**Figure 6.10**).

Figure 6.10

This is the code to be integrated into the site, which you'll do next.

INTEGRATING PAYPAL

Once you've created the test accounts and the PayPal button, you can tie your site into the fake PayPal. Doing so is a snap:

1. Add the button code where appropriate.

2. Create the **thanks.php** page.

3. Create the **cancel.php** page.

There will be a couple of catches, however, so after you integrate and test PayPal, you'll learn a way to improve the system.

Updating the Registration Page

With this particular Web site, the user should go to PayPal (by clicking the button) after successfully completing the registration process. To pull that off, start by changing the thank you message in **register.php** so that it tells the user what to do next:

echo "<h3>Thanks!</h3><p>Thank you for registering! To complete the
➡process, please now click the button below so that you may pay for your
➡site access via PayPal. The cost is $10 (US) per year. <strong>Note: When
➡you complete your payment at PayPal, please click the button to return to
➡this site.</strong></p>";

Next, drop in the PayPal-generated code in order to add the button (**Figure 6.11**):

Figure 6.11

tip

Remember that you can download all the source code for this example from **www.DMCInsights.com/ecom/**.

```
echo '<form action="https://www.sandbox.paypal.com/cgi-bin/webscr"
⇒method="post">
<input type="hidden" name="cmd" value="_s-xclick">
<input type="hidden" name="hosted_button_id" value=
⇒"8YW8FZDELF296">
<input type="image" src="https://www.sandbox.paypal.com/en_US/i/
⇒btn/btn_subscribeCC_LG.gif" border="0" name="submit" alt="PayPal -
⇒The safer, easier way to pay online!">
<img alt="" border="0" src="https://www.sandbox.paypal.com/en_US/i/
⇒scr/pixel.gif" width="1" height="1">
</form>';
```

The above code should be placed just after the thank you message and before the footer is included.

There are two more changes that need to be made. First, the original **INSERT** query gave the new user access for the next month. Now it should be changed so that the user's access is good until yesterday (that is, their account isn't active):

```
$q = "INSERT INTO users (username, email, pass, first_name, last_name,
⇒date_expires) VALUES ('$u', '$e', '" . get_password_hash($p) . "', '$fn',
⇒'$ln', SUBDATE(NOW(), INTERVAL 1 DAY) )";
```

Second, let's store the user's new ID value in a session so that their record may be updated when they return from PayPal. To do so, just add the following code anywhere after you confirm that **mysqli_affected_row($dbc)** equals 1:

```
$uid = mysqli_insert_id($dbc);
$_SESSION['reg_user_id'] = $uid;
```

I'm specifically naming this *reg_user_id* instead of *user_id* so as not to confuse the system into thinking the user has logged in when they haven't (the login process creates **$_SESSION['user_id']**). You'll see **$_SESSION['reg_user_id']** used in **thanks.php**.

Creating thanks.php

The customer ends up at the **thanks.php** page after completing their PayPal order and clicking a button to return to this site. This page needs to update the database, adding a year of access to the user's account (**Figure 6.12**). Here's how it might be defined:

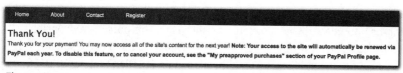

Figure 6.12

thanks.php

```php
1   <?php
2   require ('./includes/config.inc.php');
3   redirect_invalid_user('reg_user_id');
4   require (MYSQL);
5   $page_title = 'Thanks!';
6   include ('./includes/header.html');
7   $q = "UPDATE users SET date_expires = ADDDATE(date_expires,
    ➥INTERVAL 1 YEAR) WHERE id={$_SESSION['reg_user_id']}";
8   $r = mysqli_query ($dbc, $q);
9   unset($_SESSION['reg_user_id']);
10  ?><h3>Thank You!</h3>
11  <p>Thank you for your payment! You may now access all of the site's
    ➥content for the next year! <strong>Note: Your access to the site will
    ➥automatically be renewed via PayPal each year. To disable this feature,
    ➥or to cancel your account, see the "My preapproved purchases"
    ➥section of your PayPal Profile page.</strong></p>
12  <?php include ('./includes/footer.html'); ?>
```

Three key lines are highlighted. First, this script should be accessed only if the **reg_user_id** element exists in the session, meaning the page is accessible only after registering.

Second, the query runs an **UPDATE** command on the **users** table, adding one year to the expiration date for this user.

Third, the **$_SESSION['reg_user_id']** element is unset after the query. By taking this step, the page can be loaded only once. That check prevents hackers from adding years to their account by just reloading this page.

From a security standpoint, there's one problem with this script: It assumes that the user has paid, but you don't actually know that for certain. If you register a new account and then change the URL to **thanks.php**, without going through PayPal, the net effect will be the same. That would be bad.

 note

As a courtesy, the customer is told that payments will automatically recur and what they can do to prevent that.

From a customer standpoint, there are three problems. First, they'll be credited for their purchase only if they return to this page. This puts the responsibility on the customer, where the responsibility is really yours to make sure they get what they've paid for. Second, there's no confirmation that the **UPDATE** query worked properly (that is, that one row was affected). And third, there's no record anywhere associating the customer's PayPal order with their account on this site.

All four of these issues will be remedied in a few pages by using something called *IPN*.

Creating cancel.php

If the customer cancels the PayPal transaction, they will end up at the **cancel.php** page. This page should just indicate to the customer where their account now stands (**Figure 6.13**). Here's how that script might look:

Figure 6.13

cancel.php

```
1   <?php
2   require ('./includes/config.inc.php');
3   require (MYSQL);
4   $page_title = 'Oops!';
5   include ('./includes/header.html');
6   ?><h3>Oops!</h3>
7   <p>The payment through PayPal was not completed. You have a valid
    ➥membership at this site, but you will not be able to view any content
    ➥until you complete the PayPal transaction. You can do so by clicking on
    ➥the Renew link after logging in.</p>
8   <?php include ('./includes/footer.html'); ?>
```

The important thing is for this script to indicate that:

1. The customer has successfully registered at the site.

2. The customer still can't access any content.

3. To change #2, the customer should log in and click renew.

tip

The renew process will be implemented toward the end of the chapter.

TESTING THE SITE

By this point in time, the site is really very close to being a complete and real-world e-commerce project. To verify this, let's test the system as it currently stands.

1. Successfully register with the *Knowledge is Power* site.

   If you want, after registering and before Step 2, you could take a look at the database (using phpMyAdmin or another tool) to confirm that the user was registered but with a **date_expires** value in the past. You could also log in to the site with this new account (in a new browser window or tab) to confirm this.

2. Click the PayPal button shown on the registration page.

3. On the PayPal site, use one of the test-buyer accounts to log in (**Figure 6.14**).

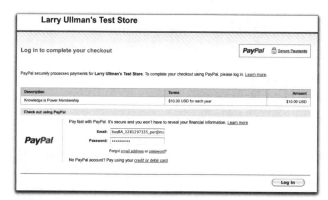

Figure 6.14

4. On the next page, click the Agree and Pay button (**Figure 6.15**).

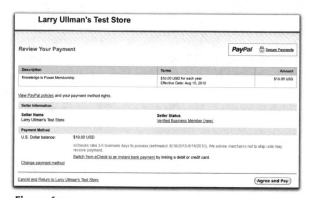

Figure 6.15

 note

You'll still need to be logged in to the PayPal Sandbox (**http://developer.paypal.com**) to use the PayPal Sandbox Test Site.

 tip

If you click the *Cancel and Return* link, you'll be taken to the site's cancel page.

5. Once the purchase has been completed, click the Return to... button to return to the *Knowledge is Power* site (**Figure 6.16**).

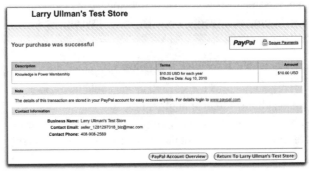

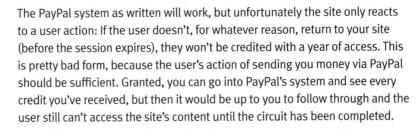

Figure 6.16

6. Look at the database again, or log in, to confirm that the expiration date now works.

7. Log in to the PayPal Sandbox Test Site using the seller account to view the orders.

USING IPN

The PayPal system as written will work, but unfortunately the site only reacts to a user action: If the user doesn't, for whatever reason, return to your site (before the session expires), they won't be credited with a year of access. This is pretty bad form, because the user's action of sending you money via PayPal should be sufficient. Granted, you can go into PayPal's system and see every credit you've received, but then it would be up to you to follow through and the user still can't access the site's content until the circuit has been completed.

Fortunately, PayPal thought of this and created something called *Instant Payment Notification* (IPN). IPN, when set up, will notify a Web site when a payment has been processed. This isn't "notify" in the sense of sending you an email—PayPal will already do that, but rather a server-to-server communication that neither the customer nor the site's administrator will witness. Through these communications, the e-commerce site can verify the transaction and update the database accordingly. More importantly, this communication will take place automatically no matter what the customer does after completing their order within PayPal.

Integrating IPN is a two-part process: enabling it on a PayPal account and creating the listening script on the server.

tip

The PayPal Sandbox will not actually send emails, but the emails that would be sent are viewable in the Sandbox's Test Email section.

tip

IPN is triggered for any kind of transaction, including purchases, refunds, disputes, and more.

tip

An alternative to IPN is PDT (Payment Data Transfer). Through PDT, you can confirm the results of a PayPal order, but PDT is only invoked when the user returns to your site.

Enabling IPN

The first part of the two-part process to integrate IPN is enabling IPN in your PayPal account.

1. Log in to the PayPal Sandbox Text Site using the steps already outlined.

You'll need to log in using your merchant account.

2. Click *Profile*.

3. Click *Instant Payment Notification Preferences*, under Selling Preferences.

4. On the subsequent page, enter the Notification URL (**Figure 6.17**).

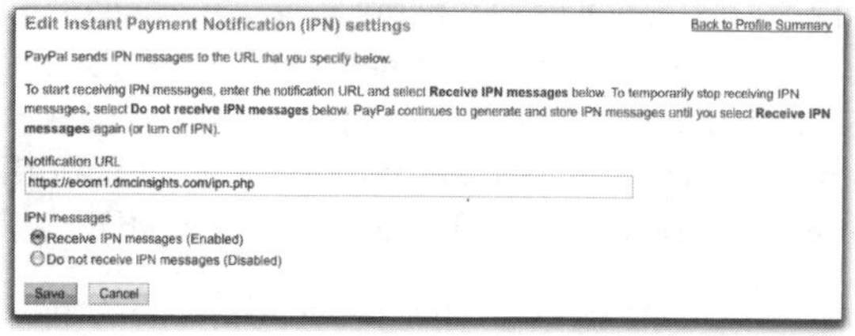

Figure 6.17

The notification URL needs to be a page on your site accessed via HTTPS. I'm naming it **ipn.php**, but you may want to use a more original name than that.

5. Select the Receive IPN messages (Enabled) option.

You can disable IPN through these preferences by selecting the Do not receive IPN messages (Disabled) option.

6. Click Save.

Updating the Registration Script

Yes, yes: I said that integrating IPN was a two-part process and here I am introducing a third. I stand by my two-part statement because this third step may or may not be necessary. I'll explain...

For the user to be properly credited, there needs to be a way to tie their account on the e-commerce site to the PayPal purchase. In the previous **register.php-PayPal-thanks.php** system, the tie-in was accomplished by storing the user's ID value in a session and then retrieving it on the **thanks.php** page. Since this new version of the process won't rely upon the **thanks.php** page to perform the update, the user must be tracked in another way. To do so, the updated site will use IPN to pass all sorts of information back to the e-commerce site.

One theoretical option would be to use the customer's email address to update the account. This is information that the IPN will return in the **$_POST['payer_email']** variable. I say "theoretical," because if the customer registered with one email address but signed in to PayPal with another, this won't work. My more foolproof solution is to pass the user's ID along to PayPal so that PayPal may return it as part of the IPN data. Here's how **register.php** should be altered to implement this technique:

1. Remove the line that stored the user ID in the session.

2. Add the following code to the PayPal form:

```
<input type="hidden" name="custom" value="'" . $uid . "'">
```

This code is output by an **echo** statement as part of the larger form and PayPal button. The code creates a hidden form input with a **name** of *custom*. You must use that exact name for the input, because *custom* is a special way to pass any data to PayPal with the express intent of having it returned to the site. The value is the user's ID, already determined by calling **mysqli_insert_id()**.

While you are expanding the code and functionality, go ahead and pass the user's email address to PayPal as well, so that the PayPal login form will be prepopulated with it (and this may also be usable as a fallback way to connect site users with PayPal transactions). There are many hidden-form inputs that PayPal will recognize, like *first_name*, *last_name*, and *email*. Here's the new **echo** statement in **register.php**:

```
echo '<form action="https://www.sandbox.paypal.com/cgi-bin/webscr"
➥method="post">
<input type="hidden" name="cmd" value="_s-xclick">
<input type="hidden" name="custom" value="'" . $uid . "'">
<input type="hidden" name="email" value="'" . $e . "'">
<input type="hidden" name="hosted_button_id" value=
➥"8YW8FZDELF296">
<input type="image" src="https://www.sandbox.paypal.com/en_US/i/
➥btn/btn_subscribeCC_LG.gif" border="0" name="submit" alt="PayPal -
➥The safer, easier way to pay online!">
<img alt="" border="0" src="https://www.sandbox.paypal.com/en_US/i/
➥scr/pixel.gif" width="1" height="1">
</form>
';
```

For the email value, you'll see that I'm using the **$e** variable, which would have just been used in the **INSERT** query.

Creating the IPN Script

The next part of the process of implementing IPN is the listener script. The IPN listener script—the file on the e-commerce site with which PayPal will automatically and behind-the-scenes communicate—is clearly important and is accordingly complex. Most of the code in this script, which I'll explain in detail, was suggested by PayPal. The process goes like this:

1. When this page is requested, it must immediately confirm the request with PayPal. This keeps the script from being fraudulently used.

2. The page reads in the response from PayPal.

3. The page validates and validates and validates the response.

4. If the data is valid, the database is updated.

What this script does not have to do is generate any HTML because it'll never be run through a Web browser.

 tip

For every transaction, PayPal will continue requesting an IPN script until the request is acknowledged.

1. Create a new PHP script in your text editor or IDE to be named **ipn.php** (or something more original) and stored in the Web root directory:

```php
<?php
require ('./includes/config.inc.php');
```

This script needs access to the configuration file for the purposes of error reporting and connecting to the database.

2. Start by creating a request variable:

```php
$req = 'cmd=_notify-validate';
```

The **$req** variable is first assigned the *cmd=_notify-validate* string value. This value indicates the command being made to PayPal (that is, the purpose for the communication).

3. Add each received *key=value* pair to the request:

```php
foreach ($_POST as $key => $value) {
    $value = urlencode(stripslashes($value));
    $req .= "&$key=$value";
}
```

The confirmation of the request needs to contain all the data that this script originally received via POST. For each element in **$_POST**, a *key=value* pair is added to the **$req** variable.

4. Open a socket connection to PayPal:

```php
$fp = fsockopen ('ssl://www.sandbox.paypal.com', 443, $errno, $errstr,
➡30); // Test
```

tip

Alternatively, you could define the live and test URLs in the configuration file, so the URL is changed automatically when the site goes live.

tip

As a useful debugging or logging tool, you could write every IPN transaction to a text file. The **ipn_log.php** example file in the downloadable scripts does this.

This is a bit complicated and may be new to you. The PayPal request will be made using the **fsockopen()** function, which opens a socket connection. The function is used similarly to **fopen()**, except that the code will be reading from and writing to another computer through a socket connection, instead of from and to a file. The address to connect to for testing purposes is **ssl://www.sandbox.paypal.com**, using port 443. The **$errno** and **$errstr** variables will store any errors that occurred during the connection process. The last argument in the function tells the script to take up to 30 seconds to make the connection.

When the site goes live, the connection will be made to just **ssl://www.paypal.com**, with the other settings the same:

$fp = fsockopen ('ssl://www.paypal.com', 443, $errno, $errstr, 30);

5. If no connection was made, trigger an error:

if (!$fp) {
    trigger_error('Could not connect for the IPN!');

If the **$fp** variable does not have a positive value, then no connection was made and an error should be triggered. The assumption is that the site is live at this point, so the error is sent in an email to the administrator. Otherwise the error messages would be printed out, for no one to see.

The **$errno** and **$errstr** variables might provide clues as to what the problem was (and they'll be available through the backtrace in the error handler.)

6. If a connection was made, send the request to PayPal:

} else {
    $header = "POST /cgi-bin/webscr HTTP/1.0\r\n";
    $header .= "Content-Type: application/x-www-form-urlencoded\r\n";
    $header .= "Content-Length: " . strlen($req) . "\r\n\r\n";
    fputs ($fp, $header . $req);

The first three lines define headers to include with the request. The first indicates that a POST request should be made to **/cgi-bin/webscr** using the HTTP 1.0 protocol. The second line says that the content type will be URL-encoded form data. The third line indicates the length of the request.

The last line sends the headers and request data to PayPal (it "puts" it to PayPal's server).

7. Read in the response:

while (!feof($fp)) {
    $res = fgets ($fp, 1024);

This code is similar to what you might use to read from a file, but instead the script is reading in the response from PayPal. The **while** loop is true until the script has reached the end of the file of the open connection (that is, the loop is true until there's nothing more to be read). Then the **fgets()** function fetches up to one kilobyte of data (1,024 bytes) or until the end of the line—into the **$res** variable (short for *response*).

8. If the response equals *VERIFIED*, process the response:

if (strcmp ($res, "VERIFIED") == 0) {

After reading in a line of the PayPal response, examine it to confirm that a valid request is being made. If the just-read line of the response equals *VERIFIED* (case-sensitive), the request is valid.

9. Check for the right values:

if (isset($_POST['payment_status'])
&& ($_POST['payment_status'] == 'Completed')
&& ($_POST['receiver_email'] == 'you@example.com')
&& ($_POST['mc_gross'] == 10.00)
&& ($_POST['mc_currency'] == 'USD')
&& (!empty($_POST['txn_id']))
) {

Just looking for a verified response is not sufficient. For the transaction to be official enough to warrant updating the site's database, several other qualities should exist. For starters, the **payment_status** needs to equal *Completed*, because there will be other possible statuses that don't warrant changes (such as *Pending*). You should confirm that the payment was received by the proper email address (the one that matches the e-commerce site's merchant PayPal account). This check prevents the site from taking action based upon a payment that didn't go to it (because someone attempted a hack).

Next, the **mc_gross** and **mc_currency** values should match the gross cost and currency for the transaction. This keeps someone from trying to pay you just one cent or 10.00 Thai baht (equivalent to 30 cents as I write this). Finally, you want to make sure that the transaction ID is not empty.

All these values are available in **$_POST**, because they're part of the original request of this script.

10. Check for this transaction in the database:

require (MYSQL);
$txn_id = mysqli_real_escape_string($dbc, $_POST['txn_id']);
$q = "SELECT id FROM orders WHERE transaction_id='$txn_id'";
$r = mysqli_query ($dbc, $q);
if (mysqli_num_rows($r) == 0) {

note

The result of calling **strcmp()** must be equal to the number zero, not the lowercase letter "O."

tip

Validating the values posted to the script are key to preventing users from defrauding your site.

note

Make sure you use your actual PayPal-associated email address for the **receiver_email** comparison.

tip

If you change any of your site's parameters, such as the cost of a subscription, you'll need to change this script, too.

note

The **$uid** variable is assigned the number zero if **$_POST['custom']** is not set.

tip

As an extra check, you could confirm that **$_POST['custom']** is a valid integer.

tip

As written, I'm only logging successful, new transactions in the **orders** table, but you could easily modify the script to log every IPN request, but still only update the **users** table for successful, new ones.

It's possible, through nefarious actions or normal operations, that the IPN script might get a repeated request for the same transaction. To prevent such an occurrence from crediting a user's account again, this query checks if the transaction ID is already listed in the **orders** table. If the query returns no records, then this is a new, proper transaction.

11. Add this transaction to the **orders** table:

```
$uid = (isset($_POST['custom'])) ? (int) $_POST['custom'] : 0;
$status = mysqli_real_escape_string($dbc, $_POST['payment_status']);
$amount = (float) $_POST['mc_gross'];
$q = "INSERT INTO orders (user_id, transaction_id, payment_status,
➥payment_amount) VALUES ($uid, '$txn_id', '$status', $amount)";
$r = mysqli_query ($dbc, $q);
if (mysqli_affected_rows($dbc) == 1) {
```

First, three more values are made safe to use in a query. You'll see here a reference to **$_POST['custom']**, which is the user's ID originally stored in the **register.php** script, then passed to PayPal, and now returned home like a loyal pet. This value gets passed back to the site, via IPN, whether the customer immediately returns to the site or not.

The **orders** table also records the transaction ID, payment status, and payment amount.

12. Update the **users** table:

```
if ($uid > 0) {
    $q = "UPDATE users SET date_expires = IF(date_expires > NOW(),
➥ADDDATE(date_expires, INTERVAL 1 YEAR), ADDDATE(NOW(),
➥INTERVAL 1 YEAR)), date_modified=NOW() WHERE id=$uid";
    $r = mysqli_query ($dbc, $q);
    if (mysqli_affected_rows($dbc) != 1) {
        trigger_error('The user\'s expiration date could not be updated!');
    }
}
```

Finally, the script is at the point where the user's account can be updated (assuming a valid user ID). To do that, an **UPDATE** query is run, providing a new value for both the **date_expires** column and **date_modified**. I improved the updating of the **date_expires** value to allow for users whose accounts lapsed and were later renewed.

In the original **thanks.php**, the query added a year to the current **date_expires** value. But if the **date_expires** value is in the past, the user would be credited a year from that date in the past: not a full year at all. So instead, the new value for **date_expires** will be a year from its current value, if its current value is greater than **NOW()**, or it will be a year from now, otherwise.

If one row was not affected by the query, an error is triggered.

13. Complete several conditionals:

```
    } else { // Problem inserting the order!
        trigger_error('The transaction could not be stored in the orders
        ↪table!');
    }
    } // The order has already been stored!
} // The right values don't exist in $_POST!
```

The **else** clause applies if the order couldn't be inserted into the **orders** table, in which case an error needs to be triggered. The two other curly brackets close earlier **IF** conditionals, but take no further actions.

14. If the PayPal response is *INVALID*, log the request:

```
} elseif (strcmp ($res, "INVALID") == 0) {
    // Log for further investigation.
}
```

If this is an invalid request, as opposed to a verified one, you may want to trigger an error or log the request so that you can investigate whether someone is trying to manipulate the system.

15. Complete the remaining control structures and close the socket connection:

```
    } // End of the WHILE loop.
    fclose ($fp);
} // End of $fp IF-ELSE.
```

16. Complete the script:

```
?>
```

17. Save the file.

Don't test it quite yet: there's still one more step in this *two-step* incorporation of IPN!

Updating the Thanks Script

And now there's Step 4 in the two-part series on integrating IPN (math is not my strong suit). With the current version of **thanks.php**, if the customer successfully goes through PayPal and returns to the site, their expiration date will be updated twice: once in **thanks.php** and once in **ipn.php**. To fix that, remove or comment out the following lines of code:

```
redirect_invalid_user('reg_user_id');
$q = "UPDATE users SET date_expires = ADDDATE(date_expires, INTERVAL 1
➥YEAR) WHERE id={$_SESSION['reg_user_id']}";
$r = mysqli_query ($dbc, $q);
unset($_SESSION['reg_user_id']);
```

Now you can test the new system by repeating the steps outlined in the "Testing the Site" section of this chapter.

RENEWING ACCOUNTS

The last addition to the site that must be created is the ability to renew an account. Given the recurring payment system setup within PayPal, there are only two situations in which a customer might need to renew their account:

- The customer registered but did not complete payment at PayPal.

- The customer registered and completed payment at PayPal, but later canceled the recurring payment and now wants to renew the account some time after it has expired.

A renewal page should only be accessible to logged-in users and should display the same PayPal button code that the registration page does. Everything else about the process would be exactly the same. Here's **renew.php**:

renew.php

```
1   <?php
2   require ('./includes/config.inc.php');
3   redirect_invalid_user();
4   $page_title = 'Renew Your Account';
5   include ('./includes/header.html');
6   require (MYSQL);
7   ?><h3>Thanks!</h3><p>Thank you for your interest in renewing your
    ➥account! To complete the process, please now click the button below
    ➥so that you may pay for your renewal via PayPal. The cost is $10 (US)
    ➥per year.</p>
8
9   <form action="https://www.sandbox.paypal.com/cgi-bin/webscr"
    ➥method="post">
10  <input type="hidden" name="cmd" value="_s-xclick">
```

```
11    <input type="hidden" name="custom" value="<?php echo $_SESSION
      →['user_id']; ?>">
12    <input type="hidden" name="hosted_button_id"
      value="8YW8FZDELF296">
13    <input type="submit" name="submit_button" value="Renew &rarr;"
      →id="submit_button" class="formbutton" />
14    </form>
15    <?php include ('./includes/footer.html'); ?>
```

To show you something different and to make the button more like the rest of the site, I changed the button itself from an **<IMG>** tag, pointing to a file on PayPal's server, to a submit input with the same class used for other submit buttons on the e-commerce site. **Figure 6.18** shows the result. This change doesn't affect the PayPal system at all, because the button is used just as something for the user to click; the true functionality is in the hidden inputs. Speaking of which, you should note that the custom value is coming from the session in this case.

Figure 6.18

GOING LIVE

When you've thoroughly tested how your site works with PayPal and you're ready to take the whole project live, you need to perform just a few simple steps.

1. Create a real Premiere or Business PayPal account, if you do not already have one.

2. Customize the PayPal experience (see the sidebar).

3. Using the real PayPal account, create the button code to be used your e-commerce site.

4. Replace the button code in **register.php** and **renew.php** with the new, real PayPal-generated button code (variations of the same code can be used for both).

5. Also in PayPal, enable IPN for the account (see the steps earlier in the chapter).

6. Update the **ipn.php** script.

You'll want to:

- Change the **fsockopen()** line to connect to the real PayPal.
- Make sure the right email address is being used for comparison to **$_POST['receiver_email']**.
- Make sure the right payment amount is being used for comparison to **$_POST['mc_gross']**.
- Make sure the right currency abbreviation is being used for comparison to **$_POST['mc_currency']**.

7. Change the value of the **$live** variable in **config.inc.php** to **true**.

Me being me, after doing all this, I would probably execute a couple of real transactions, just to confirm that the system is working. By doing so you'll cost yourself a few bucks (in the transaction fees, because the money will be going from you to you), but you'll get peace of mind. Also, be certain to routinely compare the transactions in your PayPal history with those in your **orders** table so that you know no customer is being cheated or cheating you.

tip

The four **ipn.php** factors listed could be defined in the configuration file instead.

CUSTOMIZING THE PAYPAL EXPERIENCE

Although using PayPal's Website Payments Standard system means the customer will leave your site and spend some time at PayPal, the experience does not need to be too jarring. If you log in to PayPal and click *Profile*, there's quite a lot you can do under the *Selling Preferences* banner. This is where you can establish tax and shipping policies. You can also view and update your buttons there. More importantly from a customer-experience point of view, you can create a specific *Customer Service Message* and define templates to act as *Custom Payment Pages*. *Custom Payment Pages* can use your own images and colors—to some degree—so that the PayPal interface looks similar to your own Web site. How you go about doing this is well documented in links found on PayPal's Custom Payment Pages document.

PART THREE
SELLING PHYSICAL PRODUCTS

7 | SECOND SITE: STRUCTURE AND DESIGN

The second e-commerce site that you will develop with the help of this book will sell physical products: coffee (beans, not brewed!) and coffee-related goodies. The *Coffee* site will have these primary features:

- Increased complexity in the use of HTML, PHP, and MySQL

- Browsable catalog, complete with sales information

- User's shopping cart and wish-list feature

- Inline payment processing via Authorize.net

- Administrative ability to create products, discount items, manage inventory, and process orders

The five chapters in Part Three, "Selling Physical Products," of this book will walk you through this combination of common e-commerce features and more advanced techniques. As a fail-safe, I'll present alternatives for some of the more complex code that you might find confusing or that might be beyond your server's capability.

ABOUT THE SITE

Because this coffee shop example will be much more complex than the content management one, I want to talk about its goals and functionality in some detail before getting into the actual implementation.

What's Being Sold

The aim of this book is to present the widest possible range of what it means to perform e-commerce, so the first goal of the *Coffee* site example is to sell a physical product, which requires a different approach than selling virtual content. One implication is that the *Coffee* site will need to be prudent about when customers are charged for orders relative to when the orders actually ship. Selling physical products also requires using SKUs (Stock-Keeping Unit): unique identifiers for each item sold. Without SKUs, there's no inventory management or certainty that a customer is receiving the exact item they wanted.

Physical products come in two broad categories:

- Individual, unrelated items, such as works of art

- Variations on a theme, such as a book that's available in hardcover, paperback, or electronic format

The distinction between these categories is important. For example, if you're selling books, you'll want the customer to be able to select the format from among the available options, all on the same page. But each available format still needs its own unique identifier. Conversely, a work of art or any product that's not available in different formats or with different attributes is much easier to present to the customer and to manage as inventory. As you can tell, how you handle SKUs and other product attributes differs between these two types, so the *Coffee* e-commerce store sells both categories of physical products: goodies, such as mugs, biscotti, and so on, which are treated individually (**Figure 7.1**); and coffee that has common generic properties but is purchased in specific formats (for example, size or ground versus whole beans, **Figure 7.2**).

note

Selling virtual products may also require SKUs, although you don't have to consider inventory management.

Figure 7.1

Figure 7.2

Most of the work and code in this part of the book will involve using SKUs in the database, in the displayed catalog of products, in the shopping cart, and in the administrative interface. In your own e-commerce projects, you can apply these same theories and code to sell music in different formats, clothes in different sizes and colors, and so forth.

The database and code is further complicated by supporting the ability to offer products at a discounted price. This is a nice feature, and that can go a long way toward increasing business.

tip

To simplify the example a bit, I've opted to ignore some coffee bean variables and entirely ignore the issues that arise with selling perishable goods.

No Customer Registration

Another way in which the *Coffee* e-commerce project differs from the *Knowledge is Power* site is that this site does not obligate customers to register in order to make their purchases. Required registration, which is mandatory in a content access example, has actually been proven to hurt sales (truth be told, Amazon.com gets away with required registration just fine). So this site will focus on the purchases, not on the customer. This approach will have some interesting ramifications in terms of the database and how the site operates, as you'll learn in this chapter.

If you'd rather, you could provide your customers with the option of registering or not. In such a case, you would take the code from the *Knowledge is Power* example and modify it in order to add registration and login capability to your site.

Implementing MVC

For this coffee shop site, I've decided to implement somewhat of an MVC approach. MVC, which stands for *Model-View-Controller*, is a very popular way to design more complex Web (and other) applications. Within MVC, a project's code and files are divided into their discernible parts:

- **Model** is the data involved.

- **View** is the presentation layer (what the user sees).

- **Controller** is the logic that ties everything together and reacts to user activity.

By implementing MVC, you'll have a project that's easier to develop—especially when working on a team—and easier to maintain, with cleaner code. Further, the site will potentially be more scalable. *Scalability* is the ability to handle an increased load implicitly through an increase in resources. A Web site may start with one server and be able to handle up to X number of concurrent visitors. If the site can "scale well," then it will also be able to handle, say, four times the concurrent visitors by just adding another server or two database servers. Conversely, a site that doesn't scale well could not properly handle four times the concurrent load even if you were to throw four or eight more servers at the problem. With the hope that an e-commerce site will take off, the ability for the site to scale well is a reasonable consideration.

So what does MVC mean in terms of real code? It's actually simple in theory, although I'm applying MVC in a casual manner. The controller is represented by PHP code, which handles user behavior and reacts accordingly, often as an agent between the model and the view. The data, with few exceptions, is represented by the database. The view is HTML. To keep these three things separate, the *Coffee* shop site first moves much of the model functionality into the database, using something called *stored procedures* (discussed at the end of the chapter). Second, the site stores almost all the HTML in separate files, included as appropriate by the PHP scripts. The end result will be little to no SQL or HTML intermingled with PHP. In fact, many of the PHP scripts will be quite short.

Another benefit of this MVC approach is that you will be able to look at and edit any facet of the site without having to wade through unrelated code. For example, you can adjust an SQL query without seeing any PHP and tweak the PHP without mucking about in HTML. You can also address performance issues by focusing on individual pieces. If you look back at Figure 1.4, in which I point out the three areas in which caching can be applied to improve performance, you will see that the MVC approach isolates these same three areas of the process. This means that when your site takes off and multiple servers are appropriate, each server can focus on a specific aspect: say two or three for just the database (that is, the models) and one or two for the PHP and HTML. You can also offload specific parts to cloud computing, if you want to go that route.

There are a couple of obvious downsides to using an MVC approach. First, you'll end up with *a lot* more files. Whereas one PHP script could query the database and generate the HTML output, now you'll have one PHP script, one stored procedure in the database, and one or more HTML files to accomplish the same task. Second, MVC requires that assumptions be made about what has happened previous to certain points. Third, pushing model functionality into the database will require a level of database access that not everyone will necessarily have.

Heightened Security

The significant distinction between the two e-commerce examples in this book is the level of required security. Because this site will briefly handle credit card information and permanently store more user information, extra precautions will be taken. To start, the site will be more exacting about using SSL (in the *Knowledge is Power* content management example, SSL was used to send the user to PayPal and back, but otherwise ignored). The first checkout page in the *Coffee* site will use SSL, and SSL will continue to be required throughout the checkout process and on every administration page.

The second security distinction will be the placement of every administration page in a separate, password-protected directory. Third, as previously mentioned, the site will use *stored procedures*, which is a more secure way to interact with the database.

 tip

If you find that you can't follow or don't appreciate the MVC approach used in this example, feel free to use the more direct PHP-MySQL-HTML approach used in Part Two, "Selling Virtual Products."

DATABASE DESIGN

Since the *Coffee* site is more complex than the *Knowledge is Power* example, the database is correspondingly more involved. I've come up with 12 tables, evenly split between those for representing the catalog of products and those associated with the customers and orders.

Product Tables

Six customer-related tables represent the specifics about all the products available on the *Coffee* site (**Figure 7.3**).

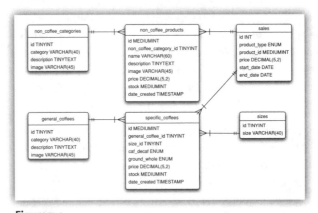

Figure 7.3

The **non_coffee_categories** table represents the types of non-coffee products that will be sold: books, mugs, edibles, and so on. This table stores the category name, a description, and an image (the image will display on a page that lists the categories). The **non_coffee_products** table has a many-to-one relationship with **non_coffee_categories**. Each product will be in one category and each category will have multiple products (Figure 7.3). The **non_coffee_products** table has a foreign key, name, description, image, price, stock, and creation-date columns. This table represents the specific non-coffee products that customers will purchase, and its **id** field will become part of the product's SKU. The **stock** field contains an indication of the quantity of the item in stock, not a simple *Yes/No*.

The **general_coffees** and **specific_coffees** tables have a parallel relationship to the two non-coffee tables. The **general_coffees** table is defined exactly like **non_coffee_categories** and will represent the primary types of coffee sold. For those types, I'm using a somewhat pedestrian organization, mixing roasts, bean types, and flavors: original, dark roast, vanilla, Kona, and so on. If the customer knew they wanted to purchase Kona coffee, they'd look into that coffee "category." The **specific_coffees** table lists the actual items the customer would purchase, which is a combination of the coffee "category," a size, ground or whole beans, and caffeinated or decaffeinated. Each combination of these qualities gets its own record in this table, and therefore its own SKU, price, and quantity in stock. This allows the customer to purchase a pound of ground Kona coffee or two pounds of decaffeinated whole beans. The available sizes come from the **sizes** table.

The sixth table pertaining to products is **sales**. A sale is defined by overriding the price of an item. The easy way to do this would be to change the price in one of the products tables, but then you wouldn't have any indication that the new price is a sale price, as opposed to just the new default price. The **sales** table has a price column, plus start- and end-date columns, with the end date allowed to be **NULL**, indicating an open-ended sale. To associate the price override with a specific product, the product's type and ID numbers are stored. If the **product_type** is *coffee*, the **product_id** will be the **id** value from the **specific_coffees** table. If the **product_type** is *other*, the **product_id** will be the **id** value from the **non_coffee_products** table.

Customer Tables

Four customer-related tables will represent an individual order, starting with **customers**, which stores the customer's name, mailing address, email address, and phone number (**Figure 7.4**).

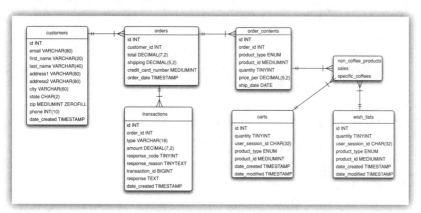

note

Figure 7.4 loosely reflects the relationships between the product-related tables— **sales, specific_coffees,** and **non_coffee_products** tables— and the order-related tables: **order_contents, carts,** and **wish_lists.**

note

Because no customer registration is required, or allowed, the same customer may be repeated multiple times in the customers table.

Figure 7.4

The **orders** table will store individual, completed orders. It stores a foreign key to the **customers** table, the total of the order, the cost of shipping, the date and time the order was entered, and part of the customer's credit card number.

Note that the site will not be storing the full credit card number, just the last four digits (so that the site can indicate the card used, as in *####).

The **order_contents** table represents the actual items purchased in an order. It has a foreign key to the **orders** table, plus the **product_type** and **product_id** columns as in the **sales** table. The **quantity** and **price** columns indicate the number ordered and the price paid per item. This is necessary because there may be a sale price and, over time, the prices in the two products tables will change. Finally, the **ship_date** column is **NULL** by default, indicating that the item has not shipped. When the item ships, this column's value will be set to that ship date and the customer will be billed for that part of the order.

The **transactions** table will be used to record every interaction between this Web application and the payment gateway, Authorize.net. The first four columns are for internal use, tying the transactions to a specific order and recording exactly what was being attempted. The bulk of the columns then store parts of the Authorize.net response. You'll see how this table is used in Chapter 10, "Checking Out."

The **carts** and **wish_lists** tables have mirrored definitions and require a bit of explanation. I decided that this project would not use sessions at all, in part because the user isn't logging in and out, and therefore isn't being tracked. But, if I forgo formal PHP sessions and move session-like functionality to the database, the site can have data permanence. By storing the customer's shopping cart contents and wish-list items in the database, the customer can leave and return (in a day, a week, or a month) and still have their previous actions recorded and available, without ever logging in. This is a very nice feature that requires a single cookie. To accomplish all this, the **carts** table records everything that's in the customer's cart (the items the customer intends to purchase now) and the **wish_lists** table records everything that the customer has saved for later (items the customer intends to purchase down the road). Each item gets listed as its own record, indicating the quantity, product type, and product ID. Each item stored is associated with a **user_session_id**, which will be a unique representative value that's stored in the user's cookie (it's not an actual session ID).

From a marketing standpoint, this system means that customers could be emailed to:

- Remind them to complete an order (gently: you want to be careful about this)
- Let them know that an item they are interested in has just gone on sale
- Let them know about similar items they may like
- Warn them that a sale item is about to go off sale

tip

Go to **www.DMCInsights.com/ecom/** to read some extra ideas as to how the database could be designed.

Of course to do any of these, the site would need to get their email address at some point and store it in the **carts** and **wish_lists** tables. The site should also have the customer formally opt in to such communications.

The SQL

The complete SQL commands for creating the tables are:

tip

You can download the SQL commands from **www.DMCInsights.com/ecom/**.

```
CREATE TABLE `carts` (
    `id` INT UNSIGNED NOT NULL AUTO_INCREMENT,
    `quantity` TINYINT UNSIGNED NOT NULL,
    `user_session_id` CHAR(32) NOT NULL,
    `product_type` ENUM('coffee','other') NOT NULL,
    `product_id` MEDIUMINT UNSIGNED NOT NULL,
    `date_created` TIMESTAMP NOT NULL DEFAULT CURRENT_TIMESTAMP,
    `date_modified` TIMESTAMP NOT NULL DEFAULT '0000-00-00 00:00:00',
    PRIMARY KEY (`id`),
    KEY `product_type` (`product_type`,`product_id`),
    KEY `user_session_id` (`user_session_id`)
) ENGINE=MyISAM  DEFAULT CHARSET=utf8;
CREATE TABLE `customers` (
    `id` INT UNSIGNED NOT NULL AUTO_INCREMENT,
    `email` VARCHAR(80) NOT NULL,
    `first_name` VARCHAR(20) NOT NULL,
    `last_name` VARCHAR(40) NOT NULL,
    `address1` VARCHAR(80) NOT NULL,
    `address2` VARCHAR(80) DEFAULT NULL,
    `city` VARCHAR(60) NOT NULL,
    `state` CHAR(2) NOT NULL,
    `zip` MEDIUMINT(5) UNSIGNED ZEROFILL NOT NULL,
    `phone` INT NOT NULL,
    `date_created` TIMESTAMP NOT NULL DEFAULT CURRENT_TIMESTAMP,
    PRIMARY KEY (`id`),
    KEY `email` (`email`)
) ENGINE=MyISAM  DEFAULT CHARSET=utf8;
CREATE TABLE `general_coffees` (
    `id` TINYINT UNSIGNED NOT NULL AUTO_INCREMENT,
    `category` VARCHAR(40) NOT NULL,
    `description` TINYTEXT,
    `image` VARCHAR(45) NOT NULL,
    PRIMARY KEY (`id`),
    UNIQUE KEY `type` (`category`)
) ENGINE=MyISAM  DEFAULT CHARSET=utf8;
```
(continues on next page)

```sql
CREATE TABLE `non_coffee_categories` (
  `id` TINYINT UNSIGNED NOT NULL AUTO_INCREMENT,
  `category` VARCHAR(40) NOT NULL,
  `description` TINYTEXT NOT NULL,
  `image` VARCHAR(45) NOT NULL,
  PRIMARY KEY (`id`),
  UNIQUE KEY `category` (`category`)
) ENGINE=MyISAM  DEFAULT CHARSET=utf8;
CREATE TABLE `non_coffee_products` (
  `id` MEDIUMINT UNSIGNED NOT NULL AUTO_INCREMENT,
  `non_coffee_category_id` TINYINT UNSIGNED NOT NULL,
  `name` VARCHAR(60) NOT NULL,
  `description` TINYTEXT,
  `image` VARCHAR(45) NOT NULL,
  `price` DECIMAL(5,2) UNSIGNED NOT NULL,
  `stock` MEDIUMINT UNSIGNED NOT NULL DEFAULT '0',
  `date_created` TIMESTAMP NOT NULL DEFAULT CURRENT_TIMESTAMP,
  PRIMARY KEY (`id`),
  KEY `non_coffee_category_id` (`non_coffee_category_id`)
) ENGINE=MyISAM  DEFAULT CHARSET=utf8;
CREATE TABLE `orders` (
  `id` INT UNSIGNED NOT NULL AUTO_INCREMENT,
  `customer_id` INT UNSIGNED NOT NULL,
  `total` DECIMAL(7,2) UNSIGNED DEFAULT NULL,
  `shipping` DECIMAL(5,2) UNSIGNED NOT NULL,
  `credit_card_number` mediumint(4) UNSIGNED NOT NULL,
  `order_date` TIMESTAMP NOT NULL DEFAULT CURRENT_TIMESTAMP,
  PRIMARY KEY (`id`),
  KEY `customer_id` (`customer_id`),
  KEY `order_date` (`order_date`)
) ENGINE=InnoDB  DEFAULT CHARSET=utf8;
CREATE TABLE `order_contents` (
  `id` INT UNSIGNED NOT NULL AUTO_INCREMENT,
  `order_id` INT UNSIGNED NOT NULL,
  `product_type` ENUM('coffee','other') DEFAULT NULL,
  `product_id` MEDIUMINT UNSIGNED NOT NULL,
  `quantity` TINYINT UNSIGNED NOT NULL,
  `price_per` DECIMAL(5,2) UNSIGNED NOT NULL,
  `ship_date` date DEFAULT NULL,
  PRIMARY KEY (`id`),
  KEY `ship_date` (`ship_date`),
  KEY `product_type` (`product_type`,`product_id`)
```

```
) ENGINE=InnoDB  DEFAULT CHARSET=utf8;
CREATE TABLE `sales` (
  `id` INT UNSIGNED NOT NULL AUTO_INCREMENT,
  `product_type` ENUM('coffee','other') DEFAULT NULL,
  `product_id` MEDIUMINT UNSIGNED NOT NULL,
  `price` DECIMAL(5,2) UNSIGNED NOT NULL,
  `start_date` date NOT NULL,
  `end_date` date DEFAULT NULL,
  PRIMARY KEY (`id`),
  KEY `start_date` (`start_date`),
  KEY `product_type` (`product_type`,`product_id`)
) ENGINE=MyISAM  DEFAULT CHARSET=utf8;
CREATE TABLE `sizes` (
  `id` TINYINT UNSIGNED NOT NULL AUTO_INCREMENT,
  `size` VARCHAR(40) NOT NULL,
  PRIMARY KEY (`id`),
  UNIQUE KEY `size` (`size`)
) ENGINE=MyISAM  DEFAULT CHARSET=utf8;
CREATE TABLE `specific_coffees` (
  `id` MEDIUMINT UNSIGNED NOT NULL AUTO_INCREMENT,
  `general_coffee_id` TINYINT UNSIGNED NOT NULL,
  `size_id` TINYINT UNSIGNED NOT NULL,
  `caf_decaf` ENUM('caf','decaf') DEFAULT NULL,
  `ground_whole` ENUM('ground','whole') DEFAULT NULL,
  `price` DECIMAL(5,2) UNSIGNED NOT NULL,
  `stock` MEDIUMINT UNSIGNED NOT NULL DEFAULT '0',
  `date_created` TIMESTAMP NOT NULL DEFAULT CURRENT_TIMESTAMP,
  PRIMARY KEY (`id`),
  KEY `general_coffee_id` (`general_coffee_id`),
  KEY `size` (`size_id`)
) ENGINE=MyISAM  DEFAULT CHARSET=utf8;
CREATE TABLE `transactions` (
  `id` INT UNSIGNED NOT NULL AUTO_INCREMENT,
  `order_id` INT UNSIGNED NOT NULL,
  `type` VARCHAR(18) NOT NULL,
  `amount` DECIMAL(7,2) NOT NULL,
  `response_code` TINYINT(1) UNSIGNED NOT NULL,
  `response_reason` TINYTEXT,
  `transaction_id` BIGINT(20) UNSIGNED NOT NULL,
  `response` text NOT NULL,
  `date_created` TIMESTAMP NOT NULL DEFAULT CURRENT_TIMESTAMP,
  PRIMARY KEY (`id`),
```
(continues on next page)

```
      KEY `order_id` (`order_id`)
) ENGINE=MyISAM  DEFAULT CHARSET=utf8;
CREATE TABLE `wish_lists` (
    `id` INT UNSIGNED NOT NULL AUTO_INCREMENT,
    `quantity` TINYINT UNSIGNED NOT NULL,
    `user_session_id` CHAR(32) NOT NULL,
    `product_type` ENUM('coffee','other') DEFAULT NULL,
    `product_id` MEDIUMINT UNSIGNED NOT NULL,
    `date_created` TIMESTAMP NOT NULL DEFAULT CURRENT_TIMESTAMP,
    `date_modified` TIMESTAMP NOT NULL DEFAULT '0000-00-00 00:00:00',
    PRIMARY KEY (`id`),
    KEY `product_type` (`product_type`,`product_id`),
    KEY `user_session_id` (`user_session_id`)
) ENGINE=MyISAM  DEFAULT CHARSET=utf8;
```

The table definitions and column types should be easily understood, given the descriptions of the tables already provided. I want to point out that the **orders** and **order_contents** tables use the *InnoDB* storage engine. InnoDB supports database transactions, meaning that a series of commands that populate both tables can be set to either completely succeed or entirely roll back.

SERVER SETUP

There are a few more server needs in the *Coffee* e-commerce example than in the *Knowledge is Power* site, so let's look at that in detail.

Server Organization

The server organization—how the files and folders are laid out—is represented in **Figure 7.5**. One file, the MySQL connection script, is stored outside the Web root directory. Within the Web root directory are folders for the CSS, images, and JavaScript. All the administrative pages will go in the **admin** directory, which you should rename to something less obvious. The **includes** directory will contain PHP and HTML scripts included by other PHP scripts, such as the configuration file, the HTML header, and the HTML footer.

The **products** directory is a special case in that it'll store the images for the products sold on the site. Those products will be added via PHP, so this directory needs to be writable by the Web server. For even more security, you could place this directory outside the Web root and use a proxy script to serve every image (just like the PDF handling in Part Two). However, the admin script will have plenty of precautions to prevent abuse of this open directory. As an extra

tip

For extra security, you could put the administration pages in a subdomain, such as **https://admin.example.com**.

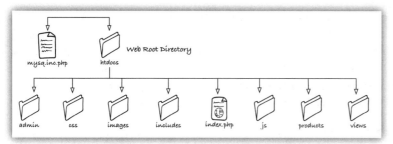

Figure 7.5

security technique to keep people from browsing the contents of this directory, place a blank **index.html** file in the **products** folder. By doing so, the Web
server will not provide to a nosy visitor a list of the folder's files.

The **views** directory will store files that represent individual snippets of HTML.
These will be used to display elements such as:

- The contents of the home page

- The shopping cart

- The wish list

- A listing of categories

- A listing of products

The **views** directory is part of the MVC breakdown that the site uses. Next, you'll
see how to protect this and the other sensitive directories from prying eyes.

Customizing the Server Behavior

For this site, you need to customize how your server runs in four ways. Your
ability to perform any of these alterations will depend upon your hosting situation, although most hosts will allow at least two of the four alterations. The
specific steps involved will depend upon your hosting situation and the Web
server application (such as, Apache, IIS, and so on) involved. Here, I'll provide
instructions for Apache, the most common Web server.

APPLYING PASSWORD PROTECTION

The administration directory needs to be password protected so that only
authenticated users can access its contents. If you want to get your hands
dirty, you can accomplish this by connecting to your server via a command-line
interface and executing the proper commands (search online for what those
would be). Or, most likely, your Web host provides a way to password protect
a directory through the site's control panel (**Figure 7.6**).

note

Make sure you know what Web
server application is being used
on your server!

Figure 7.6

The control panel should take you to a form where you can indicate what directory to protect, as well as what message should be provided to someone attempting to access that directory (**Figure 7.7**). This message will appear in the Web browser's login prompt (**Figure 7.8**). Depending upon your control panel, you might use another form to establish the username and password required to access the protected directory (**Figure 7.9**).

Figure 7.7

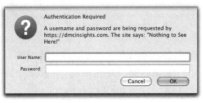

Figure 7.8

Figure 7.9

PROTECTING OTHER DIRECTORIES

Beyond password protection, there are other ways you can keep a folder safe from unwanted visitors. The process of password protecting a directory creates (or modifies) an **.htaccess** file, which alters how the Apache Web server treats that directory and its contents (other Web servers use other approaches). This file, literally named **.htaccess** and placed in the directory you want to affect, has a specific syntax for achieving different effects.

For example, you can use the **.htaccess** file to make a directory entirely unavailable through the Web browser. The syntax for that is:

```
# Disable indexing:
Options All -Indexes
# Ignore every file:
IndexIgnore *
# Prevent access to any file:
<FilesMatch "^.*$">
Order Allow,Deny
Deny from all
</FilesMatch>
```

As the comments indicate (comments in an **.htaccess** are preceded by a **#**), the first command allows every option except for indexing, which is to say the Web browser should not create an index of the directory. The second command says that every file should be ignored by any indexing (this is an extra precaution).

The final block applies a set of rules to a group of files, that group being every file in the directory (**^.*$**). The **Order Allow,Deny** command indicates that all *allow* rules should be checked first, then all *deny* rules. Then, the **Deny from all** command says that no one should be allowed access.

If you create a file with a name of **.htaccess** that contains that code and place it in both your **includes** and **views** directories, no one will be able to see the contents of those directories, or a specific file therein, through a Web browser (**Figure 7.10**).

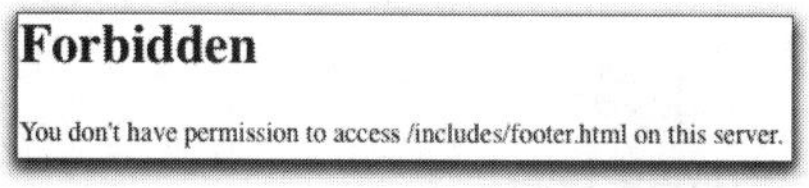

Forbidden

You don't have permission to access /includes/footer.html on this server.

Figure 7.10

Most likely, your Web host will not have a control panel tool for editing **.htaccess** files, but you might be able to create one in any text editor, and then FTP it to the Web server. Or, you could create one on the server via a command-line interface and a command-line text editor like vi or Emacs. Using **.htaccess** files will only work if the Web server is configured to allow changes on a directory basis. This setting is dictated by the server's primary configuration file, which is likely outside your influence, unless you've got your own server.

USING MOD_REWRITE

The next server alteration, which also requires **.htaccess** files, is to use Apache's *mod_rewrite* feature.

As mentioned in Chapter 5, "Managing Site Content," one way to improve the search-engine rankings of your site is to use descriptive URLs. To accomplish this—to create so-called "pretty" URLs—requires using *mod_rewrite*, which is Apache's rewrite module. This tool can transform URLs from one format to another, behind-the-scenes, so that the browser (that is, the user) is unaware of the change.

For the *Coffee* site, two public URLs need to be rewritten: **shop.php** and **browse.php**. The shop page will list the general coffee and non-coffee product categories. To know which to display, the page needs to receive a *type* value in the URL. Instead of having URLs like **shop.php?type=coffee**, let's use **shop/coffee/**. To accomplish this, you would create a **.htaccess** file in the Web root directory that starts off with:

```
<IfModule mod_rewrite.c>
RewriteEngine on
</IfModule>
```

tip

This section packs a lot of information about **.htaccess** files and Apache configuration into a small area. Look online to expand your knowledge of these important subjects.

tip

If you can't use **mod_rewrite** on your server, just skip this section and change every URL in the HTML files accordingly.

These lines say: If the **mod_rewrite** module exists, turn on the rewrite engine. After turning on the rewrite engine and before the closing **IfModule**, you define rules. Here is the complete set of rules that will be defined, to be explained later in detail:

```
<IfModule mod_rewrite.c>
RewriteEngine on
# For sales:
RewriteRule ^shop/sales/?$ sales.php
# For the primary categories:
RewriteRule ^shop/([A-Za-z\+]+)/?$ shop.php?type=$1
# For specific products:
RewriteRule ^browse/([A-Za-z\+\-]+)/([A-Za-z\+\-]+)/([0-9]+)$
➥browse.php?type=$1&category=$2&id=$3
# For HTTPS pages:
RewriteCond %{HTTPS} off
RewriteRule ^(checkout\.php|billing\.php|final\.php|admin/(.*))$
➥https://%{HTTP_HOST}/$1 [R=301,L]
</IfModule>
```

For the **shop.php** script, the rule is:

RewriteRule ^shop/([A-Za-z\+]+)/?$ shop.php?type=$1

Regular expressions are in use here, so if you're unfamiliar with them, this may seem like hieroglyphics to you. I'll explain it in pieces...

The middle chunk (between *RewriteRule* and *shop.php?type=$1*) identifies the URLs to match. That regular expression matches any URL that has text beginning (the caret **^**) with *shop* followed by a slash. That should be followed by some combination of letters and the plus sign: **([A-Za-z\+])+**. The square brackets create a *class* of characters. The specific class matches upper and lowercase letters and the plus sign, which is how spaces are represented in URLs (such as, *Kona Coffee* in a URL is *Kona+Coffee*). This class is followed by the plus sign, which is a quantity modifier that matches one or more of whatever the plus sign follows. So **shop/Mugs** matches **^shop/([A-Za-z\+]+)** but just **shop** does not and neither does **shop/123**.

The class and plus sign quantity modifier is wrapped in parentheses to make a *grouping,* which will be relevant at the end of the rule. This is followed by an *optional* slash. This slash is optional because it's followed by the question mark, another quantifier modifier. The question mark says that zero or one of the things it follows is acceptable. At this point, **^shop/([A-Za-z\+]+)/?** matches **shop/Mugs** or **shop/Mugs/**.

tip

The rewrite rules apply to the part of the URL after the hostname. In **www.example.com/ shop/coffee**, the matching begins after **www.example.com/**.

The dollar sign that concludes the matching rule indicates the end of the string. This means that if any characters follow what's been matched to this point, the match is invalidated. Put another way, the final dollar sign still allows for **shop/Mugs** or **shop/Mugs/** but does not allow for **shop/Mugs/a** or **shop/Mugs/123**.

When a match is made, the URL will be rewritten to **shop.php?type=$1**. The **$1** represents whatever string matched the first grouping: **([A-Za-z\+]+)**. This is called *backreferencing* because it refers back to something already found. The end result is that **shop/coffee** and **shop/coffee/** become **shop.php?type=coffee** and **shop/goodies** becomes **shop.php?type=goodies**. In both cases, **$_GET['type']** will be available to the **shop.php** script because the rewrite module will create it and assign it a value.

Whereas all the products are available through **shop.php**, the sale items will be listed on the **sales.php** script. But to make the URLs consistent, let's add a rule for that situation:

RewriteRule ^shop/sales/?$ sales.php

This rule specifically matches either **shop/sales** or **shop/sales/** and rewrites that as **sales.php**. This rule must be defined before the previous one, though, as the previous rule would also apply to **shop/sales**, and we don't want the URL rewritten as **shop.php?type=sales**.

Continuing along, the **browse.php** page will list specific products in a general category: all the Kona coffees available or all the mugs. The browse script needs to know the category type and the specific category ID. For Search Engine Optimization (SEO) purposes and to make the URL more accessible to the customer as well, the URL will be in the format **browse/*type*/*CategoryName*/*id***, such as **browse/coffee/Kona/3**. The rule to handle this is:

RewriteRule ^browse/([A-Za-z\+]+)/([A-Za-z\+\-]+)/([0-9]+)$
↪ browse.php?type=$1&category=$2&id=$3

This matches any URL that begins with *browse*, followed by a slash and some combination of letters and the plus sign. This first grouping represents the **type** value, such as *coffee* or *goodies*. After that should come a slash, and some combination of letters, the plus sign, and a hyphen. This second grouping matches the *category*, such as *Kona* or *Gift+Baskets*. The match should conclude with one or more numbers, which will be the ID value.

Such a match gets rewritten as **browse.php?type=$1&category=$2&id=$3**, where **$1**, **$2**, and **$3** represent the first, second, and third matched groupings. Hence, **www.example.com/browse/coffee/Kona/3** becomes (behind the scenes) **www.example.com/browse.php?type=coffee&category=Kona&id=3**.

ENFORCING SSL

While the site is using **mod_rewrite**, let's enforce SSL for several pages:

- The entire administration directory
- **checkout.php**
- **billing.php**
- **final.php**

To do this, you must have SSL enabled (see the "Enabling SSL" sidebar), and add this code to your **.htaccess** file, within the same **<IfModule mod_rewrite.c>** block:

RewriteCond %{HTTPS} off
RewriteRule ^(checkout\.php|billing\.php|final\.php|admin/(.*))$
➥https://%{HTTP_HOST}/$1 [R=301,L]

The first line checks for the condition where HTTPS is off: **%{something}** refers to a server environmental variable. Then the rule attempts to match **checkout.php**, **billing.php**, **final.php**, or **admin/***anything*. If a match is made, the URL is rewritten to **https://***hostname***/$1**, where **$1** is the matched item.

The **R=301,L** part says that this should be a permanent redirection type, associated with the server code 301, and that this should be the last rule evaluated.

By adding this rule, the server will not allow the browser to load any of those pages over a non-secure connection.

ENABLING SSL

Enabling SSL on your server is an important step to take for any e-commerce project, but unfortunately one for which I can't provide you with specific directions: There are just too many factors involved, from the hosting company, to the server type, to where you get your SSL certificate. In Chapter 2, "Security Fundamentals," I talked about some of the sites that offer digital certificates and what features you should consider. If you buy one through your hosting company, they will likely install it for you, which is a benefit. If you buy one through a third party, you may save money but have to install it yourself (although the third party should provide some instructions). In that case, you may be able to install the certificate through your Web-hosting control panel. If that's not an option, then installation is a matter of using the command line to put the right files in the right places and then editing the server's configuration files. There are plenty of tutorials online that will explain the steps in detail.

HELPER FILES

The *Coffee* site will use several helper files, not including the HTML templates and views. The first two discussed here are largely the same, in syntax and usage, as the corresponding scripts in Part Two, but let's look at them individually.

Connecting to the Database

The first helper script will connect to the database. This file, named **mysql.inc.php**, should ideally be stored outside the Web directory (see Figure 7.5). It's defined as:

mysql.inc.php

```
1   <?php
2   // Set the database access information as constants:
3   DEFINE ('DB_USER', 'username');
4   DEFINE ('DB_PASSWORD', 'password');
5   DEFINE ('DB_HOST', 'localhost');
6   DEFINE ('DB_NAME', 'ecommerce2');
7
8   // Make the connection:
9   $dbc = mysqli_connect (DB_HOST, DB_USER, DB_PASSWORD,
    ➥DB_NAME);
9
10  // Set the character set:
11  mysqli_set_charset($dbc, 'utf8');
12
13  // Omit the closing PHP tag to avoid 'headers already sent' errors!
```

As I said, this code is pretty much the same as that in Chapter 3, "First Site: Structure and Design," except that the connection constants will have different values, and there's no need for the **get_password_hash()** or **escape_data()** functions. The latter isn't required because stored procedures and prepared statements will be used instead (covered near the end of this chapter).

If you want to improve the security of this example, you could create different MySQL users that have different permissions on specific tables. The most common MySQL user would have **SELECT** permissions on all the non-customer-related tables; another MySQL user would have **SELECT** plus **INSERT**, **UPDATE**, and **DELETE** permissions on the **carts** and **wish_lists** tables; and a third would have only **INSERT** permissions on the order-related tables. To switch the

 note

Make sure you're using unique and secure usernames and passwords, unlike my purposefully obvious ones!

MySQL user on a page-by-page basis, you would indicate the user type prior to including the MySQL connection script:

```
$user = 'general';
require (MYSQL);
```

Then, in the connection script, you would have:

```
DEFINE ('DB_HOST', 'localhost');
DEFINE ('DB_NAME', 'ecommerce2');
if (isset($user) && ('user' == 'general')) {
    DEFINE ('DB_USER', 'username');
    DEFINE ('DB_PASSWORD', 'password');
} elseif (isset($user) && ('user' == 'cart')) {...
    DEFINE ('DB_USER', 'otherUser');
    DEFINE ('DB_PASSWORD', 'otherPassword');
```

The Config File

The configuration file in this site does pretty much what the configuration file in the *Knowledge is Power* site did: define site settings, constants, and declare an error handler. The *Coffee* site will not use sessions, though, so that's omitted from the configuration file, as is the redirection function.

includes/config.php

```
1   <?php
2
3   // Are we live?
4   $live = false;
5
6   // Errors are emailed here:
7   $contact_email = 'you@example.com';
8
9   // Determine location of files and the URL of the site:
10  define ('BASE_URI', '/path/to/Web/parent/folder/');
11  define ('BASE_URL', 'www.example.com/');
12  define ('MYSQL', '/path/to/mysql.inc.php');
13
14  // Function for handling errors:
15  function my_error_handler ($e_number, $e_message, $e_file, $e_line,
    ⇒$e_vars) {
16      global $live, $contact_email;
```

```
17
18    // Build the error message:
19    $message = "An error occurred in script '$e_file' on line
      ⇒$e_line:\n$e_message\n";
20
21    // Add the backtrace:
22    $message .= "<pre>" .print_r(debug_backtrace(), 1) . "</pre>\n";
23
24    if (!$live) { // Show the error in the browser.
25        echo '<div class="error">' . nl2br($message) . '</div>';
25    } else { // Development (print the error).
27        // Send the error in an email:
28        error_log ($message, 1, $contact_email,
          ⇒'From:admin@example.com');
29        // Only print an error message in the browser, if the error isn't
          ⇒a notice:
30        if ($e_number != E_NOTICE) {
31            echo '<div class="error">A system error occurred. We
              ⇒apologize for the inconvenience.</div>';
32        }
33    } // End of $live IF-ELSE.
34
35    return true; // So that PHP doesn't try to handle the error, too.
36
37  } // End of my_error_handler() definition.
38
39  // Use my error handler:
40  set_error_handler ('my_error_handler');
41
42  // Omit the closing PHP tag to avoid 'headers already sent' errors!
```

I should point out an inconsistency introduced by the error handler that may become apparent in the next couple chapters. Every PHP script in this site uses *view files*—separate HTML pages—to display content. Technically, a separate view file should be created for displaying errors, too. Without such a file, you may see errors displayed in odd places. I've omitted a dedicated error view file here so as not to complicate things even further, but you can find it among the downloadable code available at **www.DMCInsights.com/ecom/**.

 tip

If you're unsure about any of the code in the three helper files, see Part Two, where each is explained in detail.

THE HTML TEMPLATE

I feel that the HTML design for the *Coffee* site needs to be more graphically interesting than that used in the *Knowledge is Power* site. Selling physical products requires that you appeal to the user's eye: Customers want to see what they're buying. Once again, designing something like that is well beyond my abilities. This time around, I'm turning to the Coffee template (**Figure 7.11**) offered by Templates.com (**www.templates.com**).

Figure 7.11

There's nothing particularly fancy from a PHP perspective in the HTML template, so rather than walking through the files in detail, I'll just present them in entirety. You'll see that what follows is only moderately modified from the Templates.com original. I have instituted the dynamic page title system in the header, which I explained in Part Two of the book.

includes/header.html:

```
1  <!DOCTYPE html PUBLIC "-//W3C//DTD XHTML 1.0 Strict//EN"
   ➥"http://www.w3.org/TR/xhtml1/DTD/xhtml1-strict.dtd">
2  <html xmlns="http://www.w3.org/1999/xhtml" xml:lang="en"
   ➥lang="en">
```

```
3   <head>
4   <title>    <?php // Use a default page title if one wasn't provided...
5      if (isset($page_title)) {
6             echo $page_title;
7      } else {
8             echo 'Coffee - Wouldn\'t You Love a Cup Right Now?';
9      }
10     ?></title>
11  <meta http-equiv="Content-Type" content="text/html;
    ⇒charset=utf-8" />
12  <meta name="description" content="Place your description here" />
13  <meta name="keywords" content="put, your, keyword, here" />
14  <meta name="author" content="Templates.com - website templates
    ⇒provider" />
15  <link href="/css/style.css" rel="stylesheet" type="text/css" />
16  <!--[if lt IE 7]>
17     <script type="text/javascript" src="/js/ie_png.js"></script>
18     <script type="text/javascript">
19        ie_png.fix('.png, .logo h1, .box .left-top-corner, .box
           ⇒.right-top-corner, .box .left-bot-corner, .box .right-bot-corner,
           ⇒.box .border-left, .box .border-right, .box .border-top, .box
           ⇒.border-bot, .box 20 .inner, .special dd, #contacts-form input,
           ⇒#contacts-form textarea');
21     </script>
22  <![endif]-->
23  </head>
24
25  <body id="page1">
26     <!-- header -->
27     <div id="header">
28        <div class="container">
29           <div class="wrapper">
30              <ul class="top-links">
31                 <li><a href="/index.php" class="first"><img alt=""
                    ⇒src="/images/icon-home.gif" /></a></li>
32                 <li><a href="/cart.php"><img alt=""
                    ⇒src="/images/icon-cart.gif" /></a></li>
33                 <li><a href="/contact.php"><img alt=""
                    ⇒src="/images/icon-mail.gif" /></a></li>
34                 <li><a href="/sitemap.php"><img alt=""
                    ⇒src="/images/icon-map.gif" /></a></li>
```

(continues on next page)

```
35            </ul>
36            <div class="logo">
37              <h1><a href="/index.php">Coffee</a><span>Wouldn't
              ↪you love a cup right now?</span></h1>
38            </div>
39          </div>
40          <ul class="nav">
41          <!-- MENU -->
42          <li><a href="/shop/coffee/">Coffee</a></li>
43          <li><a href="/shop/goodies/">Goodies</a></li>
44          <li><a href="/shop/sales/">Sales</a></li>
45          <li><a href="/wishlist.php">Wish List</a></li>
46          <li><a href="/cart.php">Cart</a></li>
47          <!-- END MENU -->
48          </ul>
49        </div>
50      </div>
51      <!-- content -->
52      <div id="content">
53        <div class="container">
54          <div class="inside">
```

The footer file completes all the **<DIV>** tags, prints a small copyright, and links to Templates.com, which created the template in the first place.

includes/footer.html:

```
1   </div>
2         </div>
3   </div>
4   <!-- footer -->
5   <div id="footer">
6     <div class="container">
7       <div class="indent">
8         <div class="fleft"> &copy; - Clever Coffee, Inc.</div>
9         <div class="fright">Site designed by: <a href="http://
          ↪www.templates.com">Templates.com</a></div>
10      </div>
11    </div>
12  </div>
13  </body>
14  </html>
```

The only thing to note in both files is the use of absolute references in all links, images, CSS, and JavaScript. Because the URLs for some of the pages will be **/something/something**, such as **shop/coffee**, the Web browser will get confused if you just use **./images** or **css/style.css**. Instead, you'll see **/images** and **/css/style.css**, where the initial slash says to begin at the Web root.

NEWER MYSQL FEATURES

For improved security and to separate some database activity from the PHP code, this project will use a couple of features that are relatively new to MySQL. Just as important, support for these features is also relatively new to PHP. I'm specifically speaking of *prepared statements* and *stored procedures*. In this chapter, I want to talk about the benefits of each feature as well as provide you with alternative approaches should you not meet the minimum requirements. That way, when you see the actual implementation of these features, you'll be informed as to how you'll need to change your code accordingly.

The first thing you need to do, before reading any further, is confirm for certain what versions of PHP and MySQL you'll be using. These values will also likely differ between your testing environment (perhaps your computer) and the live destination server. Prepared statements were added to MySQL in version 4.1, which was released in 2004, so every host should at least meet this requirement. Stored procedures were added in version 5, released in 2005.

Along with the proper version of MySQL, you'll need the properly configured version of PHP. To use prepared statements and stored procedures from PHP, you'll need at least PHP 5, with the *MySQL Improved* extension enabled (allowing you to use the **mysqli_*** functions). You can confirm the version of PHP you're running and its support for the MySQL improved functions by running this code (as a PHP script) on your Web server (**Figures 7.12** and **7.13**):

```php
<?php phpinfo(); ?>
```

Figure 7.12

Figure 7.13

Once you've confirmed what versions you're using, you can continue reading. If you have PHP 5+ and MySQL 5+, you should be fine. If you don't, pay attention to what changes you'll need to make in order to adapt the code to your situation.

Prepared Statements

In database-based applications, many times the same query will be executed repeatedly using just slightly different parameters. For example, a query that paginates some results varies in its **LIMIT** clause:

SELECT * FROM *tablename* **LIMIT 0, 20**
SELECT * FROM *tablename* **LIMIT 20, 20**
SELECT * FROM *tablename* **LIMIT 40, 20**

An **INSERT** query varies in the values being inserted:

INSERT INTO *tablename* **(***column1, column2***) VALUES ('value1', 'value2')**
INSERT INTO *tablename* **(***column1, column2***) VALUES ('valueX', 'valueY')**

Unlike those five queries, which include the table references and the data to be used, a prepared statement separates the static content from the dynamic values, using placeholders for the latter:

SELECT * FROM *tablename* **LIMIT ?, 20**
INSERT INTO *tablename* **(***column1, column2***) VALUES (?, ?)**

The database is then asked to "prepare" the statement, at which point the database will confirm that the query is syntactically valid (assuming that values will later be provided for each placeholder). There can be a performance benefit to this approach, since the database can cache the preparation of the query, making subsequent uses of the same prepared statement faster. The next steps provide a value for all the placeholders and execute the query.

In terms of your PHP code, this is how you go about using a prepared statement...

Start by defining the query, using question marks to indicate the values to be provided later. For example, if the site had a login functionality, its query might look like:

$q = 'SELECT id, username, type, IF(date_expires >= NOW(), true, false)
➥FROM users WHERE (email=? and password=?)';

Then, call the **mysqli_prepare()** function, providing it with the database connection and the query:

$stmt = mysqli_prepare($dbc, $q);

This function returns a **MySQLi_STMT** object, which will be used by later functions.

tip

This query comes from Chapter 4, "User Accounts."

note

It's very important that you don't quote any placeholders, even if their values will be strings.

If you want to see any error that might have occurred, you could next do this:

if (!$stmt) echo mysqli_stmt_error($stmt);

The next step is to *bind* the variables, which is to associate each placeholder with a PHP variable:

mysqli_stmt_bind_param($stmt, 'ss', $email, $pass);

The first argument is the statement representative variable. The next is an indicator of the formats of the various placeholders, using one symbol for each placeholder. The available symbols are in **Table 7.1**.

Table 7.1 Bound Value Types

Letter	Represents
d	Decimal
i	Integer
b	Blob (binary data)
s	All other types

For this query, there are two placeholders and both will be strings (that is, not decimals, integers, or blobs). The **mysqli_stmt_bind_params()** function then takes one variable for each placeholder. These variables can have any valid name and wouldn't necessarily be existing variables prior to this point, because it's after this point that each variable is normally assigned a value:

$email = $_POST['email'];
$pass = get_password_hash($_POST['pass']);

Finally, execute the statement:

mysqli_stmt_execute($stmt);

To clarify a common point of confusion, the variables bound to the placeholders must have their appropriate values when the **mysqli_stmt_execute()** function is called. As you'll see in a later chapter, this means that you can prepare and bind a statement, then associate values to use within a loop or other control structure.

Also, and more importantly, **you do not need to take any extra steps to prevent SQL Injection attacks** because the prepared statements already prevent those simply by separating the values from the rest of the query.

For **UPDATE** and **INSERT** queries, you can confirm that a record was affected using:

if (mysqli_stmt_affected_rows($stmt) == 1) {

For **SELECT** queries, to count the number of returned rows, do this:

mysqli_stmt_store_result($stmt);
if (mysqli_stmt_num_rows($stmt) >= 1) {

Once you're finished with the prepared statement, you can close it and free up the resources:

mysqli_stmt_close($stmt);

All the previous code demonstrates *inbound* prepared statements, in which the values used in a query come from variables. You can also use *outbound* prepared statements—with or without inbound parameters—in which case the query's results are assigned to variables. Assuming the earlier query returned a row, you could then use:

mysqli_stmt_store_result($stmt);
if (mysqli_stmt_num_rows($stmt) == 1) {
mysqli_stmt_bind_result($stmt, $id, $username, $type, $expired);
mysqli_stmt_fetch($stmt);

At this point, the **$id**, **$username**, **$type**, and **$expired** variables have the values returned by the database.

If your server configuration does not support prepared statements, the solution is simple: Use **mysqli_query()** and the other standard functions as you normally would. Just make sure you use an escaping function and other techniques to prevent SQL Injection attacks.

Stored Procedures

Stored procedures, new(-ish) to MySQL but present in other database applications for years, is simply a way to define blocks of code within the database itself. Instead of running a query on the database, you call the corresponding stored procedure, which will do the querying for you.

Stored procedures can offer the following benefits:

- Improved security
- Better performance
- Cleaner model-controller separation
- Increased application portability

tip

Chapter 11, "Site Administration," will use prepared statements exclusively.

note

Both *stored procedures* and *stored functions* fall under the general category of *stored routines*.

note

I'm just introducing the concept of stored procedures here; later chapters will present much more context and syntax.

The most important of these is security. Because routines are stored within the database itself, the programming interface—PHP in this case—will not have direct access to the underlying tables and data. In fact, the interface wouldn't even need to know what tables and columns exist when stored procedures are used.

You can get better performance with a stored procedure in two ways. First, as you'll see, stored procedures require that less data be sent to the database, because you'll mostly be sending just values without any SQL (this is another security benefit). Second, stored procedures can be cached and managed so that the database executes them as efficiently as possible.

The cleaner model-controller separation is obvious: more logic goes into the database, removing SQL from the PHP code.

As for the increased application portability, this is both true and not. Because the logic will be stored in the database, other interfaces, like a Java application or the command line, can invoke the stored procedures in exactly the same way (this may or may not be beneficial to you). On the other hand, with the logic stored in the database, you could not as easily change the database application in use. But to be frank, I've been doing Web development for over a decade now and have had to change a Web application from one database server to another...just about never.

Stored procedures are created using this SQL command:

CREATE PROCEDURE name (arguments)
BEGIN
    CODE
END

The procedure's name can contain letters, numbers, and the underscore, but avoid using the same name as an existing MySQL function, keyword, database name, or table name.

For the procedure's arguments, give each argument a name and a MySQL-defined type, with multiple arguments separated by a comma:

CREATE PROCEDURE do_this(age INT, name VARCHAR(20)...

Again, stick to letters, numbers, and the underscore, and avoid using existing names and keywords for the argument names. **Note that these are MySQL stored procedure variables, not PHP ones, so there are no dollar signs.** The variable types are also basic, omitting extra qualities such as **UNSIGNED** or **NOT NULL**.

 note

I ran a few informal benchmarks and saw this book's stored procedures running significantly faster than the literal queries.

 note

Stored procedures are associated with a specific database and become part of its definition.

 note

As stored procedures transfer more of the processing load from the Web server to the database server, you may find the database server becomes overloaded more quickly.

 note

Banks and other extremely secure environments rely on stored procedures for increased security.

 note

You must use parentheses for the procedure's arguments, even if there are none.

The **BEGIN** and **END** blocks aren't required with only a single command, but I think it's best to still use them.

The *CODE* part is where the magic happens. In this section you can execute SQL queries, create and manipulate variables, use control structures (conditionals and loops), and so forth. In layman's terms, whatever is the result of the *CODE* section will be what's returned by the stored procedure (that is, what you'd have to work with after invoking the stored procedure in PHP).

There is, however, one little catch: Because MySQL, by default, uses the semicolon to terminate SQL commands, any use of a semicolon within the procedure's definition will terminate the definition itself. The workaround is to change the delimiter prior to the definition:

note

As with prepared statements, don't quote the arguments used *within* a stored procedure query, even if they are strings.

DELIMITER $$
CREATE PROCEDURE *name* (*arguments*)
BEGIN
    CODE
END$$

Figure 7.14 shows a stored procedure being defined using the command-line MySQL client.

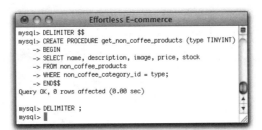

Figure 7.14

To execute a stored procedure, use **CALL** *name* (*arguments*) (**Figure 7.15**).

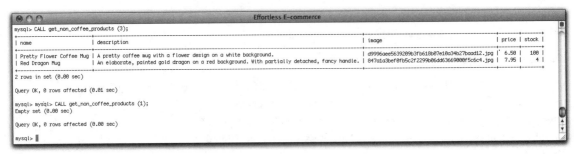

Figure 7.15

In PHP, you can use the **mysqli_query()** function to execute a stored procedure:

$r = mysqli_query("CALL get_non_coffee_products($id)");

Then you can use the **mysqli_fetch_array()** function to get the results.

The last thing you should know is that you can create stored procedures, using phpMyAdmin, the mysql command-line client, or whatever, just as you can execute any other query, provided that you're connected to the database as a user with that permission. This is to say that the MySQL user involved must have **CREATE ROUTINE** permissions, which will normally also mean they have **ALTER ROUTINE** and **EXECUTE** permissions. Unfortunately, I can't personally say how common it is for different Web hosts to allow stored procedures.

If your server environment makes using stored procedures impossible, you'll need to move all the logic and SQL back into your PHP scripts, and execute the SQL commands as you would standard queries.

 note

MySQL permissions with respect to stored procedures are more complicated than I'm presenting here. See the MySQL manual if you want all the details.

8 | CREATING A CATALOG

After preparing the server for the site (see the previous chapter), the next step is to start creating the catalog, because the customer can't shop without it. To do so, you'll need to prepopulate the database with some products, since you won't develop the administrative scripts for adding products until Chapter 11, "Site Administration." Then you can write the two PHP scripts for generating the catalog: one for browsing by category and a second for listing specific products.

After that, the chapter demonstrates better ways to show the availability of products and any applicable sale prices. From there, you'll write new PHP scripts for showing the sale items on their own.

If you have intermediate PHP and MySQL experience, nothing in this chapter should be too challenging for you, although you will learn some new tricks. The SQL queries in this chapter are some of the most complex in the book, and they'll be wrapped inside stored procedures to boot. You'll also see a real-world way of implementing the MVC design pattern in a moderately complex site.

PREPARING THE DATABASE

Half of the database tables will be used by the code in this chapter. In order to see any results in the Web browser, you'll need to insert some records into these first. For three of these tables—**general_coffees**, **non_coffee_categories**, and **sizes**, there will not be an administration page. The data in all three tables should be fairly stable, and if you want administrative capability over them, it would be easy enough for you to create corresponding administrative pages yourself. For the other three tables—**specific_coffees**, **non_coffee_products**, and **sales**, you'll create administrative scripts, but not until Chapter 11. For now, you'll populate these tables using just SQL, and then create the three stored procedures used by the PHP scripts in this chapter.

Populating the Tables Using SQL

You can populate any database table via any interface to the MySQL database, the two most common being the Web-based *phpMyAdmin* and the command-line **mysql** client. With phpMyAdmin, which is what your Web host likely provides (perhaps indirectly through another control panel), you can use the SQL tab or the SQL query window (**Figure 8.1**) to enter SQL commands.

Figure 8.1

With the command-line **mysql** client, you first need to access the server via a command-line interface (even if that's your own computer). How you do this will depend upon the operating system you're using:

- On Windows, click Start, and then Run. Enter **cmd** in the Run prompt and click OK.

- On Mac OS X, open the **/Applications/Utilities/Terminal** program.

- Most versions of Linux also have a Terminal application.

Once you're in the command-line environment, you can access the database using:

mysql -u *username* -p ecommerce2

Provide a real username and, at the prompt, enter that user's password. This command, should it work (that is, should the username and password be correct), will also select the **ecommerce2** database automatically. Change that part of the command if your database is named differently.

If you're using an all-in-one installer, such as XAMPP (**www.apachefriends.org**) or MAMP (**www.mamp.info**), you'll need to specify the full path to that version of the **mysql** client (**Figure 8.2** on the next page):

/Applications/MAMP/Library/bin/mysql -u *username* -p ecommerce2

Figure 8.2

Once you've accessed the database via any interface, you can start populating the tables (assuming you've already defined them).

1. Populate the **sizes** table:

   INSERT INTO `sizes` (`size`) VALUES
   ('2 oz. Sample'), ('Half Pound'), ('1 lb.'), ('2 lbs.'), ('5 lbs.');

   The **sizes** table is used by the **specific_coffees** table to indicate in what quantities someone can buy coffee. The table only has a primary key column and a **size** column. This query adds five values to the table.

2. Populate the **non_coffee_categories** table:

   INSERT INTO `non_coffee_categories` (`category`, `description`, `image`)
   ↪VALUES
   ('Edibles', 'A wonderful assortment of goodies to eat. Includes biscotti,
   ↪baklava, lemon bars, and more!', 'goodies.jpg'),
   ('Gift Baskets', 'Gift baskets for any occasion! Including our many coffees
   ↪and other goodies.', 'gift_basket.jpg'),
   ('Mugs', 'A selection of lovely mugs for enjoying your coffee, tea, hot
   ↪cocoa or other hot beverages.', '781426_32573620.jpg'),
   ('Books', 'Our recommended books about coffee, goodies, plus anything
   ↪written by Larry Ullman!', 'books.jpg');

   The **non_coffee_categories** table represents the categories of non-coffee items the site will sell. The three non-primary key columns are **category**, **description**, and **image**. For the images, you'll need to create a representative image for each category, with a matching image name. The images should be placed within the **products** directory (see Figure 7.5). You can, of course, just copy the images available in the downloadable code from the book's corresponding Web site.

3. Populate the **general_coffees** table:

   INSERT INTO `general_coffees` (`category`, `description`, `image`) VALUES
   ('Original Blend', 'Our original blend, featuring a quality mixture of
   ↪bean and a medium roast for a rich color and smooth flavor.',
   ↪'original_coffee.jpg'),

tip

All the SQL commands can be downloaded from **www.DMCInsights.com/ecom/**.

tip

See Chapter 7, "Second Site: Structure and Design," for a discussion of the database's tables.

('Dark Roast', 'Our darkest, non-espresso roast, with a full flavor and a
➥slightly bitter aftertaste.', 'dark_roast.jpg'),
('Kona', 'A real treat! Kona coffee, fresh from the lush mountains of
➥Hawaii. Smooth in flavor and perfectly roasted!', 'kona.jpg');

This table has the exact same structure as **non_coffee_categories**. Again, grab the images from the downloadable stuff and place them in your **products** folder.

4. Populate the **non_coffee_products** table:

INSERT INTO `non_coffee_products` (`non_coffee_category_id`, `name`,
➥`description`, `image`, `price`, `stock`, `date_created`) VALUES
(3, 'Pretty Flower Coffee Mug', 'A pretty coffee mug with a flower design on a
➥white background.', 'd9996aee5639209b3fb618b07e10a34b27baad12.jpg',
➥6.50, 100, NOW()),
(3, 'Red Dragon Mug', 'An elaborate, painted gold dragon on
➥a red background. With partially detached, fancy handle.',
➥'847a1a3befofb5c2f2299b06dd63669000f5c6c4.jpg', 7.95, 4, NOW());

In Chapter 11, you'll create a PHP script that does all the heavy lifting for you, so let's just create a couple of records in this table for now. Each product has a **non_coffee_category_id** of 3, which is *Mugs*. A specific name and description is provided, along with an image's name (also to be placed in the **products** directory). Next come the price and the quantity in stock. To test how stock availability will be handled, one product has plenty of stock and another very little.

5. Populate the **specific_coffees** table:

INSERT INTO `specific_coffees` (`general_coffee_id`, `size_id`,
➥`caf_decaf`, `ground_whole`, `price`, `stock`, `date_created`) VALUES
(3, 1, 'caf', 'ground', 2.00, 20, NOW()),
(3, 2, 'caf', 'ground', 4.50, 30, NOW()),
(3, 2, 'decaf', 'ground', 5.00, 20, NOW()),
(3, 3, 'caf', 'ground', 8.00, 50, NOW()),
(3, 3, 'decaf', 'ground', 8.50, 20, NOW()),
(3, 3, 'caf', 'whole', 7.50, 50, NOW()),
(3, 3, 'decaf', 'whole', 8.00, 20, NOW()),
(3, 4, 'caf', 'whole', 15.00, 30, NOW()),
(3, 4, 'decaf', 'whole', 15.50, 15, NOW()),
(3, 5, 'caf', 'whole', 32.50, 5, NOW());

To create specific coffee products to sell, you're actually creating multiple products of one coffee type (*Kona*, with a **general_coffee_id** of 3).

The products come in varying sizes and combinations of caffeinated, decaffeinated, ground beans, and whole beans. The products have different prices and quantities in stock.

6. Populate the **sales** table:

INSERT INTO `sales` (`product_type`, `product_id`, `price`, `start_date`, ➥`end_date`) VALUES
('other', 1, 5.00, '2010-08-16', '2010-08-31'),
('coffee', 7, 7.00, '2010-08-19', NULL),
('coffee', 9, 13.00, '2010-08-19', '2010-08-26'),
('other', 2, 7.00, '2010-08-22', NULL),
('coffee', 8, 13.00, '2010-08-22', '2010-08-31'),
('coffee', 10, 30.00, '2010-08-22', '2010-09-30');

Finally, let's put some items on sale by discounting their prices. For each sale item, you need to indicate a product type, the item's product ID (from the corresponding **specific_coffees** or **non_coffee_products** tables), the new price, and the starting date for the sale. The ending date is optional. Unless you're reading this book as I'm writing it, which would freak me out, you'll need to change the dates to be current for you.

Looking at the Stored Procedure Queries

The three stored procedures about to be created will use six queries, four of which are relatively complex. Those four select:

- All the specific coffee products in a general coffee category

- All the specific non-coffee products in a general non-coffee category

- All the sale items

- A few, random sale items to be listed on the home page

Before moving onto the stored procedures themselves, let's look at these queries in detail.

SELECTING EVERY COFFEE PRODUCT

The query for selecting every coffee product is:

SELECT gc.description, gc.image, CONCAT("C", sc.id) AS sku,
CONCAT_WS(" - ", s.size, sc.caf_decaf, sc.ground_whole, sc.price) AS name,
sc.stock
FROM specific_coffees AS sc INNER JOIN sizes AS s ON s.id=sc.size_id
INNER JOIN general_coffees AS gc ON gc.id=sc.general_coffee_id

tip

If you want, you can run some basic **SELECT** queries to confirm the database's contents.

tip

For help with complex SQL, search online, see the MySQL manual, or check out my book, *MySQL: Visual QuickStart Guide* (2nd Edition, Peachpit Press).

WHERE general_coffee_id=<*some_category_id*> AND stock>0
ORDER by name ASC;

Figure 8.3 shows the MySQL output for the query, when replacing
<*some_category_id*> with the number 3 (for Kona coffee).

```
Effortless E-commerce
mysql> SELECT gc.description, gc.image, CONCAT("C", sc.id) AS sku,
    -> CONCAT_WS(" - ", s.size, sc.caf_decaf, sc.ground_whole, sc.price) AS name,
    -> sc.stock
    -> FROM specific_coffees AS sc INNER JOIN sizes AS s ON s.id=sc.size_id
    -> INNER JOIN general_coffees AS gc ON gc.id=sc.general_coffee_id
    -> WHERE general_coffee_id=3 AND stock>0
    -> ORDER by name ASC;
+----------------------------------------------------------------------------------------------+----------+-----+-------------------------------+-------+
| description                                                                                  | image    | sku | name                          | stock |
+----------------------------------------------------------------------------------------------+----------+-----+-------------------------------+-------+
| A real treat! Kona coffee, fresh from the lush mountains of Hawaii. Smooth in flavor and perfectly roasted! | kona.jpg | C4  | 1 lb. - caf - ground - 8.00   | 50    |
| A real treat! Kona coffee, fresh from the lush mountains of Hawaii. Smooth in flavor and perfectly roasted! | kona.jpg | C6  | 1 lb. - caf - whole - 7.50    | 50    |
| A real treat! Kona coffee, fresh from the lush mountains of Hawaii. Smooth in flavor and perfectly roasted! | kona.jpg | C5  | 1 lb. - decaf - ground - 8.50 | 20    |
| A real treat! Kona coffee, fresh from the lush mountains of Hawaii. Smooth in flavor and perfectly roasted! | kona.jpg | C7  | 1 lb. - decaf - whole - 8.00  | 20    |
| A real treat! Kona coffee, fresh from the lush mountains of Hawaii. Smooth in flavor and perfectly roasted! | kona.jpg | C8  | 2 lbs. - caf - whole - 15.00  | 30    |
| A real treat! Kona coffee, fresh from the lush mountains of Hawaii. Smooth in flavor and perfectly roasted! | kona.jpg | C9  | 2 lbs. - decaf - whole - 15.50| 15    |
| A real treat! Kona coffee, fresh from the lush mountains of Hawaii. Smooth in flavor and perfectly roasted! | kona.jpg | C1  | 2 oz. Sample - caf - ground - 2.00 | 20 |
| A real treat! Kona coffee, fresh from the lush mountains of Hawaii. Smooth in flavor and perfectly roasted! | kona.jpg | C10 | 5 lbs. - caf - whole - 32.50  | 5     |
| A real treat! Kona coffee, fresh from the lush mountains of Hawaii. Smooth in flavor and perfectly roasted! | kona.jpg | C2  | Half Pound - caf - ground - 4.50 | 30 |
| A real treat! Kona coffee, fresh from the lush mountains of Hawaii. Smooth in flavor and perfectly roasted! | kona.jpg | C3  | Half Pound - decaf - ground - 5.00 | 20 |
+----------------------------------------------------------------------------------------------+----------+-----+-------------------------------+-------+
10 rows in set (0.00 sec)

mysql>
```

Figure 8.3

To understand what's happening in this query, it will probably help to see how
the data is being used in a Web page (**Figure 8.4**). For the coffee products, the
general coffee type's **image** and **description** will be used, so those need to be
selected. The product's SKU will be a combination of the capital letter "C" (for
coffee) and the product's ID value, so these are concatenated together in the
query. You can't tell this from the figure, but the SKUs are used as the values
for each option in the drop-down menu, as in:

<select name="sku">
<option value="C4">1 lb. - caf - ground - 8.00</option>
<option value="C6">1 lb. - caf - whole - 7.50</option>

The select menu's label—what the customer sees—is the concatenation
of the coffee's size, caffeinated/decaffeinated status, ground/whole bean
status, and price. You can see this in Figure 8.4. To generate this value, use
the **CONCAT_WS()** function, short for *concatenation with separator*, where
the first argument provided will be used in between each concatenated value.
This whole construct is given the alias of *name*. The product's **stock** value is
selected as well, to be used later.

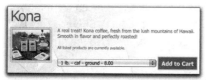

Figure 8.4

tip

If your records in the **sizes** table are in ascending size order, you could select the coffee products ordered by **size_id** first.

tip

Ending a query with **\G** instead of a semicolon returns the query results as a vertical list (as in Figure 8.5), rather than a horizontal table. This is sometimes easier to read.

The query uses a **JOIN** across three tables: **specific_coffees**, **general_coffees**, and **sizes**. The **WHERE** conditional restricts the results to a general coffee type, and retrieves only those products that are currently in stock. And the whole record set is returned in order by name, so that similar products will appear near each other.

SELECTING EVERY NON-COFFEE PRODUCT

The query for selecting every non-coffee product is:

**SELECT ncc.description AS g_description, ncc.image AS g_image, CONCAT("O", ncp.id) AS sku, ncp.name, ncp.description, ncp.image, ncp.price, ncp.stock
FROM non_coffee_products AS ncp INNER JOIN non_coffee_categories AS ncc
ON ncc.id=ncp.non_coffee_category_id
WHERE non_coffee_category_id=<some_category_id> ORDER by
⇢date_created DESC;**

Figure 8.5 shows the output for the query when replacing *<some_category_id>* with the number 3 (for *Mugs*). **Figure 8.6** shows how this data will be used in the site.

Figure 8.5

Figure 8.6

This query is more straightforward, because it only performs a **JOIN** across two tables. The query selects the **description** and **image** values from the **non_coffee_categories** tables, aliasing them as **g_description** and **g_image** accordingly (the *g_* is short for *general*). Again, the product's SKU is created in the query, by concatenating the capital letter "O" (for *other*) to the product's ID value. The specific product's **name, description, image, price,** and **stock** values are also retrieved. The only condition in this query is for restricting the results to a specific category, and the results are ordered from newest items to oldest.

SELECTING EVERY SALE ITEM

The query for selecting every sale item is:

**SELECT CONCAT("O", ncp.id) AS sku, sa.price AS sale_price, ncc.category,
ncp.image, ncp.name, ncp.price, ncp.stock, ncp.description
FROM sales AS sa
INNER JOIN non_coffee_products AS ncp ON sa.product_id=ncp.id
INNER JOIN non_coffee_categories AS ncc ON
➥ncc.id=ncp.non_coffee_category_id
WHERE sa.product_type="other" AND
((NOW() BETWEEN sa.start_date AND sa.end_date) OR (NOW() >
➥sa.start_date AND sa.end_date IS NULL))
UNION
SELECT CONCAT("C", sc.id), sa.price, gc.category, gc.image,
CONCAT_WS(" - ", s.size, sc.caf_decaf, sc.ground_whole), sc.price,
sc.stock, gc.description
FROM sales AS sa
INNER JOIN specific_coffees AS sc ON sa.product_id=sc.id
INNER JOIN sizes AS s ON s.id=sc.size_id
INNER JOIN general_coffees AS gc ON gc.id=sc.general_coffee_id
WHERE sa.product_type="coffee" AND
((NOW() BETWEEN sa.start_date AND sa.end_date) OR (NOW() >
➥sa.start_date AND sa.end_date IS NULL));**

Figure 8.7 shows the output for the query.

tip

Because of the order of the two **SELECT** queries, the non-coffee products will be returned first, followed by the coffee products.

sku	sale_price	category	image	name	price	stock	description
O1	5.00	Mugs	d9996aee5639209b3fb618b07e10a34b27baad12.jpg	Pretty Flower Coffee Mug	6.50	100	A pretty coffee mug with a flower design on a white background.
O2	7.00	Mugs	847a1a3bef0fb5c2f2299b06dd63669000f5c6c4.jpg	Red Dragon Mug	7.95	4	An elaborate, painted gold dragon on a red background. With partially detached, fancy handle.
C7	7.00	Kona	kona.jpg	1 lb. - decaf - whole	8.00	20	A real treat! Kona coffee, fresh from the lush mountains of Hawaii. Smooth in flavor and perfectly roasted!
C8	13.00	Kona	kona.jpg	2 lbs. - caf - whole	15.00	30	A real treat! Kona coffee, fresh from the lush mountains of Hawaii. Smooth in flavor and perfectly roasted!
C9	13.00	Kona	kona.jpg	2 lbs. - decaf - whole	15.50	15	A real treat! Kona coffee, fresh from the lush mountains of Hawaii. Smooth in flavor and perfectly roasted!
C10	30.00	Kona	kona.jpg	5 lbs. - caf - whole	32.50	5	A real treat! Kona coffee, fresh from the lush mountains of Hawaii. Smooth in flavor and perfectly roasted!

6 rows in set (0.00 sec)

mysql>

Figure 8.7

This query is relatively complex, because it performs a **UNION** of two **SELECT** queries, one of which is a **JOIN** across three tables and the other of which is a **JOIN** across four! The complexity derives from the fact that some records in the **sales** table will relate to the **specific_coffees** table (when the **sales** table's **product_type** value is *coffee*), and other records will relate to the **non_coffee_products** table (when the **sales** table's **product_type** value is *other*). To perform both of these **JOIN**s at one time requires the **UNION** statement, which is a way of combining two similar but unrelated queries to create one result set.

The individual **SELECT** queries are similar to those just explained, but without a **WHERE** condition on the category. However, both **SELECT** queries do require a conditional that confirms that the item is currently on sale:

((NOW() BETWEEN sa.start_date AND sa.end_date) OR (NOW() >
↪sa.start_date AND sa.end_date IS NULL))

An item's sale price is applicable if the current moment is between the start and end dates of that sale, or if the current moment is after the start date and there is no end date.

For both **SELECT** queries, the SKU is manufactured (as in the other queries), and the product's category, image, name, regular price, stock, and description are also returned. For the non-coffee products, the name will simply be the **name** value from the **non_coffee_products** table, and the **image** and **description** will come from there as well. For the coffee products, **name** will be the concatenation of several values, and **image** and **description** will come from the **general_coffees** table.

SELECTING A FEW RANDOM SALE ITEMS

The last complex query selects up to four random sale items:

(SELECT CONCAT("O", ncp.id) AS sku, sa.price AS sale_price, ncc.category,
ncp.image, ncp.name
FROM sales AS sa
INNER JOIN non_coffee_products AS ncp ON sa.product_id=ncp.id
INNER JOIN non_coffee_categories AS ncc ON
↪ncc.id=ncp.non_coffee_category_id
WHERE sa.product_type="other" AND
((NOW() BETWEEN sa.start_date AND sa.end_date) OR (NOW() >
↪sa.start_date AND sa.end_date IS NULL))
ORDER BY RAND() LIMIT 2)
UNION
(SELECT CONCAT("C", sc.id), sa.price, gc.category, gc.image,
CONCAT_WS(" - ", s.size, sc.caf_decaf, sc.ground_whole)
FROM sales AS sa
INNER JOIN specific_coffees AS sc ON sa.product_id=sc.id
INNER JOIN sizes AS s ON s.id=sc.size_id
INNER JOIN general_coffees AS gc ON gc.id=sc.general_coffee_id
WHERE sa.product_type="coffee" AND
((NOW() BETWEEN sa.start_date AND sa.end_date) OR (NOW() >
↪sa.start_date AND sa.end_date IS NULL))
ORDER BY RAND() LIMIT 2);

Figure 8.8 shows the output for the query, running it twice to see the variety of results (although with only six sale items in the database, the differences are not that pronounced).

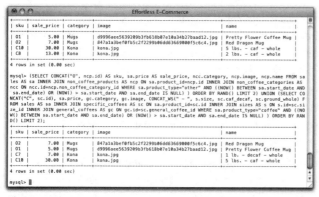

Figure 8.8

This **UNION** contains the same two **SELECT** queries as are used to find every sale item, with the addition of **ORDER BY RAND() LIMIT 2**. This query will be used on the home page, where only a couple of sale products can be advertised. For that reason, each **SELECT** query returns up to two randomly selected items: two random non-coffee products and two random coffee products. Because the **ORDER BY** and **LIMIT** clauses can confuse the **UNION** statement, both **SELECT** statements are individually wrapped in parentheses, making the general structure: **(SELECT...) UNION (SELECT...)**.

Creating Stored Procedures

This project will primarily use stored procedures, at least on the public side of the site. For the functionality being developed in this chapter, three stored procedures are required, each of which runs one of two **SELECT** queries. You can create stored procedures using most MySQL interfaces, although you must be connecting to the database as a MySQL user with **CREATE ROUTINES** permissions.

1. Create the **select_categories()** procedure:

```
DELIMITER $$
CREATE PROCEDURE select_categories (type VARCHAR(6))
BEGIN
    IF type = 'coffee' THEN
        SELECT * FROM general_coffees ORDER by category;
    ELSEIF type = 'other' THEN
```
(continues on next page)

tip

To sort the entire result set, use this structure: **(SELECT... UNION SELECT...) ORDER BY...**

note

A common problem with stored procedures is trying to create them as a MySQL user that lacks permission to create stored routines.

tip

Procedure names are case-insensitive and can be up to 64 characters long.

tip

I've included indentations in the procedures here for improved legibility, but you may need to remove the indents when pasting these commands into the **mysql** client.

note

Because this is a MySQL stored procedure, not PHP code, the syntax for the conditional itself and the equality condition (note the single equals sign, not a double) differs slightly.

note

Your stored procedure arguments should not have the same name as any column or table in the database, or as any MySQL keyword.

note

To improve legibility, I've not used the backticks around table and column names in the stored procedure queries, but you may prefer to use them.

```
    SELECT * FROM non_coffee_categories ORDER by category;
  END IF;
END$$
DELIMITER ;
```

The first line changes the delimiter from the default semicolon to something else so that the semicolons within the procedure don't cause problems. The procedure itself is named **select_categories()**, which is a clear indication of what the procedure does.

The procedure takes one argument, named **type**, and of MySQL data type **VARCHAR(6)**. The procedure executes one of two possible **SELECT** queries, depending upon the value of **type**. An **IF-ELSE IF** conditional accomplishes this.

The last line reverts the delimiter back to the default semicolon. If you're going to be creating multiple procedures at once, as in these steps, you only have to change the delimiter before the first definition and change it back after the last, but I'm changing it with each definition to avoid confusion and possible errors.

2. Create the **select_products()** procedure:

```
DELIMITER $$
CREATE PROCEDURE select_products(type VARCHAR(6), cat TINYINT)
BEGIN
  IF type = 'coffee' THEN
    SELECT  gc.description, gc.image, CONCAT("C", sc.id) AS sku,
    ➥CONCAT_WS(" - ", s.size, sc.caf_decaf, sc.ground_whole, sc.price)
    ➥AS name, sc.stock FROM specific_coffees AS sc INNER JOIN sizes
    ➥AS s ON s.id=sc.size_id INNER JOIN general_coffees AS gc ON
    ➥gc.id=sc.general_coffee_id WHERE general_coffee_id=cat AND
    ➥stock>0
ORDER by name ASC;
  ELSEIF type = 'other' THEN
    SELECT ncc.description AS g_description, ncc.image AS g_image,
    ➥CONCAT("O", ncp.id) AS sku, ncp.name, ncp.description,
    ➥ncp.image, ncp.price, ncp.stock FROM non_coffee_products AS
    ➥ncp INNER JOIN non_coffee_categories AS ncc ON
    ➥ncc.id=ncp.non_coffee_category_id
WHERE non_coffee_category_id=cat ORDER by date_created DESC;
  END IF;
END$$
DELIMITER ;
```

This procedure takes two arguments: a **type** and a **category**. If **type** equals *coffee*, then a **SELECT** runs to retrieve every specific coffee product. If **type** equals *other*, then a **SELECT** runs to retrieve every non-coffee product. These are the same queries already explained, just compressed (that is, the breaks have been removed).

3. Create the **select_sale_items()** procedure:

```
DELIMITER $$
CREATE PROCEDURE select_sale_items (get_all BOOLEAN)
BEGIN
IF get_all = 1 THEN
SELECT CONCAT("O", ncp.id) AS sku, sa.price AS sale_price, ncc.category,
➥ncp.image, ncp.name, ncp.price, ncp.stock, ncp.description FROM sales
➥AS sa INNER JOIN non_coffee_products AS ncp ON
➥sa.product_id=ncp.id INNER JOIN non_coffee_categories AS ncc ON
➥ncc.id=ncp.non_coffee_category_id WHERE sa.product_type="other"
➥AND ((NOW() BETWEEN sa.start_date AND sa.end_date) OR (NOW() >
➥sa.start_date AND sa.end_date IS NULL) )
UNION SELECT CONCAT("C", sc.id), sa.price, gc.category, gc.image,
CONCAT_WS(" - ", s.size, sc.caf_decaf, sc.ground_whole), sc.price,
sc.stock, gc.description FROM sales AS sa INNER JOIN specific_coffees
AS sc ON sa.product_id=sc.id INNER JOIN sizes AS s ON s.id=sc.size_id
INNER JOIN general_coffees AS gc ON gc.id=sc.general_coffee_id WHERE
sa.product_type="coffee" AND ((NOW() BETWEEN sa.start_date AND
sa.end_date) OR (NOW() > sa.start_date AND sa.end_date IS NULL) );
ELSE
(SELECT CONCAT("O", ncp.id) AS sku, sa.price AS sale_price,
➥ncc.category, ncp.image, ncp.name FROM sales AS sa INNER JOIN
➥non_coffee_products AS ncp ON sa.product_id=ncp.id INNER JOIN
➥non_coffee_categories AS ncc ON ncc.id=ncp.non_coffee_category_id
➥WHERE sa.product_type="other" AND ((NOW() BETWEEN sa.start_date
➥AND sa.end_date) OR (NOW() > sa.start_date AND sa.end_date
➥IS NULL) ) ORDER BY RAND() LIMIT 2) UNION (SELECT CONCAT("C",
➥sc.id), sa.price, gc.category, gc.image, CONCAT_WS(" - ", s.size,
➥sc.caf_decaf, sc.ground_whole) FROM sales AS sa INNER JOIN
➥specific_coffees AS sc ON sa.product_id=sc.id INNER JOIN sizes AS s
➥ON s.id=sc.size_id INNER JOIN general_coffees AS gc ON
➥gc.id=sc.general_coffee_id WHERE sa.product_type="coffee" AND
➥((NOW() BETWEEN sa.start_date AND sa.end_date) OR (NOW() >
➥sa.start_date AND sa.end_date IS NULL) ) ORDER BY RAND() LIMIT 2);
END IF;
END$$
DELIMITER ;
```

 tip

Queries in stored procedures, when written as I have in these examples, are just as safe as prepared statements, so you don't need to worry about using the arguments in the queries.

This stored procedure uses the two sale-related queries already explained. It takes only one argument: a Boolean value indicating whether or not every sale item should be returned (that is to say, is this the sales page or the home page?).

4. Test the stored procedures by calling them:

CALL select_categories('coffee');
CALL select_categories('other');
CALL select_products('coffee', 3);
CALL select_products('other', 3);
CALL select_sale_items(false);
CALL select_sale_items(true);

The results of these procedure calls should be exactly as those shown in the earlier figures (wherein the same queries are run directly).

SHOPPING BY CATEGORY

With the stored procedures and the overall HTML template in place (that is, two parts of an MVC approach have been written), the PHP script that lists the available categories becomes quite simple. All this file has to do is:

- Validate the received type

- Invoke the stored procedure

- Include the HTML template and specific view files

tip

See Chapter 7 for an explanation of **mod_rewrite** and how this *Coffee* site uses it.

As a reminder, the PHP script for listing the product categories is called **shop.php**, and it's linked in the header as either **/shop/coffee/** or **/shop/goodies/**. The Web server's **mod_rewrite** module will convert that URL (unbeknownst to the user) into either **shop.php?type=coffee** or **shop.php?type=goodies**. Let's write the PHP script first, then the view files it uses.

Creating the PHP Script

In keeping with the MVC approach, this PHP script should have little-to-no HTML (technically, none) and as little SQL as possible. The end result is a smattering of logic and the inclusion of several files.

1. Create a new PHP script in your text editor or IDE to be named **shop.php** and stored in the Web root directory.

2. Include the configuration file:

```php
<?php
require ('./includes/config.inc.php');
```

3. Validate the product type:

```php
if (isset($_GET['type']) && ($_GET['type'] == 'goodies')) {
    $page_title = 'Our Goodies, by Category';
    $sp_type = 'other';
    $type = 'goodies';
} else { // Default is coffee!
    $page_title = 'Our Coffee Products';
    $type = $sp_type = 'coffee';
}
```

The product type can be one of only two values: *goodies* or *coffee*. The default product type to display will always be coffee, so the first part of the conditional just checks if **$_GET['type']** is set and if it equals *goodies*. For each condition, the page's title is determined, and the **$type** and **$sp_type** variables are assigned appropriate values. Two variables are required here because the Web site uses the term *goodies,* but the database uses the term *other.* If the same term were used in both cases, you could use just one variable. The **$sp_type** variable represents what the stored procedure expects.

The assignation of *coffee* to both **$sp_type** and **$type** in one line is possible as the assignment will occur from right to left. First, **$sp_type** is assigned the value *coffee,* then **$type** is assigned the value of **$sp_type**.

4. Include the header file and the database connection:

```php
include ('./includes/header.html');
require (MYSQL);
```

5. Call the stored procedure:

```php
$r = mysqli_query($dbc, "CALL select_categories('$sp_type')");
```

This one line is all you need to invoke the stored procedure for either type. Because the **$sp_type** value will be a string, it must be quoted when you pass it to the stored procedure. The root SQL command is the same that would be run in the **mysql** client or phpMyAdmin:

CALL select_categories('coffee')

or

CALL select_categories('other')

 note

I use "goodies" in the viewable site instead of "other" because it's more meaningful to users and search engines (in theory).

note

The MySQL user that the PHP script is connecting as must have **EXECUTE** permissions in order to call a stored procedure.

For debugging purposes, you could include this line next, although you wouldn't want to use it on a live site:

if (!$r) echo mysqli_error($dbc);

This line will print any MySQL errors that occurred, if **$r** doesn't have a positive value.

6. If records were returned, include the view file:

if (mysqli_num_rows($r) >= 1) {
    include ('./views/list_categories.html');

You can use the **mysqli_num_rows()** function to confirm that results were returned by this stored procedure, as if the script had executed a standard **SELECT** query. If some rows were returned, the **list_categories.html** file, found within the **views** directory, will be included. That file will handle the actual retrieval and display of the returned rows.

7. If no records were returned, include the error view:

} else { // Include the error page:
    include ('./views/error.html');
}

The **error.html** view file will be included any time a query did not return sufficient results. You could also, at this point, write an error message to a log or send it to an email address.

8. Complete the PHP page:

include ('./includes/footer.html');
?>

9. Save the file.

Creating the View Files

The **shop.php** script uses two view files: **list_categories.html** and **error.html**. Remember that these view files just represent a snippet of HTML: a subset of the entire page, representing a small portion of what the user sees. Each view file uses a **.html** extension to indicate its basic nature, and should have a bare minimum of PHP code and logic.

Looking at the **error.html** file, all it needs to do is display a message within the context of the HTML template. For the *Coffee* template, the context is a box generated by several **<DIV>** tags.

views/error.html

```
1    <!-- box begin -->
2      <div class="box alt">
3        <div class="left-top-corner">
4        <div class="right-top-corner">
5        <div class="border-top"></div>
6      </div>
7      </div>
8      <div class="border-left">
9        <div class="border-right">
10       <div class="inner">
11         <h2>Error!</h2>
12         Unfortunately a system error has occurred. Please use the
              ➥links at the top of the page to continue shopping. We
              ➥apologize for the inconvenience.
13       </div>
14       </div>
15     </div>
16     <div class="left-bot-corner">
17       <div class="right-bot-corner">
18       <div class="border-bot"></div>
19       </div>
20       </div>
21     </div>
22     <!-- box end -->
```

Unfortunately, the template is a bit **<DIV>**-happy; yet another reason that putting this in its own file is beneficial. Should the stored procedure not return any results, the user will see the message shown in **Figure 8.9**. This would occur only if the database wasn't available, if it wasn't populated, or if the connecting MySQL user does not have **EXECUTE** permissions (the right to run a stored procedure).

Figure 8.9

The **list_categories.html** file is a bit more complicated, but only slightly (view files shouldn't be truly complex). It uses a loop to run through the query results, and writes them within the proper context.

1. Create a new HTML file in your text editor or IDE to be named **list_categories.html** and stored in the **views** folder.

2. Begin with the contextual HTML:

```
<!-- box begin -->
<div class="box alt"><div class="left-top-corner"><div class=
"right-top-corner"><div class="border-top"></div></div></div>
<div class="border-left"><div class="border-right"><div class=
"inner">
<ul class="items-list">
```

For the *Coffee* template that I'm using, everything goes within a series of **<DIV>** tags that create a box. These lines start that box and conclude by starting an unordered list.

3. Begin a **while** loop:

```
<?php while ($row = mysqli_fetch_array($r, MYSQLI_ASSOC)) {
```

As I wrote in Chapter 7, the MVC approach requires that assumptions are made, such as the assumption here that there are records to be fetched. As an extra precaution, you could add a conditional before the loop:

if ($r) {...

That being said, this **while** loop is as complicated as the view gets.

4. Print each item:

```
echo '<li><h3>' . $row['category'] . ' </h3>
<p><img alt="' . $row['category'] . '" src="/products/' . $row['image'] . '"
/>' . $row['description'] . '<br />
<a href="/browse/' . $type . '/' . urlencode($row['category']) . '/' .
$row['id'] . '" class="h4">View All ' . $row['category'] . ' Products
</a></p>
</li>';
```

The goal is to generate HTML that looks like (as a single example):

```
<li><h3>Gift Baskets</h3>
    <p><img alt="Gift Baskets" src="/products/imagename.ext" />
    Actual Description<br />
    <a href="/browse/goodies/Gift+Baskets/2" class="h4">View All
    Gift Baskets Products</a></p>
</li>
```

note

I'm compressing some of the HTML to save space in the book and because you're probably not typing in all this HTML from scratch anyway.

tip

There's a lot of PHP and HTML interspersed, so be careful of the syntax.

For the image's **src** and the link's **href** attributes, absolute paths are used (that is, each begins with a slash). This is necessary because the current page might be **www.example.com/shop/goodies/,** in which case the references to files in the **products** folder must start at the root directory.

The link to view all the products in the category is to **/browse/*type*/ *category*/*ID*,** where *type* comes from **shop.php** (and, therefore, the URL), and *category* and *ID* come from the returned database record. The **browse.php** page will use these values.

5. Complete the **while** loop and the PHP:

} ?>

6. Complete the HTML:

</ul>
</div></div></div><div class="left-bot-corner"><div class=
⇀"right-bot-corner"><div class="border-bot"></div></div></div>
⇀</div>
<!-- box end -->

7. Save the file and test it in your Web browser (**Figures 8.10** and **8.11**).

You can test this by clicking either shopping link—*coffee* or *goodies,* although clicking the links displayed on the **shop.php** page won't work, because **browse.php** has not yet been written.

Figure 8.10

Figure 8.11

LISTING PRODUCTS

Now that customers can shop by type—coffee and goodies—they need to be able to browse through the actual products they can purchase, within each type. The page for doing that, **browse.php**, is written in a very similar manner to **shop.php**, although it uses a different view file to display each product type.

Creating the PHP Script

The primary difference between **shop.php** and **browse.php** is that the latter has three values to validate—type, category, and ID—instead of just one. Still, even with lots of spacing and comments, the result is less than 70 lines long.

1. Create a new PHP script in your text editor or IDE to be named **browse.php** and stored in the Web root directory.

2. Include the configuration file:

```php
<?php
require ('./includes/config.inc.php');
```

3. Start validating the required values:

```php
$type = $sp_type = $sp_cat = $category = false;
if (isset($_GET['type'], $_GET['category'], $_GET['id']) &&
    filter_var($_GET['id'], FILTER_VALIDATE_INT, array('min_range' => 1)))
{
    $category = $_GET['category'];
    $sp_cat = $_GET['id'];
```

To start the validation process, four necessary variables are initially set to **false**, requiring the script to prove that everything's okay. Next, the condition checks for the presence of three variables in the URL—**type**, **category**, and **id**—and that the ID value is an integer greater than 1.

If all of these conditions are true, then two variables are assigned values from the URL. The **category** value will be used as a header in the HTML page. The **$sp_cat** variable will be used in the stored procedure. You really don't need to worry about these variables having inappropriate values here. The ID will have already been validated using **filter_var()** and the **category** value has to match the rewrite rule in the **.htaccess** file (see Chapter 7).

4. Validate the product type:

```php
if ($_GET['type'] == 'goodies') {
    $sp_type = 'other';
```

```
      $type = 'goodies';
   } elseif ($_GET['type'] == 'coffee') {
      $type = $sp_type = 'coffee';
   }
```

Similar to the **shop.php** script, the validation routine creates **$sp_type** and **$type** variables, used in the stored procedure and the view file, respectively. Unlike **shop.php**, this script does not assume a default type: If an invalid type is somehow used, the customer will see an error page (because, frankly, they're probably the ones that deliberately did something to cause the problem).

5. If there is a problem, display the error page:

```
   if (!$type || !$sp_type || !$sp_cat || !$category) {
      $page_title = 'Error!';
      include ('./includes/header.html');
      include ('./views/error.html');
      include ('./includes/footer.html');
      exit();
   }
```

If any of the four variables still has a **false** value, an error page should be displayed and the script terminated.

6. Create a page title and include the header file:

```
   $page_title = ucfirst($type) . ' to Buy::' . $category;
   include ('./includes/header.html');
```

The page title will be something like *Coffee to Buy::Kona* or *Goodies to Buy::Mugs*. It will appear at the top of the browser window.

7. Include the database connection and execute the stored procedure:

```
   require (MYSQL);
   $r = mysqli_query($dbc, "CALL select_products('$sp_type', $sp_cat)");
```

The stored procedure is **select_products()**, which takes two arguments: the product type and a category value. The former is quoted, because it's a string; the latter is an unquoted integer.

8. If records were returned, include the view file:

```
   if (mysqli_num_rows($r) >= 1) {
      if ($type == 'goodies') {
         include ('./views/list_products.html');
      } elseif ($type == 'coffee') {
         include ('./views/list_coffees.html');
```

 tip

The double pipe characters (II) are an alternative way of saying "or" in a PHP conditional.

```
    }
```

As long as some rows were returned, the view file (which will display the results) will be included. There are two different view files: one for non-coffee products and one for coffee products.

9. If no records were returned, include the "no products" view:

```
} else {
    include ('./views/noproducts.html');
}
```

This will be a new view file, which neither indicates an error nor attempts to list any products, because there aren't any.

10. Complete the PHP page:

```
include ('./includes/footer.html');
?>
```

11. Save the file.

Creating the View Files

The **browse.php** script uses three new files: **list_products.html**, **list_coffees.html**, and **noproducts.html**. There are two different products-listing files because the customer will buy a category of coffee in a specific format (based upon the size, caffeine, and bean type, see Figure 8.4) but will purchase other products individually (Figure 8.6). For each product type, the page should display general information about the category as a whole; hence, each view uses a trick to show that information only once.

CREATING THE PRODUCTS LIST

This view file should first show the general category information, then each specific product. It will create two HTML boxes (from the original template) to do so (again, see Figure 8.6).

1. Create a new HTML file in your text editor or IDE to be named **list_products.html** and stored in the **views** folder.

2. Begin by creating a flag variable:

```
<?php
$header = false;
```

This variable will be used to know whether or not the initial information has been printed (so that it's only printed once). By default, the value is **false**.

3. Create the **while** loop and check the **$header** value:

```
while ($row = mysqli_fetch_array($r, MYSQLI_ASSOC)) {
    if (!$header) { ?>
```

The loop will be executed once for each returned row. If you look at the query results shown in Figure 8.5, you'll see that the general category information is included in each returned row. This information will be used to create the header only for the first record fetched. To test for that situation, a conditional sees if **$header** is still **false**. In that case, a big block of HTML and PHP will be executed. Because that block is mostly HTML, it's easier to just leave the PHP code as the result of this condition, which is perfectly valid.

4. Add the header box:

```
<!-- box begin -->
<div class="box alt"><div class="left-top-corner"><div class=
"right-top-corner"><div class="border-top"></div></div></div>
<div class="border-left"><div class="border-right">
<div class="inner">
   <h2><?php echo $category; ?></h2>
   <div class="img-box">
   <p><img alt="<?php echo $category; ?>" src="/products/<?php
   echo $row['g_image']; ?>" /><?php echo $row['g_description'];
   ?></p>
   </div>
   </div></div><div class="left-bot-corner"><div class=
   "right-bot-corner"><div class="border-bot"></div></div></div>
   </div>
<!-- box end --><p> <br clear="all" /></p>
```

This box will be at the top of the page, displaying the category's name, image, and description. The **$category** variable, used as a caption, is defined in the **browse.php** page; the other two values come from the returned row.

5. Begin the next box and complete the **$header** if:

```
<!-- box begin -->
<div class="box"><div class="left-top-corner"><div class=
"right-top-corner"><div class="border-top"></div></div></div>
<div class="border-left"><div class="border-right"><div class=
"inner">
<?php
    $header = true;
} // End of $header IF.
```

tip

Instead of fetching the general category information with each specific product, you could run two queries: one for the general category info and another for all the products in that category.

As already said, the HTML template, while stylish, is over-stuffed with **<DIV>** tags. You may prefer to use the download-able code.

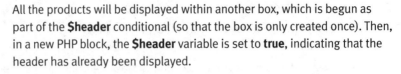

All the products will be displayed within another box, which is begun as part of the **$header** conditional (so that the box is only created once). Then, in a new PHP block, the **$header** variable is set to **true**, indicating that the header has already been displayed.

6. Print each item:

```
echo '<h3>' . $row['name'] . '</h3>
<div class="img-box">
    <p><img alt="' . $row['name'] . '" src="/products/' . $row['image']
    . '" />' . $row['description'] . '<br />
    <strong>Price:</strong> $' . $row['price'] . '<br />
    <strong>Availability:</strong> ' . $row['stock'] . '</p>
    <p><a href="/cart.php?sku=' . $row['sku'] . '&action=add"
    class="button">Add to Cart</a></p></div>';
```

The goal is to generate HTML that looks like (as a single example):

```
<h3>Red Dragon Mug</h3>
<div class="img-box">
    <p><img alt="Red Dragon Mug" src="/products/imagename.ext" />
    Actual Description<br />
    <strong>Price:</strong> $4.50<br /> <strong>Availability:</strong>
    67</p>
    <p><a href="/cart.php?sku=023&action=add" class="button">
    Add to Cart</a></p></div>
```

As with **list_categories.html**, the image's **src** and the link's **href** attributes use absolute paths. For now, the quantity in stock is just displayed; you'll improve on this later. The link is a button to add the item to the cart. It passes the SKU and an *action* value to the **cart.php** page, to be written in the next chapter.

7. Complete the **while** loop and the PHP:

```
} ?>
```

8. Complete the HTML:

```
<p> <br clear="all" /></p>
    </div></div><div class="left-bot-corner"><div class=
    "right-bot-corner"><div class="border-bot"></div></div></div>
    </div>
<!-- box end -->
```

9. Save the file and test it in your Web browser.

You can test this view by clicking any category listed on the "goodies" shopping page (again, Figure 8.6 is a representative image of this page).

Make your Add to Cart buttons big and obvious!

CREATING THE COFFEES LIST

The **list_coffees.html** view should display the general coffee name, image, and description, then provide a drop-down menu through which the user can select which coffee to order (see Figure 8.4). Unlike **list_products.html**, this view creates one HTML box.

1. Create a new HTML file in your text editor or IDE to be named **list_coffees.html** and stored in the **views** folder.

2. Begin by creating a flag variable:

```php
<?php
$header = false;
```

This variable will be used the same way here as in **list_products.html**.

3. Create the **while** loop and check the **$header** value:

```php
while ($row = mysqli_fetch_array($r, MYSQLI_ASSOC)) {
    if (!$header) { ?>
```

This is still the same as in **list_products.html**.

4. Create the start of the box and the general information:

```html
<!-- box begin -->
<div class="box alt"><div class="left-top-corner"><div class=
"right-top-corner"><div class="border-top"></div></div></div>
<div class="border-left"><div class="border-right"><div
class="inner">
<h2><?php echo $category; ?></h2>
    <div class="img-box">
    <p><img alt="<?php echo $category; ?>" src="/products/<?php
echo $row['image']; ?>" /><?php echo $row['description']; ?></p>
```

The header for the coffees page includes the start of the HTML box, the coffee category as a caption (this comes from **browse.php**), and the general coffee's image and description from the first returned row.

5. Begin the form and complete the header:

```html
<p><small>All listed products are currently available.</small>
<form action="/cart.php" method="get"><input type="hidden"
name="action" value="add" /><select name="sku">
<?php // The header has now been shown:
    $header = true;
} // End of $header IF.
```

The form uses the GET method and will be submitted to **cart.php**. The form contains a hidden input, named **action**, with a value of *add*.

In Chapter 9, "Building a Shopping Cart," you'll create that script. Next, a **<SELECT>** menu, named *sku*, is begun.

6. Print each item:

echo "<option value=\"{$row['sku']}\">{$row['name']}</option>\n";

The goal here is to generate an **<OPTION>** tag, whose value is the SKU and whose label is the concatenated name (**Figure 8.12**).

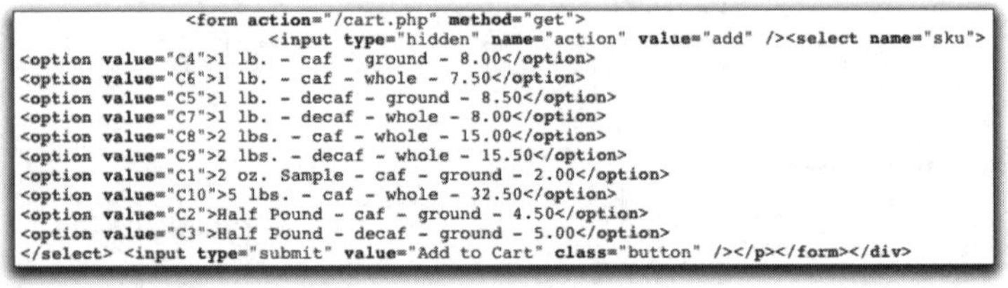

```
                    <form action="/cart.php" method="get">
                        <input type="hidden" name="action" value="add" /><select name="sku">
<option value="C4">1 lb. - caf - ground - 8.00</option>
<option value="C6">1 lb. - caf - whole - 7.50</option>
<option value="C5">1 lb. - decaf - ground - 8.50</option>
<option value="C7">1 lb. - decaf - whole - 8.00</option>
<option value="C8">2 lbs. - caf - whole - 15.00</option>
<option value="C9">2 lbs. - decaf - whole - 15.50</option>
<option value="C1">2 oz. Sample - caf - ground - 2.00</option>
<option value="C10">5 lbs. - caf - whole - 32.50</option>
<option value="C2">Half Pound - caf - ground - 4.50</option>
<option value="C3">Half Pound - decaf - ground - 5.00</option>
</select> <input type="submit" value="Add to Cart" class="button" /></p></form></div>
```

Figure 8.12

7. Complete the **while** loop and the PHP block:

} ?>

8. Complete the HTML:

</select> <input type="submit" value="Add to Cart" class="button" />
⮑</p></form></div></div></div></div><div class="left-bot-corner">
⮑<div class="right-bot-corner"><div class="border-bot"></div>
⮑</div></div>
</div><!-- box end -->

The rest of the HTML closes the **<SELECT>** tag and creates the Add to Cart button.

9. Save the file and test it in your Web browser.

You can test this by clicking any category listed on the "coffee" shopping page (again, Figure 8.4 is a representative image of this page).

Creating the "No Products" View

The **noproducts.html** view is similar to **error.html**—it primarily displays a static message, but it includes the name of the category involved (**Figure 8.13**), generated in **browse.php**. Here are that file's contents:

tip

It's really best not to have, except perhaps for search results, pages in your site that don't show products available to be purchased.

Gift Baskets

Unfortunately there are no products to list in this category. Please use the links at the top of the page to continue shopping. We apologize for the inconvenience.

Figure 8.13

views/noproducts.html

```
1    <!-- box begin -->
2    <div class="box alt">
3       <div class="left-top-corner">
4       <div class="right-top-corner">
5       <div class="border-top"></div>
6       </div>
7       </div>
8       <div class="border-left">
9       <div class="border-right">
10      <div class="inner">
11         <h2><?php echo $category; ?></h2>
12         Unfortunately there are no products to list in this category. Please
           use the links at the top of the page to continue shopping. We
           apologize for the inconvenience.
13      </div>
14      </div>
15      </div>
16      <div class="left-bot-corner">
17         <div class="right-bot-corner">
18            <div class="border-bot"></div>
19         </div>
20      </div>
21   </div>
22   <!-- box end -->
```

INDICATING AVAILABILITY

For the list of coffee products, the stored procedure only retrieves those currently in stock. For the other products, though, the stock is currently represented as the quantity on hand (see Figure 8.6), which you probably don't want to show the customer. Instead, let's create a function that will display the availability in a friendlier and purchase-encouraging, manner. The function will be defined in a new script named **product_functions.inc.php**.

1. Create a new PHP script in your text editor or IDE to be named
product_functions.inc.php and stored in the **includes** directory.

```
<?php
```

2. Begin defining the function:

function get_stock_status($stock) {

The function takes one argument, assigned to the variable **$stock**.

3. Return different messages based upon the value of **$stock**:

if ($stock > 5) {
   return 'In Stock';
} elseif ($stock >= 1) {
   return 'Low Stock';
} else {
   return 'Currently Out of Stock';
}

In reality, the amount of concern to be conveyed regarding an item's quantity in stock actually depends upon how quickly the item sells. Having 4 of an item that gets purchased a couple of times a year isn't really an issue, whereas having 10 of a product that averages 15 purchases a day will be problematic. Still, for representative purposes, this function returns a different message based upon the value of **$stock**.

4. Complete the function:

} // End of get_stock_status() function.

5. Save the file.

As with all PHP scripts included by other pages, this one does not use a closing PHP tag.

To use this function, you'll need to include the PHP file in the **list_products.html** script:

include ('./includes/product_functions.inc.php');

Note that the reference to the file is relative to the **browse.php**—the PHP script that includes **list_products.html**—because it's **browse.php** that will actually be executing this code.

Next, also in **list_products.html**, change the availability indication to:

<strong>Availability:</strong> ' . get_stock_status($row['stock']) ...

The complete echo statement should now be:

echo '<h3>' . $row['name'] . '</h3>
<div class="img-box">
   <p><img alt="' . $row['name'] . '" src="/products/' . $row['image']
  ⇥**. '" />' . $row['description'] . '
**
   **<strong>Price:</strong> $' . $row['price'] . '
**

tip

In the downloadable code, you'll see this modified view file, named **list_products2.html**, to avoid confusion.

```
<strong>Availability:</strong> ' . get_stock_status($row['stock']) . '
➥</p>
<p><a href="/cart.php?sku=' . $row['sku'] . '&action=add"
class="button">Add to Cart</a></p></div>';
```

And that's it! You can now test this in your browser to see how it looks
(**Figure 8.14**).

Figure 8.14

SHOWING SALE PRICES

Another problem with the products listings in their current formats is that they
don't reflect any applicable sale prices. This is an important issue because the
sale price for a product should appear everywhere the product is listed, not
just on the actual sales page (**Figures 8.15** and **8.16**).

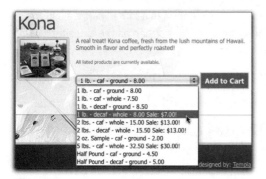

Figure 8.15

Figure 8.16

In order to make this change, the two queries in the stored procedure that
fetches every product will need to be altered so that the sale price is also
retrieved. Second, the **list_coffees.html** and **list_products.html** view files
will need some additional logic to indicate the sale price, when one exists.

Updating the Stored Procedure

The original stored procedure, as complex as its queries were, did not check for any sale prices. To do that, another **JOIN** must be added to each query to check the **sales** table. However, most items normally won't be on sale, so instead of an *inner join*, which only returns matches (records found in both joined tables), the queries will have to use an *outer join*. By adding an outer join, the query will continue to select every product currently being selected but also add in any matching rows in the **sales** table. In other words, an *inner join* is *exclusive*, in that it does not select any records without a corresponding match, whereas an *outer join* is *inclusive*: it also selects records that do match.

The first new query for the **select_products()** procedure is:

tip

This query is a good example how a simple thought—allowing items to be for sale without a clear ending date—can complicate queries and logic.

```
SELECT gc.description, gc.image, CONCAT("C", sc.id) AS sku,
CONCAT_WS(" - ", s.size, sc.caf_decaf, sc.ground_whole, sc.price) AS name,
sc.stock, sc.price, sales.price AS sale_price
FROM specific_coffees AS sc INNER JOIN sizes AS s ON s.id=sc.size_id
INNER JOIN general_coffees AS gc ON gc.id=sc.general_coffee_id
LEFT OUTER JOIN sales ON (sales.product_id=sc.id
AND sales.product_type='coffee' AND
((NOW() BETWEEN sales.start_date AND sales.end_date)
OR (NOW() > sales.start_date AND sales.end_date IS NULL)) )
WHERE general_coffee_id=<some_category_id> AND stock>0
ORDER by name;
```

This query selects specific coffee products. The first alteration (highlighted in the code) is the selection of the original price and the sale price. You'll see why the price needs to be selected again—even though it already appears in the item's name—shortly. Next, the left outer join is added on the **sales** table. The condition for the **JOIN** has three parts to it:

1. The **sales.product_id** must equal the product's ID value.

2. The **sales.product_type** value must be *coffee*.

3. The dates that the product is on sale must start before right now and end after right now, or, the sale's date must start before right now and be open-ended.

Figure 8.17 shows the results of running this query, using a category ID of 3 and without selecting the description or image (to save space). The important thing to note is that the **sale_price** column will have a **NULL** value for those products not currently on sale.

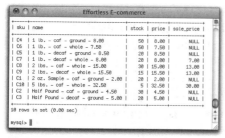

Figure 8.17

The second new query for the **select_products()** procedure is:

**SELECT ncc.description AS g_description, ncc.image AS g_image,
CONCAT("O", ncp.id) AS sku, ncp.name, ncp.description, ncp.image,
ncp.price, ncp.stock, sales.price AS sale_price
FROM non_coffee_products AS ncp INNER JOIN non_coffee_categories
➥AS ncc
ON ncc.id=ncp.non_coffee_category_id
LEFT OUTER JOIN sales ON (sales.product_id=ncp.id
AND sales.product_type='other' AND
((NOW() BETWEEN sales.start_date AND sales.end_date) OR (NOW() >
➥sales.start_date AND sales.end_date IS NULL)))
WHERE non_coffee_category_id=<some_category_id> ORDER by
➥date_created DESC;**

The update to the query that selects every non-coffee product has the same additional outer join, with similar criteria except that the product type should be *other*. And the sale price is selected now as well.

There are a few ways you can go about updating the stored procedure: You could use an **ALTER ROUTINE** syntax; you could create the procedure using a new name; or you could just drop the routine and redefine it:

**DROP PROCEDURE select_products;
DELIMITER $$
CREATE PROCEDURE select_products(type VARCHAR(6), cat TINYINT)
BEGIN
IF type = 'coffee' THEN
SELECT gc.description, gc.image, CONCAT("C", sc.id) AS sku,
CONCAT_WS(" - ", s.size, sc.caf_decaf, sc.ground_whole, sc.price) AS name,
sc.stock, sc.price, sales.price AS sale_price
FROM specific_coffees AS sc INNER JOIN sizes AS s ON s.id=sc.size_id
INNER JOIN general_coffees AS gc ON gc.id=sc.general_coffee_id
LEFT OUTER JOIN sales ON (sales.product_id=sc.id
AND sales.product_type='coffee' AND**   *(continues on next page)*

```
((NOW() BETWEEN sales.start_date AND sales.end_date)
OR (NOW() > sales.start_date AND sales.end_date IS NULL)) )
WHERE general_coffee_id=cat AND stock>o
ORDER by name;
ELSEIF type = 'other' THEN
SELECT ncc.description AS g_description, ncc.image AS g_image,
CONCAT("O", ncp.id) AS sku, ncp.name, ncp.description, ncp.image,
ncp.price, ncp.stock, sales.price AS sale_price
FROM non_coffee_products AS ncp INNER JOIN non_coffee_categories
↩AS ncc
ON ncc.id=ncp.non_coffee_category_id
LEFT OUTER JOIN sales ON (sales.product_id=ncp.id
AND sales.product_type='other' AND
((NOW() BETWEEN sales.start_date AND sales.end_date) OR (NOW() >
↩sales.start_date AND sales.end_date IS NULL)) )
WHERE non_coffee_category_id=cat ORDER by date_created DESC;
END IF;
END$$
DELIMITER ;
```

You should update the procedure, using any interface to the database, before moving forward.

Updating product_functions.inc.php

The logic for displaying the price of a product is a bit complex to write into the view file, so it'll go into a new function, also defined in **product_functions.inc.php**.

1. Open **product_functions.inc.php** in your text editor or IDE.

2. After the **get_stock_status()** definition, begin a new function:

   function get_price($type, $regular, $sales) {

   This function takes three arguments: the type of product, its regular price, and its sale price.

3. Check if the product's type equals *coffee*:

   if ($type == 'coffee') {

   As it stands, the list of coffee products is displayed as a drop-down menu (see Figure 8.15). In that context, there's a limit as to how much additional information can be displayed, compared to how the non-coffee products are displayed. For this reason, the sale price of each product type is treated a bit differently.

4. Return the sale price, if appropriate:

if ((0 < $sales) && ($sales < $regular)) {
    return ' Sale: $' . $sales . '!';
}

The value of **$sales** will be **NULL** if no sale price exists (see Figure 8.17), so this conditional confirms that the value is greater than zero but not greater than the regular price (on account of some sort of administrative error). If so, then the word *Sale*, followed by a colon and the sale price is returned (for coffee products).

5. Check if the type equals *goodies*:

} elseif ($type == 'goodies') {

For the non-coffee products, the sale price can be displayed with more information and flare.

6. Return the appropriate price:

if ((0 < $sales) && ($sales < $regular)) {
    return "Sale Price: \$$sales! (normally
↪**\$$regular)
";**
} else {
    return 'Price: $' . $regular . '<br />';
}

If the sale price is greater than zero but less than the regular price, the sale price will be returned with the regular price in parentheses (so the customer can see the extra value, Figure 8.16). Otherwise, just the regular price is returned.

7. Complete the **if-elseif** conditional and the function definition:

    }
} // End of get_price() function.

8. Save the file.

Updating list_products.html

For **list_products.html** to take advantage of the new function, you just need to replace the reference to **$row['price']** with:

get_sale_price($type, $row['price'], $row['sale_price'])

Within a larger context, **list_products.html** now has:

```
echo '<h3>' . $row['name'] . '</h3>
<div class="img-box">
    <p><img alt="' . $row['name'] . '" src="/products/' . $row['image']
    ➥. '" />' . $row['description'] . '<br />' .
    get_sale_price($type, $row['price'], $row['sale_price']) .
    '<strong>Availability:</strong> ' . get_stock_status($row['stock']) . '
    ➥</p>
    <p><a href="/cart.php?sku=' . $row['sku'] . '&action=add"
    ➥class="button">Add to Cart</a></p></div>';
```

Now you can test this additional code by viewing in your Web browser a list of goodies available in one category (as in Figure 8.16).

Updating list_coffees.html

For **list_coffees.html** to take advantage of the new function, you just need to replace this line:

```
echo "<option value=\"{$row['sku']}\">{$row['name']}</option>\n";
```

with:

```
echo '<option value="' . $row['sku'] . '">' . $row['name'] .
➥get_sale_price($type, $row['price'], $row['sale_price']) . '</option>';
```

You'll notice that I purposefully switched from using double to single quotation marks here. When you use which quotation marks is a personal preference, but because a function call cannot be integrated into double quotation marks anyway, I thought a switch to single quotation marks would be logical.

You can now test this additional code by viewing in your Web browser a specific coffee (as in Figure 8.15).

HIGHLIGHTING SALES

The preceding few pages performed the important task of reflecting sale prices on the regular products listing pages, but sale items will appear in two other places:

- On the home page (**Figure 8.18**).

- On a dedicated sales page (**Figure 8.19**).

Figure 8.18

Figure 8.19

You have already completed the stored procedure for performing both tasks, now you just need to write the PHP scripts and view files.

Creating the Home Page

Because the home page doesn't have to perform any of the validation that the shop and browse scripts perform, it ends up being the simplest of the PHP scripts in this chapter. It uses one view file, which represents all the page's content.

CREATING THE PHP SCRIPT

The **index.php** script, placed in the Web root directory, is simple enough that there's no need to walk through it in detail. It includes the three base files: configuration, header, and footer. To retrieve some sale items, it invokes the **select_sale_items()** procedure, passing it a value of **false** to indicate that not every item should be retrieved. And it includes the **home.html** view.

index.php

```
1   <?php
2   require ('./includes/config.inc.php');
3   $page_title = 'Coffee - Wouldn\'t You Love a Cup Right Now?';
4   include ('./includes/header.html');
5   require (MYSQL);
6   $r = mysqli_query ($dbc, "CALL select_sale_items(false)");
7   include('./views/home.html');
8   include ('./includes/footer.html');
9   ?>
```

CREATING THE VIEW FILE

The view file for the home page should create all the content the customer sees, including an introduction to the site and a few of the sale items. With the theory that there may or may not be any current sale items, this view file will actually confirm that there are sales records to return.

1. Create a new HTML script in your text editor or IDE to be named **home.html** and stored in the **views** directory.

2. Start with the initial HTML for creating a box:

```
<!-- box begin -->
<div class="box alt"><div class="left-top-corner"><div class=
"right-top-corner"><div class="border-top"></div></div></div>
<div class="border-left"><div class="border-right"><div
class="inner"><div class="wrapper">
```

3. Check for any sales:

```
<?php
if (mysqli_num_rows($r) >= 1) {
    echo '<dl class="special fright">
        <dt><a href="/shop/sales/">Sale Items</a></dt>';
```

If the stored procedure called in **index.php** returns some rows, then a definition list is begun (that's how the template handles the inset products) and a header is printed. The header is linked to **/shop/sales/**, which will be turned into **sales.php**, thanks to **mod_rewrite** (see Chapter 7).

4. Print each sale item:

```
while ($row = mysqli_fetch_array($r, MYSQLI_ASSOC)) {
    echo '<dd><a href="/shop/sales/#' . $row['sku'] . '" title="View This
    Product"><img alt="" src="/products/' . $row['image'] . '" />
    <span>' . $row['sale_price'] . '</span></a></dd>';
}
```

Each sale item on the home page is displayed within **<DD>** tags. The HTML is just an image and a **<SPAN>** (for the price), plus a link to view the sale item in more detail and where the customer can purchase it. The link is to **/show/sales/#*SKU***, where *#SKU* will be an anchored location on the sales page.

tip

The anchor on the sales page works without changing the **mod_rewrite** definition.

5. Complete the sales section of the page:

```
    echo '</dl>';
} // End of mysqli_num_rows() IF.
?>
```

6. Complete the rest of the page's content:

```
<h2>Welcome to Our Online Coffee House!</h2>
<p>We're so glad you made it. Have a seat. Let me get you a fresh, hot
➥cup o' Joe. Cream and sugar? There you go.</p>
<p>Please use the links at the top to browse through our catalog. If
➥you've been here before, you can find things you bookmarked by
➥clicking on your Wish List and Cart links. </p>
</div></div></div></div><div class="left-bot-corner"><div class=
➥"right-bot-corner"><div class="border-bot"></div></div></div>
</div>
<!-- box end -->
<!-- box begin -->
<div class="box"><div class="left-top-corner"><div class=
➥"right-top-corner"><div class="border-top"></div></div></div>
➥<div class="border-left"><div class="border-right"><div
➥class="inner">
<h3>About Clever Coffee, Inc.</h3>
<p>Clever Coffee, Inc. has been selling coffee online since 1923.
➥For years, Clever Coffee, Inc. failed to make a profit, due to the lack of
➥computers and the Internet. Yadda, yadda, yadda.</p>
<p>It's safe to shop here, promise!</p>
</div></div></div><div class="left-bot-corner"><div class=
➥"right-bot-corner"><div class="border-bot"></div></div></div>
➥</div>
<!-- box end -->
```

The rest of the page's content is mostly bragging about the site and encouraging the customer to shop there.

7. Save the file and test the home page in your Web browser (see Figure 8.18).

Creating the Sales Page

The final Web page you'll develop in this chapter displays every sale item on a single page (see Figure 8.19). Let's quickly look at this page's PHP script and corresponding view file.

CREATING THE PHP SCRIPT

As with the **index.php** script, **sales.php** is very simple: there's no validation, just the invocation of a stored procedure. In fact, this is the same stored procedure used on the home page, this time passing along a value of **true,** so that every sale item is fetched from the database.

sales.php

```
1   <?php
2   require ('./includes/config.inc.php');
3   $page_title = 'Sale Items';
4   include ('./includes/header.html');
5   require (MYSQL);
6   $r = mysqli_query ($dbc, 'CALL select_sale_items(true)');
7   if (mysqli_num_rows($r) > o) {
8       include ('./views/list_sales.html');
9   } else {
10      include ('./views/noproducts.html');
11  }
12  include ('./includes/footer.html');
13  ?>
```

One difference here is that this script checks that some records are returned by the stored procedure. If so, the **list_sales.html** view is included. If not, the previously covered **noproducts.html** view is included.

CREATING THE VIEW FILE

The view file for the sales page just lists each product on sale. For all products, the output will be exactly like that on the pages that list non-coffee products (see Figure 8.19). This means a slightly different format for coffee products.

1. Create a new HTML script in your text editor or IDE to be named **list_sales.html** and stored in the **views** directory.

2. Include the **product_functions.inc.php** script:

```
<?php include ('./includes/product_functions.inc.php'); ?>
```

This view will use both functions defined in this file.

3. Start the initial HTML box:

```
<!-- box begin -->
<div class="box alt"><div class="left-top-corner"><div class=
"right-top-corner"><div class="border-top"></div></div></div>
<div class="border-left"><div class="border-right">
<div class="inner">
  <h2>Current Sale Items</h2>
```

4. Loop through each returned item:

```php
<?php
while ($row = mysqli_fetch_array($r, MYSQLI_ASSOC)) {
```

5. Print each item:

```php
echo '<h3 id="' . $row['sku'] . '">' . $row['category'] . '::' . $row['name']
.'</h3>
<div class="img-box">
    <p><img alt="' . $row['name'] . '" src="/products/' . $row['image']
. '" />' . $row['description'] . '<br />' .
    get_price('goodies', $row['price'], $row['sale_price']) . '
    <strong>Availability:</strong> ' . get_stock_status($row['stock'])
. '</p>
    <p><a href="/cart.php?sku=' . $row['sku'] . '&action=add"
class="button">Add to Cart</a></p></div>';
```

You should notice that this code is similar to that in **list_products.html**, at least in terms of how the product's image, description, price, availability, and Add to Cart buttons are generated. One difference is that the name for each product also reflects the category that the product is in. And by adding an **id** attribute to each **<H3>** tag, with a value of the product's SKU, the links from the home page to a specific product on this page will work.

6. Complete the **while** loop and the PHP code:

```php
} ?>
```

7. Complete the HTML:

```html
</div></div></div><div class="left-bot-corner"><div class=
"right-bot-corner"><div class="border-bot"></div></div></div>
</div>
<!-- box end -->
```

8. Save the file and test it in your Web browser.

You can test the sales listing page in two ways: by clicking the *SALES* link at the top of the page or by clicking a sale item on the home page.

 tip

For an ongoing discussion of ways to extend this project, see my support forum or blog, both linked from **www.DMCInsights.com/ecom/**.

9 | BUILDING A SHOPPING CART

In the previous chapter, an online catalog of products was developed, complete with buttons for adding items to the customer's shopping cart. Now it's time to implement the cart itself. A good shopping cart shows customers exactly what they have in their basket and provides ways to remove items, update the quantities, and to check out. For this Web site, there's also a "wish-list" feature, allowing the customer to save cart items for later.

The bulk of this chapter will focus on writing the shopping cart and wish-list features. First, though, new stored procedures are required. The chapter ends with various ways to factor in shipping as well as a discussion of other additions you could add to this process.

DEFINING THE PROCEDURES

Because this site uses an MVC approach, the chapter begins by looking at the *model* aspect of the project, which is to say the database. Eight stored procedures will be defined in this chapter: four for the shopping cart and four for the wish list. Only two of the queries involved come close to being as complex as those in Chapter 8, "Creating a Catalog," although the procedures themselves will use a bit more logic than the ones you've already seen. Because the **carts** and **wish_lists** tables have the exact same structure and because they'll be used identically, I'll just explain the stored procedures for the cart. To create the corresponding procedures for the wish list feature, you'll just need to replace every occurrence of "cart" with "wish_list."

Adding Products

The **add_to_cart()** stored procedure will be invoked when the customer requests that a product be added to their shopping cart. The procedure needs to take four pieces of information—a unique user ID, the product type (*coffee* or *other*), the product ID, and the quantity being added. As an extra bit of logic, the procedure should *add* the product to the cart if it doesn't already exist there but *add more quantity* of the product if it is already in the cart. Here is the stored procedure, and I'll explain its logic afterward:

```
DELIMITER $$
CREATE PROCEDURE add_to_cart (uid CHAR(32), type VARCHAR(6), pid
➥MEDIUMINT, qty TINYINT)
BEGIN
    DECLARE cid INT;
    SELECT id INTO cid FROM carts WHERE user_session_id=uid AND
    ➥product_type=type AND product_id=pid;
    IF cid > 0 THEN
        UPDATE carts SET quantity=quantity+qty, date_modified=NOW()
        ➥WHERE id=cid;
    ELSE
        INSERT INTO carts (user_session_id, product_type, product_id,
        ➥quantity) VALUES (uid, type, pid, qty);
    END IF;
END$$
DELIMITER ;
```

First, in keeping with how stored procedures are created, the delimiter is immediately changed to the combination of two dollar signs together. Next, the procedure's *signature* is created, which is to say the combination of its name and arguments. The first argument is the user's session ID, which will be exactly 32 characters long. Next is the product type, which will be either five or six characters long (*other* or *coffee*). The last two arguments are the product's ID and the quantity being added.

To incorporate the logic that checks if the product is already in the cart, an internal variable is necessary. You can create one using **DECLARE**, followed by the variable's name and its MySQL data type. The variable named **cid** is created, short for *cart ID*.

Next, a **SELECT** query checks the **carts** table for the submitted product. If the product is already represented in the table, then its **id** value will be assigned to the **cid** variable, thanks to the **SELECT...INTO** syntax.

 tip

See Chapter 8 for instructions on creating stored procedures in your database.

 tip

You can download all the SQL and files for this project from **www.DMCInsights.com/ecom/**.

 tip

The delimiter just needs to be changed to something other than a semicolon.

 note

Variables must be declared immediately after the **BEGIN** statement.

After the **SELECT** query, an **IF-ELSE** conditional will run either an **UPDATE** or an **INSERT** query, depending upon the value of **cid**. If it's greater than zero, then the product is already in the table, and the submitted quantity should be added to the existing quantity. Otherwise, a new record is inserted. The **date_modified** column is updated to the current moment only for an **UPDATE** query.

Removing Products

The stored procedure for removing products from the cart is the simplest of the four procedures. It requires three of the four arguments that **add_to_cart()** uses (obviously no quantity needs to be indicated when removing something). The procedure just runs a **DELETE** query:

```
DELIMITER $$
CREATE PROCEDURE remove_from_cart (uid CHAR(32), type VARCHAR(6),
➥pid MEDIUMINT)
BEGIN
    DELETE FROM carts WHERE user_session_id=uid AND product_type=type
    ➥AND product_id=pid;
END$$
DELIMITER ;
```

Updating the Cart

The stored procedure for updating the shopping cart will be invoked after the user clicks the update button on the shopping cart page (**Figure 9.1**). The procedure takes the same four arguments as **add_to_cart()**, but doesn't have to confirm that the product already exists in the database (unless the user did something tricky, the product has to exist in order to show up in the cart form). However, if the user enters zero for the quantity of the item, the procedure should go ahead and remove that from the cart. Rather than write the removal

Figure 9.1

functionality into this procedure, the procedure will just invoke the already defined **remove_from_cart()** procedure if the quantity is zero.

```
DELIMITER $$
CREATE PROCEDURE update_cart (uid CHAR(32), type VARCHAR(6), pid
➥MEDIUMINT, qty TINYINT)
BEGIN
    IF qty > 0 THEN
        UPDATE carts SET quantity=qty, date_modified=NOW() WHERE
        ➥user_session_id=uid AND product_type=type AND product_id=pid;
    ELSEIF qty = 0 THEN
        CALL remove_from_cart (uid, type, pid);
    END IF;
END$$
DELIMITER ;
```

 tip

Whenever the quantity of an item in the **carts** or **wish_lists** table changes (without the product being removed), the item's **date_modified** value is updated, too.

Fetching the Cart's Contents

The fourth and final stored procedure (for the shopping cart, that is) runs a **SELECT** query to retrieve all the contents of the cart. How tricky this **SELECT** query is depends upon how much information you want to display, but at its base, the query looks a lot like the sales-related queries from Chapter 8. The query is a **UNION** of two **SELECT** statements: the first a **JOIN** across four tables and the second a **JOIN** across five. In the procedure, I've written out the query over multiple lines for clarity. This procedure only needs the user's session ID as an argument.

```
DELIMITER $$
CREATE PROCEDURE get_shopping_cart_contents (uid CHAR(32))
BEGIN
    SELECT CONCAT("O", ncp.id) AS sku, c.quantity, ncc.category,
ncp.name, ncp.price, ncp.stock, sales.price AS sale_price
FROM carts AS c
INNER JOIN non_coffee_products AS ncp ON c.product_id=ncp.id
INNER JOIN non_coffee_categories AS ncc ON ncc.id=ncp.non_coffee_
➥category_id
LEFT OUTER JOIN sales ON
(sales.product_id=ncp.id AND sales.product_type='other' AND
((NOW() BETWEEN sales.start_date AND sales.end_date) OR (NOW() >
➥sales.start_date AND sales.end_date IS NULL)) )
WHERE c.product_type="other" AND c.user_session_id=uid
    UNION
```
(continues on next page)

```
    SELECT CONCAT("C", sc.id), c.quantity, gc.category,
CONCAT_WS(" - ", s.size, sc.caf_decaf, sc.ground_whole), sc.price,
sc.stock, sales.price
FROM carts AS c
INNER JOIN specific_coffees AS sc ON c.product_id=sc.id
INNER JOIN sizes AS s ON s.id=sc.size_id
INNER JOIN general_coffees AS gc ON gc.id=sc.general_coffee_id
LEFT OUTER JOIN sales ON
(sales.product_id=sc.id AND sales.product_type='coffee' AND
((NOW() BETWEEN sales.start_date AND sales.end_date) OR (NOW() >
➥sales.start_date AND sales.end_date IS NULL)) )
WHERE c.product_type="coffee" AND c.user_session_id=uid;
END$$
DELIMITER ;
```

Figure 9.2 shows the result of calling this procedure. You'll notice that the query returns the default price (under the heading *price*), the quantity in stock, and the sale price, if any. This information will be needed later.

Figure 9.2

DEFINING THE HELPER FUNCTIONS

Before getting into the shopping cart itself, there are two helper functions that will be useful to this chapter's code. The first function takes two possible prices—the regular and the sale price—and returns the appropriate price for the product:

```
function get_just_price($regular, $sales) {
    if ((0 < $sales) && ($sales < $regular)) {
        return number_format($sales, 2);
    } else {
        return number_format($regular, 2);
    }
}
```

This is similar to the **get_price()** function already defined in Chapter 8, but just returns the numeric price (**get_price()** returned the price within some context).

The second function will parse a SKU, which is to say convert a value like *C12* into *coffee* and *12*, accordingly. This conversion will often be necessary, because the database uses each product's type and ID number individually. The function for parsing the SKU takes one argument—the SKU itself—and returns an array containing two elements:

```
function parse_sku($sku) {

    // Grab the first character:
    $type_abbr = substr($sku, 0, 1);

    // Grab the remaining characters:
    $pid = substr($sku, 1);

    // Validate the type:
    if ($type_abbr == 'C') {
        $sp_type = 'coffee';
    } elseif ($type_abbr == 'O') {
        $sp_type = 'other';
    } else {
        $sp_type = NULL;
    }

    // Validate the product ID:
    $pid = (filter_var($pid, FILTER_VALIDATE_INT, array('min_range' => 1)))
    ➥? $pid : NULL;

    // Return the values:
    return array($sp_type, $pid);

} // End of parse_sku() function.
```

The two uses of **substr()** breaks the SKU into its parts. Next, the product type is validated based upon the first character in the SKU, which must be either *C*, for *coffee*, or *O*, for *other*. If neither is the case, the **$sp_type** variable is assigned the value **NULL**.

The remaining characters must be an integer greater than 1. The **filter_var()** function can test for that. If the value is an integer greater than 1, the value is assigned to **$pid**. Otherwise, the value **NULL** will be assigned.

Finally, both values are returned as an array. Because this function returns an array, you must use the **list()** function when calling it:

list($type, $id) = parse_sku($sku);

The **list()** function assigns to the variables—**$type** and **$id**—the values returned by the code on the right side of the equation.

The most appropriate place to define these two functions is within the already existing **product_functions.inc.php** script, found in the **includes** directory. Go ahead and do that before proceeding.

MAKING A SHOPPING CART

After defining the stored procedures and the helper functions, three files must be created:

- **cart.php** will do all the work (it's the controller).

- **cart.html** is the view file for the cart.

- **emptycart.html** is the view file if there's nothing in the cart.

Let's create these files now, starting with the PHP script.

Creating the PHP Script

As in Chapter 8, thanks to the use of stored procedures and included HTML files, the PHP script itself becomes surprisingly short and quite tidy. The entire **cart.php** is only 50 lines of code, including comments and blank lines! Most of the script is logic that invokes the correct stored procedure based on how the script is accessed.

1. Create a new PHP script in your text editor or IDE to be named **cart.php** and stored in the Web root directory.

2. Include the configuration file:
   ```php
   <?php
   require ('./includes/config.inc.php');
   ```

3. Check for, or create, a user session ID:
   ```php
   if (isset($_COOKIE['SESSION'])) {
       $uid = $_COOKIE['SESSION'];
   ```

```
} else {
   $uid = md5(uniqid('biped',true));
}
```

This site only needs one cookie to handle the cart and wish-list functionality. The cookie's name is *SESSION*. Even though it's not a real PHP session, the name is indicative of how the cookie is used, and should the user check the cookies a site sends, this particular cookie will have an air of familiarity to it.

If the cookie does exist, its value is assigned to the **$uid** variable. If the cookie does not exist, a new session ID must be created. That's done by using a combination of **uniqid()** and **md5()**.

4. Send the cookie:

   setcookie('SESSION', $uid, time()+(60*60*24*30));

   Whether the user is returning to this page, or just coming here for the first time, a cookie will be sent. For new users, this is obviously necessary. For returning visitors, this call will update an existing cookie, so that it lasts longer. The cookie is set to expire in 30 days from now.

5. Include the header file:

   $page_title = 'Coffee - Your Shopping Cart';
   include ('./includes/header.html');

6. Require the database connection and the functions file:

   require (MYSQL);
   include ('./includes/product_functions.inc.php');

7. If there's a SKU value in the URL, break it down into its parts:

   ```
   if (isset($_GET['sku'])) {
      list($sp_type, $pid) = parse_sku($_GET['sku']);
   }
   ```

   By calling the user-defined **parse_sku()** function, the SKU, which might be present in the URL, is turned into its two components: the type and ID.

8. Check for a product to be added to the cart:

   ```
   if (isset ($sp_type, $pid, $_GET['action']) && ($_GET['action'] ==
   ‑'add') ) {
      $r = mysqli_query($dbc, "CALL add_to_cart('$uid', '$sp_type',
      ‑$pid, 1)");
   ```

   The logic for this script is a longish **IF-ELSEIF** conditional that checks for the various possible ways in which this script would be accessed. The first way a user might get to this page is by clicking an *Add to Cart* link, which will

tip

The **md5()** function returns a string exactly 32 characters long.

note

Cookies must be sent prior to anything being sent to the Web browser.

tip

The **isset()** function can be used to validate that multiple variables are set in one function call.

tip

have a URL like **http://*hostname*/cart.php?sku=C8&action=add**. In that case, the SKU would be broken down into **$sp_type** and **$pid** values, and **$_GET['action']** would equal *add*.

If all these conditions are true, the **add_to_cart()** stored procedure is called, passing along the user's session ID, the type of product, the product ID, and a quantity of 1.

9. Check for a product to be removed from the cart:

```
} elseif (isset ($sp_type, $pid, $_GET['action']) && ($_GET['action'] ==
'remove') ) {
    $r = mysqli_query($dbc, "CALL remove_from_cart('$uid', '$sp_type',
    $pid)");
```

The **isset()** conditional is the same as that for adding products, but if **$_GET['action']** equals *remove*, the **remove_from_cart()** stored procedure will be called. This will be the case when the user clicks the *Remove from Cart* link (see Figure 9.1).

10. Check for a product to be moved into the cart:

```
} elseif (isset ($sp_type, $pid, $_GET['action'], $_GET['qty']) &&
($_GET['action'] == 'move') ) {
    $qty = (filter_var($_GET['qty'], FILTER_VALIDATE_INT,
    array('min_range' => 1))) ? $_GET['qty'] : 1;
    $r = mysqli_query($dbc, "CALL add_to_cart('$uid', '$sp_type',
    $pid, $qty)");
    $r = mysqli_query($dbc, "CALL remove_from_wish_list('$uid',
    '$sp_type', $pid)");
```

The customer has the option of moving items back and forth between their cart and their wish list. If something is in the wish list and gets moved to the cart, the program's response should be similar to adding a product to the cart directly, with two differences. First, the quantities will be transferred over, too: If the customer has three of something in their wish list, all three will be added to the cart. Second, when this transfer occurs, the item should be removed from the wish list.

To make all this happen, the conditional checks that **$_GET['qty']** is set and that **$_GET['action']** equals *move*. The quantity value is then validated to be an integer greater than 1.

For every stored procedure call in this script, the results are assigned to the **$r** variable, even though only one of the procedure's results will actually be used (the procedure that returns the cart's contents). Still, I'm leaving these assignations in place for your own debugging purposes.

If you have problems with the script, you could include the following line of code after a procedure call:

if (!$r) echo mysqli_error($dbc);

11. Check for a form submission:

} elseif (isset($_POST['quantity'])) {

All the previous conditions apply to GET requests, but this page can be invoked using a POST request, too. This will happen when the user submits the cart form in order to update the quantities.

12. Loop through each item:

```
foreach ($_POST['quantity'] as $sku => $qty) {
    list($sp_type, $pid) = parse_sku($sku);
    if (isset($sp_type, $pid)) {
        $qty = (filter_var($qty, FILTER_VALIDATE_INT, array('min_range'
        => 0))) ? $qty : 1;
        $r = mysqli_query($dbc, "CALL update_cart('$uid', '$sp_type',
        $pid, $qty)");
    }
}
```

$_POST['quantity'] will be an array of elements, in the format *SKU => quantity*. For each element in **$_POST['quantity']**, the corresponding product in the cart must be updated. To do that, first the SKU is parsed and validated. Then the quantity is validated. If it's an integer greater than or equal to zero (because the customer can enter a quantity of zero to remove an item), that value will be used. If, for whatever reason, the customer enters an invalid quantity for a product, the value 1 will be used instead. Finally, the **update_cart()** stored procedure is executed, passing along the proper values.

13. Complete the primary conditional and retrieve the cart's contents:

}// End of main IF.
$r = mysqli_query($dbc, "CALL get_shopping_cart_contents('$uid')");

Regardless of what action just took place, the cart's current contents will be displayed.

14. Include the appropriate view:

```
if (mysqli_num_rows($r) > 0) {
    include ('./views/cart.html');
} else { // Empty cart!
    include ('./views/emptycart.html');
}
```

15. Complete the page:

include ('./includes/footer.html');

16. Save the file.

Creating the Views

note

Both view files go in the **views** directory, of course.

The shopping cart uses two view files: one for displaying products and one indicating an empty cart. The latter one, named **emptycart.html**, is simple (**Figure 9.3**):

Figure 9.3

```
<!-- box begin -->
<div class="box alt"><div class="left-top-corner"><div class=
"right-top-corner"><div class="border-top"></div></div></div>
<div class="border-left"><div class="border-right"><div class="inner">
<h2>Your Shopping Cart</h2>
<p>Your shopping cart is currently empty.</p>
</div></div></div><div class="left-bot-corner"><div class=
"right-bot-corner"><div class="border-bot"></div></div></div></div>
<!-- box end -->
```

The second view file is more complicated, naturally. It must display every item retrieved by the stored procedure—every product in the cart—but it must do so as an HTML form so that the user can update the quantities. Secondarily, each product should have its own links for removing the product from the cart or for moving it to the wish list. Finally, subtotals and an order total should be calculated and displayed (**Figure 9.4** shows the initial version of the view; Figure 9.1 shows how it will be updated later).

Figure 9.4

1. Create a new HTML file in your text editor or IDE to be named **cart.html** and stored in the **views** directory.

2. Begin the HTML box and the header:

```
<div class="box alt"><div class="left-top-corner"><div class=
"right-top-corner"><div class="border-top"></div></div></div>
<div class="border-left"><div class="border-right"><div class=
"inner">
<h2>Your Shopping Cart</h2>
    <p>Please use this form to update your shopping cart. You may change
```

⇒**the quantities, move items to your wish list for future purchasing, or**
⇒**remove items entirely. The shipping and handling cost is based upon**
⇒**the order total. When you are ready to complete your purchase, please**
⇒**click Checkout to be taken to a secure page for processing.</p>**

For the instructions on the cart page, you'll need to strike a balance between being informative and not being too busy. Remember that the primary purpose of the cart page is to get the customer to check out!

3. Begin the form:

<form action="/cart.php" method="POST">

The form is submitted back to **cart.php** and uses the POST method. The action value starts with a slash to indicate that **cart.php** is in the Web root directory. The slash isn't absolutely required for the **cart.php** script, but is required with many other links and references used by the site, so it's here for consistency.

4. Begin the table:

<table border="0" cellspacing="8" cellpadding="6">
  <tr>
    <th align="center">Item</th>
    <th align="center">Quantity</th>
    <th align="right">Price</th>
    <th align="right">Subtotal</th>
    <th align="center">Options</th>
  </tr>

In an old-school way, I'm using a standard HTML table to display the cart's contents. There are five columns in the table.

5. Begin a PHP block:

<?php
$total = 0;

Within the PHP block, the total variable is initialized to zero, so that a proper order total can be calculated.

6. Fetch each item:

while ($row = mysqli_fetch_array($r, MYSQLI_ASSOC)) {
  $price = get_just_price($row['price'], $row['sale_price']);
  $subtotal = $price * $row['quantity'];

Within the loop, the item's price is first determined by passing the regular and sale prices to the **get_just_price()** function. Then a subtotal is calculated by multiplying the price times the quantity in the cart.

 tip

For security purposes, the price is always coming from the database; it's not possible for the customer to manipulate it.

7. Print a table row:

```
echo '<tr>
    <td>' . $row['category'] . '::' . $row['name'] . '</td>
    <td align="center"><input type="text" name="quantity['.
    ⇒$row['sku'] . ']" value="' . $row['quantity'] . '" size="2" /></td>
    <td align="right">$' . $price . '</td>
    <td align="right">$' . number_format($subtotal, 2) . '</td>
    <td align="right"><a href="/wishlist.php?sku=' . $row['sku'] .
    ⇒'&action=move&qty=' . $row['quantity'] .'">Move to Wish List</a>
    ⇒<br /><a href="/cart.php?sku=' . $row['sku'] . '&action=remove">
    ⇒Remove from Cart</a></td>
</tr>
';
```

For each item, a table row is generated. The first column is the displayed name of the product. For the name, the cart shows a combination of the product's category and its specific name, as on the sales page. In the second column, the quantity is displayed. So that this value is editable, it's displayed within a text input. The name for each input will be *quantity[sku]*, so that both the SKU and the new quantity will be available when the form is submitted (**Figure 9.5**).

```
<tr><td>Mugs::Red Dragon Mug</td>
        <td align="center"><input type="text" name="quantity[O2]" value="4" size="2" /></td>
        <td align="right">$7.00</td>
        <td align="right">$28.00</td>
        <td align="right"><a href="/wishlist.php?sku=O2&action=move&qty=4">Move to Wish List</a>
    </tr>
    <tr><td>Kona::1 lb. - caf - ground</td>
        <td align="center"><input type="text" name="quantity[C4]" value="1" size="2" /></td>
        <td align="right">$8.00</td>
        <td align="right">$8.00</td>
        <td align="right"><a href="/wishlist.php?sku=C4&action=move&qty=1">Move to Wish List</a>
    </tr>
```

Figure 9.5

The third and fourth columns are the price and subtotal. In the fifth column are two links. The first is to move the item to the wish list. That link passes to **wishlist.php**, the SKU, the current quantity, and an action value of *move*. The second link is back to this page for removing the product.

8. Add an error message if the product is not sufficiently stocked:

```
if ($row['stock'] < $row['quantity']) {
    echo '<tr class="error"><td colspan="5" align="center">There are
    ⇒only ' . $row['stock'] . ' left in stock of the ' . $row['name'] . '. Please
    ⇒update the quantity, remove the item entirely, or move it to your
    ⇒wish list.</td></tr>';
}
```

If the user has more of an item in their cart than is currently in stock, they need to be notified of the problem (**Figure 9.6**). At this point in the process, the customer is told exactly how many are left and asked to remedy the issue themselves. In the next chapter, an insufficiently stocked item will be dropped from the order automatically.

Figure 9.6

9. Add the subtotal to the total and complete the loop:

```
$total += $subtotal;
} // End of WHILE loop.
```

10. Add the total to the table and complete the PHP block:

```
echo '<tr>
    <td colspan="3" align="right"><strong>Total</strong></td>
    <td align="right">$' . number_format($total, 2) . '</td>
    <td> </td>
</tr>
';
?>
```

11. Complete the table and create two buttons:

```
</table><br /><p align="center"><input type="submit" value=
➥"Update Quantities" class="button" /></form></p><br />
➥<p align="center"><a href="https://<?php echo BASE_URL; ?>
➥"checkout.php?session=<?php echo $uid; ?> class="button">
➥Checkout</a></p></div>
```

The first button is used to submit this form (to update the quantities). The second button is to start the checkout process. That link goes to **checkout.php**, but via an https connection. To generate that link's value, the **BASE_URL** constant is required. Notice, as well, that the user's session ID is being passed along in the URL, so that **checkout.php** can use it. You'll see why this is necessary in the next chapter.

12. Complete the page:

```
</div></div><div class="left-bot-corner"><div class=
➥"right-bot-corner"><div class="border-bot"></div></div></div>
➥</div>
<!-- box end -->
```

13. Save the file and test the shopping cart in your Web browser.

Now you should be able to test everything except for the interactions with the wish list. You can add products, update quantities, and remove items.

 note

The checkout process must begin on a secure page for the customer to feel safe (and to actually be safe)!

MAKING A WISH LIST

Just as the stored procedures for managing the wish list are virtually the same as those for managing the shopping cart, the PHP script and HTML files involved here will be extraordinarily similar to the ones just written. The chapter will post all three files in entirety, but for a full description of any of the code or logic, review the previous several pages.

Creating the PHP Script

The **wishlist.php** script, stored in the Web root directory, is exactly like **cart.php** except:

- Its page title is different.

- The wish list versions of the stored procedures are called.

- Different HTML files are used for the views.

- There's no conditional checking for adding an item.

Really, aside from this last difference, you can almost do a search and replace to create this script using a copy of **cart.php**. As for this last item, as written, items are added to the wish list by moving them from the cart.

```php
<?php // wishlist.php
require ('./includes/config.inc.php');
if (isset($_COOKIE['SESSION'])) {
    $uid = $_COOKIE['SESSION'];
} else {
    $uid = md5(uniqid('biped',true));
}
setcookie('SESSION', $uid, time()+(60*60*24*30));
$page_title = 'Coffee - Your Wish List';
include ('./includes/header.html');
require (MYSQL);
include ('./includes/product_functions.inc.php');
if (isset($_GET['sku'])) {
    list($sp_type, $pid) = parse_sku($_GET['sku']);
}
if (isset ($sp_type, $pid, $_GET['action']) && ($_GET['action'] == 'remove')
➥) {
    $r = mysqli_query($dbc, "CALL remove_from_wish_list('$uid',
    ➥'$sp_type', $pid)");
} elseif (isset ($sp_type, $pid, $_GET['action'], $_GET['qty']) &&
➥($_GET['action'] == 'move') ) {
```

```
$qty = (filter_var($_GET['qty'], FILTER_VALIDATE_INT, array('min_range'
⇒ => 1))) ? $_GET['qty'] : 1;
$r = mysqli_query($dbc, "CALL add_to_wish_list('$uid', '$sp_type',
⇒$pid, $qty)");
$r = mysqli_query($dbc, "CALL remove_from_cart('$uid', '$sp_type',
⇒$pid)");
} elseif (isset($_POST['quantity'])) {
    foreach ($_POST['quantity'] as $sku => $qty) {
        list($sp_type, $pid) = parse_sku($sku);
        if (isset($sp_type, $pid)) {
            $qty = (filter_var($qty, FILTER_VALIDATE_INT, array('min_range'
            ⇒ => 0))) ? $qty : 1;
            $r = mysqli_query($dbc, "CALL update_wish_list('$uid',
            ⇒'$sp_type', $pid, $qty)");
        }
    }
}
$r = mysqli_query($dbc, "CALL get_wish_list_contents('$uid')");
if (mysqli_num_rows($r) > 0) {
    include ('./views/wishlist.html');
} else {
    include ('./views/emptylist.html');
}
include ('./includes/footer.html');
?>
```

Creating the Views

The **emptylist.html** view is used when the customer's wish list is empty
(Figure 9.7).

note

Of course, the two view files go
in the **views** directory.

Figure 9.7

```
<!-- box begin -->
<div class="box alt"><div class="left-top-corner"><div class=
⇒"right-top-corner"><div class="border-top"></div></div></div>
⇒<div class="border-left"><div class="border-right"><div class="inner">
<h2>Your Wish List</h2>
<p>Your wish list is currently empty.</p>
```
(continues on next page)

```
</div></div></div><div class="left-bot-corner"><div class=
➥"right-bot-corner"><div class="border-bot"></div></div></div></div>
<!-- box end -->
```

The **wishlist.html** view file displays the wish list in an HTML table. As with the shopping cart, the wish list contents can be altered in a couple of ways:

- Their quantities can be changed.

- Items can be moved to the shopping cart.

- Items can be removed from the wish list.

Unlike the shopping cart page, the wish list does not display an order total or a link to checkout (**Figure 9.8**). Also, instead of indicating that insufficient quantity of a product is in stock, the wish list will indicate those items that are running low, in the hopes of inducing the customer to purchase the items now (**Figure 9.9**).

Figure 9.8

Figure 9.9

```
<div class="box alt"><div class="left-top-corner"><div class=
➥"right-top-corner"><div class="border-top"></div></div></div>
➥<div class="border-left"><div class="border-right"><div class="inner">
<h2>Your Wish List</h2>
<p>Please use this form to update your wish list. You may change the
➥quantities, move items to your cart for purchasing, or remove items
➥entirely.</p>
<form action="/wishlist.php" method="POST">
<table border="0" cellspacing="8" cellpadding="6">
   <tr>
      <th align="center">Item</th>
      <th align="center">Quantity</th>
      <th align="right">Price</th>
      <th align="right">Subtotal</th>
      <th align="center">Options</th>
   </tr>
```

```php
<?php
while ($row = mysqli_fetch_array($r, MYSQLI_ASSOC)) {
    $price = get_just_price($row['price'], $row['sale_price']);
    $subtotal = $price * $row['quantity'];
    echo '<tr>
        <td>' . $row['category'] . '::' . $row['name'] . '</td>
        <td align="center"><input type="text" name="quantity[' .
        $row['sku'] . ']" value="' . $row['quantity'] . '" size="2" /></td>
        <td align="right">$' . number_format($price, 2) . '</td>
        <td align="right">$' . number_format($subtotal, 2) . '</td>
        <td align="right"><a href="/cart.php?sku=' . $row['sku'] .
        '&action=move&qty=' . $row['quantity'] .'">Move to Cart</a><br />
        <a href="/wishlist.php?sku=' . $row['sku'] . '&action=remove">
        Remove from Wish List</a></td>
    </tr>
    ';
    // Check the stock status:
    if ( ($row['stock'] > 0) && ($row['stock'] < 10)) {
        echo '<tr class="error"><td colspan="5" align="center">There are
        only ' . $row['stock'] . ' left in stock of the ' . $row['name'] . '.</td>
        </tr>';
    }
} // End of WHILE loop.
?>      </table><p align="center"><input type="submit" value="Update
        Quantities" class="button" /></form></p></div>
        </div></div><div class="left-bot-corner"><div class=
        "right-bot-corner"><div class="border-bot"></div></div>
        </div></div>
<!-- box end -->
```

CALCULATING SHIPPING

A nice feature worth adding to the shopping cart is an indication of how much the shipping will be. For many customers, the shipping and handling charges are a significant factor when deciding whether or not to make an online purchase. The shipping cost may be a fixed price or be based upon:

- The total weight of the order
- The distance between the origination and destination
- The physical size of the order (for example, large furniture costs extra)
- The total amount of the sale

This site will use this last criterion.

The first step is to define a function that will calculate the shipping using a formula. As an example, let's say that shipping starts with a base rate, which covers the simple fact that some employee has to be paid to assemble and box the order. Added to that should be an amount that's partly based on the amount of the order: Presumably, as the order total increases, more items are being shipped, but at the same time the site is making more money. Therefore, the bulk of the shipping cost will be proportional to the order total, and that proportion will decrease for larger orders. Here, then, is the function:

```
function get_shipping($total = o) {
    // Set the base handling charges:
    $shipping = 3;
    // Rate is based upon the total:
    if ($total < 10) {
        $rate = .25;
    } elseif ($total < 20) {
        $rate = .20;
    } elseif ($total < 50) {
        $rate = .18;
    } elseif ($total < 100) {
        $rate = .16;
    } else {
        $rate = .15;
    }
    // Calculate the shipping total:
    $shipping = $shipping + ($total * $rate);
    // Return the shipping total:
    return number_format($shipping, 2);
} // End of get_shipping() function.
```

Logically, this function should be defined in the **product_functions.inc.php** script so that it's available to multiple scripts (such as **cart.php** and **checkout.php**, which will be written in the next chapter).

To use this function in **cart.php** (the wish list does not display a total), add this code before displaying the total (**Figure 9.10**):

```
$shipping = get_shipping($total);
$total += $shipping;
echo '<tr>
```

```
<td colspan="3" align="right"><strong>Shipping &amp; Handling
➥</strong></td>
<td align="right">$' . $shipping . '</td>
<td> </td>
</tr>
';
```

Figure 9.10

10 | CHECKING OUT

The next step in the evolution of the *Coffee* site is to incorporate the payment processing system that will allow customers to complete their order. For this project, I've chosen Authorize.net as the payment processor. The first several pages of the chapter talk about Authorize.net and walk you through setting up a test account there. Once you have a test account, you can write the entire checkout process.

There are four parts to the checkout process:

1. Take and validate the shipping information.

2. Take and validate the billing information.

3. Process the payment.

4. Wrap it up (send an email, create a receipt, and so on).

This chapter probably has the most complicated code of any in the book. But this chapter also conveys the information that many readers need the most, so ample space is dedicated to explaining the code as thoroughly as possible.

ABOUT AUTHORIZE.NET

Authorize.net is perhaps the largest payment gateway out there and was most certainly one of the first available for e-commerce. How Authorize.net functions is different than PayPal, used in Chapter 6, "Using PayPal." PayPal fetches monies from customers' credit cards (or PayPal accounts) and deposits those amounts into *your PayPal account* (which you can later move to a bank account). By comparison, Authorize.net coordinates with several networked systems to transfer funds from credit cards to *your merchant bank account*. Authorize.net is an agent in the process, a true payment gateway, and when the transaction is completed, the money will automatically be transferred to your bank account. For this reason, you must have a merchant bank account (with an actual bank) that supports the Authorize.net system.

Authorize.net accepts all major credit cards and offers:

- Advanced fraud detection
- PCI DSS compliance
- Support for recurring payments
- International transactions
- An online virtual terminal
- Customer information management
- eCheck acceptance
- Multiple administrators with different permissions
- Good documentation and support

Authorize.net provides what they call the *Merchant Interface*, where you can configure your account, manage transactions, view statements, generate reports, and so forth. This chapter will mention the Merchant Interface a few times, but keep in mind that the Merchant Interface is how a site administrator manages an Authorize.net account, it's not how the site itself communicates with the payment system.

As with PayPal and many other payment systems, there are multiple ways you can use Authorize.net: *Simple Checkout*, *Server Integration Method* (SIM), and *Advanced Integration Method* (AIM). When using the first two, the customer will be taken to the Authorize.net Web site, similar to the PayPal example in Chapter 6. In this chapter, the Advanced Integration Method will be demonstrated instead.

 tip

To test Authorize.net, you don't need an actual merchant account.

 tip

Authorize.net has a Verified Merchant Seal image that you can display on your Web site to imply your site's credibility.

 tip

AIM is the Authorize.net recommended system, but requires programming and Web security skills.

To communicate with the Authorize.net service using PHP, a POST request will need to be made over SSL. Instead of the customer sending a form of data to Authorize.net, PHP will do that behind the scenes. This requires using *libcurl*, the *cURL* library (**http://curl.haxx.se**). cURL, if you're not familiar with it, is a command-line utility for performing network communications. The standalone application may already exist on your own computer and most likely on your server. libcurl is a cURL library that can be integrated into other software, such as PHP. If your version of PHP is installed with libcurl, scripts can use the **curl_*** functions to perform the communications. To confirm support for libcurl, run a **phpinfo()** script (**Figure 10.1**).

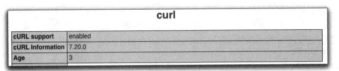

curl	
cURL support	enabled
cURL Information	7.20.0
Age	3

Figure 10.1

tip

It's not 100 percent clear what cURL stands for, except for the "URL" part (Uniform Resource Locator).

If your PHP installation does not support libcurl, you can have PHP invoke the command-line cURL application via the **exec()** function:

exec('curl *<arguments>*', $response);

The response of the cURL request will be stored in the **$response** variable, after the execution is complete. You'll need to look online for how to use the command-line cURL directly.

Because this site uses cURL, you may be able to test the entire system on your development server (for example, your own computer). This differs from the *Knowledge is Power* example (developed in Part Two, "Selling Virtual Products"), which had to be online, because PayPal needs to communicate directly with the e-commerce Web site.

CREATING A TEST ACCOUNT

tip

If you know you'll be using Authorize.net for a real project, go ahead and create a real account with Authorize.net now.

There are two ways you can create an account for testing the Authorize.net system. First, if you create a *real* Authorize.net account, associated with your business and tied to your merchant bank account, that account will initially be in a testing mode. Once you've finished testing the account, you only need to go into the Merchant Interface to take the account live. The second option is to create a true test account: an account with limited functionality that cannot be later turned into an actual account. This is the route taken in the next series of steps.

1. Go to **http://developer.authorize.net/testaccount/**.

2. Fill out the simple form (**Figure 10.2**) and click Submit.

   For this chapter, you'll need to select the Card Not Present (CNP) account type (as opposed to in-person commercial transactions, where the card is present). Also select the Advanced Integration Method (AIM) check box.

3. Check your email.

   You'll receive an email with the basic information you'll need to continue. You'll be provided with the login values for accessing the Merchant Interface. And the email will contain the API login ID and transaction-key values used by the Web site to communicate with Authorize.net.

Figure 10.2

PREPARING THE SITE

Before implementing the actual **checkout.php** script (the first in the checkout process), there's some background work to do. This includes creating the required stored procedures (for every database query), creating a modified HTML template, and defining one helper function. Let's look at the template first, because it's the simplest task to complete.

The New HTML Template

At car dealerships, customers are able to roam around the lot and look at all the pretty, shiny vehicles. They can look at this one, then that one, and then compare those with another. But when it comes time to buy, the dealership locks the customer in a room with a salesperson whose job it is to close the sale without any distractions. With an e-commerce site, you want to pretty much do the same thing...

At first, the customer should be free to roam about the site, eyeing the products, and enjoying the "window shopping" opportunity. The online catalog, developed in Chapter 8, "Creating a Catalog," has this approach: It's designed so that it's easy for the customer to get around, look at products, and put them into his or her cart. But the checkout process should be different: The sole purpose is to get the customer to complete the sale. Toward that end, the HTML template needs to be changed for this process, discouraging the customer from doing anything but completing the sale. Specifically, the template should remove the shopping-related links so that the customer stays on track

 tip

Do not attempt to change the password of a test account, because multiple test users share the same credentials.

 tip

A different template is also a visual cue to the customer that they are in "purchase" mode instead of "browsing" mode.

(**Figure 10.3**). Still, the customer shouldn't be trapped in the checkout process (car dealerships don't literally lock the door), so the less obvious links at the top of the page are still required.

Figure 10.3

The entire checkout process will require an SSL connection. This means that any links in the template to non-checkout pages need to be absolute, to a non-SSL version (that is, to **http://*whatever***).

1. Make a copy of **header.html** to be named **checkout_header.html** and stored in the **includes** directory.

2. Remove the big shopping links by deleting this code:

```
<ul class="nav">
    <li><a href="/shop/coffee/">Coffee</a></li>
    <li><a href="/shop/goodies/">Goodies</a></li>
    <li><a href="/shop/sales/">Sales</a></li>
    <li><a href="/wishlist.php">Wish List</a></li>
    <li><a href="/cart.php">Cart</a></li>
</ul>
```

3. Change the remaining links to **index.php**, **cart.php**, **contact.php**, and **sitemap.php** so that they use *HTTP* instead of *HTTPS*.

   For example, the code should be:

   http://<?php echo BASE_URL; ?>/index.php

   These other links, as originally defined, were *relative*. On an HTTPS page, such links would take the customer to an HTTPS version of the shopping pages, which isn't necessary (and could adversely affect the server's performance).

4. Save the file.

When viewing the pages that use this new header, the user can still return to the shopping part of the site, but it's not obvious, which is a good thing. If you want to be more generous, you could create an overt *Return to Shopping* link somewhere (just make sure it's an absolute reference using HTTP). Also, the footer does not need to be changed.

The Helper Function

For the checkout process, one helper function will be defined. Because this process involves a couple of forms (for taking the shipping and billing information), a function for creating and managing form inputs will be quite useful. In Chapter 4, "User Accounts," the **create_form_input()** function was defined. That function creates a form element, handles any existing values, and indicates errors when appropriate. That version of the function created only text, password, and textarea inputs. It also looked for existing element values only in the **$_POST** array. This site will use a new version of that function, generating both text inputs and select menus. The function also needs to be able to find existing values in **$_SESSION**, not just **$_POST**. A third alteration is that the function will allow for extra HTML to be added to inputs. You'll see why shortly.

1. Create a new PHP script in your text editor or IDE to be named **form_functions.inc.php** and stored in the **includes** directory.

   As in Part Two of the book, this script will only define a single function, but the file's name will still be plural, in case more functions are added later.

2. Begin defining the function:

   function create_form_input($name, $type, $errors, $values = 'POST',
   ⇒$extras = '') {

   The function takes five arguments, two of which are optional. The first argument is the name for the element. The second is its type (for example, *text* or *select*). The third is an array in which any errors would be stored. These three arguments are the same as in the book's previous version of this function.

   The fourth argument is the name of the array where existing values are to be found, for the purpose of making the form sticky. For the checkout process, the value will be either *POST* or *SESSION*. In theory, you could pass the array itself—**$_POST**, **$_SESSION** (even **$_GET** or **$_COOKIE**, if you wanted)—to the function, just as the **$errors** array is passed. But since these arrays are global in scope, they'll be available to the function without being sent along as a second copy.

   The fifth argument is for passing extra HTML. This chapter will provide one value for this argument: **autocomplete="off"**. You'll see why and how later in the chapter.

tip

Just as the checkout process should minimize links that take the customer elsewhere, it should maximize those links and buttons that move the process onward.

3. Look for and process any existing value:

```
$value = false;
if ($values == 'SESSION') {
    if (isset($_SESSION[$name])) $value = $_SESSION[$name];
} elseif ($values == 'POST') {
    if (isset($_POST[$name])) $value = $_POST[$name];
    if ($value && get_magic_quotes_gpc()) $value = stripslashes($value);
}
```

First, the **$value** variable is set to **false**, thereby assuming that no value exists. A conditional then checks in which array an existing value could be found. In each case, any existing value is assigned to **$value**. Since posted values could be affected by Magic Quotes, **stripslashes()** is applied to those values, but only if Magic Quotes is enabled.

4. Determine what kind of element to create:

```
if ( ($type == 'text') || ($type == 'password') ) {
```

This version of the function will be used only to create text and select elements, but I'm leaving the password type in (as in the original version of this function), because it's defined in the same way as text inputs.

5. Create the text input:

```
echo '<input type="' . $type . '" name="' . $name . '" id="' . $name . '"';
if ($value) echo ' value="' . htmlspecialchars($value) . '"';
if (!empty($extras)) echo " $extras";
if (array_key_exists($name, $errors)) {
    echo 'class="error" /><br /><span class="error">' . $errors[$name]
    ➥. '</span>';
} else {
    echo ' />';
}
```

All this code is the same as that explained in Chapter 4, save for two differences. First, if the **$extras** variable is not empty, its value is added to the input. As you'll see, this will allow the site to disable *autocomplete* for the credit card number field. This will be explained in more detail a bit later.

The second change is that a break is added after the input and before the error message itself, should one exist. This change is necessary because of the template in use, which makes a mess of the form if errors are placed immediately beside form elements.

6. Check for the select type:

```
} elseif ($type == 'select') {
```

The previous incarnation of this function didn't handle **<SELECT>** menus, but this one will (four will be required by the checkout process).

7. If a states menu is being created, define the data source:

```
if (($name == 'state') || ($name == 'cc_state')) {
    $data = array('AL' => 'Alabama', 'AK' => 'Alaska', 'AZ' => 'Arizona',
    ➥'AR' => 'Arkansas', 'CA' => 'California', 'CO' => 'Colorado', 'CT' =>
    ➥'Connecticut', 'DE' => 'Delaware', 'FL' => 'Florida', 'GA' =>
    ➥'Georgia', 'HI' => 'Hawaii', 'ID' => 'Idaho', 'IL' => 'Illinois', 'IN'
    ➥=> 'Indiana', 'IA' => 'Iowa', 'KS' => 'Kansas', 'KY' => 'Kentucky',
    ➥'LA' => 'Louisiana', 'ME' => 'Maine', 'MD' => 'Maryland', 'MA'
    ➥=> 'Massachusetts', 'MI' => 'Michigan', 'MN' => 'Minnesota', 'MS'
    ➥=> 'Mississippi', 'MO' => 'Missouri', 'MT' => 'Montana', 'NE' =>
    ➥'Nebraska', 'NV' => 'Nevada', 'NH' => 'New Hampshire', 'NJ' =>
    ➥'New Jersey', 'NM' => 'New Mexico', 'NY' => 'New York', 'NC' =>
    ➥'North Carolina', 'ND' => 'North Dakota', 'OH' => 'Ohio', 'OK' =>
    ➥'Oklahoma', 'OR' => 'Oregon', 'PA' => 'Pennsylvania', 'RI' =>
    ➥'Rhode Island', 'SC' => 'South Carolina', 'SD' => 'South Dakota',
    ➥'TN' => 'Tennessee', 'TX' => 'Texas', 'UT' => 'Utah', 'VT' =>
    ➥'Vermont', 'VA' => 'Virginia', 'WA' => 'Washington', 'WV' => 'West
    ➥Virginia', 'WI' => 'Wisconsin', 'WY' => 'Wyoming');
```

The only difference among the four select menus used in this chapter will be their names and their data sources. For each menu, a different data source is defined as the **$data** array. Two menus, named *state* and *cc_state*, will use this list of US states.

8. If an expiration month menu is being created, define that data source:

```
} elseif ($name == 'cc_exp_month') {
    $data = array(1 => 'January', 'February', 'March', 'April', 'May', 'June',
    ➥'July', 'August',  'September', 'October', 'November', 'December');
```

For the credit card's expiration month, a select menu will display the month name but use the numbers 1 through 12 as the values.

9. If an expiration year menu is being created, define that data source:

```
} elseif ($name == 'cc_exp_year') {
    $data = array();
    $start = date('Y');
    for ($i = $start; $i <= $start + 5; $i++) {
        $data[$i] = $i;
    }
} // End of $name IF-ELSEIF.
```

 tip

If the server's time zone is not set in PHP, you'll need to set it using **date_default_timezone_set()** prior to calling any date-related function.

For the credit card's expiration year, a list of years will be presented. This list will always start with the current year and then display five more from there. The combination of the **date()** function, to return the current year, and a **foreach** loop will populate the array.

10. Create the opening **<SELECT>** tag:

echo '<select name="' . $name . '"';

11. Add the *error* class, if applicable, and close the opening tag:

if (array_key_exists($name, $errors)) echo ' class="error"';
echo '>';

If an error exists for this element, the *error* class is added to the opening tag. The effect will be the element outlined in red (in accordance with the definition of the *error* class in the CSS file).

12. Create each option:

foreach ($data as $k => $v) {
    echo "<option value=\"$k\"";
    if ($value == $k) echo ' selected="selected"';
    echo ">$v</option>\n";
} // End of FOREACH.

A **foreach** loop iterates through the data source, creating an **<OPTION>** tag for each element. If there is an existing value, that will be selected as well (**Figure 10.4**).

```
<option value="NH">New Hampshire</option>
<option value="NJ">New Jersey</option>
<option value="NM" selected="selected">New Mexico</option>
<option value="NY">New York</option>
```

Figure 10.4

13. Complete the tag:

echo '</select>';

14. Add an error message, if one exists:

if (array_key_exists($name, $errors)) {
    **echo '
<span class="error">' . $errors[$name] . '</span>';**
}

The error message is displayed on the line after the menu.

15. Complete the function:

    } // End of primary IF-ELSE.
} // End of the create_form_input() function.

16. Save the file.

Creating the Procedures

This chapter requires five new stored procedures. Each one applies to an important part of the checkout process:

- The customer

- The shopping cart

- The order

- The order's contents

- The payment transaction

Three of these are simple, one is not too complicated, and one is, well, complicated. Let's look at the easy ones first.

CLEARING THE SHOPPING CART

After the customer has completed a purchase, the shopping cart needs to be emptied of its contents. That stored procedure is short and simple:

```
DELIMITER $$
CREATE PROCEDURE clear_cart (uid CHAR(32))
BEGIN
    DELETE FROM carts WHERE user_session_id=uid;
END$$
DELIMITER ;
```

This procedure takes one argument: the customer's cart session ID. The procedure then runs a **DELETE** query on the **carts** table.

ADDING TRANSACTIONS

The **transactions** table stores a record of every call to the payment gateway: what order the transaction was tied to and what the response was. All this information will also be available through the Merchant Interface, but it'd be nice to have it on this server as well: When it comes to databases, it's always better to store more information. There's nothing of a sensitive nature in the transaction data (that is, no billing information), so storing it does not constitute a security risk.

The **transactions** table has nine columns: **id**, **order_id**, **type**, **amount**, **response_code**, **response_reason**, **transaction_id**, **response**, and **date_created**. Most of these columns, and their values, will be explained later in the chapter when the payment response is covered in detail. But for now,

tip

All the book's SQL commands can be downloaded from **www.DMCInsights.com/ecom/**.

tip

Chapter 8 provides instructions on using the command-line mysql client or the browser-based phpMyAdmin to create stored procedures.

tip

If you're looking for a good third-party tool for MySQL development, check out Toad (**www.quest.com**). It's available free for Windows.

tip

As a reminder, the lines that change the delimiter aren't part of the stored procedure itself, but are necessary in order to use semicolons within the definition.

seven of these values need to be provided when the procedure is called. Here is that definition:

```
DELIMITER $$
CREATE PROCEDURE add_transaction (oid INT, trans_type VARCHAR(18),
➥amt DECIMAL(7,2), rc TINYINT, rrc TINYTEXT, tid BIGINT, r TEXT)
BEGIN
    INSERT INTO transactions VALUES (NULL, oid, trans_type, amt, rc, rrc,
    ➥tid, r, NOW());
END$$
DELIMITER ;
```

ADDING CUSTOMERS

The stored procedure for adding a customer isn't that complicated, but it uses a new stored procedure concept: *outbound arguments* (new in that they have not been discussed previously in this book). Stored procedures can be written to take arguments, just like a function in PHP. By default, all procedure arguments are *inbound*, meaning that values are assigned to the arguments when the procedure is called. You can also create *outbound arguments*. Outbound arguments are assigned values within the procedure itself, not when the procedure is called. The values assigned within the procedure can then be available outside of the procedure, after it has been called.

As a practical example of how outbound arguments might be used, take this next stored procedure, which inserts a record into the **customers** table. The rest of the checkout process will need the new record's ID value, so using an outbound argument is appropriate. Here is the procedure's definition:

```
DELIMITER $$
CREATE PROCEDURE add_customer (e VARCHAR(80), f VARCHAR(20),
➥l VARCHAR(40), a1 VARCHAR(80), a2 VARCHAR(80), c VARCHAR(60),
➥s CHAR(2), z MEDIUMINT, p INT, OUT cid INT)
BEGIN
    INSERT INTO customers VALUES (NULL, e, f, l, a1, a2, c, s, z, p, NOW());
    SELECT LAST_INSERT_ID() INTO cid;
END$$
DELIMITER ;
```

The first nine arguments are typical inbound ones. They represent the customer's email address, first name, last name, street address, additional street address, city, state, zip code, and phone. The argument names are cryptic, but they aren't referenced more than once within the procedure and, more impor-

note

The argument names used in a stored procedure should not be the same as any table's column names or as any MySQL keyword.

tip

Since the default parameter type is inbound, the **IN** keyword declaring them as such is optional.

tantly, they don't conflict with the table's actual column names this way. These nine arguments are used as the values for the **INSERT** query.

The tenth argument, **cid**, is defined as outbound, thanks to the **OUT** keyword. The last thing the procedure does is call the **LAST_INSERT_ID()** function, which returns the primary key value for the previously run **INSERT**. This value is selected and assigned to **cid**.

RETRIEVING ORDER CONTENTS

After the order has been completed, many site pages will need to retrieve the details of an order. For example, the PHP script that generates a receipt will need to fetch those order details, as will an administrative script. Doing so only requires the order ID, which can then be used to query the **order_contents** table. The **order_contents** table stores the number of items purchased, the quantity, and the price. By performing a **JOIN** from this table to the various product-related tables, similar to the **JOIN**s in the **get_shopping_cart_contents()** procedure, each product's descriptive name can also be retrieved. The query also joins in the **orders** table, so that it may select the order total and shipping cost.

```
DELIMITER $$
CREATE PROCEDURE get_order_contents (oid INT)
BEGIN
    SELECT oc.quantity, oc.price_per, (oc.quantity*oc.price_per) AS subtotal,
ncc.category, ncp.name, o.total, o.shipping
FROM order_contents AS oc
INNER JOIN non_coffee_products AS ncp ON oc.product_id=ncp.id
INNER JOIN non_coffee_categories AS ncc
ON ncc.id=ncp.non_coffee_category_id
INNER JOIN orders AS o ON oc.order_id=o.id
WHERE oc.product_type="other" AND oc.order_id=oid
    UNION
    SELECT oc.quantity, oc.price_per, (oc.quantity*oc.price_per),
gc.category, CONCAT_WS(" - ", s.size, sc.caf_decaf, sc.ground_whole),
➥o.total, o.shipping
FROM order_contents AS oc
INNER JOIN specific_coffees AS sc ON oc.product_id=sc.id
INNER JOIN sizes AS s ON s.id=sc.size_id
INNER JOIN general_coffees AS gc ON gc.id=sc.general_coffee_id
INNER JOIN orders AS o ON oc.order_id=o.id
WHERE oc.product_type="coffee" AND oc.order_id=oid;
END$$
DELIMITER ;
```

tip

Stored procedures can also have **INOUT** arguments, which can be used for both inbound and outbound purposes.

tip

Because the **get_order_contents()** procedure will be used to confirm to the customer what they just purchased, the query does not retrieve any of the customer data.

tip

To fetch the order total and shipping cost, it must be selected as part of each returned row, or a second **SELECT** query would be required and the procedure's results would be that much harder to handle.

Figure 10.5 shows the result of executing this procedure.

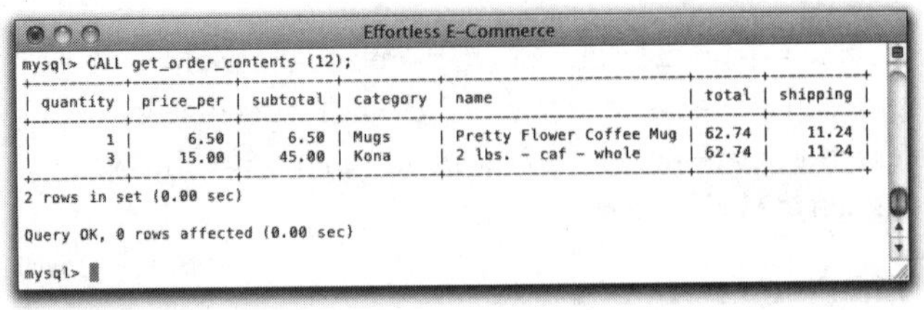

```
mysql> CALL get_order_contents (12);
+----------+-----------+----------+----------+------------------------+--------+----------+
| quantity | price_per | subtotal | category | name                   | total  | shipping |
+----------+-----------+----------+----------+------------------------+--------+----------+
|        1 |      6.50 |     6.50 | Mugs     | Pretty Flower Coffee Mug | 62.74 |    11.24 |
|        3 |     15.00 |    45.00 | Kona     | 2 lbs. - caf - whole   | 62.74  |    11.24 |
+----------+-----------+----------+----------+------------------------+--------+----------+
2 rows in set (0.00 sec)

Query OK, 0 rows affected (0.00 sec)

mysql>
```

Figure 10.5

ADDING ORDERS

The final stored procedure for this chapter is perhaps the most complicated one in the book. At its core, the procedure needs to add a new order to the database. This involves populating both the **orders** and **order_contents** tables. Let's look at the queries and the process separately, before revealing the complete procedure definition.

Adding records to the **orders** table is easy: The **INSERT** just requires the customer ID, the total, the shipping cost (which is also part of the total), the last four digits of the credit card number (for the customer's reference), and the date of the order. That query is:

INSERT INTO orders (customer_id, shipping, credit_card_number,
order_date) VALUES (cid, ship, cc, NOW());

For now, let's ignore the total column, as that value is unknown without adding up all the items in the order.

Next, the order ID will be required to populate the **order_contents** table, so that information will need to be selected into a variable:

SELECT LAST_INSERT_ID() INTO oid;

This is exactly how the customer ID value is retrieved in the **add_customer()** stored procedure.

The **order_contents** table is going to store the order ID, the product type (*coffee* or *other*), the product ID, the quantity, and the price being paid for each. The interesting thing is that all this information is readily available to the **add_order()** procedure without it being passed as arguments. And that's where things get complicated…

The order ID was just created, so that's not a problem. The product type, product ID, and quantity can come from the **carts** table, assuming that this procedure can access the user's cart ID. But to determine the price to be paid, factoring in sale prices, requires a **JOIN** across **carts, sales,** and either **non_coffee_products** or **specific_coffees**. Because this last **JOIN** is across one of two tables, a **UNION** is required, just like the **get_shopping_cart_contents()** procedure uses.

Fetching the product's information and the correct price for just non-coffee products requires this **SELECT** statement (**Figure 10.6**):

```
SELECT c.product_type, c.product_id, c.quantity,
IFNULL(sales.price, ncp.price)
FROM carts AS c
INNER JOIN non_coffee_products AS ncp ON c.product_id=ncp.id
LEFT OUTER JOIN sales ON (sales.product_id=ncp.id AND
➥sales.product_type='other' AND
((NOW() BETWEEN sales.start_date AND sales.end_date) OR (NOW() >
➥sales.start_date AND sales.end_date IS NULL)) )
WHERE c.product_type="other" AND c.user_session_id=<user_cart_id>
```

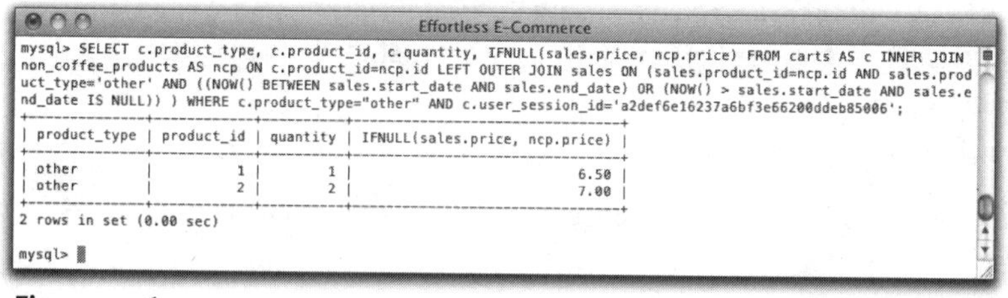

```
mysql> SELECT c.product_type, c.product_id, c.quantity, IFNULL(sales.price, ncp.price) FROM carts AS c INNER JOIN
non_coffee_products AS ncp ON c.product_id=ncp.id LEFT OUTER JOIN sales ON (sales.product_id=ncp.id AND sales.prod
uct_type='other' AND ((NOW() BETWEEN sales.start_date AND sales.end_date) OR (NOW() > sales.start_date AND sales.e
nd_date IS NULL)) ) WHERE c.product_type="other" AND c.user_session_id='a2def6e16237a6bf3e66200ddeb85006';
+--------------+------------+----------+--------------------------------+
| product_type | product_id | quantity | IFNULL(sales.price, ncp.price) |
+--------------+------------+----------+--------------------------------+
| other        |          1 |        1 |                           6.50 |
| other        |          2 |        2 |                           7.00 |
+--------------+------------+----------+--------------------------------+
2 rows in set (0.00 sec)

mysql>
```

Figure 10.6

For the price, the query uses the **IFNULL()** construct, which selects the first value if it's not **NULL** and the second value if it is. Thus, **IFNULL(sales.price, ncp.price)** will select **sales.price** if it exists, and select **ncp.price** otherwise. You can confirm this by also selecting the two prices, too (**Figure 10.7**).

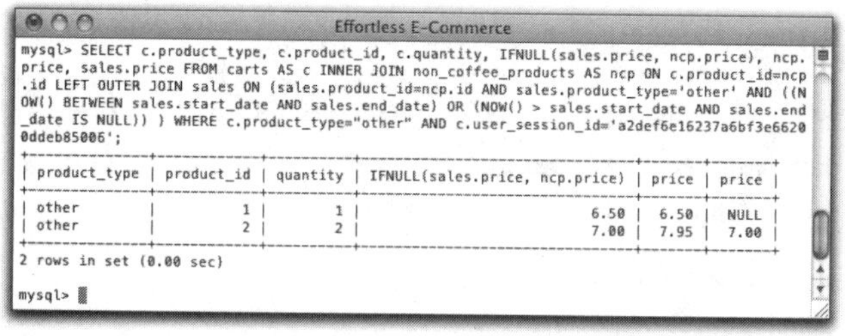

```
mysql> SELECT c.product_type, c.product_id, c.quantity, IFNULL(sales.price, ncp.price), ncp.
price, sales.price FROM carts AS c INNER JOIN non_coffee_products AS ncp ON c.product_id=ncp
.id LEFT OUTER JOIN sales ON (sales.product_id=ncp.id AND sales.product_type='other' AND ((N
OW() BETWEEN sales.start_date AND sales.end_date) OR (NOW() > sales.start_date AND sales.end
_date IS NULL)) ) WHERE c.product_type="other" AND c.user_session_id='a2def6e16237a6bf3e6620
0ddeb85006';
+--------------+------------+----------+--------------------------------+-------+-------+
| product_type | product_id | quantity | IFNULL(sales.price, ncp.price) | price | price |
+--------------+------------+----------+--------------------------------+-------+-------+
| other        |          1 |        1 |                           6.50 |  6.50 |  NULL |
| other        |          2 |        2 |                           7.00 |  7.95 |  7.00 |
+--------------+------------+----------+--------------------------------+-------+-------+
2 rows in set (0.00 sec)

mysql>
```

Figure 10.7

Now that you (hopefully) understand how the **SELECT** query works, consider that the **SELECT** query can be used immediately as the values for an **INSERT** query, thanks to the **INSERT...SELECT** construct. The **INSERT** for order_contents is:

INSERT INTO order_contents (order_id, product_type, product_id, quantity,
➥price_per) VALUES (...

Putting together the **INSERT** and **SELECT** queries, the entire query becomes:

INSERT INTO order_contents (order_id, product_type, product_id, quantity,
➥price_per)
SELECT oid, c.product_type, c.product_id, c.quantity,
IFNULL(sales.price, ncp.price)
FROM carts AS c
INNER JOIN non_coffee_products AS ncp ON c.product_id=ncp.id
LEFT OUTER JOIN sales ON (sales.product_id=ncp.id AND
➥sales.product_type='other' AND
((NOW() BETWEEN sales.start_date AND sales.end_date) OR (NOW() >
➥sales.start_date AND sales.end_date IS NULL)))
WHERE c.product_type="other" AND c.user_session_id=<*user_cart_id*>
UNION
SELECT oid,...

By adding the selection of the **oid** variable, that value can be inserted into **order_contents** at the same time.

Moving on in the procedure, the last step is to update the **orders** table for the order total. The total can be determined by running an aggregating query on **order_contents** for the current order:

SELECT SUM(quantity*price_per) INTO subtotal FROM order_contents
➥WHERE order_id=oid;

And now the **orders** table can be updated:

UPDATE orders SET total = (subtotal + ship) WHERE id=oid;

Finally, the order total will be necessary outside of the procedure (as part of the payment processing). To make that possible, the total should also be assigned to an outbound argument:

SELECT (subtotal + ship) INTO total;

The complete stored procedure is therefore:

```
DELIMITER $$
CREATE PROCEDURE add_order (cid INT, uid CHAR(32), ship DECIMAL(5,2),
⇒cc MEDIUMINT, OUT total DECIMAL(7,2), OUT oid INT)
BEGIN
    DECLARE subtotal DECIMAL(7,2);
    INSERT INTO orders (customer_id, shipping, credit_card_number,
    ⇒order_date) VALUES (cid, ship, cc, NOW());
    SELECT LAST_INSERT_ID() INTO oid;
    INSERT INTO order_contents (order_id, product_type, product_id,
    ⇒quantity, price_per) SELECT oid, c.product_type, c.product_id,
    ⇒c.quantity, IFNULL(sales.price, ncp.price) FROM carts AS c INNER JOIN
    ⇒non_coffee_products AS ncp ON c.product_id=ncp.id LEFT OUTER JOIN
    ⇒sales ON (sales.product_id=ncp.id AND sales.product_type='other'
    ⇒AND ((NOW() BETWEEN sales.start_date AND sales.end_date)
    ⇒OR (NOW() > sales.start_date AND sales.end_date IS NULL)) ) WHERE
    ⇒c.product_type="other" AND c.user_session_id=uid UNION SELECT
    ⇒oid, c.product_type, c.product_id, c.quantity, IFNULL(sales.price,
    ⇒sc.price) FROM carts AS c INNER JOIN specific_coffees AS sc ON
    ⇒c.product_id=sc.id LEFT OUTER JOIN sales ON (sales.product_id=sc.id
    ⇒AND sales.product_type='coffee' AND ((NOW() BETWEEN
    ⇒sales.start_date AND sales.end_date) OR (NOW() > sales.start_date
    ⇒AND sales.end_date IS NULL)) ) WHERE c.product_type="coffee" AND
    ⇒c.user_session_id=uid;
    SELECT SUM(quantity*price_per) INTO subtotal FROM order_contents
    ⇒WHERE order_id=oid;
    UPDATE orders SET total = (subtotal + ship) WHERE id=oid;
    SELECT (subtotal + ship) INTO total;
END$$
DELIMITER ;
```

The procedure takes the customer ID, the customer's cart ID, the ship-ping amount, and the credit card number (the last four digits) as inbound arguments. There are two outbound arguments: **total** and **oid**. Within a **BEGIN** block, a local variable named **subtotal** is defined. Next, the record is added to the **orders** table, and the just-created ID is selected and assigned to **oid**. After that, the **order_contents** table is populated, using the **INSERT...SELECT UNION SELECT** query.

The last three lines calculate the subtotal of the order, update the **total** column in the **orders** table, and assign the total order value to the **total** variable.

 note

Remember that variables in stored procedures do not use a dollar sign like PHP variables.

STORED PROCEDURES REVISITED

The modestly complex **add_order()** stored procedure demonstrates the security and performance benefits that can be had by using stored procedures. The procedure takes just four arguments—the customer ID, the customer's cart session ID, the shipping total, and the credit card representation—and does a lot of work with that little information. The procedure could even be cut down to just two inbound arguments if the shipping were to be calculated by a database-stored function and the credit card numbers were omitted (they'll be stored in the **transactions** table anyway). From a performance standpoint, there's very little information that PHP needs to send to the database, and, more critically, the PHP script only needs to execute a single query—the procedure call itself. Since query executions are one of the most demanding things a PHP script does, limiting those can have a huge performance gain. (Although that burden is therefore moved to the database server.)

From a security standpoint, much of the key information—like the price a product is sold for—never leaves the database, making it that much harder to be manipulated. And no PHP script directly accesses any of the database tables, adding a layer of obfuscation.

I should add that you might logically use transactions in this stored procedure, which stored procedures do support. By using transactions, every query would have to work properly or else the entire process would be reverted. Such an approach prevents an incomplete order from being recorded. Still, I opted not to use transactions, because they would further complicate an already complicated process.

TAKING THE SHIPPING INFORMATION

Once the customer is finished shopping and is ready to purchase items, he or she will click a button on the shopping cart page that will go to **checkout.php** (over HTTPS). This page needs to:

1. Take the customer's shipping information.

2. Validate the provided data.

3. If valid, store the data and send the customer on to the next step in the checkout process.

4. If invalid, redisplay the form with errors.

In terms of displaying and validating the form, **checkout.php** behaves like **register.php** from Chapter 4. But there are some additional considerations that make this script more complicated than that one. Let's first define the PHP script, then the two view files it uses.

Creating the PHP Script

The PHP script should be accessed at least twice: originally as a GET request, at which point the form should be loaded, and as a POST request, when the form is submitted. The latter action demands about 100 lines of validation, which is the bulk of the script.

Unlike the shopping area of the Web site, the checkout process will use PHP sessions. This is necessary because multiple scripts will all need access to some of the same information. By default, PHP will store the session identifier in a cookie. You might not be aware of this, but with respect to cookies, **http://www.example.com** and **https://www.example.com** are separate realms, meaning that a cookie sent over HTTP is available only to pages accessed via HTTP (and the same goes for HTTPS). I mention this now, because the sessions used by the checkout process will not be available on the shopping side of the site, and the cookie used on the shopping side of the site is not available in the checkout process.

1. Create a new PHP script in your text editor or IDE to be named **checkout.php** and stored in the Web root directory.

2. Include the configuration file:

   <?php
   require ('./includes/config.inc.php');

3. Check for the user's cart ID, available in the URL:

   if ($_SERVER['REQUEST_METHOD'] == 'GET') {
   **   if (isset($_GET['session'])) {**
   ** $uid = $_GET['session'];**

   In order to access the customer's shopping cart, this script needs the user's shopping cart session ID, stored in a cookie in the user's browser. However, that cookie was sent over HTTP, meaning that it's not available to **checkout.php**, because this script is being accessed via HTTPS. The remedy is to pass the cookie value to this script when the user clicks the checkout button on **cart.php**. This script first confirms that a session value was passed along in the URL. If so, it's assigned to the **$uid** variable for later use.

4. Use the cart ID as the session ID, and begin the session:

   session_id($uid);
   session_start();

   The shopping part of the site purposefully does not use sessions (in order to give longevity to the customer's cart and wish list), but the checkout process will. For continuity, and because the shopping cart ID will be

tip

The **.htaccess** modifications in Chapter 7, "Second Site: Structure and Design," ensure that **checkout.php** is accessible only over HTTPS.

tip

When the user returns to the shopping side of the site, the wish list and cart cookie will still be usable, even after checking out.

required by the checkout process, the user's existing cart ID will be used as the session ID. This can be arranged by providing a session ID value to the **session_id()** function prior to calling **session_start()**.

The net result will be two cookies in the user's browser: *SESSION*, sent over HTTP, and *PHP_SESSION_ID*, sent over HTTPS. Both will have the same value.

5. If no session value was present in the URL (for a GET request), redirect the user:

```
} else {
    $location = 'http://' . BASE_URL . 'cart.php';
    header("Location: $location");
    exit();
}
```

There's no point in checking out if there's nothing to purchase. And without a cart session ID, there will be nothing to purchase! In that case, the customer is redirected back to **cart.php**, over HTTP. That page will display the checkout button only if the cart is not empty.

6. If the request method isn't GET, start the session and retrieve the session ID:

```
} else { // POST request.
    session_start();
    $uid = session_id();
}
```

This **else** clause will apply when the customer submits the form for validation. In that case, the session needs to be started. The session ID would have already been set the first time this script was accessed, so that value can be retrieved (by calling **session_id()** with no arguments) to be used later in this script.

7. Include the database connection and create an array for validation errors:

```
require (MYSQL);
$shipping_errors = array();
```

8. If the form was submitted, validate the first and last names:

```
if ($_SERVER['REQUEST_METHOD'] == 'POST') {
    if (preg_match ('/^[A-Z \'.-]{2,20}$/i', $_POST['first_name'])) {
        $fn= addslashes($_POST['first_name']);
    } else {
        $shipping_errors['first_name'] = 'Please enter your first name!';
    }
```

```
if (preg_match ('/^[A-Z \'.-]{2,40}$/i', $_POST['last_name'])) {
    $ln = addslashes($_POST['last_name']);
} else {
    $shipping_errors['last_name'] = 'Please enter your last name!';
}
```

The validation routines for the customer's first and last names match those from **register.php** in Chapter 4. To make the values safe to use in the stored procedure call, each value is run through **addslashes()**.

If there's a chance that Magic Quotes may be enabled on your server, you'll also need to apply **stripslashes()** prior to validation:

```
if (get_magic_quotes_gpc()) {
    $_POST['first_name'] = stripslashes($_POST['first_name']);
    // Repeat for other variables that could be affected.
}
```

If Magic Quotes is enabled, a valid last name, such as *O'Toole*, will become *O\'Toole*, which won't pass the regular expression test. But when the stored procedure is invoked, the query will be **CALL add_customer('$fn', '$ln', . . .)**, so **addslashes()** must be applied to the query data to prevent the apostrophe in *O'Toole* from breaking that procedure call: **CALL add_customer('Peter', 'O'Toole', . . .)**

9. Validate the street addresses:

```
if (preg_match ('/^[A-Z0-9 \',.#-]{2,80}$/i', $_POST['address1'])) {
    $a1 = addslashes($_POST['address1']);
} else {
    $shipping_errors['address1'] = 'Please enter your street address!';
}
if (empty($_POST['address2'])) {
    $a2 = NULL;
} elseif (preg_match ('/^[A-Z0-9 \',.#-]{2,80}$/i', $_POST['address2'])) {
    $a2 = addslashes($_POST['address2']);
} else {
    $shipping_errors['address2'] = 'Please enter your street address!';
}
```

Addresses are trickier to validate because they can contain many characters besides alphanumeric ones. The regular expression pattern allows for any letter, any number, a space, an apostrophe, a comma, a period, the number sign, and a dash.

The second street address (for longer addresses) is optional, so it's only validated if it's not empty.

 tip

As a formality, you could add **isset()** to each validation conditional, as in

**if (isset($_POST['var'])
&& preg_match(...**

10. Validate the city:

```
if (preg_match ('/^[A-Z \'.-]{2,60}$/i', $_POST['city'])) {
    $c = addslashes($_POST['city']);
} else {
    $shipping_errors['city'] = 'Please enter your city!';
}
```

11. Validate the state:

```
if (preg_match ('/^[A-Z]{2}$/', $_POST['state'])) {
    $s = $_POST['state'];
} else {
    $shipping_errors['state'] = 'Please enter your state!';
}
```

There's no need to apply either **stripslashes()**, with Magic Quotes enabled, or **addslashes()** to this variable, because a valid value can contain exactly two capital letters.

tip

All address and phone number validation routines would need to be altered if the site is serving non-U.S. customers.

12. Validate the zip code:

```
if (preg_match ('/^(\d{5}$)|(^\d{5}-\d{4})$/', $_POST['zip'])) {
    $z = $_POST['zip'];
} else {
    $shipping_errors['zip'] = 'Please enter your zip code!';
}
```

The zip code can be in either the five digit or five plus four format (12345 or 12345-6789).

13. Validate the phone number:

```
$phone = str_replace(array(' ', '-', '(', ')'), '', $_POST['phone']);
if (preg_match ('/^[0-9]{10}$/', $phone)) {
    $p = $phone;
} else {
    $shipping_errors['phone'] = 'Please enter your phone number!';
}
```

The phone number must be exactly ten digits long, which is easy to check. But as users commonly enter phone numbers with and without spaces, hyphens, and parentheses, any of those characters that may be present are first removed via **str_replace()**. Its first argument is an array of values to find—space, hyphen, opening parenthesis, closing parenthesis; its second argument is the replacement value (here, an empty string).

tip

The **str_replace()** function is a faster alternative to **preg_replace()**, usable when fancy pattern matching isn't required.

14. Validate the email address:

```
if (filter_var($_POST['email'], FILTER_VALIDATE_EMAIL)) {
    $e = $_POST['email'];
    $_SESSION['email'] = $_POST['email'];
} else {
    $shipping_errors['email'] = 'Please enter a valid email address!';
}
```

Thanks to the **filter_var()** function, this is the most straightforward of all these validation routines. If your PHP installation does not support the Filter extension, you can search online for the Perl-Compatible Regular Expression (PCRE) pattern to use instead.

Unlike every other variable, the customer's email address will be stored automatically in the session so that a receipt can be sent to the customer once the order has gone through.

15. Store the data in the session if the shipping information matches the billing:

```
if (isset($_POST['use']) && ($_POST['use'] == 'Y')) {
    $_SESSION['shipping_for_billing'] = true;
    $_SESSION['cc_first_name'] = $_POST['first_name'];
    $_SESSION['cc_last_name'] = $_POST['last_name'];
    $_SESSION['cc_address'] = $_POST['address1'] . ' '
    ➡. $_POST['address2'];
    $_SESSION['cc_city'] = $_POST['city'];
    $_SESSION['cc_state'] = $_POST['state'];
    $_SESSION['cc_zip'] = $_POST['zip'];
}
```

 note

Fraudulent credit card charges often use different shipping and billing addresses. If your site allows for this, make sure your payment gateway has stringent fraud-protection tools.

The checkout form will present the customer with a check box to select if they want the shipping information to be used as the billing address, too (**Figure 10.8**). In that case, the customer's name and address need to be stored in the session for use in the next PHP script. Also, a value is stored in the session indicating this choice.

Authorize.net takes the customer's street address as a single item, so the two potential street addresses are concatenated together in the session.

Your Shipping Information

Please enter your shipping information. On the next page, you'll be able to enter your billing information and complete the order. Please check the first box if your shipping and billing addresses are the same. * Indicates a required field.

Use Same Address for Billing?

Figure 10.8

16. If no errors occurred, add the user to the database:

```
if (empty($shipping_errors)) {
    $r = mysqli_query($dbc, "CALL add_customer('$e', '$fn', '$ln', '$a1',
    ➥'$a2', '$c', '$s', $z, $p, @cid)");
```

To add the customer to the database, the **add_customer()** stored procedure is invoked. The first nine arguments are the PHP variables assigned during the validation process. The tenth is a MySQL user-defined variable. This will match up with the outbound parameter in the stored procedure, to be further explained in the next step.

17. If the procedure worked, retrieve the customer ID:

```
if ($r) {
    $r = mysqli_query($dbc, 'SELECT @cid');
    if (mysqli_num_rows($r) == 1) {
        list($_SESSION['customer_id']) = mysqli_fetch_array($r);
```

To get the customer ID generated by the stored procedure, a second query must select **@cid**. This query is run, then the results of the query are fetched into **$_SESSION['customer_id']**. If you find this concept to be confusing, it may help to think about this in MySQL terms, as if the procedure were being called from the command-line **mysql** client (**Figure 10.9**), not a PHP script...

Figure 10.9

The first query itself is a call to a MySQL stored procedure. When the query is executed, a reference to a user-defined variable—**@cid**—is created. This is a variable that exists within MySQL, but outside of the stored procedure (variables in MySQL outside of stored procedures begin with **@**). Within the stored procedure, a value is assigned to the internal variable **cid**, as explained earlier in the chapter. This variable is associated with **@cid**, thanks to the procedure call and the outbound argument. When the procedure call is complete, **@cid** still exists (because it's outside of the procedure), but will now have a value. But **@cid** only exists within the MySQL world; to get it to a PHP script, it must be selected and fetched.

18. Redirect the customer to the billing page:

```
$location = 'https://' . BASE_URL . 'billing.php';
header("Location: $location");
exit();
```

At this point, the customer can be sent to **billing.php** where the billing information will be requested and processed.

19. If there was a problem, indicate an error:

```
    }

}

trigger_error('Your order could not be processed due to a system error.
➥We apologize for the inconvenience.');
```

The two closing brackets complete the two query-related conditionals. If the customer got to this point in the script, it means that they did everything right but the system is not working. In that case, you should log the error, email the administrator—pretty much panic—but let the customer know that a problem occurred through no fault of their own. The site's support team or administrator would be able to contact the customer immediately, as both the customer's email address and phone number would be stored in the error log.

20. Complete the **$shipping_errors** and request method conditionals:

```
    } // Errors occurred IF.
} // End of REQUEST_METHOD IF.
```

This concludes the end of the form validation process. The rest of the script will apply to the initial GET request. It will also apply should there be errors in the form data after the POST request.

21. Include the header file:

```
$page_title = 'Coffee - Checkout - Your Shipping Information';
include ('./includes/checkout_header.html');
```

Note that this script includes the new **checkout_header.html** file, not the original **header.html**.

22. Retrieve the shopping cart contents:

```
$r = mysqli_query($dbc, "CALL get_shopping_cart_contents('$uid')");
```

The customer's shopping cart ID is necessary at this point in order to retrieve and later display what the customer is purchasing. This is the same stored procedure used by **cart.php** in Chapter 9, "Building a Shopping Cart."

23. Complete the script:

```
if (mysqli_num_rows($r) > 0) {
    include ('./views/checkout.html');
} else { // Empty cart!
    include ('./views/emptycart.html');
}
```

If the stored procedure returned some records, then the **checkout.html** view file will be included (this will be a new file). If the stored procedure did not return any records, the **emptycart.html** file will be included instead. It was defined in Chapter 9. Its inclusion means that the customer will not be able to continue the checkout process, which is entirely appropriate.

24. Finish the page:

```
include ('./includes/footer.html');
?>
```

The checkout process scripts include the standard footer.

25. Save the file.

Creating the View Files

The **checkout.php** script uses three view files:

- **checkout.html**
- **checkout_cart.html**
- **emptycart.html**

The first file is included if there are products in the shopping cart. The second file is included by the first (which is why there's no reference to it in **checkout.php**). The third has already been defined.

Let's write **checkout_cart.html** first.

CREATING CHECKOUT_CART.HTML

The **checkout_cart.html** view file displays the contents of the cart—what the customer is actually about to purchase (**Figure 10.10**). It's defined as its own script so that it can be used by both of the first two steps of the checkout process. Unlike the **cart.html** view file, this one doesn't allow the customer to update the quantities, remove items, or move items to the wish list. More importantly, this script needs to watch out for situations in which the customer is attempting to purchase an item that is insufficiently stocked. In such cases, the original shopping cart page recommends that the customer update the quantity of the item or move it to their wish list (see Figure 9.6). This script will forcibly move the item to the wish list if it's still in the cart but can't be fulfilled.

Figure 10.10

1. Create a new HTML page in your text editor or IDE to be named **checkout_cart.html** and stored in the **views** directory.

2. Begin the HTML box and the cart table:

```
<div class="box alt"><div class="left-top-corner"><div class=
➥"right-top-corner"><div class="border-top"></div></div></div>
➥<div class="border-left"><div class="border-right"><div class=
➥"inner">
   <h2>Your Shopping Cart</h2>
   <table border="0" cellspacing="8" cellpadding="6"
➥width="100%">
   <tr>
      <th align="center">Item</th>
      <th align="center">Quantity</th>
      <th align="right">Price</th>
      <th align="right">Subtotal</th>
   </tr>
```

3. Begin a PHP block and include the product functions file:

```
<?php
include ('./includes/product_functions.inc.php');
```

The **product_functions.inc.php** script was begun in Chapter 8 and expanded in Chapter 9. It defines a couple of necessary functions for displaying the shopping cart.

4. Initialize a variable to represent the order total:

```
$total = 0;
```

5. Create an array for identifying problematic items:

$remove = array();

With the site as written, it's possible that the customer is still trying to purchase items that aren't available. There are a couple of ways you can handle this. First, you could remove those items from the cart and place them in the wish list, as this page will do. Alternatively, you could allow the sale to go through with the thinking that the item would be available relatively soon. The risk of such a policy depends upon what's being sold and how readily it's available. This site will not actually charge a customer's card until a product ships, so allowing an order to go through that may not be fulfilled at that moment is not fraudulent.

In any case, the **$remove** array will be used to store insufficiently stocked products found in the customer's cart so that they can later be removed.

6. Fetch each product:

while ($row = mysqli_fetch_array($r, MYSQLI_ASSOC)) {

tip

You could also write logic that will sell a partial order: If the customer wants four of something and only three are available, sell three and move one to the wish list. Or the site could ask the customer how they want the item to be handled.

7. If the quantity of the item in the cart is greater than the stock on hand, make a note of the item:

if ($row['stock'] < $row['quantity']) {
    echo '<tr class="error"><td colspan="4" align="center">There are
    ⇒**only ' . $row['stock'] . ' left in stock of the ' . $row['name'] . '. This**
    ⇒**item has been removed from your cart and placed in your wish list.**
    ⇒**</td></tr>';**
    $remove[$row['sku']] = $row['quantity'];

If the store does not have enough of an item in stock to cover the number in the cart, a message is added to the table indicating the problem to the customer (**Figure 10.11**). Then, the problematic item is added to the **$remove** array, using the syntax *SKU => quantity*.

Figure 10.11

8. If the stock is fine, display the item:

```
} else {
    $price = get_just_price($row['price'], $row['sale_price']);
    $subtotal = $price * $row['quantity'];
    echo '<tr><td>' . $row['category'] . '::' . $row['name'] . '</td>
        <td align="center">' . $row['quantity'] . '</td>
        <td align="right">$' . $price . '</td>
        <td align="right">$' . number_format($subtotal, 2) . '</td>
    </tr>
    ';
    $total += $subtotal;
}
```

This code is similar to that in **cart.html**, except for the particulars of each table row: The quantity is not alterable and there are no links to remove or move the item.

9. Complete the loop and add the shipping:

```
} // End of WHILE loop.
$shipping = get_shipping($total);
$total += $shipping;
echo '<tr>
    <td colspan="2"> </td><th align="right">Shipping &amp;
    ➥Handling</th>
    <td align="right">$' . $shipping . '</td>
</tr>
';
```

Again, this code is largely similar to that in **cart.html**. Figures 10.9 and 10.10 show the result.

10. Add the shipping to the session:

```
$_SESSION['shipping'] = $shipping;
```

The shipping cost is calculated by the **get_shipping()** function, defined in **product_functions.inc.php**. Because the shipping amount will be needed by the next PHP script, it's now stored in the session (at this point the order itself has been finalized, so the shipping can be finalized, too).

11. Display the total:

```
echo '<tr>
    <td colspan="2"> </td><th align="right">Total</th>
    <td align="right">$' . number_format($total, 2) . '</td>
    <td> </td>
</tr>
';
```

12. If the **$remove** array isn't empty, remove the problematic items:

```
if (!empty($remove)) {
    mysqli_next_result($dbc);
    foreach ($remove as $sku => $qty) {
        list($sp_type, $pid) = parse_sku($sku);
        $r = mysqli_multi_query($dbc, "CALL add_to_wish_list('$uid',
        ⇒'$sp_type', $pid, $qty);CALL remove_from_cart('$uid',
        ⇒'$sp_type', $pid)");
    }
}
```

If the **$remove** array isn't empty, then at least one product in the customer's cart needs to be moved to their wish list. You can accomplish that by parsing the SKU, then calling the **add_to_wish_list()** and **remove_from_cart()** stored procedures for each item. That's what the **foreach** loop accomplishes.

But first, the **get_shopping_cart_contents()** stored procedure, like any procedure that runs a **SELECT** query, returns two sets of results: the **SELECT** results and results indicating the success of running the procedure. These latter results must be addressed before calling another stored procedure. The invocation of the **mysqli_next_result()** function will take care of that. It clears this secondary result set.

To execute the two stored procedures, the **mysqli_multi_query()** function is used instead of two executions of **mysqli_query()**. This function, as its name implies, allows more than one query to be executed with a single database call.

13. Complete the page:

```
?></table>
</div></div></div><div class="left-bot-corner"><div class=
⇒"right-bot-corner"><div class="border-bot"></div></div></div>
⇒</div>
<!-- box end -->
```

14. Save the file.

tip

If, when using stored procedures, you see a "commands out of sync" error message, it means that stored procedure results exist that have not been retrieved.

CREATING CHECKOUT.HTML

The **checkout.html** view file is included by **checkout.php**. It must include **checkout_cart.html** and then display the form for obtaining the customer's shipping information (**Figure 10.12**).

Figure 10.12

1. Create a new HTML page in your text editor or IDE to be named **checkout.html** and stored in the **views** directory.

2. Add the progress indicator:

   ```
   <div align="center"><img src="/images/checkout_indicator1.png" />
   ➥</div>
   <br clear="all" />
   ```

   To make the checkout process clear to the customer, and where they are in that process, a *progress indicator* or *progress tracker* will be used (see Figure 10.3).

3. Include the **checkout_cart.html** view:

   ```
   <?php include ('./views/checkout_cart.html'); ?>
   ```

   This includes the script just created. The file reference is relative to **checkout.php**, which is including this **checkout.html** view file (which is why the code is **./views/checkout_cart.html** instead of just **checkout_cart.html**).

4. Begin the HTML box and the form:

```
<div class="box alt"><div class="left-top-corner"><div class=
➥"right-top-corner"><div class="border-top"></div></div></div>
➥<div class="border-left"><div class="border-right"><div class=
➥"inner">
<h2>Your Shipping Information</h2>
<p>Please enter your shipping information. On the next page, you'll be
➥able to enter your billing information and complete the order. Please
➥check the first box if your shipping and billing addresses are the same.
➥<span class="required">*</span> Indicates a required field. </p>
<form action="/checkout.php" method="POST">
```

Before the form are some simple instructions to the customer. Then the form is begun, which will be submitted to **checkout.php**.

5. Include the form functions:

```
<?php include ('./includes/form_functions.inc.php'); ?>
```

The **form_functions.inc.php** script defines the **create_form_input()** function written earlier in the chapter. The function will be used repeatedly by this form.

6. Create the Use Same Address for Billing check box:

```
<fieldset>
    <div class="field"><label for="use"><strong>Use Same Address
➥for Billing?</strong></label><br /><input type="checkbox"
➥name="use" value="Y" id="use" <?php if (isset($_POST['use']))
➥echo 'checked="checked" ';?>/></div>
```

If the customer selects this check box, they won't need to enter their address on the next page because their shipping address will be stored in the session. To make the check box sticky, a PHP conditional is added within the input.

7. Create the first name input:

```
<div class="field"><label for="first_name"><strong>First Name
➥<span class="required">*</span></strong></label><br /><?php
➥create_form_input('first_name', 'text', $shipping_errors); ?></div>
```

The **<DIV>** is used by the template to style form elements. Then comes the label, along with an indication that this is a required field. After a break, the **create_form_input()** function is called, creating a text box with a name of *first_name*. The **$shipping_errors** array is passed to the function. When the page is first loaded, **$shipping_errors** will be empty (it's initialized in **checkout.php**); if an error occurs, the error will be stored in it.

8. Create the last name, addresses, and city inputs:

```
<div class="field"><label for="last_name"><strong>Last Name
➥<span class="required">*</span></strong></label><br /><?php
➥create_form_input('last_name', 'text', $shipping_errors); ?></div>
<div class="field"><label for="address1"><strong>Street Address
➥<span class="required">*</span></strong></label><br /><?php
➥create_form_input('address1', 'text', $shipping_errors); ?></div>
<div class="field"><label for="address2"><strong>Street Address,
➥Continued</strong></label><br /><?php create_form_input(
➥'address2', 'text', $shipping_errors); ?></div>
<div class="field"><label for="city"><strong>City
➥<span class="required">*</span></strong></label><br />
➥<?php create_form_input('city', 'text', $shipping_errors); ?></div>
```

These four inputs are repetitions of the first name input, except that the second address field is not required.

9. Create the state select menu:

```
<div class="field"><label for="state"><strong>State
➥<span class="required">*</span></strong> </label><br />
➥<?php create_form_input('state', 'select', $shipping_errors); ?></div>
```

To create the select menu using the **create_form_input()** function, the second argument just needs to be *select*. The data used in the menu is based upon the element's name.

10. Create the zip code, phone number, and email address inputs:

```
<div class="field"><label for="zip"><strong>Zip Code
➥<span class="required">*</span></strong></label><br />
➥<?php create_form_input('zip', 'text', $shipping_errors); ?></div>
<div class="field"><label for="phone"><strong>Phone Number
➥<span class="required">*</span></strong></label><br />
➥<?php create_form_input('phone', 'text', $shipping_errors); ?></div>
<div class="field"><label for="email"><strong>Email Address
➥<span class="required">*</span></strong></label><br />
➥<?php create_form_input('email', 'text', $shipping_errors); ?></div>
```

11. Complete the form:

```
    <br clear="all" />
<div align="center"><input type="submit" value="Continue onto
➥Billing" class="button" /></fieldset></form></div>
```

As mentioned earlier, this button, which continues the checkout process, needs to be impossible to miss.

Figure 10.13

12. Complete the page:

    </div></div><div class="left-bot-corner"><div class=
    ➥"right-bot-corner"><div class="border-bot"></div></div></div>
    ➥</div>
    <!-- box end -->

13. Save the file.

Now you can test the **checkout.php** process. If you fill out the form *incorrectly*, it will be displayed again (**Figure 10.13**). If you fill it out correctly, you'll be sent to **billing.php**, which will be written next.

TAKING THE BILLING INFORMATION

After the customer has properly provided her or his shipping information, the site will ask for the customer's billing information. When accepting credit cards to be processed by Authorize.net, the billing information equates to their credit card data plus the billing address. This is the most sensitive information requested and handled by any script in the entire book. This is therefore the most complex and important script in the book (well, coupled with the next two). The entire billing process is reflected in **Figure 10.14**.

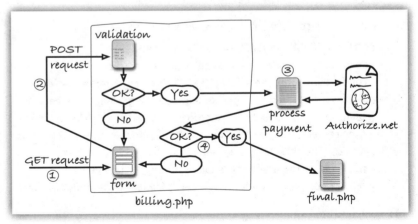

Figure 10.14

To make this script easier to comprehend, let's look at it piecemeal: the GET part (that displays the order contents and the form), the POST part (that validates the form data), and the payment processing part.

Creating the Basic PHP Script

To start, the basic PHP script will address all of the GET functionality. It's rather similar to **checkout.php** and really short (without all the form validation and billing processing stuff).

1. Create a new PHP script in your text editor or IDE to be named **billing.php** and stored in the Web root directory.

2. Include the configuration file:

```php
<?php
require ('./includes/config.inc.php');
```

3. Begin the session and retrieve the session ID:

```php
session_start();
$uid = session_id();
```

This page will be able to access the same session data as **checkout.php**, because both pages are being accessed over HTTPS. The session ID needs to be assigned to the **$uid** variable so that it can be used many times over in this page (to access the user's cart).

4. Redirect invalid users:

```php
if (!isset($_SESSION['customer_id'])) {
    $location = 'https://' . BASE_URL . 'checkout.php';
    header("Location: $location");
    exit();
}
```

If **$_SESSION['customer_id']** is not set, the user hasn't come to this page via **checkout.php**, meaning their order can't be completed. In that case, the customer is redirected back to the checkout page to begin again.

5. Require the database connection and create an array for storing errors:

```php
require (MYSQL);
$billing_errors = array();
```

6. Include the header file:

```php
$page_title = 'Coffee - Checkout - Your Billing Information';
include ('./includes/checkout_header.html');
```

Again, the newer, custom **checkout_header.html** file is included, not the older **header.html**.

7. Get the shopping cart contents:

```php
$r = mysqli_query($dbc, "CALL get_shopping_cart_contents('$uid')");
```

8. Include the view files:

```
if (mysqli_num_rows($r) > o) {
    if (isset($_SESSION['shipping_for_billing']) &&
    ⇥($_SERVER['REQUEST_METHOD'] != 'POST')) {
        $values = 'SESSION';
    } else {
        $values = 'POST';
    }
    include ('./views/billing.html');
} else { // Empty cart!
    include ('./views/emptycart.html');
}
```

You've seen most of this code several times over by now, the one difference being the conditional that checks for the **$_SESSION['shipping_for_billing']** element. This conditional is necessary because the HTML form in the view file could be prepopulated with values in two situations.

In the first case, the customer selected the check box (on **checkout.php**) to use their shipping information as their billing information. If so, the values already stored in **$_SESSION** should be used for the form elements.

The second situation in which there will be values to display in the form is when the customer submitted the form but errors occurred. If so, the values should come from **$_POST**. Note that even if the user opted to use the same information for shipping and billing, once they've submitted the form, only the posted values will count. This way, if the customer altered any of the prepopulated values, the changes will be reflected when the form is redisplayed. Still, if the customer did not alter the original session-based values, those same values will be used again after any errors.

9. Complete the page:

```
include ('./includes/footer.html');
?>
```

10. Save the file.

Creating the View File

The next step is to create the **billing.html** view file. Like **checkout.html**, this script should include **checkout_cart.html** (to display the cart), and then create an HTML form, primarily using the **create_form_input()** function (**Figure 10.15**).

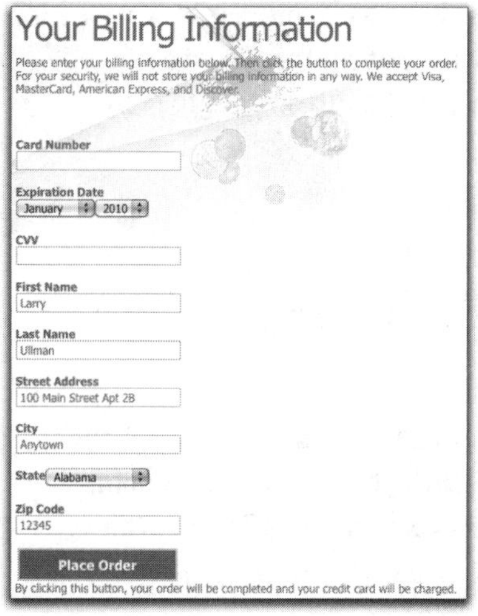

Figure 10.15

1. Create a new HTML page in your text editor or IDE to be named **billing.html** and stored in the **views** directory.

2. Add the progress indicator:

   <div align="center"><img src="/images/checkout_indicator2.png" />
   </div>
   <br clear="all" />

   The progress indicator for this page uses a different image showing that this is the second step in the process (I'd include a figure, but the changes are too subtle in black and white).

3. Include the checkout_cart.html view:

   <?php include ('./views/checkout_cart.html'); ?>

   This is the same view file included by **checkout.html**.

4. Begin the HTML box and the form:

   <div class="box alt"><div class="left-top-corner"><div class=
   "right-top-corner"><div class="border-top"></div></div></div>
   <div class="border-left"><div class="border-right"><div class=
   "inner">
   **   <h2>Your Billing Information</h2>**
   **   <p>Please enter your billing information below. Then click the button**
   **   to complete your order. For your security, we will not store your**
   **   billing information in any way. We accept Visa, MasterCard, American**
   **   Express, and Discover.</p>**
   <form action="/billing.php" method="POST">

Again, there are some simple instructions, plus an indication that their data will be safe. The instructions also indicate what card types are accepted. You may choose to make this more prominent or use images to represent the accepted cards.

The form gets submitted back to **billing.php**.

5. Include the form function file:

<?php include ('./includes/form_functions.inc.php'); ?>

6. Create the credit card number input:

**<div class="field"><label for="cc_number"><strong>Card Number
↪</strong></label>
<?php create_form_input('cc_number',
↪'text', $billing_errors, 'POST', 'autocomplete="off"'); ?></div>**

The element for taking the customer's credit card number is just a text input. The potential existing value for this input can come only from POST, because the credit card number will never be stored in the session.

The input uses the extra HTML **autocomplete="off"**, which is a necessary security measure. If you don't use this attribute, and the user's browser is set to remember their form data, then the browser will record the user's credit card number in plain text on the customer's computer. That's not good. (It may still happen because of less diligent e-commerce sites, though.)

7. Create the expiration date elements:

**<div class="field"><label for="exp_date"><strong>Expiration Date
↪</strong></label>
<?php create_form_input('cc_exp_month',
↪'select', $billing_errors); ?><?php create_form_input('cc_exp_year',
↪'select', $billing_errors); ?></div>**

The expiration date is generated using two select menus. The first is the expiration month and the second is the year. Because the fourth argument to the **create_form_input()** function—for indicating where existing values come from—is not provided, the default (**$_POST**) will be used.

8. Create the Card Verification Value (CVV) input:

**<div class="field"><label for="cc_cvv"><strong>CVV</strong>
↪</label>
<?php create_form_input('cc_cvv', 'text',
↪$billing_errors, 'POST', 'autocomplete="off"'); ?></div>**

The CVV code is an extra security measure used to limit fraud. What the customer should enter here are three digits on the back of Visa, Master-Card, and Discover cards or the four digits on the front of American Express cards. This is an extremely sensitive piece of information, so like the card

note

You don't actually have to ask the customer what type of card they're using, because the card number is indicative of the card type.

tip

The acronyms CVV, CCV, CVC, and CVVC all refer to the Card Security Code (CSC).

note

Merchants are not allowed to store CVV numbers.

number input, the **autocomplete="off"** code will be added to the input HTML. And, as with the card number, the value can only come from **$_POST**.

9. Create the first and last name inputs:

```
<fieldset>
<div class="field"><label for="cc_first_name"><strong>First Name
➥</strong></label><br /><?php create_form_input('cc_first_name',
➥'text', $billing_errors, $values); ?></div>
<div class="field"><label for="cc_last_name"><strong>Last Name
➥</strong></label><br /><?php create_form_input('cc_last_name',
➥'text', $billing_errors, $values); ?></div>
```

The rest of this form is largely like the shipping form, except that each input is prefaced with *cc_*. An important addition is that each call to **create_form_input()** includes the fourth argument. The fourth argument indicates where an existing value should exist: in **$_SESSION** or **$_POST**. The value of the **$values** variable will have been determined in the **billing.php** script (as you've already seen).

10. Create the address input:

```
<div class="field"><label for="address"><strong>Street
➥Address</strong></label><br /><?php create_form_input(
➥'cc_address', 'text', $billing_errors, $values); ?></div>
<div class="field"><label for="city"><strong>City</strong>
➥</label><br /><?php create_form_input('cc_city', 'text',
➥$billing_errors, $values); ?></div>
<div class="field"><label for="state"><strong>State</strong>
➥</label><br /><?php create_form_input('cc_state', 'select',
➥$billing_errors, $values); ?></div>
<div class="field"><label for="zip"><strong>Zip Code</strong>
➥</label><br /><?php create_form_input('cc_zip', 'text',
➥$billing_errors, $values); ?></div>
```

These are just like the inputs on the shipping information form, plus the additional fourth argument indicating the source of the value. If the customer selected the Use Shipping for Billing check box, these inputs will be prepopulated with data from the session the first time the page is loaded. If the form is redisplayed, the values will come from **$_POST**.

There is only one street address field, though, because Authorize.net is set up to accept only a single street address.

tip

You could add a little help button next to the CVV input that creates a pop-up window indicating where the customer can find their CVV number.

11. Complete the form:

```
<br clear="all" />
<div align="center"> <input type="submit" value="Place Order"
➥class="button" /></div></fieldset></form>
```

12. Complete the page:

```
<div>By clicking this button, your order will be completed and your
➥credit card will be charged.</div>
</div></div></div><div class="left-bot-corner"><div class=
➥"right-bot-corner"><div class="border-bot"></div></div></div>
➥</div>
<!-- box end -->
```

The instructions make it clear that the act of clicking the button completes the order.

13. Save the file.

Now you can load the billing page in your Web browser, although submitting the form will have no effect.

Validating the Form Data

Now that the shell of the script has been written, as has the view file for creating the form, it's time to add the code that processes the form data. This is largely like the validation in **checkout.php**, with additional validation of the credit card data. Needless to say, it's very important that you treat that credit card data with the utmost security. For example, you might think it is safe to store such information in the session, even temporarily:

$_SESSION['cc_number'] = $_POST['cc_number'];

But that one, seemingly harmless line just stored the customer's credit card number in a plain text file, in a publicly available directory on the server! Conversely, the way this script is written, all the ultimately sensitive information will exist only on the server (in memory) for the time it takes this script to execute.

1. Open **billing.php** in your text editor or IDE, if it is not already.

2. After creating the **$billing_errors** array, but before including the header file, check for the form submission:

if ($_SERVER['REQUEST_METHOD'] == 'POST') {

Again, if Magic Quotes might be enabled on your server, you'll need to add code applying **stripslashes()** to some of the variables at this point:

```
if (get_magic_quotes_gpc()) {
    $_POST['cc_first_name'] = stripslashes($_POST['cc_first_name']);
    // Repeat for other variables that could be affected.
}
```

3. Validate the first and last names:

```
if (preg_match ('/^[A-Z \'.-]{2,20}$/i', $_POST['cc_first_name'])) {
    $cc_first_name = $_POST['cc_first_name'];
} else {
    $billing_errors['cc_first_name'] = 'Please enter your first name!';
}
if (preg_match ('/^[A-Z \'.-]{2,40}$/i', $_POST['cc_last_name'])) {
    $cc_last_name  = $_POST['cc_last_name'];
} else {
    $billing_errors['cc_last_name'] = 'Please enter your last name!';
}
```

These regular expressions are the same as those used in **checkout.php**.
Unlike in the **checkout.php** script, **addslashes()** does not need to be applied
to any values, because no strings will be used in any stored procedure calls.

4. Remove any spaces or dashes from the credit card number:

$cc_number = str_replace(array(' ', '-'), '', $_POST[cc_number]);

As with the phone number in **checkout.php**, the first step in validating
the credit card number is to remove any spaces or numbers from the submitted credit card number. This allows the customer to enter the number
however they prefer.

5. Validate the card number against allowed types:

```
if (!preg_match ('/^4[0-9]{12}(?:[0-9]{3})?$/', $cc_number) // Visa
&& !preg_match ('/^5[1-5][0-9]{14}$/', $cc_number) // MasterCard
&& !preg_match ('/^3[47][0-9]{13}$/', $cc_number) // American Express
&& !preg_match ('/^6(?:011|5[0-9]{2})[0-9]{12}$/', $cc_number) //
➡Discover
) {
    $billing_errors['cc_number'] = 'Please enter your credit card number!';
}
```

All credit card numbers adhere to a specific formula, based upon the type
of credit card. For example, all Visa cards start with 4 and are either 13 or
16 characters long. All American Express cards start with either 34 or 37 but
must be exactly 15 characters long. These four patterns can confirm that
the supplied credit card number matches an allowed pattern. By checking

 tip

You may want to add to the
form an indicator as to how
the credit card number can
be entered (for example,
####).

that the number follows an acceptable format, the script won't attempt to process clearly unacceptable credit cards.

Note that nothing else is done with the card number at this point; however, an error message is created if the number doesn't match one of the four patterns.

6. Validate the expiration date:

```
if ( ($_POST['cc_exp_month'] < 1 || $_POST['cc_exp_month'] > 12)) {
    $billing_errors['cc_exp_month'] = 'Please enter your expiration
    ↪month!';
}
if ($_POST['cc_exp_year'] < date('Y')) {
    $billing_errors['cc_exp_year'] = 'Please enter your expiration year!';
}
```

There are two parts to the expiration date: the month and the year. The month must be between 1 and 12 and the year cannot be before the current year.

As an added check, you could confirm that if the expiration year is the current year, the expiration month is not before the current month (meaning that the card hasn't already expired).

7. Validate the CVV:

```
if (preg_match ('/^[0-9]{3,4}$/', $_POST['cc_cvv'])) {
    $cc_ccv = $_POST['cc_cvv'];
} else {
    $billing_errors['cc_cvv'] = 'Please enter your CVV!';
}
```

The CVV will be either three or four digits long.

8. Validate the street address:

```
if (preg_match ('/^[A-Z0-9 \',.#-]{2,160}$/i', $_POST['cc_address'])) {
    $cc_address = $_POST['cc_address'];
} else {
    $shipping_errors['cc_address'] = 'Please enter your street address!';
}
```

Since the billing form uses a single street address, the maximum length is doubled from those in the shipping form.

9. Validate the city, state, and zip code:

```
if (preg_match ('/^[A-Z \'.-]{2,60}$/i', $_POST['cc_city'])) {
    $cc_city = $_POST['cc_city'];
```

```
   } else {
      $billing_errors['cc_city'] = 'Please enter your city!';
   }
   if (preg_match ('/^[A-Z]{2}$/', $_POST['cc_state'])) {
      $cc_state = $_POST['cc_state'];
   } else {
      $billing_errors['cc_state'] = 'Please enter your state!';
   }
   if (preg_match ('/^(\d{5}$)|(^\d{5}-\d{4})$/', $_POST['cc_zip'])) {
      $cc_zip = $_POST['cc_zip'];
   } else {
      $billing_errors['cc_zip'] = 'Please enter your zip code!';
   }
```

10. If no errors occurred, convert the expiration date to the correct format:

```
if (empty($billing_errors)) {
   $cc_exp = sprintf('%02d%d', $_POST['cc_exp_month'],
   ➥$_POST['cc_exp_year']);
```

Authorize.net can accept the expiration date in many different formats: *MMYY*, *MM-YY*, *MMYYYY*, *MM/YYYY*, and so on; this site will submit it as *MMYYYY*. The year will already be four digits long, but the month could be either one or two digits. To turn the month into a two-digit value, the **sprintf()** function can be used. Its first argument is the formatting pattern: **%02d%d**. The **%02d** will format an integer as two digits, adding extra zeros as necessary. The subsequent **%d** just represents an integer without any additional formatting. The second and third arguments in this **sprintf()** call are the values to be used for the two placeholders. The end result will be values like 012011 or 102011.

11. Check for an existing order ID in the session:

```
if (isset($_SESSION['order_id'])) {
   $order_id = $_SESSION['order_id'];
   $order_total = $_SESSION['order_total'];
```

The next bit of code needs to create a new order ID, which is to say a new set of records in the **orders** and **order_contents** tables. However, the billing form could be submitted more than once, so the script shouldn't automatically call the associated stored procedure to do that.

For example, if the payment gateway said there was a problem with the provided credit card, the customer would correct that information (in the form) and resubmit the form. In such a case, the site should not create a second, duplicate order. To prevent that from happening, the script will look in the session for a previously stored order ID. If one is found, the previously stored ID and total will be assigned to local variables, to be used by the payment process.

12. If there is no existing order ID, get the last four digits of the credit card number:

```
} else { // Create a new order record:
    $cc_last_four = substr($cc_number, -4);
```

The site will store, in the **orders** table, the last four digits of the credit card number used, which is a safe and general practice. By doing so, there is a reference as to what card was used without storing the actual credit card number (which would be bad).

13. Store the order:

```
$r = mysqli_query($dbc, "CALL add_order({$_SESSION['customer_id']},
➥'$uid', {$_SESSION['shipping']}, $cc_last_four, @total, @oid)");
```

If all the user-supplied data is valid, the script needs to store the order information in the **orders** table. By doing so prior to calling the payment gateway, the order's ID number can be sent along as part of the payment gateway transaction. More importantly, the **add_order()** procedure calculates the order total, which is required for the payment gateway request as well.

Even though the complete order will now be stored in the database—prior to authorizing the payment—the site will not treat this order as successful, because, as you'll see in the next chapter, the success of an order also depends upon the transaction record found in the **transactions** table.

 note

The code that invokes the **add_order()** stored procedure will be executed only once, no matter how many times the billing form has to be resubmitted.

14. Retrieve the total and order ID:

```
if ($r) {
    $r = mysqli_query($dbc, 'SELECT @total, @oid');
    if (mysqli_num_rows($r) == 1) {
        list($order_total, $order_id) = mysqli_fetch_array($r);
        // Process the payment!
```

To retrieve the order total and ID, select those two user-defined MySQL variables. This is similar to how the customer ID was selected after calling the **add_customer()** procedure.

15. Store the order ID and total in the session:

```
$_SESSION['order_total'] = $order_total;
$_SESSION['order_id'] = $order_id;
```

Should the billing form be submitted a second time, the conditional defined in Step 11 will be true now.

16. If the order ID and total could not be retrieved, trigger an error:

> **} else { // Could not retrieve the order ID and total.**
> **unset($cc_number, $cc_cvv);**
> **trigger_error('Your order could not be processed due to a system**
> **➥error. We apologize for the inconvenience.');**
> **}**

As with the **checkout.php** script, if the PHP code gets to the **trigger_error()** point, it means that the customer did everything right but the system failed. That is really one of the worst things that could happen (and really shouldn't on a live, tested site). I've only included the **trigger_error()** call, but you should make sure that something significant—like emailing the administrator—happens in this case so that the problem gets fixed immediately. Fortunately, the customer's contact information—name, phone number, and email address—are stored in the session, making them available to any error logging that **trigger_error()** does.

On that note, because the error-handling function, as defined, records every variable that existed at the time of the error, the customer's credit card number and CVV value would be sent in an unsecured email or stored in a plain text log file. Such an occurrence would be a terrible security violation and a failure to abide by PCI DSS standards. To prevent this, before triggering the error, those two variables are deleted.

17. If the **add_order()** procedure failed, trigger an error:

> **} else { // The add_order() procedure failed.**
> **unset($cc_number, $cc_cvv);**
> **trigger_error('Your order could not be processed due to a system**
> **➥error. We apologize for the inconvenience.');**
> **}**

This is a replication of the code in Step 16, applicable if the **add_order()** procedure call does not return a positive result.

18. Complete the form-handling conditionals:

> **} // End of isset($_SESSION['order_id']) IF-ELSE.**
> **} // Errors occurred IF.**
> **} // End of REQUEST_METHOD IF.**

19. Save the file.

Now you can test the **billing.php** script as long as you purposefully create errors (because the payment-processing aspect hasn't been defined yet).

 note

The error-handling function will send an email when an error occurs on a live site.

 note

Think about what might happen to any customer-supplied data should an error occur at any point in the checkout process!

 tip

For these errors, you would want to also indicate to the customer what will happen next: The customer shouldn't resubmit the order, they'll be contacted shortly, and so forth.

PROCESSING CREDIT CARDS

The next step in the checkout sequence is to actually process the payment (this is number 3 in Figure 10.14). To do so, the customer information, payment data, and order specifics need to be sent to the payment gateway, and the returned response needs to be confirmed. With the Authorize.net system, this really isn't that difficult. The site just needs to establish the right settings and use libcurl to contact Authorize.net.

I've broken the gateway communication into two scripts: one that establishes the particulars to be sent to Authorize.net for a new order and another script that performs the actual communication. I separated the functionality this way because the administrative pages will also communicate with Authorize.net, passing along slightly different information. After completing Chapter 11, "Site Administration," there will be two setup scripts and one process script:

- **gateway_setup.php** establishes new order parameters.

- **gateway_setup_admin.php** establishes existing order parameters.

- **gateway_process.php** establishes common parameters and performs the request.

After defining two of these here, **billing.php** will need to be updated to use them.

Creating gateway_setup.php

The payment gateway needs to receive a large number of *name=value* pairs in each request. These pairs communicate to the gateway everything required to process the transaction:

- The site's merchant information

- The customer's billing information

- The order information

- How data should be returned

- And more

Each payment gateway differs as to what information needs to be transferred and under what naming scheme. For Authorize.net, each name begins with $x\_$.

The easiest way to start this process is to create an array, which will later be turned into the *name=value* pairs. The **gateway_setup.php** should create the array and populate it with all the information particular to the customer completing a new order. Here is that script, in its entirety:

gateway_setup.php:

```php
1   <?php
2   // Create an array for the information:
3   $data = array();
4
5   // Transaction type:
6   $data['x_type'] = 'AUTH_ONLY';
7
8   // Billing info:
9   $data['x_card_num'] = $cc_number;
10  $data['x_exp_date'] = $cc_exp;
11  $data['x_card_code'] = $cc_cvv;
12  $data['x_first_name'] = $cc_first_name;
13  $data['x_last_name'] = $cc_last_name;
14  $data['x_address'] = $cc_address;
15  $data['x_state'] = $cc_state;
16  $data['x_city'] = $cc_city;
17  $data['x_zip'] = $cc_zip;
```

First, an empty array is created. Next, the transaction type is set as *AUTH_ONLY*. This means that the request will authorize that funds be reserved for this merchant from this customer. Later, after taking steps in the administration area, a *capture* request will be made, at which point Authorize.net will actually charge the card and transfer the funds. To immediately charge the card, the transaction type would be *AUTH_CAPTURE*.

Next, the customer's billing information is assigned. This includes the credit card number, the expiration date, the CVV code, the customer's name, and their address. All of these values come from local variables found in **billing.php**.

This is all that needs to be transmitted particular to an original order. The merchant information, the order total, order ID, and the customer ID will all be added in the next script.

Because the payment-processing scripts will contain sensitive information (the next one will especially), I recommend storing it outside the Web root directory, if at all possible. If not, place **gateway_setup.php** in the **includes** directory, but prevent that directory from being accessible over the Internet. See Chapter 7 for instructions.

 note

When the customer is charged for their order is a policy decision that each business will need to make.

 note

Different card companies will reserve authorized funds for different lengths of time, anywhere from three days to some months.

 note

The PHP script does not have the closing PHP tag, because this file will be included by **billing.php**.

Defining gateway_process.php

The **gateway_process.php** script needs to do several things:

- Add to the **$data** array information that's common to all transactions
- Convert the **$data** array to a string
- Perform the request
- Convert the request response into an array

This code isn't that complicated, but let's walk through it step by step just to be safe.

1. Create a new PHP script in your text editor or IDE to be named **gateway_process.php** and stored in the same location as **gateway_setup.php**.

   Again, it'd be best to store this outside the Web root directory. If that's not possible, place it in the most secure location you can.

2. Define the access URL:

   ```php
   <?php
   if ($live) {
       define ('GATEWAY_API_URL', 'https://secure.authorize.net/gateway/
       ⟶transact.dll');
   } else {
       define ('GATEWAY_API_URL', 'https://test.authorize.net/gateway/
       ⟶transact.dll');
   }
   ```

   As with most payment gateways, Authorize.net uses different URLs for live and testing purposes. Based upon the value of **$live** set in the configuration file, the correct URL is assigned to a constant.

3. Define your Authorize.net merchant information:

   ```php
   $data['x_login'] = '75sqQ96qHEP8';
   $data['x_tran_key'] = '7r83Sb4HUd58Tz5p';
   ```

   These two pieces of information uniquely identify you to the Authorize.net system. You should use the values emailed to you by Authorize.net in your code.

4. Define the Advanced Integration Method values:

   ```php
   $data['x_version'] = '3.1';
   $data['x_delim_data'] = 'TRUE';
   $data['x_delim_char'] = '|';
   $data['x_relay_response'] = 'FALSE';
   ```

tip

Authorize.net also allows you to use the live URL for tests when using a real account in testing mode.

tip

Your login ID and transaction key must be kept safe. Having this information, hackers could credit their cards from your account.

These four items are required when using the Advanced Integration Method (AIM). The first indicates the version of AIM in use. The second says that the returned response data should be delimited. The third dictates the delimiting character to be used (here, the pipe). The *relay_response* is used by Authorize.net's SIM system, so it should be set to **false** for AIM connections (this is Authorize.net's recommendation).

5. Indicate the transaction method:

$data['x_method'] = 'CC';

A method value of *CC* means this is a credit card transaction. An alternative is *ECHECK*.

6. Add the order information:

$data['x_amount'] = $order_total;
$data['x_invoice_num'] = $order_id;
$data['x_cust_id'] = $customer_id;

The *amount* value is obviously one of the most important. The invoice number and customer ID values aren't required, but by providing them, that information will be stored in the Authorize.net system, making it easy to look up information there, relative to orders on this site.

For each of these values, variables created in **billing.php** will be used. In Chapter 11, this same script will be invoked, but these three values will come from variables defined in an administrative script.

7. Convert the data to a series of *name=value* pairs:

```
$post_string = '';
foreach( $data as $k => $v ) {
    $post_string .= "$k=" . urlencode($v) . "&";
}
$post_string = rtrim($post_string, '& ');
```

Using a **foreach** loop, each element in **$data** will be turned into the format *name=value*. Each value is URL-encoded, to make it safe to use in a request, and each *name=value* pair is separated by an ampersand. The final ampersand is chopped off as a last step. The result will be a string like:

x_type=AUTH_ONLY&x_card_num=4556510523894&x_exp_date=
➥**062010&x_card_code=890&x_first_name=Larry&x_last_name=**
➥**Ullman&x_address=100+Main+Street+Apt+2B&x_state=NH**
➥**&x_city=Anytown&x_zip=65894&x_login=75sqQ96qHEP8**
➥**&x_tran_key=7r83Sb4HUd58Tz5p&x_version=3.1&x_delim_data=**
➥**TRUE&x_delim_char=%7C&x_relay_response=FALSE&x_method=**
➥**CC&x_amount=309.82&x_invoice_num=21&x_cust_id=27**

8. Set up the cURL request:

$request = curl_init(GATEWAY_API_URL);
curl_setopt($request, CURLOPT_HEADER, 0);
curl_setopt($request, CURLOPT_RETURNTRANSFER, 1);
curl_setopt($request, CURLOPT_POSTFIELDS, $post_string);
curl_setopt($request, CURLOPT_SSL_VERIFYPEER, FALSE);

The first line initializes a cURL request, providing it with the URL to be communicated with. The second line says that header information should be omitted from the response (only the data is necessary). The third line, setting **CURLOPT_RETURNTRANSFER** to 1, confirms that actual data should be returned as a response. On the fourth line, the **$post_string** data is added as **CURLOPT_POSTFIELDS**.

On the last line, the option of verifying the SSL connection of the server is disabled. By doing so, you're improving the odds of the connection going through. If you don't include this line and cURL hiccups at the validity of the gateway's certificate, the request will fail. This doesn't mean the transaction won't be secure, it's just more likely to succeed.

9. Execute the cURL request:

$response = curl_exec($request);
curl_close ($request);

10. Convert the response into an array:

$response_array = explode($data["x_delim_char"], $post_response);

The cURL response will be returned as a long string of data. To make it easier to use, it can be converted to an array by exploding the string on the delimiting character (previously set to be the pipe).

11. Save the file.

Again, no closing PHP tag is used.

Examining the Server Response

Before updating the billing script to use the gateway scripts, let's take a quick look at the Authorize.net response. When using AIM, the server response will be a long string of data in the format of (the actual delimiter will be whatever you choose):

1|1|1|This transaction has been approved.|iJUUAm|Y|2390|. . .

After applying the **explode()** function to this response, the string will be broken into an array. The first 68 elements in that array are reserved for Authorize.net's purposes; most will not have values. **Table 10.1** lists many of these.

tip

For the full list of cURL options, see **www.php.net/curl_setopt**.

note

Because arrays are indexed beginning at zero, Table 10.1 starts listing the fields at zero.

Table 10.1 Some Authorize.net Response Fields

Field	Name
0	Response Code
1	Response Subcode
2	Response Reason Code
3	Response Reason Text
4	Authorization Code
5	AVS Response
6	Transaction ID
7	Invoice Number
8	Description
9	Amount
10	Method
11	Transaction Type
12	Customer ID
13–31	Customer Information
38	CCV/CVV Response Code
50	Last Four Digits of Card
51	Card Type

The full breakdown is available in the Authorize.net manual. The most important of these is really the *response code*. The possible values are:

- Approved
- Declined
- Error
- Held for Review

In short, if the first element returned by the response has a value of 1, the payment was authorized. If it's not 1, then a problem occurred. The specific type of problem will be reflected by the *response reason code* and the *response reason text*. Again, the Authorize.net AIM manual and online documentation lists all the possible codes and messages.

Updating billing.php

Now that the two payment-related scripts have been written, they should be incorporated into **billing.php**. By including the two scripts, the payment transaction will be processed. After that, the transaction should be recorded in the database and the script should respond accordingly (item number 4 in Figure 10.14).

1. Open **billing.php** in your text editor or IDE, if it is not already.

2. After the **isset($_SESSION['order_id']) IF-ELSE**, check that the order ID and total are set:

if (isset($order_id, $order_total)) {

The **IF-ELSE** conditional that should precede this line creates these two variables either by retrieving them from the session or by executing the stored procedure. As long as both variables exist, the payment request can be processed.

3. Assign the customer ID value to a variable:

$customer_id = $_SESSION['customer_id'];

The customer ID is currently stored in the session, but **gateway_process.php** expects it to be in a variable named **$customer_id**. (I wrote it this way because the administrative script that also uses **gateway_process.php** won't have the customer ID in a session.)

4. Include the two scripts:

require_once(BASE_URI . 'gateway_setup.php');
require_once(BASE_URI . 'gateway_process.php');

The scripts must be included in this order. The first establishes the **$data** array and populates it with some information for this particular kind of transaction. The second script adds more information to **$data** and then contacts Authorize.net.

You'll need to change the references to the scripts so that the paths are accurate for your setup.

5. Add addslashes to two of the text fields:

$reason = addslashes($response_array[3]);
$response = addslashes($response);

The reason text and the full response could have problematic characters (namely, the single quotation mark), so **addslashes()** needs to be applied before using these values in the stored procedure.

6. Record the transaction in the database:

```
$r = mysqli_query($dbc, "CALL add_transaction($order_id,
➥'{$data['x_type']}', $response_array[9], $response_array[0], '$reason',
➥$response_array[6], '$response')");
```

To record the transaction in the database, call the **add_transaction()** stored procedure. Its first argument is the order ID. The second is the transaction type. The third is the amount involved, which can be found in **$response_array[9]** (or **$order_total**). The fourth argument is the response code. This is the value 1, 2, 3, or 4 and is the first element in the parsed **$response_array**. The next argument is the transaction ID. This is a value returned by Authorize.net that reflects this transaction in their system. Finally, the entire cURL response, as a string, is stored in the table. Admittedly, this response contains all this other information, but in a less accessible way.

7. If the transaction was a success, store the response code in the session:

```
if ($response_array[0] == 1) {
    $_SESSION['response_code'] = $response_array[0];
```

This value will be required by the last script in the process.

8. Redirect the user:

```
$location = 'https://' . BASE_URL . 'final.php';
header("Location: $location");
exit();
```

The **final.php** script is the last page in the checkout process. It should indicate the success to the customer, send an email, create a receipt, and so on.

9. If the transaction was not a success, respond accordingly:

```
} else {
    if ($response_array[0] == 2) { // Declined
        $message = $response_array[3] . 'Please fix the error or try another
        ➥card.';
    } elseif ($response_array[0] == 3) { // Error
        $message = $response_array[3] . ' Please fix the error or try
        ➥another card.';
    } elseif ($response_array[0] == 4) { // Held for review
        $message = "The transaction is being held for review. You
        ➥will be contacted ASAP about your order. We apologize for any
        ➥inconvenience.";
    }
}
```

For each possible response, numbered 2 through 4, a message is created. In the first two cases, the message includes the textual reason from the response. Some example reasons are:

- The credit card number is invalid.

- The credit card has expired.

- The merchant does not accept this type of credit card.

In any of these cases, the billing form will be shown again (because the user is not being redirected).

10. Complete the **isset($order_id, $order_total)** conditional:

} // End of isset($order_id, $order_total) IF.

This line should come just before the curly bracket that closes the **if (empty($billing_errors)) {** conditional.

11. Save the file.

Lastly, **billing.html** needs to be updated to display a message if it exists. To do so, add this code after the instructions but before the form is begun:

<?php if (isset($message)) echo "<p class=\"error\">$message</p>"; ?>

Figure 10.16 shows how this might look.

Figure 10.16

COMPLETING THE ORDER

The **final.php** script is the last page in the checkout process. It should be accessed only after a completed sale. In terms of the database, the script should clear the **carts** table, since now those items have been purchased. In terms of the customer, the script should:

- Indicate completion of the order

- Offer a receipt

- Send an email confirmation

- Tell the customer what will happen next

This last item is important: Just because the customer has already given you money doesn't mean they couldn't use a little extra reassurance about that decision. The site should provide a sense of when the order will be processed and even ship, if possible.

You could also use the **final.php** script to take user feedback, attempt to sell other products, and so forth.

Let's start with the PHP script, and then create the view file. The code for generating an HTML email receipt will be created separately.

Creating the PHP Script

The PHP script is the simplest of those in this chapter, but let's still walk through it explicitly.

1. Create a new PHP script in your text editor or IDE to be named **final.php** and stored in the Web root directory.

2. Include the configuration file:

```
<?php
require ('./includes/config.inc.php');
```

3. Begin the session and get the session ID:

```
session_start();
$uid = session_id();
```

This code is the same as in **billing.php**.

4. Validate that the page is being accessed appropriately:

```
if (!isset($_SESSION['customer_id'])) {
    $location = 'https://' . BASE_URL . 'checkout.php';
    header("Location: $location");
    exit();
} elseif (!isset($_SESSION['response_code']) ||
➥($_SESSION['response_code'] != 1)) {
    $location = 'https://' . BASE_URL . 'billing.php';
    header("Location: $location");
    exit();
}
```

The first conditional is the same as in **billing.php** and implies that the user attempted to skip the **checkout.php** page. If so, the customer is redirected back to it. The second conditional implies that the user skipped the **billing.php** page and redirects the browser there.

5. Require the database connection:

require (MYSQL);

6. Clear the shopping cart:

$r = mysqli_query($dbc, "CALL clear_cart('$uid')");

Now that the order has been completed, the contents of the user's shopping cart should be cleared. This is accomplished by calling the **clear_cart()** stored procedure.

7. Include the script that will send the email:

include('./includes/email_receipt.php');

The **email_receipt.php** script isn't that complicated, but is verbose enough that it merits standing on its own. It will be created in just a few pages.

8. Include the header file:

$page_title = 'Coffee - Checkout - Your Order is Complete';
include ('./includes/checkout_header.html');

9. Include the view:

include('./views/final.html');

10. Clear the session:

$_SESSION = array();
session_destroy();

Clearing the session prevents a second immediate order by the same customer from conflicting with the order just submitted. That may not be a common occurrence, but without this code, if the customer does go back and purchase something else, the existing order ID will be erroneously used.

11. Complete the page:

include ('./includes/footer.html');
?>

12. Save the file.

Creating the View File

tip

You may want to add to the final checkout page an obvious link back to the shopping area.

The view file can be as simple or as complex as you want it to be, just ensure that it's appreciative and communicative. For **final.html**, stored in the **views** directory, a couple of messages are printed, providing the customer with the order ID and total, along with an indication of what will happen next (**Figure 10.17**).

Figure 10.17

```
<!-- box begin -->
<div class="box alt"><div class="left-top-corner"><div class=
"right-top-corner"><div class="border-top"></div></div></div>
<div class="border-left"><div class="border-right"><div class="inner">
  <h2>Your Order is Complete</h2>
  <p>Thank you for your order (#<?php echo $_SESSION['order_id']; ?>).
  Please use this order number in any correspondence with us.</p>
  <p>A charge of $<?php echo $_SESSION['order_total']; ?> will appear
  on your credit card when the order ships. All orders are processed on the
  next business day. You will be contacted in case of any delays.</p>
  <p>An email confirmation has been sent to your email address.
  <a href="receipt.php">Click here </a>to create a printable receipt of
  your order.</p>
</div></div></div><div class="left-bot-corner"><div class=
"right-bot-corner"><div class="border-bot"></div></div></div>
</div><!-- box end -->
```

In the view, a link exists to **receipt.php**, which is not actually created in this book. Such a file would be just a combination of the order information and the shopping cart information, without any extra HTML, images, and so forth (in fact, you could use the **checkout_cart.html** view as part of it). In short, the receipt would look much like the HTML email, which you'll design next.

Note that if you want to create the receipt page, that PHP script will need access to the order ID. This is a bit tricky, as that value will be cleared out of the session in **final.php**. The solution would be to pass the order ID along in the link to **receipt.php**. However, you wouldn't want to pass along just the order ID, as in **receipt.php?oid=X**, because the user could easily change the value of X to view other orders. One workaround would be to pass two pieces of information, such as the order ID and the total. The **receipt.php** script would display the order information only if both received values match those in the database.

TESTING THE SITE

With all the code written, you can fully test the site. You could use your own information—including credit card data—to test the payment gateway, but that's not the best of ideas. Here are syntactically valid, test credit card numbers:

- 370000000000002, American Express
- 6011000000000012, Discover
- 5555555555554444, MasterCard
- 4007000000027, Visa

Those numbers will work, regardless of the address and CVV values used with them. If you want to make them fail, one option is to use an expiration date in the past.

Authorize.net has its own method for triggering specific responses. If you use the faux-Visa number 4222222222222, the *amount* value can trigger a specific error response. For example, the response reason code of 6 means the credit card number is invalid. If you process a test transaction using that Visa number and an amount of 6.00, the returned response will be that the transaction was declined because of an invalid credit card number.

Because the amount used in the payment process is not an editable, dynamic value (which, for security purposes, is for the best), you'll have to manually alter the **gateway_process.php** script accordingly:

$data['x_amount'] = 6.00;

You also need to add this parameter:

$data['x_test_request'] = 'TRUE';

You should know that when you use the **x_test_request** setting, the returned transaction ID will always be zero. This is not a mistake.

tip

In January, the site won't accept an expiration date in the past because the year would have to be the previous year, which isn't an option.

GOING LIVE

Once you're happy with the site and it's time to go live, here's all you need to do...

1. Make sure you have an actual Authorize.net account, associated with your merchant bank.

2. Use your actual Authorize.net login ID and transaction key in the **gateway_process.php** script.

3. Set the site to live in the configuration file:

$live = true;

By changing the value of the **$live** variable, the site will hide all errors and use the live Authorize.net URL. If you still want to see the errors (for the last round of testing, Step 4), keep **$live** set to **false** in the configuration file but set **$live** equal to **true** at the top of **gateway_process.php**.

4. Test the site a couple more times, just to be safe.

Unless you go into the Merchant Interface to change your account mode, even a real Authorize.net account begins in test mode. So this round of tests just confirms that your account information is working with the live Authorize.net URL.

5. Use the Merchant Interface to take your account live.

A. Log in to the Merchant Interface at **https://account.authorize.net**.

B. Click Account in the main toolbar.

C. Click General Security Settings > Test Mode.

D. Click Turn Test Off.

6. Run one or two real transactions, as an extra precaution.

You can test the site by purchasing something inexpensive, just to be safe. Then you can go into the Merchant Interface and quickly void the transaction. (You can easily find the transaction under Search > Unsettled Transactions.)

 tip

Authorize.net, like all payment gateways, completes the processing of all transactions at a particular time each day.

11 | SITE ADMINISTRATION

The last requirement of the *Coffee* site is the ability to administer it. As a book has limited pages, there's not enough room to discuss and develop every administrative feature, but this chapter will walk through the most important and complex ones.

The site administration pertains to three categories of information:

- Products
- Sales
- Orders

For each of these, the chapter will present one or more scripts to view and manipulate the respective data, such as adding new products, defining sales, increasing inventory, viewing orders, and so on.

The administrative pages will use neither the MVC approach nor the stored procedures that the public side does. Instead of using stored procedures, the chapter will use prepared statements (when appropriate), providing you with a different approach for working securely with a database. Without using stored procedures, the MVC design will be undermined, and because the administrative side won't have the performance and maintenance demands of the public side, it makes sense to use a single, complete PHP script for each task.

The administration pages will also use the jQuery (**www.jquery.com**) JavaScript framework, which may be new to you. You'll see it integrated into the site in a couple of practical, but simple, ways.

SETTING UP THE SERVER

At this point, after all the work completed in the preceding four chapters, there's actually not much server setup to be performed. The administrative site can use the same configuration file and database connection file as the public side. It can also use the same CSS, footer, and images.

The most important setup involved is the creation of an HTML header appropriate for what the administrator will need to do. Also, a few lines of code have to be added to the **create_form_input()** function. Before that, though, I want to restate the need for folder-based authentication.

Requiring Authentication

Unlike the *Knowledge is Power* example in which administrators use the same integrated login system as the customers, the *Coffee* site has all the administrative scripts within their own directory. Since the administrative pages will allow access to some customer information—name, address, email address, and phone number (but no billing data), it's imperative that the administrative directory is secure. To start, give the directory a unique name, or, better yet, put the administrative files in a subdomain such as **http://admin.example.com** (again, using a more original value in lieu of *admin*).

Second, the admin pages should be available only via HTTPS. Chapter 7, "Second Site: Structure and Design," walks through a **mod_rewrite** definition (for the Apache Web server) that can enforce this constraint.

Third, the administrative directory must be password protected. Chapter 7 also talks about how you might use a host-provided control panel for performing this task. By protecting the directory, users will be prompted for a username and password when they attempt to access any of the administrative directory's content (see Figure 7.8).

 tip

Even if you wanted the extra security of having the administrator connect to the database as a MySQL user with different privileges, that can still be accomplished using only a single PHP connection script.

Creating a Template

Naturally, the administrative pages will use a different template than the public side, as there are different scripts with different purposes. The admin template is just a modified version of the public template (**Figure 11.1**). It features:

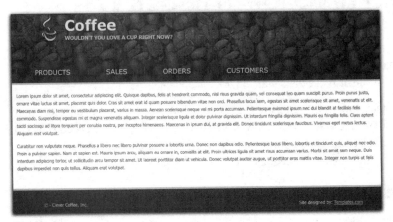

Figure 11.1

- Different primary links
- Drop-down suckerfish menus
- No background image behind the content
- A wider area for the content

Almost all these changes can be made by creating a new header file (you'll see the new, full header code shortly).

The primary links represent the three main content areas—products, sales, and orders, plus customers (although no customer-related script will be created in this chapter). The products link will reveal sublinks when the mouse hovers over it, using an approach known as *suckerfish* (if you search online for the term, you'll find thousands of results). **Figure 11.2** shows the effect.

Figure 11.2

To remove the background image behind the content, you need to override the CSS for the **#content <DIV>**. Otherwise, the admin pages can use the same CSS as the public ones.

To make a larger usable content area, the template needs to drop the following two **<DIV>** tags from the public template:

```
<div class="container">
    <div class="inside">
```

CREATING THE HEADER

Along with the features of the template just discussed (which are primarily implemented in the header), the header file will also begin the session (sessions will be used in a few spots as a convenience) and include the jQuery libraries. Here's the complete administrative header:

tip

As a reminder, all the code is available from **www.DMCInsights.com/ecom/**.

admin/includes/header.html

```
1   <?php session_start(); ?><!DOCTYPE html PUBLIC "-//W3C//DTD
    XHTML 1.0 Strict//EN" "http://www.w3.org/TR/xhtml1/DTD/xhtml1
    -strict.dtd">
2   <html xmlns="http://www.w3.org/1999/xhtml" xml:lang="en"
    lang="en">
3   <head>
4   <title><?php // Use a default page title if one wasn't provided. . .
5       if (isset($page_title)) {
6           echo $page_title;
7       } else {
8           echo 'Coffee - Administration';
9       }
10      ?></title>
11  <meta http-equiv="Content-Type" content="text/html;
    charset=utf-8" />
12  <link href="/css/style.css" rel="stylesheet" type="text/css" />
13  <script src="http://ajax.googleapis.com/ajax/libs/jquery/1.4.2/
    jquery.min.js" type="text/javascript" charset="utf-8"></script>
14  <style type="text/css" media="screen">
15      #content { background: #fff; width:100%; padding:20px 100px
        30px 0px; }
16      #header .nav li ul a { color:#ffe7be; text-decoration:none;
        text-transform:none; font-size: .75em; }
17  </style>
```
(continues on next page)

```
18  <!--[if lt IE 7]>
19      <script type="text/javascript" src="/js/ie_png.js"></script>
20      <script type="text/javascript">
21          ie_png.fix('.png, .logo h1, .box .left-top-corner, .box
            ➥.right-top-corner, .box .left-bot-corner, .box .right-bot-corner,
            ➥.box .border-left, .box .border-right, .box .border-top, .box
            ➥.border-bot, .box .inner, .special dd, #contacts-form input,
            ➥#contacts-form textarea');
22      </script>
23  <![endif]-->
24  </head>
25  <body id="page1">
26      <!-- header -->
27      <div id="header">
28          <div class="container">
29          <div class="wrapper">
30          <div class="logo"><h1><a href="/index.php">Coffee</a>
            ➥<span>Wouldn't you love a cup right now?</span></h1></div>
31          </div>
32          <ul class="nav">
33              <!-- MENU -->
34              <li class="first"><a href="#">Products</a></li>
35              <li><a href="create_sales.php">Sales</a></li>
36              <li><a href="view_orders.php">Orders</a></li>
37              <li><a href="#">Customers</a></li>
38              <!-- END MENU -->
39              </ul>
40          </div>
41      </div>
42      <!-- content -->
43      <div id="content">
44          <div class="container">
```

tip

By using the Google-hosted jQuery library, the page may load faster, if the user's browser has previously cached that same jQuery resource.

As you can see in the highlighted code, the session is begun as the first step.

Then, in the document's head, the jQuery library is included via the Google API, which means the site doesn't need its own version of the library.

After the site's primary CSS file (from the public directory) is included, the **#content** and **#header .nav li ul a** formatting is overwritten. The latter change will make the cascading (suckerfish) menu items smaller.

CREATING THE FOOTER

The footer file simply needs to complete the template.

admin/includes/footer.html

```
1   </div>
2     <!-- footer -->
3     <div id="footer"> <div class="container"><div class="indent">
4       <div class="fleft"> &copy; - Clever Coffee, Inc.</div>
5       <div class="fright">Site designed by: <a href="http://
        ⇒www.templates.com">Templates.com</a></div>
6       </div> </div> </div>
7   </body>
8   </html>
```

CREATING THE HOME PAGE

Right now, there's nothing for the home page to do, because all the key functionality is in other scripts. Create **index.php**, stored in the administrative directory, with some filler text:

admin/index.php

```
1   <?php
2   require ('../includes/config.inc.php');
3   $page_title = 'Coffee - Administration';
4   include ('./includes/header.html');
5   ?>
6   <p>Filler Text</p>
7   <?php include ('./includes/footer.html'); ?>
```

Using Superfish

The suckerfish style of cascading menus has been around for years and has become one of the de facto navigation approaches for today's Web sites. All suckerfish menus are based upon a group of nested, unordered lists that get dynamically converted into cascading menus. There are a number of tools available for creating suckerfish menus, but because the administrative pages will already use jQuery in some other places, I've turned to a jQuery-based plug-in called *Superfish* (**http://users.tpg.com.au/j_birch/plugins/superfish/**) here.

1. Download the latest version of Superfish.

2. Expand the downloaded file.

   The download will be a ZIP file.

3. Copy the **hoverIntent.js** and **superfish.js** scripts from the Superfish download's **js** directory to the site's **js** directory.

   The **hoverIntent.js** library isn't technically part of Superfish, but Superfish can use it for a better menu experience. For consistency, all the JavaScript for the entire site is being placed within the public **js** folder.

4. Copy the **superfish.css** file from the Superfish download's **css** directory to the site's **css** directory.

   This CSS file styles the Superfish menu. Again, all CSS goes into the public **css** directory.

5. Open **header.html** in your text editor or IDE, if it is not already.

6. Change the menu options to:

   ```
   <ul class="nav sf-menu">
       <!-- MENU -->
       <li class="first"><a href="#">Products</a><ul>
           <li><a href="add_specific_coffees.php">Add Coffee Products</a>
           ↪</li>
           <li><a href="add_other_products.php">Add Non-Coffee
           ↪Products</a></li>
           <li><a href="add_inventory.php">Add Inventory</a></li>
           </ul></li>
       <li><a href="create_sales.php">Sales</a></li>
       <li><a href="view_orders.php">Orders</a></li>
       <li><a href="#">Customers</a></li>
       <!-- END MENU -->
   </ul>
   ```

   There are two key changes here. First, before the closing **</LI>** tag for the products link, another unordered list is added. This list contains links to three pages. Second, an additional class of *sf-menu* (short for suckerfish menu) is added to the parent unordered list.

7. After including the site's primary CSS file, include the Superfish CSS file:

   <link href="/css/superfish.css" rel="stylesheet" type="text/css" />

tip

Unless otherwise specified, every file discussed in this chapter goes within the administrative directory.

tip

To apply multiple CSS classes to a single element, separate the class names with a space.

Again, the reference to the CSS file assumes it will be found in the *Web root directory*/**css** folder.

8. After including the jQuery library, include the **hoverIntent** and Superfish JavaScript files:

```
<script src="/js/hoverIntent.js" type="text/javascript"
➥charset="utf-8"></script>
<script src="/js/superfish.js" type="text/javascript"
➥charset="utf-8"></script>
```

Make sure you include the scripts in this order.

9. In a separate script block, apply Superfish:

```
<script type="text/javascript">
  $(function() {
    $('ul.sf-menu').superfish({
      autoArrows: false,
      speed: 'fast'
    });
  });
</script>
```

tip

The **us.sf-menu** code actually selects every unordered list with a class of *sf-menu*, but the template has only one.

This code enables the Superfish menu. The very basic JavaScript being executed is just **$();**. This is magic jQuery speak for "when the document is ready, do the following." The code to be executed when the document is ready is defined in an *anonymous function* (a function without a name). Within the function, the unordered list with a class of *sf-menu* is selected. To that selection, the **superfish()** method is applied. Two attribute-value pairs are passed to the **superfish()** method: one disabling arrows that indicate submenus exist; the other sets the Superfish speed to *fast*.

tip

If the Superfish menu doesn't work for you, use a JavaScript debugging tool, such as Firebug for the Firefox browser, to see what might be wrong.

10. Save the file and test it in your Web browser.

Updating create_form_input()

The **create_form_input()** function, first defined in Part Two, "Selling Virtual Products," then redefined in Chapter 10, "Checking Out," will be used in the administrative pages, too. As currently defined, the function works well for the public side, creating the text inputs and different select menus used by the checkout process. The administrative pages will have some forms that also require textareas, so that functionality needs to be added to the function.

As written in Chapter 10, the structure of the function is:

```
if ( ($type == 'text') || ($type == 'password') ) {
    // Lots of code.
} elseif ($type == 'select') {
    // Lots more code.
} // End of primary IF-ELSEIF.
```

To support textareas, the following code needs to be added before the closing **IF-ELSEIF** curly bracket:

```
} elseif ($type == 'textarea') {
    // Display the error first:
    if (array_key_exists($name, $errors)) echo ' <span class="error">'
    ➥. $errors[$name] . '</span>';
    // Start creating the textarea:
    echo '<textarea name="' . $name . '" id="' . $name . '" rows="5"
    ➥cols="75"';
    // Add the error class, if applicable:
    if (array_key_exists($name, $errors)) {
        echo ' class="error">';
    } else {
        echo '>';
    }
    // Add the value to the textarea:
    if ($value) echo $value;
    // Complete the textarea:
    echo '</textarea>';
```

For an explanation of this code beyond the inline comments, see Chapter 4, "User Accounts."

ADDING PRODUCTS

The e-commerce site sells two types of products: coffee and other (aka, goodies). The two products are treated differently in the database and in the catalog, so the administrative scripts for adding each will differ, too.

Adding Non-Coffee Products

Non-coffee products—books, mugs, and so on—are represented as records in the **non_coffee_products** table. For each item, there is a **non_coffee_category_id** (a reference to the values in the **non_coffee_categorties** table), a name,

tip

This chapter does not include scripts for adding general coffee or goodie types, although each would be easy to create. Turn to the book's supporting Web site if you need help implementing either.

a description, an image, a price, and the quantity in stock (**Figure 11.3**). Handling most of these values is straightforward, although the file upload is a bit tricky, requiring code similar to that used for working with PDFs in Chapter 5, "Managing Site Content."

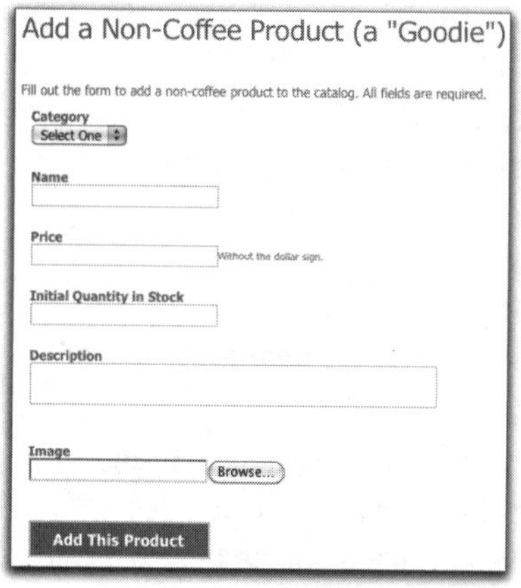

Add a Non-Coffee Product (a "Goodie")

Fill out the form to add a non-coffee product to the catalog. All fields are required.

Category
[Select One ▾]

Name
[   ]

Price
[   ] Without the dollar sign.

Initial Quantity in Stock
[   ]

Description
[   ]

Image
[   ] (Browse...)

[Add This Product]

Figure 11.3

1. Create a new PHP script in your text editor or IDE to be named **add_other_products.php** and stored in the administrative directory.

2. Include the configuration file, the header, and the database connection:

```php
<?php
require ('../includes/config.inc.php');
$page_title = 'Add a Goodie';
include ('./includes/header.html');
require(MYSQL);
```

3. Define an array for storing errors:

```php
$add_product_errors = array();
```

4. Check for a form submission:

```php
if ($_SERVER['REQUEST_METHOD'] == 'POST') {
```

5. Validate the product's category:

```php
if (!isset($_POST['category']) || !filter_var($_POST['category'],
FILTER_VALIDATE_INT, array('min_range' => 1))) {
    $add_product_errors['category'] = 'Please select a category!';
}
```

tip

A page for creating new non-coffee categories would be a slimmed-down version of the **add_other_products.php** script, taking just a category name, description, and an image file.

The product's category value should come from a select menu. It needs to be an integer with a value of at least 1. If those criteria are not met, an error is added to the errors array. Unlike validation routines seen elsewhere in the book, nothing else is done with the validated value at this point.

6. Validate the price and quantity in stock:

```
if (empty($_POST['price']) || !filter_var($_POST['price'],
➥FILTER_VALIDATE_FLOAT) || ($_POST['price'] <= 0)) {
    $add_product_errors['price'] = 'Please enter a valid price!';
}
if (empty($_POST['stock']) || !filter_var($_POST['stock'],
➥FILTER_VALIDATE_INT, array('min_range' => 1))) {
    $add_product_errors['stock'] = 'Please enter the quantity in stock!';
}
```

The price must not be empty and must be a float (a decimal) that's not less than or equal to zero. The quantity in stock must be an integer greater than or equal to 1. You could change the **min_range** to zero if you wanted to allow the administrator to add products whose inventory will be increased later.

7. Validate the name and description:

```
if (empty($_POST['name'])) {
    $add_product_errors['name'] = 'Please enter the name!';
}
if (empty($_POST['description'])) {
    $add_product_errors['description'] = 'Please enter the description!';
}
```

These two values cannot be empty.

8. Begin validating the image:

```
if (is_uploaded_file ($_FILES['image']['tmp_name']) &&
➥($_FILES['image']['error'] == UPLOAD_ERR_OK)) {
    $file = $_FILES['image'];
    $size = ROUND($file['size']/1024);
    if ($size > 512) {
        $add_product_errors['image'] = 'The uploaded file was too large.';
    }
```

This code is similar to that used in Chapter 5 to validate uploaded PDF files. The image's maximum size is 512 KB.

9. Validate the file's type:

```
$allowed_mime = array ('image/gif', 'image/pjpeg', 'image/jpeg',
➥'image/JPG', 'image/X-PNG', 'image/PNG', 'image/png',
➥'image/x-png');
$allowed_extensions = array ('.jpg', '.gif', '.png', 'jpeg');
$image_info = getimagesize($file['tmp_name']);
$ext = substr($file['name'], -4);
if ( (!in_array($file['type'], $allowed_mime))
|| (!in_array($image_info['mime'], $allowed_mime) )
|| (!in_array($ext, $allowed_extensions) )
) {
    $add_product_errors['image'] = 'The uploaded file was not of the
    ➥proper type.';
}
```

Again, this is similar to the process for uploading PDFs. First, an array of allowed MIME types is defined. Then an array of allowed extensions is defined. Third, the **getimagesize()** function is invoked, which can be used as a good server-based confirmation of an image's properties. Fourth, the last four characters in the uploaded file's name are retrieved, in order to be compared against the allowed extensions.

The code then creates an error if any of three conditions are false. The first is that the browser-supplied MIME type is appropriate. The second is that the server-supplied MIME type (from the **getimagesize()** function call) is acceptable. The third is that the file's extension is on the approved list.

10. Move the file to its final destination:

```
if (!array_key_exists('image', $add_product_errors)) {
    $new_name= (string) sha1($file['name'] . uniqid('',true));
    $new_name .= ((substr($ext, 0, 1) != '.') ? ".{$ext}" : $ext);
    $dest = "../products/$new_name";
    if (move_uploaded_file($file['tmp_name'], $dest)) {
        $_SESSION['image']['new_name'] = $new_name;
        $_SESSION['image']['file_name'] = $file['name'];
        echo '<h4>The file has been uploaded!</h4>';
    } else {
        trigger_error('The file could not be moved.');
        unlink ($file['tmp_name']);
    }
} // End of array_key_exists() IF.
```

If no image-related error exists, a new name for the image is created, starting with the application of **SHA1()** to the combination of the file's current name and a unique ID. This will generate a 40-character-long random name. Then the existing extension is appended. Finally, the file is moved to its final resting place, within the **_Web root directory_/products** folder.

The image's new name and its original file name are both stored in the session for use later.

11. If a file upload error occurred, determine what it was:

```
} elseif (!isset($_SESSION['image'])) {
    switch ($_FILES['image']['error']) {
        case 1:
        case 2:
            $add_product_errors['image'] = 'The uploaded file was too
            ⇒large.';
            break;
        case 3:
            $add_product_errors['image'] = 'The file was only partially
            ⇒uploaded.';
            break;
        case 6:
        case 7:
        case 8:
            $add_product_errors['image'] = 'The file could not be
            ⇒uploaded due to a system error.';
            break;
        case 4:
        default:
            $add_product_errors['image'] = 'No file was uploaded.';
            break;
    } // End of SWITCH.
} // End of $_FILES IF-ELSEIF-ELSE.
```

Yet again, this is all similar to that in the PDF upload script. First, the **switch** will be checked only if there's no file already represented in the session. This is necessary because it's possible that the administrator uploaded an image correctly the first time, but had another error in the form. In that case, when the administrator resubmits the form, the existing image upload should be used.

12. If there were no errors, add the record to the database:

```
if (empty($add_product_errors)) {
    $q = 'INSERT INTO non_coffee_products (non_coffee_category_id,
    ➥name, description, image, price, stock) VALUES (?, ?, ?, ?, ?, ?)';
    $stmt = mysqli_prepare($dbc, $q);
    mysqli_stmt_bind_param($stmt, 'isssdi', $_POST['category'],
    ➥$name, $desc, $_SESSION['image']['new_name'], $_POST['price'],
    ➥$_POST['stock']);
    $name = strip_tags($_POST['name']);
    $desc = strip_tags($_POST['description']);
    mysqli_stmt_execute($stmt);
```

As explained in Chapter 7, to use prepared statements, the first step is to define the query, using placeholders (the question marks) in lieu of actual values. Then the statement is *prepared*. Next, the placeholders are bound, by type, to PHP variables. The second argument to the **mysqli_stmt_bind_param()** function indicates that the first placeholder is an integer, the next three are strings, the fifth is a decimal, and the last is another integer.

Four of the values to be used in the query come from **$_POST** and **$_SESSION** directly. The other two values will come from local variables, after the **strip_tags()** function is applied.

If you have problems when executing this script, you can use the following line (after preparing the statement) to see what the problem is:

```
if (!$stmt) echo mysqli_stmt_error($stmt);
```

13. If the query created a new record, print a message and perform some cleanup:

```
if (mysqli_stmt_affected_rows($stmt) == 1) {
    echo '<h4>The product has been added!</h4>';
    $_POST = array();
    $_FILES = array();
    unset($file, $_SESSION['image']);
```

If one row was affected, a message will be printed, and the variables will be reset (because the form will be shown again, and it shouldn't display the previous values).

14. If there was a problem, trigger an error:

```
} else {
    trigger_error('The product could not be added due to a system error.
    ➥We apologize for any inconvenience.');
    unlink ($dest);
}
```

When a problem occurs, because of a database or query error, a message is displayed to the administrator and the uploaded file is removed (to prevent deadwood from cluttering the **products** directory).

15. Complete the errors array and request method conditionals:

```
    } // End of $errors IF.
} else { // Clear out the session on a GET request:
    unset($_SESSION['image']);
} // End of the submission IF.
```

The final unsetting of the session variable would apply if the administrator uploaded a file, but incompletely filled out the form, and then, for some reason, clicked the link in the header to return to this page, thereby starting the process anew.

16. Include the form functions script:

require ('../includes/form_functions.inc.php');

The **create_form_input()** function is defined in this script, in the public **includes** folder, so it must be included here.

17. Begin the form:

```
?><h3>Add a Non-Coffee Product (a "Goodie")</h3>
<form enctype="multipart/form-data" action=
➥"add_other_products.php" method="post" accept-charset="utf-8">
    <input type="hidden" name="MAX_FILE_SIZE" value="524288" />
    <fieldset><legend>Fill out the form to add a non-coffee product to
the catalog. All fields are required.</legend>
```

In order to handle the file upload, the form must use the **enctype** attribute, and it should include the **MAX_FILE_SIZE** hidden input (which recommends a maximum upload file size to the browser). That value is in bytes.

18. Create the category menu:

```
<div class="field"><label for="category"><strong>Category
➥</strong></label><br /><select name="category"<?php
➥if (array_key_exists('category', $add_product_errors)) echo '
➥class="error"'; ?>>
```

```
<option>Select One</option>
<?php
$q = 'SELECT id, category FROM non_coffee_categories ORDER BY
➥category ASC';
$r = mysqli_query ($dbc, $q);
while ($row = mysqli_fetch_array ($r, MYSQL_NUM)) {
    echo "<option value=\"$row[0]\"";
        if (isset($_POST['category']) && ($_POST['category'] ==
        ➥$row[0]) ) echo ' selected="selected"';
        echo ">$row[1]</option>\n";
}
?>
</select><?php if (array_key_exists('category',
➥$add_product_errors)) echo ' <span class="error">'
➥. $add_product_errors['category'] . '</span>'; ?></div>
```

I choose not to have the **create_form_input()** function generate this select
menu, because the menu's options require a database query (unlike the
menus currently created by that function). Therefore, all the error-handling
code has to be inline. Other than that, this code should be pretty straightforward by now.

19. Create the name, price, and stock elements:

```
<div class="field"><label for="name"><strong>Name</strong>
➥</label><br /><?php create_form_input('name', 'text',
➥$add_product_errors); ?></div>
<div class="field"><label for="price"><strong>Price</strong>
➥</label><br /><?php create_form_input('price', 'text',
➥$add_product_errors); ?><small>Without the dollar sign.</small>
➥</div>
<div class="field"><label for="stock"><strong>Initial Quantity in
➥Stock</strong></label><br /><?php create_form_input('stock',
➥'text', $add_product_errors); ?></div>
```

These are all basic text inputs.

20. Create the description element:

```
<div class="field"><label for="description"><strong>Description
➥</strong></label><br /><?php create_form_input('description',
➥'textarea', $add_product_errors); ?></div>
```

The description is a textarea.

21. Begin the image file input:

```
<div class="field"><label for="image"><strong>Image</strong>
</label><br /><?php
if (array_key_exists('image', $add_product_errors)) {
    echo '<span class="error">' . $add_product_errors['image']
    . '</span><br /><input type="file" name="image"
    class="error" />';
```

If an image-related error exists, the error message is first displayed, then the file input is created, with an assigned *error* class.

22. Complete the image file input:

```
} else {
    echo '<input type="file" name="image" />';
    if (isset($_SESSION['image'])) {
        echo "<br />Currently '{$_SESSION['image']['file_name']}'";
    }
} // end of errors IF-ELSE.
?></div>
```

If no image-related error exists, then the file input has no additional class. If a value exists in **$_SESSION['image']**, the already uploaded file's name is indicated to the administrator.

23. Complete the form:

```
<br clear="all" />
<div class="field"><input type="submit" value="Add This Product"
class="button" /></div>
</fieldset>
</form>
```

24. Complete the PHP page:

```
<?php include ('./includes/footer.html'); ?>
```

25. Save the file and test it in your Web browser.

The script does not restrict the uploaded image to a given size, nor does it resize the image to the proper dimensions (96 pixels wide by 76 pixels tall), so it's up to the administrator to use an image that's sized appropriately.

Any errors in using the form will be reflected inline (**Figure 11.4**).

tip

For more explanation of the image file input's code, see how PDFs are handled in Chapter 5.

tip

You can have PHP resize images; it just requires external libraries and a bit more code.

Figure 11.4

Adding Coffee Products

For non-coffee products, each product a customer might purchase is associated with a particular non-coffee category. For coffee products, each specific product is associated with a particular type of coffee: Dark Roast, Kona, Original Blend, and so on. For each coffee type, there can be a number of specific products available: Given five initial size options, there are already 20 possible combinations of sizes, ground beans versus whole, and caffeinated versus decaffeinated. Therefore, the fastest way for the administrator to add specific coffee products is to present multiple options as part of one form (**Figure 11.5**).

Figure 11.5

Unlike the **add_other_products.php** script, this form will not use the **create_form_input()** function or perform any error reporting. The form is easy enough to use that errors shouldn't be a problem, and the method of generating the form in this script is different enough that using **create_form_input()** would overly complicate matters.

1. Create a new PHP script in your text editor or IDE to be named **add_specific_coffees.php** and stored in the administrative directory.

2. Include the configuration file, the header, and the database connection:

```
<?php
require ('../includes/config.inc.php');
$page_title = 'Add Specific Coffees';
include ('./includes/header.html');
require(MYSQL);
```

3. Identify how many records might be created at once:

```
$count = 10;
```

The **$count** variable is the basis for how many specific coffee products can be created with each use of the page. Changing this number will alter the number of form rows generated in the table.

4. Check for a form submission:

```
if ($_SERVER['REQUEST_METHOD'] == 'POST') {
```

5. Check for a category:

```
if (isset($_POST['category']) && filter_var($_POST['category'],
FILTER_VALIDATE_INT, array('min_range' => 1))) {
```

If the administrator did not select a coffee category (using the select menu at the top of the form), there's no need to continue, so that value is validated first. The category should be an integer greater than or equal to 1.

6. Define the query and prepare the statement:

```
$q = 'INSERT INTO specific_coffees (general_coffee_id, size_id,
caf_decaf, ground_whole, price, stock) VALUES (?, ?, ?, ?, ?, ?)';
$stmt = mysqli_prepare($dbc, $q);
```

This script, which will execute the same query up to **$count** times (using different values for each execution), is an excellent place to use prepared statements. The query needs to be prepared only once, its usage can be cached by the database, and the only thing that needs to be transmitted to MySQL for each query execution are the actual values (as opposed to the whole query).

7. Bind the variables:

**mysqli_stmt_bind_param($stmt, 'iissdi', $_POST['category'], $size,
➥$caf_decaf, $ground_whole, $price, $stock);**

Six values need to be present in variables when the query is executed. The first two—the category and size values—will be integers, as will the last one (the quantity in stock). The third and fourth values—caffeinated/decaffeinated and ground/whole beans—will be strings. The fifth value, the price, will be a decimal. The first of these values will be the same for each query, and will come from $**_POST['category']**. The rest of the values will be determined within a **foreach** loop.

8. Begin looping through the submitted values:

**$affected = 0;
for ($i = 1; $i <= $count; $i++) {**

A **for** loop needs to run through **$count** iterations, matching the number of items that may be submitted. Prior to that, the **$affected** variable is initialized to zero. It will be used to track the total number of affected rows by all the executed queries.

9. Validate the required values:

**if (filter_var($_POST['stock'][$i], FILTER_VALIDATE_INT,
➥array('min_range' => 1))
&& filter_var($_POST['price'][$i], FILTER_VALIDATE_FLOAT)
&& ($_POST['price'][$i] > 0)) {**

The initial quantity in stock and the item's price will be entered by the administrator into text inputs (see Figure 11.5). For each product submission, both values are validated using the Filter extension, ensuring that the stock value is an integer greater than or equal to 1 and that the price is greater than zero.

10. Assign the values to variables:

**$size = $_POST['size'][$i];
$caf_decaf = $_POST['caf_decaf'][$i];
$ground_whole = $_POST['ground_whole'][$i];
$price = $_POST['price'][$i];
$stock = $_POST['stock'][$i];**

To use the values in the query, each needs to be assigned to a variable identified in the binding call (in Step 7).

11. Execute the query:

```
mysqli_stmt_execute($stmt);
$affected += mysqli_stmt_affected_rows($stmt);
```

First the query is executed, and then the number of affected rows is added to the existing count.

12. Complete the control structures and print the number of affected rows:

```
    } // End of IF.
} // End of FOREACH.
echo "<h4>$affected Product(s) Were Created!</h4>";
```

The script just ignores any incomplete submissions, rather than generate errors. By using this approach, the administrator isn't told that a problem exists simply because they only added six new items instead of the full ten (or whatever value **$count** has).

13. Complete the form submission conditionals:

```
    } else {
        echo '<p class="error">Please select a category.</p>';
    }
} // End of the submission IF.
```

The **else** clause applies if no category was selected.

14. Begin defining the form:

```
?><h3>Add Specific Coffees</h3>
<form action="add_specific_coffees.php" method="post"
⇒accept-charset="utf-8">
    <fieldset><legend>Fill out the form to add specific coffee products
⇒to the site.</legend>
```

15. Create the category select menu:

```
<div class="field"><label for="category"><strong>General Coffee
⇒Type</strong></label><br />
    <select name="category"><option>Select One</option>
    <?php
    $q = 'SELECT id, category FROM general_coffees ORDER BY category
⇒ASC';
    $r = mysqli_query ($dbc, $q);
    while ($row = mysqli_fetch_array ($r, MYSQLI_NUM)) {
        echo "<option value=\"$row[0]\">$row[1]</option>\n";
    }
    ?>
    </select></div>
```

The list of coffee categories will be derived from a database query. As this is a static query—it will never change, there's no need to use prepared statements.

16. Define a table:

```
<table border="0" width="100%" cellspacing="5" cellpadding="5">
  <thead>
    <tr>
      <th align="right">Size</th>
      <th align="right">Ground/Whole</th>
      <th align="right">Caf./Decaf.</th>
      <th align="center">Price</th>
      <th align="center">Quantity in Stock</th>
    </tr>
  </thead>
  <tbody>
```

The form for adding specific products uses table rows to present a series of form elements: one for each possible product quality.

17. Determine the size options:

```
<?php
$q = 'SELECT id, size FROM sizes ORDER BY id ASC';
$r = mysqli_query ($dbc, $q);
$sizes = '';
while ($row = mysqli_fetch_array ($r, MYSQLI_NUM)) {
    $sizes .= "<option value=\"$row[0]\">$row[1]</option>\n";
}
```

Each of the **$count** number of form elements will contain three select menus. Since the values for these menus will be the same for each row, it's best to define those menu options once, rather than query the database for each generated menu. To start, the **$sizes** variable will be assigned a series of **<OPTION>** tags (as a string of HTML), based upon the values retrieved from the **sizes** table.

18. Determine the grind and caffeine options:

```
$grinds = '<option value="ground">Ground</option>
➥<option value="whole">Whole</option>';
$caf_decaf = '<option value="caf">Caffeinated</option>
➥<option value="decaf">Decaffeinated</option>';
```

Both of these qualities have two possible options. Again, just the **<OPTION>** tags are defined. The **<SELECT>** tags will be given unique names for each row.

19. Create one table row of form elements for each number in **$count**:

```
for ($i = 1; $i <= $count; $i++) {
    echo '<tr>
        <td align="right"><select name="size[' . $i . ']">' . $sizes . '
        ↪</select></td>
        <td align="right"><select name="ground_whole[' . $i . ']">' .
        ↪$grinds . '</select></td>
        <td align="right"><select name="caf_decaf[' . $i . ']">' .
        ↪$caf_decaf . '</select></td>
        <td align="center"><input type="text" name="price[' . $i . ']"
        ↪id="price[]" class="small" /></td>
        <td align="center"><input type="text" name="stock[' . $i . ']"
        ↪id="stock[]" class="small" /></td>
    </tr>';
}
```

tip

The two text inputs in this form have **class="small"** attributes. Thanks to the CSS, this makes them not quite so wide as a standard input.

Each table row contains five columns, each of which contains a form element. The name of each form element is an array, using the current count number as its index. The result will be an array named **$_POST['size']**, indexed from 1 to **$count**, another named **$_POST['ground_whole']**, indexed from 1 to **$count**, and so on.

20. Complete the PHP block and the table:

```
?></tbody>
</table>
```

21. Complete the form:

```
    <div class="field"><input type="submit" value="Add These
    ↪Products" class="button" /></div>
    </fieldset>
</form>
```

22. Complete the page:

```
<?php include ('./includes/footer.html'); ?>
```

23. Save the file and test it in your Web browser (**Figure 11.6**).

10 Product(s) Were Created!
Add Specific Coffees

Figure 11.6

ADDING INVENTORY

In an e-commerce site that sells physical products, inventory management is an important feature. As you'll see later in this chapter, the inventory of an item is reduced when the item ships (you could alternatively choose to reduce the quantity on hand when the item sells). There needs to be a way to increase the inventory, too.

As I imagine it, the administrator might daily or weekly review the sales and the current inventory, then order more quantities of products to replenish the business's stock. When that shipment arrives, the added inventory needs to be reflected on the site.

To accomplish this, the administrator will be presented with a list of every product available for sale. Each will have a text input wherein the administrator enters the number just received (**Figure 11.7**).

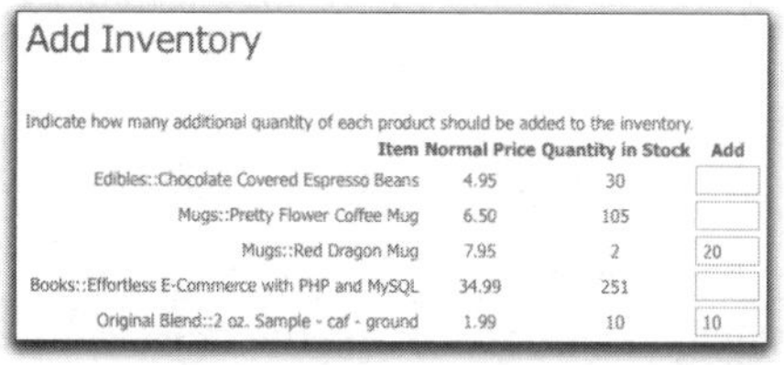

Add Inventory

Indicate how many additional quantity of each product should be added to the inventory.

	Item Normal Price	Quantity in Stock	Add
Edibles::Chocolate Covered Espresso Beans	4.95	30	
Mugs::Pretty Flower Coffee Mug	6.50	105	
Mugs::Red Dragon Mug	7.95	2	20
Books::Effortless E-Commerce with PHP and MySQL	34.99	251	
Original Blend::2 oz. Sample - caf - ground	1.99	10	10

Figure 11.7

1. Create a new PHP script in your text editor or IDE to be named **add_inventory.php** and stored in the administrative directory.

2. Include the configuration file, the header, and the database connection:

```php
<?php
require ('../includes/config.inc.php');
$page_title = 'Add Inventory';
include ('./includes/header.html');
require (MYSQL);
```

3. Check for a form submission:

```php
if ($_SERVER['REQUEST_METHOD'] == 'POST') {
    if (isset($_POST['add']) && is_array($_POST['add'])) {
        require ('../includes/product_functions.inc.php');
```

This script's form will submit an array of values in **$_POST['add']**. The only initial validation is that **$_POST['add']** is set and that it is an array. If so, the **product_functions.inc.php** (from the Web root's **includes** directory) is required, as the script will need to use the **parse_sku()** function defined therein.

4. Define two queries:

$q1 = 'UPDATE specific_coffees SET stock=stock+? WHERE id=?';
$q2 = 'UPDATE non_coffee_products SET stock=stock+? WHERE id=?';

This script will execute two different **UPDATE** queries: one to update the stock values in the **specific_coffees** table and another to update the stock values in the **non_coffee_products** table. Each is assigned to a separate variable here. The placeholders in each represent the number to be added to the inventory and the ID value (that is, which product is being updated).

5. Prepare the statements:

$stmt1 = mysqli_prepare($dbc, $q1);
$stmt2 = mysqli_prepare($dbc, $q2);

Each query is prepared separately, assigning the results to different variables.

6. Bind the variables:

mysqli_stmt_bind_param($stmt1, 'ii', $qty, $id);
mysqli_stmt_bind_param($stmt2, 'ii', $qty, $id);

For each statement, variables are bound to the parameters. The same variables are bound to each query, although for each submitted value, only one of the two queries will be executed.

7. Loop through each submitted value:

$affected = 0;
foreach ($_POST['add'] as $sku => $qty) {

First, a variable is initialized at zero, in order to count the number of affected rows. Then a **foreach** loop will go through the **$_POST['add']** array. For each item in that array, the index is assigned to **$sku** and the value to **$qty**. This is the same **$qty** variable that's been bound to the prepared statements.

8. Validate the quantity to be added:

if (filter_var($qty, FILTER_VALIDATE_INT, array('min_range' => 1))) {

The first requirement is that the number of items being added is an integer greater than or equal to 1.

9. Parse the SKU:

list($type, $id) = parse_sku($sku);

The **parse_sku()** function will turn a value such as *C23* into a type of *coffee* and an ID of 23, necessary for the queries. This **$id** variable has already been bound to the prepared statements.

10. Execute the correct prepared statement based upon the type:

```
if ($type == 'coffee') {
    mysqli_stmt_execute($stmt1);
    $affected += mysqli_stmt_affected_rows($stmt1);
} elseif ($type == 'other') {
    mysqli_stmt_execute($stmt2);
    $affected += mysqli_stmt_affected_rows($stmt1);
}
```

If the current item's type equals *coffee*, the first prepared statement will be executed, updating a record in the **specific_coffees** tables. If the type equals *other*, the second prepared statement will be executed, updating a record in the **non_coffee_products** table. The number of affected rows is added to the existing count in both cases.

11. Complete the quantity validation **IF** and the **foreach** loop. Print the results:

```
    } // End of IF.
} // End of FOREACH.
echo "<h4>$affected Items(s) Were Updated!</h4>";
```

12. Complete the form submission conditionals:

```
    } // End of $_POST['add'] IF.
} // End of the submission IF.
```

13. Begin the form:

```
?><h3>Add Inventory</h3>
<form action="add_inventory.php" method="post"
accept-charset="utf-8">
    <fieldset><legend>Indicate how many additional quantity of each
product should be added to the inventory.</legend>
```

14. Create a table:

```
<table border="0" width="100%" cellspacing="4" cellpadding="4">
    <thead>
        <tr>
            <th align="right">Item</th>
            <th align="right">Normal Price</th>
            <th align="right">Quantity in Stock</th>
            <th align="center">Add</th>
```

(continues on next page)

```
    </tr>
  </thead>
  <tbody>
```

The table will list the current products. For each product, the table shows the item's name, its normal price (as an additional point of reference), the current quantity in stock, and an input for adding more.

15. Fetch every product:

```php
<?php
$q = '(SELECT CONCAT("O", ncp.id) AS sku, ncc.category, ncp.name,
➥ncp.price, ncp.stock FROM non_coffee_products AS ncp INNER JOIN
➥non_coffee_categories AS ncc ON ncc.id=ncp.non_coffee_category_id
➥ORDER BY category, name) UNION (SELECT CONCAT("C", sc.id),
➥gc.category, CONCAT_WS(" - ", s.size, sc.caf_decaf, sc.ground_whole),
➥sc.price, sc.stock FROM specific_coffees AS sc INNER JOIN sizes AS
➥s ON s.id=sc.size_id INNER JOIN general_coffees AS gc ON
➥gc.id=sc.general_coffee_id ORDER BY sc.general_coffee_id, sc.size,
➥sc.caf_decaf, sc.ground_whole)';
$r = mysqli_query ($dbc, $q);
```

The query is a **UNION** of two **SELECT** queries, retrieving every product from the **non_coffee_products** and **specific_coffees** tables. The query returns each item's SKU, category and name, price, and current stock.

tip

This query is rather similar to the **UNION** queries used on the public side of the site. See those chapters for detailed explanations of the SQL.

16. Create a table row for each product:

```php
while ($row = mysqli_fetch_array ($r, MYSQLI_ASSOC)) {
    echo '<tr>
    <td align="right">' . $row['category'] . '::' . $row['name'] . '</td>
    <td align="center">' . $row['price'] .'</td>
    <td align="center">' . $row['stock'] .'</td>
    <td align="center"><input type="text" name="add[' . $row['sku'] .
    ➥']" id="add[' . $row['sku'] . ']" size="5" class="small" /></td>
    </tr>';
}
```

The first three columns in the row print literal values. The fourth column is a text input, whose name will be *add[SKU]*.

17. Complete the PHP block and the table:

```php
?> </tbody></table>
```

18. Complete the form:

> **<div class="field"><input type="submit" value="Add The**
> **⇒Inventory" class="button" /></div>**
> **</fieldset>**
> **</form>**

19. Complete the page:

> **<?php include ('./includes/footer.html'); ?>**

20. Save the file and test it in your Web browser (**Figure 11.8**).

CREATING SALES

The site allows the administrator to put any product on sale, for a definite or indefinite amount of time. From the perspective of the database, all that's required is the insertion of a new record into the **sales** table. To manage this process, the **create_sales.php** script will function much like **add_inventory.php**, except that instead of indicating additional quantities of each product, the administrator indicates the sale price, the start date, and, optionally, the end date for each product the site sells (**Figure 11.9**).

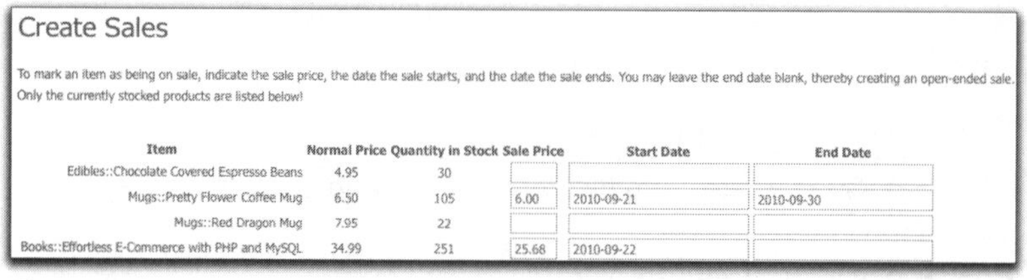

tip

The updated quantity should be reflected when the page reloads.

2 Items(s) Were Updated!
Add Inventory

Figure 11.8

Create Sales

To mark an item as being on sale, indicate the sale price, the date the sale starts, and the date the sale ends. You may leave the end date blank, thereby creating an open-ended sale. Only the currently stocked products are listed below!

Item	Normal Price	Quantity in Stock	Sale Price	Start Date	End Date
Edibles::Chocolate Covered Espresso Beans	4.95	30			
Mugs::Pretty Flower Coffee Mug	6.50	105	6.00	2010-09-21	2010-09-30
Mugs::Red Dragon Mug	7.95	22			
Books::Effortless E-Commerce with PHP and MySQL	34.99	251	25.68	2010-09-22	

Figure 11.9

To make the dates both easier to enter and to reliably guarantee they are in the proper format, the dates will be entered using jQuery's Datepicker plug-in (**Figure 11.10**), part of the jQuery User Interface (jQuery UI, **www.jqueryui.com**).

September 2010						
Su	Mo	Tu	We	Th	Fr	Sa
			1	2	3	4
5	6	7	8	9	10	11
12	13	14	15	16	17	18
19	20	21	22	23	24	25
26	27	28	29	30		

Figure 11.10

1. Create a new PHP script in your text editor or IDE to be named **create_sales.php** and stored in the administrative directory.

2. Include the configuration file, the header, and the database connection:

```
<?php
require ('../includes/config.inc.php');
$page_title = 'Create Sales';
include ('./includes/header.html');
require (MYSQL);
```

3. Check for a form submission:

```
if ($_SERVER['REQUEST_METHOD'] == 'POST') {
```

4. Confirm that the three required variables exist:

```
if (isset($_POST['sale_price'], $_POST['start_date'],
➥$_POST['end_date'])) {
```

The form will post back to this page three arrays, representing prices, start dates, and end dates.

5. Require the product functions:

```
require ('../includes/product_functions.inc.php');
```

Again, as with the add inventory page, the **parse_sku()** user-defined function will be required.

6. Prepare the query to be run:

```
$q = 'INSERT INTO sales (product_type, product_id, price, start_date,
➥end_date) VALUES (?, ?, ?, ?, ?)';
$stmt = mysqli_prepare($dbc, $q);
mysqli_stmt_bind_param($stmt, 'sidss', $type, $id, $price, $start_date,
➥$end_date);
```

The query inserts into the **sales** table a record consisting of the product's type, ID, sale price, start date, and end date. Three of these values, including the two dates, will technically be strings. The product ID will be an integer, and the price will be a decimal.

7. Loop through each submitted value:

```
$affected = o;
foreach ($_POST['sale_price'] as $sku => $price) {
```

The script should receive three arrays: **$_POST['sale_price']**, **$_POST['start_date']**, and **$_POST['end_date']**. It doesn't matter which array the code loops through, but price is a logical selection. Each array is indexed using the product's SKU.

The **$price** variable has already been bound to the query, so that its value will be used when the query is executed.

8. Validate the price and start date:

```
if (filter_var($price, FILTER_VALIDATE_FLOAT)
&& ($price > 0)
&& (!empty($_POST['start_date'][$sku]))
){
```

The new sale price must be a decimal (aka, a float) greater than zero. The starting date is checked that it's not empty.

9. Parse the SKU:

```
list($type, $id) = parse_sku($sku);
```

I'm sounding like a broken record here but...the **parse_sku()** function is invoked here because it is in the add inventory page, creating the **$type** and **$id** variables in the process. These same variables have already been bound to the prepared statement.

10. Associate the dates with variables:

```
$start_date = $_POST['start_date'][$sku];
$end_date = (empty($_POST['end_date'][$sku])) ? NULL :
➥$_POST['end_date'][$sku];
```

The starting date is available in the **$_POST['start_date']** array. For the current iteration of the **foreach** loop, the specific date to use is in **$_POST['start_date'][$sku]**. The end date is optional, so if the associated **$_POST** value is empty, **NULL** is assigned to the **$end_date** variable. Otherwise, the administrator-provided value will be used.

11. Execute the query:

```
mysqli_stmt_execute($stmt);
$affected += mysqli_stmt_affected_rows($stmt);
```

12. Complete the price and start date validation, plus the **foreach** loop:

```
    } // End of price/date validation IF.
} // End of FOREACH loop.
```

13. Indicate the results and complete the form submission conditionals:

```
        echo "<h4>$affected Sales Were Created!</h4>";
    } // $_POST variables aren't set.
} // End of the submission IF.
?>
```

 tip

A stricter validation would check that the starting date and ending date (if provided) are valid. You could also confirm that the start date is not before today, and that the end date is after the start date.

14. Begin the form:

```
<h3>Create Sales</h3>
<p>To mark an item as being on sale, indicate the sale price, the date
➥the sale starts, and the date the sale ends. You may leave the end date
➥blank, thereby creating an open-ended sale. Only the currently
➥stocked products are listed below!</p>
<form action="create_sales.php" method="post"
➥accept-charset="utf-8">
    <fieldset>
```

This form begins with some instructions, because the use of the dates could be confusing.

15. Begin a table:

```
<table border="0" width="100%" cellspacing="2" cellpadding="2">
    <thead>
    <tr>
        <th align="right">Item</th>
        <th align="right">Normal Price</th>
        <th align="right">Quantity in Stock</th>
        <th align="center">Sale Price</th>
        <th align="right">Start Date</th>
        <th align="right">End Date</th>
    </tr>
    </thead>
    <tbody>
```

16. Retrieve every product that's currently in stock:

```php
<?php
$q = '(SELECT CONCAT("O", ncp.id) AS sku, ncc.category, ncp.name,
➥ncp.price, ncp.stock FROM non_coffee_products AS ncp INNER JOIN
➥non_coffee_categories AS ncc ON ncc.id=ncp.non_coffee_category_id
➥WHERE ncp.stock > 0 ORDER BY category, name) UNION (SELECT
➥CONCAT("C", sc.id), gc.category, CONCAT_WS(" - ", s.size,
➥sc.caf_decaf, sc.ground_whole), sc.price, sc.stock FROM
➥specific_coffees AS sc INNER JOIN sizes AS s ON s.id=sc.size_id
➥INNER JOIN general_coffees AS gc ON gc.id=sc.general_coffee_id
➥WHERE sc.stock > 0 ORDER BY sc.general_coffee_id, sc.size,
➥sc.caf_decaf, sc.ground_whole)';
$r = mysqli_query ($dbc, $q);
```

This **UNION** query is essentially the same as that on the add inventory page, with the addition of a **WHERE** *table*.**stock > 0** clause. The thinking there is that the administrator would want to create sales only for products currently in stock.

17. Print each item as its own row:

```
while ($row = mysqli_fetch_array ($r, MYSQLI_ASSOC)) {
    echo '<tr>
    <td align="center">' . $row['category'] . '::' . $row['name'] . '</td>
    <td align="center">' . $row['price'] .'</td>
    <td align="center">' . $row['stock'] .'</td>
    <td align="center"><input type="text" name="sale_price[' .
    $row['sku'] . ']"  id="sale_price[' . $row['sku'] . ']" class="small"
/></td>
    <td align="center"><input type="text" name="start_date[' .
    $row['sku'] . ']" id="start_date[' . $row['sku'] . ']"
    class="calendar" /></td>
    <td align="center"><input type="text" name="end_date[' .
    $row['sku'] . ']" id="end_date[' . $row['sku'] . ']" class="calendar"
    /></td>
    </tr>';
}
```

The first three columns display values returned by the query. The last three columns each define a text input. The name of each input is an array, using the product's SKU as its index. The two date inputs have an additional **class** attribute, with a value of *calendar*. This will be used to apply the jQuery Datepicker to these inputs.

18. Complete the table and the form:

```
?> </tbody></table>
    <div class="field"><input type="submit" value="Add These Sales"
    class="button" /></div>
    </fieldset>
</form>
```

19. Include the UI-Lightness theme CSS file and the jQuery UI library:

```
<link href="/css/ui-lightness/jquery-ui-1.8.4.custom.css"
rel="stylesheet" type="text/css" />
<script src="http://ajax.googleapis.com/ajax/libs/jqueryui/1.8.5/
jquery-ui.min.js" type="text/javascript" charset="utf-8"></script>
```

tip

There are many other
jQuery UI themes available
(see **www.jqueryui.com**), or
you can roll your own.

The jQuery Datepicker tool is going to use one of jQuery's User Interface themes for its formatting. You can download the corresponding CSS file from **www.jqueryui.com** (or find it among the downloaded files from this book's corresponding Web site). The jQuery UI library will be accessed through the Google API.

20. Turn the two date columns into Datepickers:

```
<script type="text/javascript">
    $(function() {
        $(".calendar").datepicker({dateFormat: "yy-mm-dd",
        ➥minDate:0});
    });
</script>
```

To repeat what's already been said, the **$();** syntax in jQuery is a way of executing some JavaScript once the page has been loaded. The specific code to be executed is placed within an anonymous function.

The anonymous function selects every element on the page that has a class of *calendar*. To that selection, the **datepicker()** method is invoked, thereby converting them into Datepickers. Passed to the **datepicker()** method are two properties. The first, **dateFormat: "yy-mm-dd"**, indicates the format that the selected date should be in. This format matches what is usable in the database queries. The second property, **minDate:0**, indicates that the earliest date that can be selected is the current date (zero days from now).

21. Complete the page:

```
<?php include ('./includes/footer.html'); ?>
```

22. Save the file and test it in your Web browser.

VIEWING ORDERS

The scripts to this point affect the product catalog and what the customer can purchase. Once customers have completed their orders, the administrator needs a way to view and handle those orders. This will be a three-step process:

- Viewing every order
- Viewing the particulars of a single order
- Processing an order

The processing part is when the business will actually get its money. Chapter 10 authorized payment for an order. Once the order has been reviewed and processed, using the following scripts, the payment will be captured (that is, transferred).

To understand how the orders are represented in the database, you may want to review the checkout process, specifically **billing.php**, before looking at these scripts. You will notice that the database may reflect orders that have not been finalized (that is, orders for which payment wasn't processed). The corresponding administrative system can indicate to the administrator if funds could not be captured for an order, but as an extra precaution, nonfinalized orders won't be listed by this next script.

Listing Every Order

The PHP script for listing every order is short and simple: The only thing complicated about it is the query it runs (as can often be the case). **Figure 11.11** shows what it looks like.

View Orders

Order ID	Total	Customer Name	City	State	Zip	Left to Ship
19	$33.68	Ullman, Larry	Anytown	MS	65894	0
18	$73.76	Ullman, Larry	Anytown	SC	65894	0
17	$20.99	Ullman, Larry	Anytown	NV	65894	0
16	$90.00	Ullman, Larry	Anytown	MT	65894	0
15	$11.13	Ullman, Larry	Anytown	ME	12345	1
14	$52.56	Ullman, Larry	Anytown	HI	12345	3
13	$62.74	Ullman, Larry	State College	AL	16803	2

Figure 11.11

1. Create a new PHP script in your text editor or IDE to be named **view_orders.php** and stored in the administrative directory.

2. Include the configuration file, the header, and the database connection:

```php
<?php
require ('../includes/config.inc.php');
$page_title = 'View All Orders';
include ('./includes/header.html');
require (MYSQL);
```

3. Create a table:

```php
echo '<h3>View Orders</h3><table border="0" width="100%"
➥cellspacing="4" cellpadding="4">
<thead>
  <tr>
  <th align="center">Order ID</th>
```

(continues on next page)

 note

This script is named **view_orders.php** (with an "s" after "order"). The next script will be the singular **view_order.php**.

```
    <th align="center">Total</th>
    <th align="right">Customer Name</th>
    <th align="right">City</th>
    <th align="center">State</th>
    <th align="center">Zip</th>
    <th align="center">Left to Ship</th>
    </tr></thead>
<tbody>';
```

The HTML table reflects the information to be displayed about each order. This includes the order ID, the order total, the customer's name, city, state, zip code, and a count of how many items are left to be shipped in this order. This count will act as an indicator of which orders have been completed and which have not.

4. Define and execute the query:

**$q = 'SELECT o.id, total, c.id AS cid, CONCAT(last_name, ", ", first_name)
➥AS name, city, state, zip, COUNT(oc.id) AS items FROM orders AS o LEFT
➥OUTER JOIN order_contents AS oc ON (oc.order_id=o.id AND
➥oc.ship_date IS NULL) JOIN customers AS c ON (o.customer_id = c.id)
➥JOIN transactions AS t ON (t.order_id=o.id AND t.response_code=1)
➥GROUP BY o.id DESC';**

The query needs to join the **orders**, **order_contents**, **customers**, and **transactions** tables. To retrieve the count of items left to ship in an order, the query uses a **LEFT OUTER JOIN** between **orders** and **order_contents** where the order ID matches, but the **ship_date** is **NULL**. The effect of this condition is that only **order_content** records without ship dates will be matched to orders. This is strictly for the purpose of indicating nonfulfilled orders; viewing any particular order will show the complete contents, whether they have shipped or not.

Only orders that have a corresponding transaction response code of 1, indicating a successful request of the payment gateway, will be returned.

The orders are listed starting with the newest.

5. Print each record in the table:

```
while ($row = mysqli_fetch_array ($r, MYSQLI_ASSOC)) {
    echo '<tr>
    <td align="center"><a href="view_order.php?oid=' . $row['id'] . '">' .
    ➥$row['id'] . '</a></td>
    <td align="center">$' . $row['total'] .'</td>
```

```
<td align="right"><a href="view_customer.php?cid=' . $row['cid'] .
'">' . $row['name'] .'</a></td>
<td align="right">' . $row['city'] . '</td>
<td align="center">' . $row['state'] .'</td>
<td align="center">' . $row['zip'] .'</td>
<td align="center">' . $row['items'] .'</td>
</tr>';
}
```

The order ID is linked to the **view_order.php** script (to be written next), passing along the order ID in the URL. The customer ID is linked to the **view_customer.php** script, passing along the customer ID in the URL. That script is not actually written in this book.

6. Complete the table:

echo '</tbody></table>';

7. Complete the page:

include ('./includes/footer.html');
?>

8. Save the file and test it in your Web browser.

You'll have to have some orders in the database in order for the results to be meaningful.

PAGINATION AND TABLE SORTING

The **view_orders.php** script purposefully does not include pagination or a way for the administrator to sort by column (that is, by the customer's last name or zip code). Both of these features, and many, many more, can easily be added to the page by using one of the available table plug-ins for jQuery. I've used, for example, Datatables (**www.datatables.net**) before, with great success. See the Datatables Web site, or the book's corresponding site, for how it might be integrated into **view_orders.php**.

Viewing One Order

The **view_order.php** script receives the order ID in the URL and displays all the order's details (**Figure 11.12**). The administrator can then click a button to mark the order as shipped. At that point, the order cycle will be complete.

Figure 11.12

To start this process, the next series of steps will explain how to display the order's contents.

1. Create a new PHP script in your text editor or IDE to be named **view_order.php** and stored in the administrative directory.

2. Include the configuration file and the header:

```php
<?php
require ('../includes/config.inc.php');
$page_title = 'View An Order';
include ('./includes/header.html');
```

3. Validate the order ID:

```php
$order_id = false;
if (isset($_GET['oid']) && (filter_var($_GET['oid'], FILTER_VALIDATE_INT,
➥array('min_range' => 1))) ) {
    $order_id = $_GET['oid'];
    $_SESSION['order_id'] = $order_id;
} elseif (isset($_SESSION['order_id']) && (filter_var($_SESSION[
➥'order_id'], FILTER_VALIDATE_INT, array('min_range' => 1))) ) {
    $order_id = $_SESSION['order_id'];
}
```

The script can't function at all if it does not have access to a valid order ID (an integer greater than or equal to 1). The first time this page is accessed, it should receive an order ID in the URL (from the link on **view_orders.php**). If that's the case, the local **$order_id** variable is created for use in a query later in the script, and the order ID is stored in the session for use when the page is submitted back to itself.

If the order ID is not in the URL but is in the session, that order ID value is assigned to a local variable and will be used by the page instead. This would be the case when the administrator clicks the Ship This Order button.

4. Stop the page if the **$order_id** is not valid:

```
if (!$order_id) {
    echo '<h3>Error!</h3><p>This page has been accessed in error.</p>';
    include ('./includes/footer.html');
    exit();
}
```

If the page does not have a valid order ID, there's no point in continuing. An error will be printed, the footer included, and the script terminated.

5. Require the database connection:

```
require(MYSQL);
```

6. Define and execute the query:

```
$q = 'SELECT total, shipping, credit_card_number, DATE_FORMAT(
➥order_date, "%a %b %e, %Y at %h:%i%p") AS od, email,
➥CONCAT(last_name, ", ", first_name) AS name, CONCAT_WS(" ",
➥address1, address2, city, state, zip) AS address, phone, customer_id,
➥CONCAT_WS(" - ", ncc.category, ncp.name) AS item, ncp.stock,
➥quantity, price_per, DATE_FORMAT(ship_date, "%b %e, %Y") AS sd
➥FROM orders AS o INNER JOIN customers AS c ON (o.customer_id = c.id)
➥INNER JOIN order_contents AS oc ON (oc.order_id = o.id) INNER JOIN
➥non_coffee_products AS ncp ON (oc.product_id = ncp.id AND
➥oc.product_type="other") INNER JOIN non_coffee_categories AS ncc
➥ON (ncc.id = ncp.non_coffee_category_id) WHERE o.id=' . $order_id . '
UNION
SELECT total, shipping, credit_card_number, DATE_FORMAT(
➥order_date, "%a %b %e, %Y at %l:%i%p"), email,
➥CONCAT(last_name, ", ", first_name), CONCAT_WS(" ", address1,
➥address2, city, state, zip), phone, customer_id, CONCAT_WS(" - ",
➥gc.category, s.size, sc.caf_decaf, sc.ground_whole) AS item, sc.stock,
➥quantity, price_per, DATE_FORMAT(ship_date, "%b %e, %Y") FROM
➥orders AS o INNER JOIN customers AS c ON (o.customer_id = c.id)
➥INNER JOIN order_contents AS oc ON (oc.order_id = o.id) INNER
```

(continues on next page)

```
➥JOIN specific_coffees AS sc ON (oc.product_id = sc.id AND
➥oc.product_type="coffee") INNER JOIN sizes AS s ON (s.id=sc.size_id)
➥INNER JOIN general_coffees AS gc ON (gc.id=sc.general_coffee_id)
➥WHERE o.id=' . $order_id;
$r = mysqli_query($dbc, $q);
```

This query is similar to those in Chapter 9, "Building a Shopping Cart," in that it requires a **UNION** of two **SELECT** statements. Unlike that chapter's queries, this query must also join in the **customers**, **orders**, and **order_contents** tables. **Figure 11.13** shows the result of running this query.

Effortless E-Commerce

total	shipping	credit_card_number	od	email	name	address	phone	customer_id	item	stock	quantity	price_per	sd
52.56	10.56	4444	Fri Sep 10, 2010 at 12:01AM	larry@dmcinsights.com	Ullman, Larry	100 Main Street Anytown HI 12345	1234567890	18	Mugs - Pretty Flower Coffee Mug	105	2	6.50	NULL
52.56	10.56	4444	Fri Sep 10, 2010 at 12:01AM	larry@dmcinsights.com	Ullman, Larry	100 Main Street Anytown HI 12345	1234567890	18	Mugs - Red Dragon Mug	22	3	7.00	NULL
52.56	10.56	4444	Fri Sep 10, 2010 at 12:01AM	larry@dmcinsights.com	Ullman, Larry	100 Main Street Anytown HI 12345	1234567890	18	Kona - 1 lb. - caf - ground	35	1	8.00	NULL

3 rows in set (0.00 sec)

mysql>

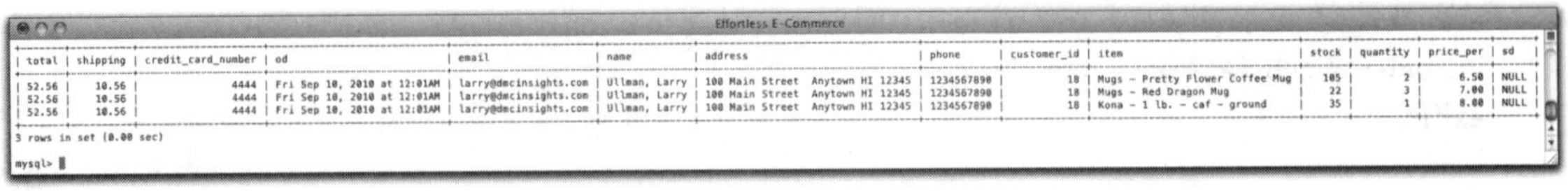

Figure 11.13

7. If rows were returned, start a form:

```
if (mysqli_num_rows($r) > 0) {
    echo '<h3>View an Order</h3>
    <form action="view_order.php" method="post" accept-charset=
    ➥"utf-8">
        <fieldset>';
```

The form posts back to this same page and only contains, as written, a submit button.

8. Fetch the first returned row and display the general information:

```
$row = mysqli_fetch_array($r, MYSQLI_ASSOC);
    echo "<p><strong>Order ID</strong>: $order_id<br /><strong>
    ➥Total</strong>: \${$row['total']}<br /><strong>Shipping
    ➥</strong>: \${$row['shipping']}<br /><strong>Order Date
    ➥</strong>: {$row['od']}<br /><strong>Customer Name
    ➥</strong>: {$row['name']}<br /><strong>Customer Address
    ➥</strong>: {$row['address']} <br /><strong>Customer Email
    ➥</strong>: {$row['email']}<br /><strong>Customer Phone
    ➥</strong>: {$row['phone']}<br /><strong>Credit Card Number
    ➥Used</strong>: *{$row['credit_card_number']}</p>";
```

The query will return the general order and customer information once for each item in the order (see Figure 11.13). To display the general information only once, and first, the first returned row is immediately fetched, outside of any loop. You'll see how and why this works shortly.

tip

As a fraud-prevention technique, you could retrieve the billing address from the payment transaction and compare it to the shipping address, looking for suspicious differences.

9. Create the table:

```
echo '<table border="0" width="100%" cellspacing="2"
➥cellpadding="2">
  <thead>
  <tr>
    <th align="center">Item</th>
    <th align="right">Price Paid</th>
    <th align="center">Quantity in Stock</th>
    <th align="center">Quantity Ordered</th>
    <th align="center">Ship?</th>
  </tr>
  </thead>
  <tbody>';
```

The table lists the ordered items, along with the price paid, the quantity currently in stock, the quantity ordered, and when the item has shipped, if applicable.

10. Create a flag variable to track if the order has already shipped:

```
$shipped = true;
```

The administrator is going to be given the option of processing the payment for this order only if it hasn't already shipped. The assumption will be that it has, and later code will change this setting if that's not the case.

11. Print each item:

```
do {
  echo '<tr>
    <th align="left">' . $row['item'] . '</thd>
    <th align="right">' . $row['price_per'] . '</thd>
    <th align="center">' . $row['stock'] . '</thd>
    <th align="center">' . $row['quantity'] . '</thd>
    <th align="center">' . $row['sd'] . '</td>
  </tr>';
```

Because one row has already been fetched, the less common **do...while** loop will be used to navigate the remaining query results. This construct performs some actions first and checks the conditional last, thereby guaranteeing that the code within the loop will be executed at least one time. Within the loop, each value is displayed within a table row.

12. Update the shipping status:

```
if (!$row['sd']) $shipped = false;
```

If **$row['sd']** is **NULL** (for any item in the order), then the entire order has not been shipped yet, and the flag variable should indicate such.

13. Complete the loop and the table:

} while ($row = mysqli_fetch_array($r));

echo '</tbody></table>';

After the contents of the loop are executed, the condition is checked. The specific condition is the fetching of another array from the query results. If another array can be found, the loop will be repeated again.

14. If the order hasn't entirely shipped, create the submit button:

if (!$shipped) {
    echo '<div class="field"><p class="error">Note that actual
    ⇒**payments will be collected once you click this button!</p>**
    ⇒**<input type="submit" value="Ship This Order " class="button" />**
    ⇒**</div>';**
}

For orders that have completely shipped, no submit button will exist (**Figure 11.14**).

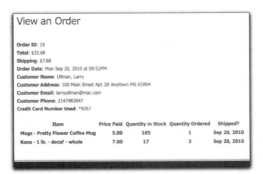

Figure 11.14

15. Complete the form:

echo '</fieldset>
</form>';

16. Complete the **mysqli_num_rows()** conditional:

} else { // No records returned!
    echo '<h3>Error!</h3><p>This page has been accessed in error.
    ⇒**</p>';**

```
    include ('./includes/footer.html');
    exit();
}
```

This **else** clause applies if no records were returned by the query.

17. Complete the page:

```
include ('./includes/footer.html');
?>
```

18. Save the file and test it in your Web browser.

At this point, clicking the submit button will have no effect, however.

SHIPPING ORDERS

To complete the **view_order.php** script, the functionality for processing completed orders has to be integrated. This entire process involves:

1. Requesting actual payment for the order

2. Recording the payment request transaction in the database

3. Updating the **order_contents** table

4. Updating the catalog inventory

5. Reporting upon the results

Although there are many steps, the code itself isn't that complicated, largely thanks to the work that's already been done for the public side of the site. First, though, a script for setting up the payment gateway for administrative purposes must be defined.

Creating gateway_setup_admin.php

In Chapter 10's **billing.php**, payments are processed by including two files. The first, **gateway_setup.php**, creates an array of values particular to the public side of the site. This includes, for example, the customer's billing information. Since a payment has already been authorized, the administrative setup script only needs to identify the transaction ID associated with the prior authorization and use a payment request type of **PRIOR_AUTH_CAPTURE**. Here, then, is the complete **gateway_setup_admin.php**, which should be stored in a secure location (such as the same place you used for **gateway_setup.php**):

gateway_setup_admin.php

```
1   <?php
2   // Create an array for the information:
3   $data = array();
4   $data['x_trans_id'] = $trans_id;
5   $data['x_type'] = 'PRIOR_AUTH_CAPTURE';
```

The second script in the payment request process, **gateway_process.php**, defines values required by both customer and administrator requests, and then performs the actual communication with the payment gateway. In that script, three values are assigned on the fly:

```
$data['x_amount'] = $order_total;
$data['x_invoice_num'] = $order_id;
$data['x_cust_id'] = $customer_id;
```

The code for assigning these values needs to be written into **view_order.php**, just as it was within **billing.php**.

Updating view_order.php

The code for processing the payment capture is about 70 lines long, well spaced, and with comments. You can place it all within an includable file, or just add it to **view_order.php**, as in these next steps.

1. Open **view_order.php** in your text editor or IDE, if it is not already.

2. After including the database connection, check for a form submission:

if ($_SERVER['REQUEST_METHOD'] == 'POST') {

3. Retrieve the customer ID, order total, and transaction ID:

$q = "SELECT customer_id, total, transaction_id FROM orders AS o JOIN ➡transactions AS t ON (o.id=t.order_id AND t.type='AUTH_ONLY' AND ➡t.response_code=1) WHERE o.id=$order_id";
$r = mysqli_query($dbc, $q);

At this point in the script, **$order_id** has already been validated to be an integer greater than or equal to 1, meaning it's safe to use in a query (you could use prepared statements, if you'd rather). The query selects three pieces of information from the **orders** and **transactions** tables. Each order can be represented in the **transactions** table multiple times, but only once in an **AUTH_ONLY** status. And the order is only valid if the **response_code** equals 1, meaning that the authorization request worked.

4. If one row was returned, get the selected values:

```
if (mysqli_num_rows($r) == 1) {
    list($customer_id, $order_total, $trans_id) =
    ⇥mysqli_fetch_array($r, MYSQL_NUM);
```

The important thing to note here is that these three variable names exactly match those expected by the **gateway_setup_admin.php** and **gateway_process.php** scripts.

5. Check for a positive order total:

```
if ($order_total > 0) {
```

As a safety check, only positive payment requests will ever be made.

6. Process the payment request:

```
require_once(BASE_URI . 'private/gateway_setup_admin.php');
require_once(BASE_URI . 'private/gateway_process.php');
```

Because these two scripts define all the requisite functionality, including them is all this page needs to do in order to make the payment request.

7. Record the transaction results:

```
$reason = addslashes($response_array[3]);
$response = addslashes($response);
$r = mysqli_query($dbc, "CALL add_transaction($order_id,
⇥'{$data['x_type']}', $response_array[9], $response_array[0], '$reason',
⇥$response_array[6], '$response')");
```

This code is exactly like that in **billing.php**.

8. If the request was successful, create a message:

```
if ($response_array[0] == 1) {
    $message = 'The payment has been made. You may now ship the
    ⇥order.';
```

As explained in Chapter 10, if the first element of the returned response has a value of 1, the request succeeded. If so, a message is assigned to a variable for use later in the script.

9. Update the **order_contents** table:

```
$q = "UPDATE order_contents SET ship_date=NOW() WHERE
⇥order_id=$order_id";
$r = mysqli_query($dbc, $q);
```

To reflect that the order has shipped (or can be shipped now), the **order_contents** table needs to be updated for every row with the current order ID.

 tip

The order total (or **x_amount** in the payment process) is only required if less than the original, authorized amount. It is best to be thorough and include it, though.

tip

The comma between the table names in the queries is equivalent to the word **JOIN**.

10. Update the site's inventory:

```
$q = 'UPDATE specific_coffees AS sc, order_contents AS oc SET
sc.stock=sc.stock-oc.quantity WHERE sc.id=oc.product_id AND
oc.product_type="coffee" AND oc.order_id=' . $order_id;
$r = mysqli_query($dbc, $q);
$q = 'UPDATE non_coffee_products AS ncp, order_contents AS oc SET
ncp.stock=ncp.stock-oc.quantity WHERE ncp.id=oc.product_id AND
oc.product_type="other" AND oc.order_id=' . $order_id;
$r = mysqli_query($dbc, $q);
```

Now that the items in the order have officially been purchased and can head out the door, the site's inventory needs to reflect the sold items. This means that for every item in the **order_contents** table (for the current order), the corresponding records in the **specific_coffees** and **non_coffee_products** tables have to be updated.

MySQL actually allows you to perform a **JOIN** on an **UPDATE** query; two such queries can update the entire inventory, no matter how many records are present in the **order_contents** table. Each query may make more sense if viewed as a standard **SELECT JOIN**:

```
SELECT sc.stock, oc.quantity FROM specific_coffees AS sc,
order_contents AS oc WHERE sc.id=oc.product_id AND
oc.product_type="coffee" and oc.order_id=X
```

Instead of selecting the two values—stock and quantity—in matching rows, the one value is used to update the value in the other.

11. If the payment request didn't succeed, create an error:

```
} else {
    $error = "The payment could not be processed because: $response_
    array[3]";
} // End of payment response IF-ELSE.
```

As in Chapter 10, **$response_array[3]** contains a textual description of the problem. This will be safe to reveal to the administrator.

12. Complete the order total **IF-ELSE**:

```
} else { // Invalid order total!
    $error = "The order total (\$$order_total) is invalid.";
} // End of $order_total IF-ELSE.
```

If the order total was not a positive number, that message is assigned to an error variable, along with the actual total.

13. If no matching order was found, indicate that:

> **} else { // No matching order!**
> **$error = 'No matching order could be found.';**
> **} // End of transaction ID IF-ELSE.**

14. Report any messages or errors:

> **echo '<h3>Order Shipping Results</h3>';**
> **if (isset($message)) echo "<p>$message</p>";**
> **if (isset($error)) echo "<p class=\"error\">$error</p>";**

> **Figures 11.15** and **11.16** show these lines in action.

Order Shipping Results

The payment has been made. You may now ship the order.

Figure 11.15

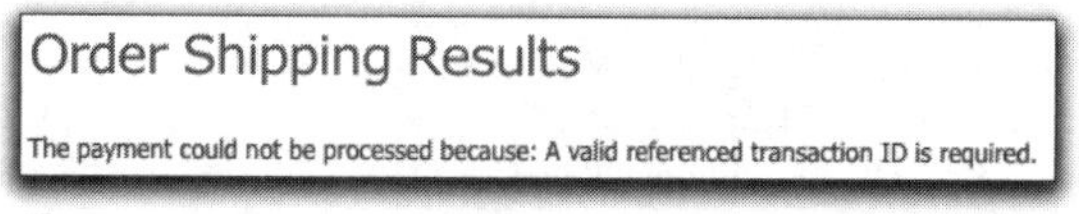

Order Shipping Results

The payment could not be processed because: A valid referenced transaction ID is required.

Figure 11.16

15. Complete the form submission **IF**:

> **} // End of the submission IF.**

16. Save the page and test it in your Web browser.

note

You'll need to use relatively recent orders to test this process, because the authorization for older orders may have since been revoked.

INDEX

WATCH
READ
CREATE

Meet Creative Edge.

A new resource of unlimited books, videos and tutorials for creatives from the world's leading experts.

Creative Edge is your one stop for inspiration, answers to technical questions and ways to stay at the top of your game so you can focus on what you do best—being creative.

All for only $24.99 per month for access—any day any time you need it.

peachpit.com/creativeedge